A VOLUME IN THE SERIES

Native Americans of the Northeast

Edited by
Colin G. Calloway
Jean M. O'Brien
Lisa T. Brooks

THROUGH
AN INDIAN'S
LOOKING-GLASS

THROUGH AN INDIAN'S LOOKING-GLASS

*A Cultural Biography
of William Apess,
Pequot*

Drew Lopenzina

University of Massachusetts Press
Amherst and Boston

ISBN 978-1-62534-259-1 (paper); 258-4 (hardcover)

Designed by Jack Harrison
Set in Adobe Garamond with Garamond Premiere display
Printed and bound by The Maple-Vail Book Manufacturing Group

Frontispiece: Illman and Pilbrow engraving of the 1830 John Paradise portrait of
William Apess as seen in the 1831 edition of *A Son of the Forest*.
Courtesy American Antiquarian Society.

Cover design by Jack Harrison
Cover art: Photomontage combining portrait of William Apess as seen in 1831 edition of
A Son of the Forest (Courtesy of American Antiquarian Society), with a Methodist camp meeting
as depicted in Harry T. Peters "America on Stone" Lithography Collection, National Museum of
American History, Smithsonian Institution (Courtesy Smithsonian Art Museum).

Library of Congress Cataloging-in-Publication Data
Names: Lopenzina, Drew, author.
Title: Through an Indian's looking-glass : a cultural biography of
William Apess, Pequot / Drew Lopenzina.
Other titles: Cultural biography of William Apess, Pequot
Description: Amherst : University of Massachusetts Press, [2017] |
Series: Native Americans of the Northeast |
Includes bibliographical references and index.
Identifiers: LCCN 2016047359| ISBN 9781625342591 (pbk. : alk. paper) |
ISBN 9781625342584 (hardcover : alk. paper)
Subjects: LCSH: Apess, William, 1798-1839. |
Pequot Indians—Biography. |Indians of North America—New England. |
Methodist Church—New England—Clergy—Biography. |
United States—History—War of 1812—Participation, Indian. |
Mashpee Indians—History. | Indians, Treatment of—New England.
Classification: LCC E99.P53 L67 2017 | DDC 974.004/97344092 [B] —dc23
LC record available at https://lccn.loc.gov/2016047359

British Library Cataloguing-in-Publication Data
A catalog record for this book is available from the British Library.

To Barbara

Contents

Acknowledgments

I am indebted to family, friends, colleagues, various institutions, and the occasional perfect stranger who helped make this difficult project possible. From the very start, the endeavor to write a book on the life and times of William Apess, locating this Pequot writer and minister within the indigenous networks that informed and inspired his activism, seemed an improbable task that nevertheless drew passionate support. I often felt invested with the cares and concerns of those who feel a strong connection to Apess's life, and for the trust that was extended to my ability to carry this task forward into print, I am immensely grateful.

To locate the life of a nineteenth-century "Indian Preacher" within indigenous networks required the expertise, knowledge, patience, and generous mentoring of a number of people in the indigenous communities of the Northeast, including Janice Hill and the Four Directions Aboriginal Student Center at Queens University in Ontario; Karen Lewis at the Kanhiate-Tyendinaga Territory First Nation Public Library; Kimberly Maracle and everyone at the L'il Crow Café at Tyendinaga; Melissa Tantaquidgeon Zobel, medicine woman and tribal historian for the Mohegan tribe; Dr. Donna (and John) Moody; Kerri Helme; Joan Avant; and, in particular, Margaret Bruchac and Lisa Brooks, who, among other things, engaged me in an impromptu tour of the indigenous history of northwestern Massachusetts and accompanied me into the backwoods of Colrain, place of Apess's birth, to seek out Apess on his own ground. I am also indebted, as always, to Siobhan Senier for her unfailing mentorship. Thank you all for your support and guidance.

Many of the findings that this book brings to the fore would not have been possible without a generous month-long residential fellowship granted by the American Antiquarian Society. I am grateful to Paul Erickson, director of academic programs, as well as the entire AAS staff, for their support and assistance. I am also grateful for the collaborative relationships forged in that time with fellow Americanist and Native studies scholars Kelly Wisecup, Katy Chiles, and Daniel Radus. It felt from the start that their sustained interest, enthusiasm, and input were essential to the success of this project.

I want to thank Kevin McBride, head of research at the Pequot Museum and Research Center, for walking me along the grounds of "Mistick Fort," site of the infamous 1637 Pequot massacre, and helping me to physically conceptualize the devastating events of that day. I received valuable information concerning Apess's Pequot networks from Jason Mancini, director of the Pequot Museum, and I am equally indebted to the research shared by Paul Grant Costa and Tobias Glaza, curators of the Yale Indian Papers Project.

In my research travels, I was the beneficiary of the expertise of countless town clerk's offices, local libraries, and historical societies, who tolerated my camping out in their offices often for days on end. In particular, I thank Keith Herkalo with the War of 1812 Museum in Plattsburgh, New York; Nancy Soderberg with the Mashpee Historical Commission in Mashpee, Massachusetts; Liz Sonnenberg and Erica Wheeler of the Colrain Historical Society in Colrain, Massachusetts; and Linda Flugrad, town clerk of Salem, Connecticut, without whom I could never have located David Furman's field, site of Apess's childhood indenture.

I am grateful for the efforts of the University of Massachusetts Press and acquisitions editor Brian Halley. Much thanks to Barry O'Connell for his expertise, exacting standards, and diligent attention to the manuscript. Along the way Lee Bebout, Lisa Brooks, Rachel Bryant, Katy Chiles, Jeff Crane, Alyssa Mt. Pleasant, Kelly Wisecup, and Hilary Wyss all provided valuable input on the manuscript. Thanks to Ashley Barnett for her assistance in preparing the appendix. I thank Terry Stigers for his brilliant mapping of forgotten landscapes and his constant willingness to take one more trek up the mountain. On my research trips I was also accompanied by Peter Lopenzina Allan Morrison, Greg Brennan, Kerry Lynch, and Bear (the best dog ever), every one of whom was essential to the journey.

Assistance always comes from unexpected sources, and my journey would not have been half so serendipitous if not for certain random and fortuitous interventions at key moments. I am most grateful to the young woman who tended bar at the Lake on the Mountain Resort in Prince Edward County, Ontario, for her encouragement; to the helpful proprietor of the Devil's Wishbone Winery, also in Ontario, who came through with a timely and important tip; and to the hawk that led me deep into the woods and safely back out again as I blindly searched vast tracts of Canadian wilderness looking for a large rock with a curious hole and a stream of water running through it—a site of great significance to William Apess's narrative as well as the concerns of this book.

Lastly, I must thank my family for their kindness, support, patience, love, and willingness to listen to my stories. My son, Dylan, and my daughter, Amelia, have been a constant source of pride and inspiration. Thanks especially to my wife, Barb, who hides little notes of encouragement in my books and reminds me to breathe.

THROUGH
AN INDIAN'S
LOOKING-GLASS

INTRODUCTION
Negative Work

Michachunck the soule, in a higher notion which is of affinity, with a word signifying looking glasse, or cleere resemblance, so that it hath its name from a cleere sight or discerning, which indeed seems very well to suit with the nature of it.
——ROGER WILLIAMS, *A Key into the Language of America*

In August of 1856 the poet Walt Whitman wrote to Ralph Waldo Emerson that, in all our literature, "not a man faces round at the rest with terrible negative voice." Whitman's lament was that there was none who dared speak out against the established creeds of church and state, none to challenge the veracity of whatever was "presented them in novels, histories, newspapers, poems, schools, lectures, everything." Absent this voice, the general populace was all too willing to be guided by the persistent pieties of conventional wisdom, a pitiful "spectacle," Whitman maintained, of falsehood, illusion, and moral cowardice.[1] Doubtless Whitman had not heard of William Apess. And even if he had, it is questionable whether he would have perceived in Apess that "terrible" voice he so earnestly sought. Never could he have apprehended that the truer challenge to America's stalled imaginary, a more piercing and provocative "negative voice" laying waste to expansive claims of American piety, imperialism, and exceptionalism, might come not from a white poet but from a Native American, an Indian, a member of that race for whom, in Whitman's own estimation, the "hour for death" had already come.[2]

And yet, as this book argues, William Apess, for a brief moment in the first half of the nineteenth century, was that terrible negative voice, pushing against the grain of American literature by directly confronting the dominant narrative structures presented in "novels, histories, newspapers, poems, schools, lectures,"—the *"everything"* constituting the discourse of settler

I

colonialism. As an indigenous American, Apess stood precariously on the margins of Whitman's vision of nationhood and as such was perfectly positioned to apprehend the fault lines running fast through the young nation's foundation, its self-congratulatory notions of enlightened democratic government, its fever-visions of Manifest Destiny. However, that same marginalized subject position that enabled Native Americans to perceive these faults also typically left them powerless to confront or alter them. In this Apess proved a rare exception, a bold and radicalizing presence who insinuated himself into channels of mainstream speech and letters, exhorting America to reconsider the long line of cultural productions that served to rationalize and ameliorate the violent disenfranchisement of Native people across this continent.

William Apess was an early nineteenth-century Pequot Indian and Methodist preacher whose life and textual legacy presents us with an evocative portrait of Native community, activism, and advocacy within the thoroughly colonized boundaries of the American Northeast. His writings, consisting of a half dozen known texts that received only scant public attention at their time of publication between 1829 and 1837, offer one of the more persuasive reminders of the persistence of Native community and resistance in a time and place that was long supposed to have settled its "Indian question" in favor of extinction. That his life emerges into view in our time at all is the result of Apess's self-willed ambition to write and publish his own story, *A Son of the Forest,* in 1829, an almost unprecedented feat for a nineteenth-century Native American. Apess was not motivated by vanity, of course, but by the awareness that his story of childhood indentures, warfare, and spiritual and economic struggle was also the story of thousands of other Natives being written out of the historical and geographical landscapes of nineteenth-century New England. To address the enormous scale of social injustice these communities faced required an attempt to make their stories and claims visible once more, something Apess labored to do throughout his lifetime in a variety of ways.

While there is no doubt that an indigenous presence actually persisted on the economic and political fringes of the nineteenth-century Northeast (evidenced by, among other things, the highly visible casinos operated today by both the Pequot and Mohegan nations in southern Connecticut), this fact could easily be dismissed by the greater populace given that their presence was either blurred or altogether elided by certain linguistic strategies and frameworks of history keeping. The nineteenth-century French tourist Alexis de Tocqueville, a contemporary of Apess's and often regarded as a shrewd observer of the American scene, imbibed these frameworks as fully as anyone. In his famous *Democracy in America,* Tocqueville observes of America's indigenous peoples that "their implacable prejudices, their uncontrolled passions, their vices, and still more, perhaps, their savage virtues, consigned them to inevitable destruction. The ruin of these tribes began from the day when Europeans landed on their shores; it has proceeded ever since, and we are now witnessing its completion."[3] Tocqueville was merely echoing a well-worn trope that the race of Native Americans, if they belonged anywhere, belonged to the past, and that their westward inclination toward the setting sun was as inevitable and self-inflicted as that of moths sputtering helplessly toward the porch light. This type of rhetoric has been so ubiquitous in American arts and letters that even today students in the Native American literature classes I teach reflexively begin most discussions employing the past tense and continue to trip over this conjugation throughout a given semester.

Tocqueville claimed to be "witnessing" the end of indigenous existence, but in fact his statement was an act of *unwitnessing,* of rhetorically erasing the inconvenient truth of the persistence of Native peoples and their cultures. His conclusions were achieved not through meticulous observation on his part but by passively deferring to the literary conventions of the times. Rather than acknowledge the human capacities of this land's original inhabitants, he diminishes them by constricting their emotional range and vitality to a species of sullen rage, uncontrolled passion, mindless vice, and a vaguely appreciated nobility (what he refers to as "savage virtues") that nonetheless offers no viable defense against the onslaught of American democratic culture and values. The only possible future for Native people envisioned by most nineteenth-century commentators was one of assimilation (something regarded as improbable due to the shortcomings of the race) or total extinction, and Toqueville proves utterly acquiescent to this line of thought.[4]

Apess's life and writings are capable of offering a powerful corrective to the worn-out assumptions that form this intellectual vortex of American history keeping. While his contribution to American letters had been relegated to a little-read footnote for the last one hundred and seventy some odd years, he has suddenly reappeared on the scene, perhaps as vital, compelling, controversial, and misunderstood as he was in his own time. For this we have largely to thank Barry O'Connell, who recognized the vibrancy of Apess's work and in 1992 assembled his known writings into a superb collection titled *On Our Own Ground.* This has facilitated a conversation on Apess that has brought him not only to the attention of scholars but into the classroom as well, where his writings serve a vital role in establishing Native presence and intellectual engagement in a period traditionally dominated by white males and a very small handful of plucky women writers. Apess's wit, his political consciousness, his provocative engagement with history, and even his bifurcated brand of Christianity all work to powerfully subvert passive notions of Native identity in this period prior to the Trail of Tears, Crazy Horse, Custer, Geronimo, Wounded Knee, Indian boarding schools, the "closing of the American frontier," and most other prominent cultural markers of the fall of the so-called wild Indian. And perhaps the most subversive aspect of all in terms of Apess's reception is the fact that *he writes*. He writes and he tackles with "terrible negative voice" the historical and cultural biases that have worked to distort and undermine the picture of Native presence in nineteenth-century America.

Many are surprised to learn that a member of this presumed vanishing race could articulate and sustain such impassioned narratives of social injustice at this particular moment in our history. While a handful of other late eighteenth- and early nineteenth-century Native writers, such as Samson Occom, Jane Johnston Schoolcraft, David Cusick, and Elias Boudinot, also managed to write and publish their own works, the relative obscurity of this body of literature only serves to reinforce that for Native individuals to pick up the pen in this period was to repeatedly run against a formidable wall of colonial history making. As O'Connell observes, "To write as a Native American could only be an unspeakable contradiction."[5] One way to resolve this seeming contradiction, for many a scholar, was to group Apess among a select few "Christianized" Indians who had cobbled together an education through extraordinary circumstances and were now assisting in the colonial project of assimilation or extinction, sweeping up the indigenous remains left after disease, warfare, and the other ills of colonialism, and preparing them for their subaltern position in the dominant cultural milieu.

Apess's rhetoric may have strained at the polite boundaries of such a discourse, but nevertheless he presented the novelty of an *Indian* preaching the gospel of Christ and, from a colonial perspective at least, this kept him at a rhetorical remove from other nineteenth-century Native figures, such as Tecumseh, Black Hawk, Geronimo, or Sitting Bull, who were involved in what might seem like more tangible struggles for land and cultural identity. By claiming Christianity and appearing to have fully turned his back on Native custom, Apess ceased being a threat to dominant paradigms of social order and, for some, he ceased even being *Indian*. Late nineteenth-century scholars were content to regard Apess as a "humbug" and the first wave of twentieth-century scholars to consider his literary contribution viewed it as "subjugated," perceiving Apess to have been exiled from the necessarily "pristine" conditions that were thought to characterize authentic indigenous identity.[6]

But if Apess's concessions to Western culture, alongside his refusal to simply vanish once having converted, rendered him either uninteresting or culturally inert to readers of an earlier generation, these are very much points of interest to contemporary scholarship. Apess is now more frequently seen as a dynamic figure of liminality or hybridity whose textual negotiations of a troubling period in Native history speak toward long-standing intellectual traditions of Native resistance and *survivance.*[7] Recognizing these traditions and creating pathways for them to be nourished, respected, and circulated within the strains of discourse that continue to affect the lives and well-being of Native communities has become a primary goal of contemporary Native scholarship. There is a vital push to produce studies that accept, in the words of Robert Warrior, "the influences and complexities of contemporary and historical American Indian life."[8] While the traditions Apess represents in his writings may not reflect precisely on the lifeways of the Pequot Indians prior to, or even during, early colonization, they are nonetheless vital to an understanding of the forces under which Natives of the Northeast survived and maintained community cohesion throughout the nineteenth century.

Warrior, whose much-heralded work on Native intellectual sovereignty has inevitably led him to Apess's oeuvre, maintains that the intellectual legacy of Apess has "less to do with celebrating culture than it does with his creative engagement in the intellectual task of understanding the experiences and contemporary situation of Native people."[9] Despite powerful forces that worked to isolate Apess in his lifetime and crush his creative and intellectual ambitions, Warrior still understands Apess's life and work to emerge precisely from "his experiences of being Native in New England."[10] Apess's articulation of that experience makes him, in Warrior's eyes, the pre-twentieth-century Native writer "who most demands the attention of contemporary Native intellectuals."[11] Abenaki scholar Lisa Brooks furthers this observation, suggesting that Apess "represents an apex of the Native northeastern intellectual tradition, writing his relations into a narrative of continuance at a time when the rest of New England was heavily invested in the tragic story of extinguishment."[12]

Other scholars, like Maureen Konkle, have examined how Apess's political discourse borrowed from active movements of nineteenth-century Native resistance, as in the case of the Cherokee removal. Phillip Round has remarked on the significance of Apess's journey into the realm of "proprietary authorship," and Jean O'Brien investigates how Apess consciously confronted the forces of history making that sought to make Natives seemingly vanish from the New England landscape. Anne Marie Dannenberg has usefully considered the way Apess's discourse intersected with the growing abolitionist movement and Karim Tiro and Mark J. Miller have studied Apess's career through the lens of his involvement with the Methodist Church. In the twenty-three years since O'Connell's collection first appeared, still more critics have worked to strengthen our understanding of how, rather than standing in isolation from networks of Native space and community, Apess moved actively within them, forging a public voice for their concerns.[13]

For Apess, however, it wasn't enough to simply speak, or write, in "negative voice" against the abuses and injustices Native people faced. As the French philosopher Michel Foucault insists, "There is a *negative work* to be carried out" prior to engaging with the totality of what is recognized as "knowledge." This "negative work" consists of a radical refiguring of concepts and tropes that have been historically taken for granted, such as tradition, history, identity, the origins of things, and, inevitably, knowledge itself—what Whitman recognized as the "everything" that stands behind and gives shape to public discourse.[14] Rather than regard "tradition" as something forged in the iron of earliest times and laboriously carried forth into the present, refining and multiplying itself along the way, Foucault suggested we attune ourselves to the production of its materials at any given moment and to how we, in fact, actively project our historical longings of the moment onto a fluid and malleable "historical" past.

For Native writers in America, it truly has been a "negative work" to combat the biases that colonial writers incorporated into their traditions of representing American Indians. Many Native intellectuals find themselves engaged in a tiresome and perpetual undoing of sorts, having to rhetorically untangle an intricate web of cultural and historical assumptions before they can clear a space in which their own narratives might emerge, their own sense of tradition be assembled from the traces of materials past. To engage in negative work means to stand in the path of history itself and imagine its alternatives—to intellectually challenge the static identity carved out in colonial manuscripts that pictured Natives as, at best, an "uncivilized" people, and, at worst, gross, beastlike, Stone Age savages of the type described in letters attributed to Christopher Columbus, John Smith, William Bradford, Alexis de Toqueville, and countless others. "Negative work" raises the question of how to offer something affirmative and meaningful concerning a people and a history that has been so effectively unwitnessed. How do we demonstrate that the line of history so meticulously drawn from past to present is but one set of markers, one temporal arrangement constructed from the materials of a fluid past? How do we show that the names and labels we have applied, the very language by which our cultural narratives are drawn, offer but one set of terms and one language among many that tell the story of how America came to be? For there are other stories, other ways of knowing, and other ways of telling "American" history that are, in fact, equally "true" and older than "America" itself.

In my own consideration of William Apess, I have labored in some manner to imagine his life, his travels, and the impressions that the world must have made on him. Unlike almost any other modern figure deserving of biographical treatment, there are no personal letters to assist us in navigating the private intricacies of Apess's life or to help us see beyond the pale of the persona he constructed for himself in print. His original book manuscripts are lost to us; there are few corroborating records to document his travels or accomplishments; and, as Jean O'Brien has demonstrated, the U.S. government in the nineteenth century felt little investment in tracking and recording the lives of its Indian populace.[15] As a result, even the most basic authenticating forms of identification, such as birth notice, property records, preacher's license, or last will and testament, seem to not exist for Apess. The private intimate exchanges that are so often available to the biographer cannot assist us in this case, making it extremely difficult to track or even partially comprehend the individual behind the complex performance of identity Apess forwarded in his books. To compensate for this, in some degree, I have attempted to cast a somewhat wider net, constructing this book as a "cultural biography" that holds up Apess's life as a lens through which to view the dynamics of Native lives in the Northeast.

But I have also hiked through the hills of Apess's birthplace in Colrain, Massachusetts, wandered the grounds of the Pequot reservation and his childhood places of indenture in and around Colchester, Connecticut. I have looked out over the East River rapids at Hell Gate, where, as a child of fifteen, he crossed for the first time into New York City under threat from the ship's captain that the "devil" was approaching on a stone canoe to beat Apess with his "iron paddle." I have walked the historic grounds of Governors Island, a place Apess described as "hell upon earth" while being drilled as a foot soldier in the subsequent war he would help his oppressors to fight against Great Britain. I have traveled the routes of his campaigns through the Champlain Valley and up into Canada, crossed back again through the Longhouse of the Haudenosaunee, and journeyed as far east as Mashpee on Cape Cod, where Apess helped engineer the 1833 Mashpee resistance. And I have paged through the newspapers and picture books of Boston and New York City of the early nineteenth century, trying to imagine what varieties of life inhabited those black-and-white stills that flatten the world into row houses, horse-drawn streetcars, brownstones, and gas-lit thoroughfares that puncture the horizon and yet refuse entry into their theaters of limitless silence. It is a history and a consciousness that I cannot ever claim to know or unravel, save, perhaps, through the negative reflection of light bouncing off the surface of a page in a book, or perhaps, if you will, through an Indian's looking-glass darkly.

To hold up an Indian's "looking-glass," however, is to assume some measure of control over the production of images. Throughout his life, Apess was forced to confront the images of Indian identity projected onto him by the dominant colonial culture. "I was nothing but a poor ignorant Indian," he wrote in *A Son of the Forest*.[16] As a child, Apess feared his own people, ran in terror at the thought of encountering wild Indians in the woods, had been plied, as he noted, with "many stories" of savage "cruelties toward the whites—how they [Natives] were in the habit of killing and scalping men, women, and children."[17] He not only internalized such negative racial constructions, but he endured a great deal of explicit racism in the form of corporal punishment, hostile crowds, hate speech, economic marginalization, segregation, physical violence, and incarceration. He wrote of his early days as a preacher when he was surprised at the "great concourse of people [who] had come to hear the Indian preach," only to then be pelted with sticks and other objects by his fellow Christians.[18]

And there is every reason to believe that Apess saw some projection of Native identity in the major works of his day, from the romanticized portrayal of frontier life in James Fenimore Cooper's "Leatherstocking Tales," to the archival documents Apess studied for the composition of his *Eulogy on King Philip*, to the Hudson River School portraits that reduced Native presence to a mere naked speck on the sublime canvas of the American wilderness. He quite possibly attended the most famous play of his era, *Metamora: Or, The Last of the Wampanoags*, and witnessed Edwin Forrest, the nineteenth century's most acclaimed white American thespian, pacing the stage in war paint and deer skins, crying out of the Indian that "I go to my happy hunting grounds . . . we are no more, yet we are forever."[19] And of course Apess was all too aware of the legal barriers constructed around Native agency, the laws and customs designed to either annihilate Native identity and culture altogether or remove it from sight, where the fragile remnants might be "dealt with" at a later date.

In every case, however, what Apess confronted was not a "reflection" but a "projection," not the reproduction of his own being, an expression of "soule" as the Algonquian understood it, but a horrid carnivalesque strutting across the stage of American history and consciousness, at once frightening and comic, bombastic and violent, an image from which he could only recoil even while white America looked on with absorbed credulity. Constantly Apess found himself having to reverse the image, turn it around, stand it on its head, and in so doing reconstitute colonial history-making processes. He reminded us that in "1620, the Pilgrims landed at Plymouth, and without asking liberty from anyone they possessed themselves of a portion of the country, and built themselves houses, and then made a treaty, and commanded them [Natives] to accede to it. This, if now done, it would be called an insult and every white man would be called to go out and act the part of a patriot to defend their country's rights."[20] As for his own image, an undistorted view of Pequot identity, we are—perhaps like Apess himself—left with only the image that penetrates but dimly through the historical glass.

As such, the object of writing a scholarly biography of Apess has presented itself as a daunting, if not, improbable task. And yet one of the true surprises of this project was just how much information concerning Apess had been left unmined up to this point. I hope general readers, as well as Apess scholars, will be as excited as I have been to finally be able to connect the various dots of his life, from the probable location of his birth in Colrain to the site of his indigenous "rebirth" at the Lake on the Mountain in Prince Edward County, Ontario, to the one-room schoolhouse where he delivered his first "exhortation" as an aspiring Methodist minister to the hall (still standing today) where he pronounced his first reading of *A Eulogy on King Philip,* not at the Odeon Theater in Boston in 1836 as presumed, but at a Unitarian meeting house in Portsmouth, New Hampshire, a full year earlier.[21]

While researching and writing this book, I was often struck by the notion that if nineteenth-century luminaries such as Whitman, Thoreau, and Emerson are deemed worthy of multiple biographical treatments, many of them roughly the size of city phone books, then William Apess's life surely must be deserving of equal attention. His is a stunning and unprecedented voice, not just of Native identity and advocacy, but of rhetorical genius in an age known for its oratory. Of course, gaps exist in the reconstruction of any life, and the unknowns still outweigh the knowns in regard to Apess. But what has emerged are not only important writings, dates, places, and facts previously unrecorded but also the full extent of Apess's courage and commitment to Native causes and his almost inexhaustible energy in pursuing those aims—an energy that kept Apess constantly on the move, one step ahead of the persistent traumas that, I argue, continuously pursued him throughout his life.

Such stamina in the face of overwhelming resistance allowed Apess to overcome the obstacles to attaining his preaching license in 1831; compelled him to write multiple books and have them published and distributed at a time when Native authorship was all but unheard of; gained Apess entry into pulpits, theaters, and town halls, where he packed every seat; and enabled Apess to become a compelling voice of dissent. Apess's writings might be viewed as studied investigations into the limits of speech, what might be said publicly and to what effect in the discourse communities within which he performed. In a climate structured around the imposition of racialized hierarchies, Apess consistently argued for a common humanity, cried out against laws prohibiting miscegenation, and was one of the few men of his era to persistently address the social vulnerability of women, whom he saw as virtually defenseless against the predation of white men. Like his contemporary, the black activist David Walker, who galvanized support for the abolitionist movement with his *Appeal to the Coloured People of America* in 1829, Apess apprehended how he might use America's foundational revolutionary rhetoric of equality among men to the advantage of all people of color. More so than Walker,

Apess determined how an evangelical calling could become a kind of armor against knee-jerk criticism and afford him a pulpit from which to advance a biting critique of the abysmal conditions suffered by both Native and black communities in America's sharply racialized landscapes.

In his 1833 sermon "An Indian's Looking-Glass for the White Man," Apess asked, "Suppose these skins [of the world] were put together, and each skin had its natural crimes written upon it—which skin do you think would have the greatest? . . . I know that when I cast my eye upon that white skin, and if I see those crimes written upon it, I should enter my protest against it immediately and cleave to that which is more honorable."[22] As an itinerant minister traveling the American Northeast in the late 1820s and 1830s, Apess honed his message before both white and colored audiences, developing a razor-sharp delivery peppered with ironic observations that not only exposed the profound prejudices of America's supposedly democratic institutions but leveled its aim fearlessly at the church as well. By holding up an Indian's looking-glass, Apess hoped to expose the blatant hypocrisies underwriting America's ongoing treatment of people of color, forcing the nation to confront its own tarnished aspect in regards to civil rights. "By what you might read, you may learn how deep your own principles are," Apess warned. "I should say they were skin-deep."[23]

The Ojibwe scholar Scott Lyons has noted the complexity and difficulty of Apess's performance, referring to his literary output as a kind of "x-mark." According to Lyons, when in early treaties Native people put their x-marks on documents, it was rarely done in a spirit of amicable agreement. Such concessions were most often made under duress in highly disruptive circumstances, but if it was understood that severe losses would follow, there was always the hope that something might be preserved as well. In this way, Lyons asserts, all Indian texts function as "x-marks" or "signs of consent in a context of coercion."[24] For an Indian to write was already a sign that cultural concessions had been made, that loss had been incurred and more sacrifice was on the way. And yet, it was also always a tacit expression of agency. Writing signaled a determination to effect change through whatever means were at hand, to define oneself in resistant terms, to speak for communities that often were prevented through myriad means from speaking for themselves. To understand the contribution of early Native writers like Apess, Lyons tells us, "requires a vigilant awareness of the discursive formations that created their contexts," just as these writers themselves "were always acutely aware of their rhetorical contexts and addressed them accordingly."[25] The mark of Apess's genius is how he would ultimately hit upon a language, a form of address, with which to transcend these rhetorical horizons and proffer a foundation of indigenous self-determinacy.

Through an Indian's Looking-Glass reflects upon the x-mark that is Apess's life and work, locating strains of Native community and resistance from within the dominant narrative framework in which he necessarily labored. At each step of the way, Apess's life becomes a kind of lens through which we might catch a glimpse of the lives Native peoples lived in the Northeast of the early nineteenth century. Like all Native peoples of this region, Apess lived under the long shadow of war, disease, and disruption, all of which contributed to a legacy of cultural trauma that persists in some measure to this day. As a Pequot, Apess carried the cultural memories of the 1636–37 Pequot War, which oversaw the intended obliteration of the Pequots as a people. The Puritan colonists pledged to "root their very name out of this Country . . . dunging the Ground with their Flesh."[26] Not a few revered colonial figures are implicated in the obscenity of this genocidal intention, understood by the Puritans to be a mandate from Heaven. The Pequots endured as a people, though not without scars to their collective psyche, and Apess's narrative addresses these wounds even as he must cope with the scars of his own experiences with war and race hatred.

Apess's narrative also crosses the intersections of sovereignty and slavery in the early republic, noting the bonded lives of Native people in New England at this time amid their struggles to retain land and identity. Economic marginalization at the hands of the dominant culture contributed to the splintering of families and communities as Native people were forced into lives of servitude or had to range far and wide searching for gainful employment. Apess's father pursued the rapid current of industrialization to newly sprung towns such as Colrain, Massachusetts, where Apess was born in 1798. Apess's mother was a slave. But the more predictable life for an Indian child born to this era was that of indentured servitude, and such was Apess's fate, subject to the whims and abuses of his masters until finally he fled and joined the U.S. Army.

Apess's familiarity with warfare was not acquired as an Indian "brave" or "savage" but as an enlisted man in the War of 1812. Although only fifteen at the time of his enrollment, Apess spent two years at the Canadian front, involved in campaigns against Montreal and in the decisive 1814 Battle of Plattsburgh. This part of Apess's life has received scant academic attention and yet it was a formative experience shared by a great many Native men, as Natives have fought alongside the United States (and the English colonists before that) in every war waged in this country's history. Apess's political consciousness truly awakened following the war as he wandered the freshly contested boundaries of Canada and the United States, forging a sense of solidarity with other borderland Native communities that helped him to heal and to begin to discover an indigenous identity for himself and his people.

When Apess finally returns home to New England, he continues to culti-
vate this emerging sense of self-empowerment as he reunites with his Pequot
community, starts a family, and pursues the life of an itinerant Methodist
minister. Apess's ministry reflects the reality of so many Native communities
of the Northeast that sought shelter within Christian revivalist movements
of the time, but it also paves the way for Apess's work as an advocate for
Native causes, resulting in the 1833 event known as the "Mashpee Revolt" in
which Apess launches America's first successful campaign of civil disobedience. Apess continued to pursue that advocacy through literary productions
and ultimately to the American stage where he offered his most poignant
effort yet at reconfiguring historical paradigms with his *Eulogy on King Philip*.
Although this will not be his final public performance, the *Eulogy* proved to
be Apess's last published work, and it affords us a parting glimpse of Apess
in his struggle to unwind the fierce and persistent machinations of colonial
power.

As we know, mirrors never reflect back to us an undistorted image of self.
They can only show us reflections of what we wish to see or what we have
been conditioned to see. In the nineteenth century, however, the mirror was a
commonly deployed metaphor for writing. It was accepted that what a mirror
reflected back to us was accurate, as was the archival body of work that com-
prised the looking-glass of a dominant colonial culture. Perhaps this is how
Apess's work becomes "negative work," as it is always necessarily dealing with
a backward image, the tricked-out darkened light that never reveals to us the
thing itself.

In Native tradition, too, the looking-glass was a window to the soul. In the
foundational narrative of the Haudenosaunee Longhouse, which Apess knew
at least in part, the cultural hero Hiawatha, after generations of war, had lost
sight of his humanity. Living on the margins of community, he reportedly
feasted on the flesh of his enemies. He is the original savage cannibal fetishized
by early explorers such as Columbus, Vespucci, and others. Until, one day, he
looks into his cooking pot and, encountering his own reflection in the broth,
sees that he is beautiful. What he doesn't realize is that the pure spirit known
in Haudenosaunee tradition as the Peacemaker has climbed to Hiawatha's
roof and is looking down through the smoke hole. What Hiawatha sees is
not his own reflection but that of the Peacemaker. From this moment on,
however, he resolves to be true to that image and spends the remainder of
his days pursuing a path of peace for himself and his people, forging the laws
and the customs that will bind the Five Nations of the Longhouse together
for generations to come. We all require that chance to see what is best in
ourselves, to have positive reflections of our identity projected outward upon

us, to believe that our lives and souls are created in beauty. William Apess had to labor against a flood tide of colonial history making to offer this impression to himself, to discern in his own image and the image of his beleaguered people that which is holy. "My image is of God," Apess tells us in his *Eulogy.* "I am not a beast."[27]

Robert Warrior notes that Apess was, indeed, "a product of the absence of traditional Pequot culture," but he also maintains that "the continuing existence of the Pequots in the face of all they experienced is testimony to the resilience of generations of political leadership that refused to give up on the idea of the Pequots as a people."[28] Apess was a product of both that absence and that resilience. And he sought to fill that absence with the materials at hand, the bits and pieces of cultural flotsam he amassed in his travels. Apess craved a Native identity and sensibility that would serve as solid ground in the cultural swamps through which he wandered, and his writings have left us a remarkable legacy, an indelible mark of that quest—a quest shared by so many peoples of the Native Northeast groping, themselves, for a like vision of permanence and unity in nineteenth-century New England.

CHAPTER ONE
The Baskets Copy Our Stories

Some think the idea for weaving baskets came from the earth, which is the holder of our cornfields. Which is the holder of our lives. Yes, the baskets just copy the land.

But others think the idea for weaving baskets came from the sky. An upside-down holder of the rain. So it falls back to us.

But I say, the idea for baskets came from our stories. The baskets hold fish and corn and beans. Just like our stories hold meaning. Yes, I say the baskets copy our stories.

—DIANE GLANCY, *Pushing the Bear*

On a chill spring evening in 1802 walks the old woman, her unsold wares lashed to her back, bumping lightly together with the rhythm of her footsteps, straw brooms, pails, and baskets, some softer vessels of wild hemp and corn leaf she herself has woven and bound, stamped and imprinted with dye made from the juice of blood-root and berries, the whole assemblage melded to her frame so that she resembles, in the dimming light, some mythic beast just wandered out from the wood. Her dress, thrown over her taut frame, is of brown homespun, embroidered with porcupine quills in roseate patterns that loop and wind, feet shoed with deerskin, hair pulled back with hemp. She walks, hunched over, not so much from weight or even age, but from other burdens she has carried. She has come many miles and her breath carries the heavy scent of rum that escapes with the curses she utters to none but the darkening sky as she presses homeward.

Upon reaching the threshold of the cabin, she unburdens herself of baskets and brooms, hangs them by a nail embedded on a rude post propping up the extended eave that shelters the doorstep. She enters the cramped quarters, her eyes moving back and forth, parsing the countenances of the five young children within whose shapes are limned by the hearthfire before which they huddle. There is a wooden table and a few handmade chairs for furniture, a small bundle of wood piled by the hearth and a pail filled with water nearby, bits of ash swirling within. Tools hang amidst grasses and dried herbs on the walls, the floor is strewn with wood shavings and straw.

The children do not appear to be engaged in anything other than staring at the flames. The youngest is not yet two years old and a doll made of corn cob and leaves lies limp in the folds of her dress. They have not eaten. There is no telling why the woman's gaze lingers on the one whose dark hair hangs slightly over his eyes, skinny, sitting on his haunches, clothed in rags, his uncertain lips proffering the slightest intimation of a smile. The others look to her as well, but she is troubled by him alone, a certain searching in his countenance that levels some unspoken claim she feels welling up inside her, mixing with the rum.

She takes a step and stumbles, nearly falling to the floor. Until this point the very rhythm of her walking, endlessly, along the dirt path had steadied her like a drumbeat, kept her moving upright and in a straight line, but now that she has paused, forfeited her momentum, her knees buckle and she lurches forward. The child does not flinch or move his eyes from hers.

"Why do you stare at me like that?" she demands of him. She is only half aware at first that she has even spoken this aloud, or how it stands apart from her other random mutterings, but as the realization sinks in she repeats it with even greater force.

"Why do you stare at me? Do you hate me?"

This child has experienced many things in his short life. He has felt love, loss, hunger, pain, and sorrow enough to cripple many a soul. He has collected these emotions, stirred them about, wrestled down some of the sharper edged fragments that cut from the inside and are not forgotten.

Yet however rich and complex his world of feeling, however deep the intelligence by which he measures his small dram of heartache and injury, he does not count hate among his reserve. He has unconsciously flirted with it, but is too young to reduce his allotment of experiences into that cold hardened lump animating so much of human endeavor. Though he is cognizant of it. Has seen it in the world already and felt its proximity. It is a force that hovers about him, creeps close upon the quarters where he and his siblings huddle on the cold floor, involves itself in his circumstances in ways that he has no ability to articulate at this young age and perhaps never will. Hate is both a presence and an absence.

When he looks around the room, sees his young sister's wasted frame close by the fire, waxen and listless, he knows hate is nearby. When he looks for the faces of his mother and father whose purposeful talk and movements once kept this space astir, he knows hate has worked to somehow cast them from his presence. And there is hate in the air both inside and out, although he wouldn't know how to name it thus or from whence it entered. He only knows it as an indeterminate force that

presses down on him and he feels it hovering around the frame of his grandmother
who has been gone since before the sun arose and who is somehow visibly wrested
by this force and speaking its name as the smell of it comes streaming in a current
of her breath.

"Do you hate me?" she demands once more.

"Yes," he answers.

"The Intensity of Our Sufferings I Cannot Tell"

William Apess was roughly thirty years old when he recorded the above events
for his 1829 autobiography *A Son of the Forest*. Already he had journeyed far
from his obscure and pathetic origins, seen a large swath of the world, served
in war, experienced combat at its most heated and brutal pitch, and labored
at many different occupations: cobbler, farmhand, baker, river boat naviga-
tor. More significantly, he had educated himself in the ways of the dominant
white culture, becoming adept enough at their spiritual practices to be considered for ordination in the Methodist Episcopal Church (a position that
would ultimately be denied him) and, in fact, to attempt what few, if any,
other Native people had essayed up to this point in time—that is, to write a
book-length story of his life. He had climbed about as high as a Native man
could expect to aspire in a world built to enable and protect the economic
and cultural propriety of whites, which is to say, he was eking out a living by
itinerant preaching and selling his books.

He had also put some manner of distance between himself and the traumas
of his youth. He had steadied himself against all odds, was married, sober,
and supporting a young family. Settling down to write his story, he was able
somehow to summon a controlled and dispassionate voice as he recalled how
his grandmother took up a club on that long ago evening and proceeded to
beat him "unmercifully," repeating the question "Do you hate me?," which,
as he recalls, "I very innocently answered in the affirmative as I did not then
know what the word meant and thought all the while I was answering aright;
and so she continued asking me the same question, and I as often answered
in the same way, whereupon she continued beating me," until "my poor little
body was mangled and my little arm broken into three pieces."[1]

Undoubtedly Apess had learned enough in his travels to appreciate the risks
of ripping open such old wounds, of trotting them out for a public viewing
and exposing his immediate family, and, by extension, the larger indigenous
community implicated in such acts, to censure and even ridicule by white
readers. And there were *personal* risks for Apess as well. Such memories must
still have carried with them a psychic residue, painful to recall and even more
painful to orchestrate in prose. One of the paradoxical symptoms of being a

victim of such violence is that it is not uncommon to entertain on some level the notion that it was somehow deserved. An affect and privilege of power is that it protects itself by channeling blame back toward the victim, and when such violence can be positioned within a discourse of race, the dynamic complicates exponentially, reaffirming deep-rooted stereotypes that operate both within and without the abused subject. Simpler by far, then, would have been to bypass the shameful history of his treatment at the hands of his own family altogether, burying such uncomfortable confessions in the darkest recesses of his consciousness or anecdotally attributing them to someone else entirely. Certainly, he could invoke sympathy for Native peoples without making them complicit in their own injury, without reaffirming the worst stereotypes maintained by the white evangelical communities most likely to read his books. He might easily be forgiven for not exposing such intimate acts of domestic cruelty to light. And yet Apess begins the narrative arc of his life journey at precisely this point. It is the very thing he must address.

Apess had arrived at an acute awareness that, whatever the risk involved, traumas left in the dark can never be healed, their wrongs never corrected. Rather than view himself as the individual object of an injustice at the hands of his grandparents, Apess apprehended larger machinations at work. He determined to boldly bear witness not only to his own mistreatment, but to the complex social forces that engendered it and to which he, his parents, his grandparents, and his entire extended community of "brethren" (as he often referred to his fellow Natives) remained entirely vulnerable. A powerful tide of history had brought both the young Apess and his grandmother to wreck upon the shores of this concentrated outbreak of violence. As he noted, "This cruel and unusual conduct was the effect of some cause." And if he could not entirely exonerate his grandmother for her behavior, he understood that "the whites were justly chargeable with at least some portion of my sufferings."[2] This chapter seeks to explicate some of the cultural and historical forces that help to account for William Apess's traumatic childhood experience.

At the time of his writing the autobiographical *A Son of the Forest*, it may have been difficult for Apess to fully unravel this long and complicated history. He may as yet have lacked the rhetorical skill, and he certainly lacked the formal education, the time, and the resources to explicate what many recognized but so few would openly acknowledge—that is, that indigenous peoples of the Northeast stood at the very epicenter of over two hundred years of the most aggressive and vindictive colonial encroachments. In fact, the deliberate annihilation of Native lifeways in New England, and in particular that of the Pequots, had proceeded to such a point that, where it had once been in the interests of the colonial power structure to violently "Root their very Name out of this Country," it had now become almost fashionable to pity the "poor child of the forest" and view the "dying race" of Natives as dependent "wards of the state" in need of charity and government oversight.[3] Such a state of cultural crisis and condescension served only to complicate the range of effective responses that could be mustered by any Native individual dedicated to improving the condition of his people.

Apess understood that there was little to gain by invoking sympathy for his troubled childhood. Sympathy, even well-intentioned sympathy, would only position him squarely back within the dominant paradigm that continued to politically disenfranchise Native people. He makes a point of noting, "I merely relate these circumstances, without any embellishment or exaggeration, to show the reader how we [he and his siblings] were treated. The intensity of our sufferings I cannot tell."[4] Apess understood that, rather than become an object of pity, he somehow needed to reverse the current of anguish, to reflect back upon the settler culture how their own actions lay at the root of the perceived injustices and were colored by the very characteristics of "savagery" with which they had attempted to tar Native peoples. Apess understood that hate didn't always come exclusively at the end of a gun or a sword, but that it continued to exert itself through other means as an ambivalent presence, a studied indifference to the social conditions achieved through violence that could be generationally perpetuated, expanded upon, and coolly rationalized through processes of racial categorization. These categories, left unchallenged, would continue to wreak devastation on Native lives, uproot entire communities, and aggressively beat down every claim to Native sovereignty and land title across the North American continent.

In 1829, Apess had just recently battled his way into the structure of the Methodist Church. If he had attained a rare status for a Native man of the early nineteenth century, he stood yet on precarious ground. As we will see, he had to overcome a great deal of institutional resistance to get to where he was and needed to frame his words of protest with the greatest care. As such, he attributed his grandmother's actions "in a great measure to the whites, inasmuch as they introduced among my countrymen that bane of comfort and happiness, ardent spirits—seduced them into a love of it and, when under its unhappy influence, wronged them out of their lawful possessions— that land where reposed the ashes of their sires."[5]

For Apess to blame his grandmother's actions on "the influence of spirituous liquor" was at best a partial indictment of colonial violence toward Native peoples, but it was an indictment that played well within the structure of the Methodist Church, where temperance sermons were the coin of the realm, and it allowed him to at least gesture toward that larger history of misuse and deceit that informed his pivotal childhood memories. Before the introduction of the "debaucheries of the whites," Apess tells us, Native people were as "unoffending and happy as they roamed over their goodly possessions as any people on whom the sun of heaven ever shone." But in the wake of colonial infiltration, "the consequence was that they [Native peoples] were scattered abroad. Now many of them were seen reeling about intoxicated with liquor, neglecting to provide for themselves and families, who were before assiduously engaged in supplying the necessities of those depending upon them for support. I do not make this statement in order to justify those who had treated me so unkindly, but simply to show that . . . I was thus treated only when they [his grandparents] were under the influence of spirituous liquor."[6]

It may be difficult for contemporary readers to grasp the limited outlets for protest confronted by someone in Apess's situation—his time, his place, and his racial profile. It may, in fact, be difficult for many contemporary readers to fathom that such an Indian as Apess even existed, given that he fails to conform to the most ubiquitous stereotypes of Native identity in circulation both then and now. Americans have long had a tendency to view Native people through a highly romanticized lens as a bundle of contradictions, typified by the Comanche and Sioux warrior type of Hollywood productions, patrolling the western plains or dense forests, bare-torsoed, in feathered headdress, pursuing buffalo or wagon trains and looking to kidnap unsuspecting white women and children—or, conversely, as hyperspiritualized stewards of the environment, in communion with animal spirits and shedding a tear, perhaps, for our current despoiled environment before dissolving into the landscape. Rarely is this figure imagined as belonging to vital community structures, in a family setting, with concerns both domestic and political. He is rather an emblem of savage passions and agendas, driven by bloodlust and revenge, melancholic, isolated by historical forces that are in the very process of rooting him from the earth. And even when we are, perhaps, conscious of the reductive nature of these stereotypes, we find ourselves armed with little to combat or replace them. In short, Indians, as the mainstream culture has come to know them, are supposed to look nothing like the evangelizing, book-writing, temperance-lecturing promoter of the Christian creed William Apess.

In the most general terms, however, Apess's circumstances were, in fact, typical of nineteenth-century Native lives in the Northeast. By 1829, the local tribes of New England, including the Wampanoags, Narragansetts, Nipmucks, Pocumtucks, Abenakis, Passamaquoddies, Montauks, Schagticokes, Mohegans, and the Pequots among them, had withstood over two centuries of sustained colonial aggression. A number of these tribes had managed, against seemingly insurmountable odds, to maintain a land base, and they had done so through elaborate processes of diplomacy, resistance, and assimilation. By Apess's time, however, Native peoples had, in the most outward manifestation of their appearance, accepted English manners and customs, like one who puts on a borrowed coat after their own has been stripped from their back.

They mostly spoke English. They were compelled to abandon communally held lands and to think of themselves instead as private property owners. They switched out their wigwams for wood-framed houses, adapted to European gender roles concerning agriculture and labor, surrendered polygamous family structures, and had invested, at least to some degree, in Christian forms of worship. Despite the forces that prompted these transformations, however, none of this prevented Native people from maintaining their own sense of themselves as Wampanoags, Narragansetts, Nipmucks, Pocumtucks, Abenakis, Passamaquoddies, Montauks, Schagticokes, Mohegans, or Pequots. If they had found it necessary to put on a borrowed coat, so to speak, they retained the memory of their old coats and still understood who they were beneath the new mantle that had been flung over them.

But even this is an unsatisfactory analogy and doesn't quite take into account the manner by which Native peoples of New England actively determined the shape and structure of their identities, at times embracing the introduction of colonial norms, at times resisting them, and other times melding them into new and useful forms to suit their own particular needs, uses, and political agendas. The very act of placing pen to paper was a tacit expression of the hybrid world Native peoples occupied. To express oneself in this manner was to imagine an audience informed in English literacy and English language, replete with all of its codes, mannerisms, spiritual guideposts, and aesthetic expectations. Apess, as a writer, was not at liberty to express an unfiltered sense of Pequot identity. Nor would he, despite all these cultural concessions, ever be regarded as on a par with white writers—not because he lacked talent or ability but because the very nature of his expression, the conditions that inspired his protest, were rooted in the racial hierarchies of colonial language and aesthetics that, in the eyes of the public, reduced his nature to a state of Indian savagery and rendered his writing an ambiguous x-mark. As a result, any form of self-expression became entangled in a kind of treacherous double bind, made of him a "child of the woods" or "son of the forest" despite the fact that he was raised mostly in white households in a largely urban environment.

When Apess attributed the abuse he had suffered as a child to "spirituous liquors" introduced by whites, he was at once locating an acceptable portal of resistance and yet playing into an established colonial construction of Native dependency. He had to pick his battles, and often found himself rhetorically hemmed in whichever way he turned. Native peoples, through a complex web of socially constructed categories and expectations, were at once doomed by their essentialized categorization as Indians, and yet tragically compromised by their attempts to conform to dominant cultural norms. To do battle with such persistent constraints meant to engage in negative work, to deal with physical and psychic wounds for which there was no possible redress, while trafficking in reflections and projections of images that had no substance and yet carried enormous weight.

These were only some of the factors that Apess was up against as he set out to tell his tale, recalling the hardships of his past and contemplating how things came to pass in such a manner. Yet, even as he began to unravel the thread of his personal history, bearing old wounds and struggling to articulate the historical processes that brought them about, we must keep in mind his own assurance that "the intensity of our sufferings I cannot tell." Apess carefully calculates what his white nineteenth-century audience might be capable of hearing, but leaves just as many gaps in his narrative, signaling the horizons of acceptable speech, the dimensions of grief and trauma that cannot be entered into with language, and leaving us with many uncertainties in regard to his life, career, and motivations.

Defining Savagery and Civilization in the Nineteenth Century

"I presume," Apess writes, "that the reader will exclaim, 'What *savages* your grandparents were to treat unoffending, helpless children in this cruel manner.'"[7] The appellation of "savage" in reference to people of Native origin was, of course, still well in vogue throughout the nineteenth century with no degree of assimilation up to the task of prying the subject loose from the stereotype. Far more than just a simple slur used by lower types to denigrate their frontier rivals, it was a figure of standard speech employed in every circle of American thought, codified in legal documents, national histories, poetry, and prose.

The world Apess was born into unproblematically equated Indian identity with savagery even when it didn't use the term explicitly, or, as noted earlier, it wrapped itself in a language of benevolence toward the "poor Indians." The earliest missionary language adopted by the Puritans who settled New England in the seventeenth century brought these tropes together seamlessly, proclaiming as its very first priority in this land the goal of spreading Christian light by setting a "good example to the poor savage heathens among whom they live."[8] The fact that the settlers were greeted with diplomatic poise and respect by the local Wampanoags was in no way attributed to the politic nature of the Indians. Rather it was characterized by Puritan leaders as the "providence of God . . . possessing the hearts of the Savages with astonishment and fear of us, whereas if God had let them loose, they might easily have swallowed us up, scarce being an handful in comparison of those forces they might have gathered together against us."[9] One can apprehend the cognitive dissonance at work here. Settlers freely expressed their own agency in setting a "good example" to the Indians. And yet they stripped agency away from

Native acts of benevolence and restraint by attributing such overall lack of aggression to "the providence of God." *Savage* acts are guided not by politics or principle but instead by base passions such as fear, envy, and revenge. The very lack of rationale presumed to be at the core of Native existence left only heavenly providence to explain the adroit diplomatic tenor of the Wampanoag response to Puritan incursions on their land.

This cognitive dissonance is set deep in the soil of the American psyche and continues to rationalize a great deal of ongoing cultural and physical exploitation of Native peoples. Locating Native identity within a discourse of "savagery" enabled Euro-Americans to define their own presumably more enlightened and progressive condition against the denigrated state of the other. Presumed racial differences became embedded not just in colonial histories and literature but in the very linguistic operations informing thought and speech, creating a set of hierarchies that have become engrained in our rhetorics. This dynamic is referred to by the philosopher Charles W. Mills as the ever present, but largely unacknowledged, "racial contract" drawn up by Western powers.[10]

Mainstream American discourse continues to have difficulty coming to terms with this "contract" because so many Americans perceive the origins of their national identity to be wrapped in an Enlightenment era discourse founded on freedom and egalitarian principles presumably recognized as good the world over. Typically we will allow that slavery was the one aberration from this set of noble ideals, but when that was inevitably done away with in the course of time, the United States went on to fulfill its grand original promise: a land of equal opportunity for all regardless of race or class. But, as Mills argues, the very authors of the Enlightenment—people like Jean-Jacques Rousseau, John Locke, and Immanuel Kant—all forwarded explicit doctrines of racial difference. Kant went so far as to write a treatise in 1775, "The Different Races of Mankind," locating Native Americans at the very lowest rung of his evolutionary scheme.[11]

The leading naturalist of the Enlightenment era, Georges-Louis Leclerc, otherwise known as Comte de Buffon, wrote of the American Indian that he was "feeble," had "smaller sex organs," and exhibited "no passion for the female." Lacking the basic motivations of hunger and thirst, Buffon asserted, the Indian "will stand around or lie down for days on end. It is pointless to seek out other explanations of the isolated life of these people, or their dislike of society: the most valuable spark of nature's fire has been denied them; they lack passion for the females, and consequently have no love for their fellow men . . . their heart is chill, their society cold, their rule harsh."[12] The fact that Buffon had never so much as visited America or witnessed Native society in action did not discourage him from advancing such utterly erroneous comments.

The American-born William Stanhope Smith, a Presbyterian minister and president of what would become Princeton University, noted in a 1787 treatise, *An Essay on the Causes of Variety of Complexion and Figure in the Human Species,* that "the Indian of North-America presents to us man completely savage, but obliged by the nature of the forest which he inhabits . . . as well as by the enemies with which he is surrounded, to employ both courage and address, for his subsistence, and defense. He is of savages, therefore, the most noble."[13] Smith was, in fact, arguing for a single species of man; however, this did not prevent him from perceiving America's indigenous peoples, as did Buffon, as lacking community, art, science, literature, and agriculture. He significantly situates his Indian in a location of spatialized savagery, "the forest which he inhabits," as though village communities sustained by agricultural practices, strong family ties, artistic pursuits, and vast trade networks were unknown to Native peoples inhabiting the North American continent. Such a framework for understanding the "savage" existence of Natives would allow for an even partially sympathetic observer like Smith to conclude, "A savage can hardly be said to have a country."[14] In other words, those imagined to dwell in unimproved forest spaces can stake no claim to the land that any civilized person is bound to respect. Such a belief, forwarded in the same year that the U.S. Constitution was ratified, carried with it significant political and cultural consequences.

George Bancroft, often referred to as "the father of American history," perfectly spells out this equating of savagery with space in his mammoth *The History of America from Colonization to Present Times* first published in 1834. The very design of this history purported to demonstrate how a "favoring Providence [has called] our institutions into being [and] conducted the country to its present happiness and glory."[15] In other words, Bancroft believed that the institutions inscribed by the success of the American Revolution were preordained by God. Such a program virtually necessitated that issues of Native land tenure quickly be addressed, and, in fact, they are, in the brief introduction of what was to become a ten-volume history. Bancroft decrees that prior to colonization the whole of the continent "was an unproductive waste. Throughout its wide extent, the arts had not erected a monument. Its only inhabitants were a few scattered tribes of feeble barbarians, destitute of commerce, of political connexion, and of morals. The axe and the ploughshare were unknown. The soil, which had been gathering fertility from the repose of centuries, was lavishing its strength in magnificent but useless vegetation. In the view of civilization the immense domain was a solitude."[16]

That such assertions are made concerning indigenous antiquity and largely still accepted speaks to the ambivalence with which Americans typically engage their own history, as well as to the phenomenon of "unwitnessing." Americans historically "unwitness" Native civilization as part of a passive process of disenfranchising indigenous peoples from their lands. To look too closely would provoke a host of extremely problematic questions piercing to the heart of national identity and legal statutes. And so we require, at least rhetorically, that Native people vanish, sucked whole cloth into a pretend poetic space often referred to as "the American forest primeval." Poets and prose writers, in chorus with philosophers and historians, helped to situate the Native within this forest space while inscribing an endless stream of premature elegies for the "vanished" red man. James Fenimore Cooper, in America's most enduring literary eulogy, *The Last of the Mohicans,* could assert without raising a single readerly eyebrow that his stock noble savage, the Mohican sagamore Chingachgook, had "never seen the sun shine but through the trees."[17] Consigning Native identity to this imagined forest existence became the primary means for internalizing the dislocation of Native civilization by the dominant culture, however much facts on the ground contradicted this formulation.

Popular colonial lore, in keeping with the savagery-and-civilization binary, would have us believe that the Pilgrims encountered dense forest when first landing on these shores. What they faced in reality were cleared lands and an abundance of Native agriculture. The first settlers of Plymouth Plantation observed of their chosen location for a new home that disease had recently carried off a great number of the original inhabitants, leaving "much plain ground, about fifty acres, fit for the plow, and some signs where the Indians had formerly planted their corn."[18] Edward Winslow recounts warding off starvation in the first few years of settlement by frantically bartering with the local Indians for corn, and yet he still might claim "that when I seriously consider of things, I cannot but think that God hath a purpose to give that Land as an inheritance to our Nation, and great pity it were that it should long lie in so desolate a state."[19]

It is a fact that without the surplus availability of Indian corn that the English were able to acquire through trade or theft, the early settlements would have floundered. Bancroft himself must repeatedly contradict his own claims regarding the rich American soil that presumably languished in a state of repose, producing only "useless vegetation." When discussing the Pequot War of 1636–37, he records the systematic destruction of Pequot crops, noting that their "every cornfield was laid to waste."[20] If it must be admitted that Indians did, in fact, have agriculture, Bancroft and others could attribute this to their "natural instinct [which] had led the Indians to select for their villages the pleasantest places, along the purest streams, and near the soil that was most easily cultivated."[21] So often in the dominant archive of American history making, the presence of Native agriculture is witnessed only in the same moment that it is being erased from historical view, the cornfields burned to the ground, and the settlers moving in to claim those "desolate" fertile spaces to which Natives had apparently been drawn not by reason but by "natural instinct." This, in fact, is the essence of *unwitnessing*—to simultaneously see and not see. The deadly irony here is that, if Native landscapes were a "waste," it was the colonists who were, in fact, responsible for wasting them.

Hector St. John de Crèvecoeur, the French immigrant who in 1782 famously defined what it means to be an "American," referred to his Native neighbors on the New York–Pennsylvania frontier as "a race doomed to recede and disappear before the superior genius of the Europeans."[22] While immigrants such as Crèvecoeur could plow the American soil and find their very identities transformed by the generative vapors therein, Native people were deemed too savage to benefit from this alchemy. Even the Declaration of Independence, America's founding document and most sacred text, offers only one reference to Native peoples, when it asserts that King George "had endeavored to bring on the inhabitants of our frontiers, *the merciless Indian savages* whose known rule of warfare is an undistinguished destruction of all ages, sexes & conditions."[23] This characterization was offered within the framework of "self-evident" truths and the equal capacities of all men. There were compelling reasons, however, for Native peoples to see it the other way around.

Both America's historical patriarch, George Bancroft, and America's cultural orphan, William Apess, were composing their texts at the precise same historical moment, one with the implicit assurance that his words would be received with applause in the halls of power, and the other under the explicit assumption that one of his race and social standing had nothing to contribute to art, culture, or civilization. As Mills notes of the racial contract, "The spread of colonialism would consolidate an intellectual world in which this bestial state of nature would be reserved for non-white savages, to be despotically governed, while civil Europeans would enjoy the benefits of liberal parliamentarianism."[24] By rigidly policing the lines of racial difference from the dawn of colonial history right up until the present day, the dominant white culture reserves the highest privileges of economic and political freedoms for themselves.

Basket Cases: First Encounters in Native Space

So, what were the external circumstances that lead to Apess's abusive treatment at the hands of his grandmother? What can we hope to know of these effects, and how might the dominant culture, aside from cognitively denigrating Native peoples as "savages" and introducing "spirituous liquors," have been at least partly to blame for such ills? All we really know for certain of

Apess's grandmother is that she resided in the area of Colchester, Connecticut, in 1802; had a male consort whom Apess referred to as his grandfather on his mother's side; and that she lived in a cabin or hut that was divided into two apartments, with Apess's unnamed uncle living in the adjoining apartment. She was abusive when drunk and would go out "among the whites with her baskets and brooms," where, perhaps more often than not, she would foment "herself with the fiery waters of the earth, so that she had lost all her reason and judgment and, in this fit of intoxication, raged most bitterly."[25] And yet, even these thin strands of information might provide us materials to begin weaving together a more comprehensive narrative structure. For if we are to at least partially understand the actions of Apess's grandmother, we need to know something of Pequot history, and that history is, to a certain extent, woven into the baskets themselves.

Basket making was prevalent among Native men and women in early nineteenth-century New England. In continuing this art, Apess's grandparents were not only struggling to insert themselves into the settler economy but were also involving themselves in one of the enduring seasonal traditions that preceded the advent of European colonialism in their lives. To whatever extent the cultural integrity of Pequot customs were shaken and uprooted by colonial dynamics, this practice still served as a vital touchstone of the lifeways of Apess's ancestors, who had inhabited the drainage basin of the Connecticut River long before the first European visitors began sailing to these shores.

In New England, wood-splint baskets were commonly made from ash, although oak, hickory, and maple might also be used. The men would cut down the selected trees in the fall and soak the logs in water before beginning the laborious task of pounding the wood to flatten and loosen the rings, which could then be peeled off in strips to form the splints of the basket. Traditionally it was the women who would weave the baskets throughout the long winter months, although Apess, in his account, recalls that both "my father and my mother made baskets," which they would "sell to the whites" in an effort "to keep soul and body in a state of unity."[26] The baskets were decorated with patterns and designs that adhered to regional traditions going back as far as memory. For the indigenous peoples who patterned them, such designs represented features of the natural world but suggested also "the spiritual force that flows through all things," the tree of life, the dome of the sky, the four directions, and distances traveled.[27]

The Puritan Roger Williams, who lived for a time with the Narragansetts, reported that many northeastern Natives believed their ancestors had been formed from trees, "which were the Fountaines of all mankind."[28] The baskets carried something of that hereditary life force as well. A generation before Apess was born another "writing Indian," the Mohegan preacher Samson

Occom, who had relocated to the frontier settlement of Brothertown in upstate New York, sent home to his sister a small decorated box made of dark elm which patterned out the Trail of Life and Path of the Sun and, according to Native scholar Stephanie Fitzgerald, embodied "the continuity of Mohegan cultural traditions and identity in a time of tremendous change."[29] Baskets carried stories and traditions that were central to indigenous life in the Northeast, but they also served as a link in that tradition, a record of the path that indigenous peoples had journeyed and a touchstone of forces reaching back as far as Creation. For Apess they were also a link to the labor of his parents and to the memory of their last days together.

When the Pilgrims established their first beachhead on Patuxet land in 1620 (today we know it as Cape Cod), prior even to meeting with the local inhabitants face-to-face they encountered Native basketry. As told in *Mourt's Relation*, the first published tract to emerge from the colony, a landing party was sent out to explore the coastal area soon after their arrival, in search of drinking water, game, and a proper place for settlement. It was already late in the season, and the party passed through continuous fields of recently harvested corn.

As the narrator of this tract or "journal" tells it, they came upon a heap of sand, "which we digged up, and in it we found a little old basket full of fair Indian corn, and digged further and found a fine great new basket full of very fair corn of this year, with some thirty-six goodly ears of corn, some yellow, and some red, and others mixed with blue, which was a very goodly sight. The basket was round, and narrow at the top; it held about three or four bushels which was as much as two of us could lift up from the ground, and was very handsomely and cunningly made."[30] Just a few more pages in, we are told how the landing party next stumbled upon a number of empty "houses" or wigwams wherein they discovered a great deal of domestic wares, including "baskets of sundry sorts," some of which were "curiously wrought with black and white in pretty works." The narrator concludes by recounting "some of the best things we took away with us."[31] Interestingly, the basketry, described as "fine" and "curiously wrought," is rendered in greater detail than practically anything else these adventurers came across, suggesting that they greatly admired these creations and evidently appropriated them for their own use. What they were encountering, however, were vessels not only of domestic utility but intricate carriers of sustenance and tradition.

The region of southern New England occupied by the Pequots was first settled not by English Pilgrims, of course, but by indigenous peoples, who, upon the retreat of the glaciers, pushed in some eleven thousand years ago, following mastodon, caribou, and other game. These Paleo-Indian hunter-gatherers scraped out a dire living, leaving bone fragments, stone-sharpened tools, and the occasional trash midden—by which archeologists can apprehend something of the lives they managed. With the passage of another ten thousand years and a helpful increase in global temperatures, the climate became suitable for agriculture and the production of maize. By this point, stable village communities had secured a place for some three to four thousand years, and peoples of the Northeast had learned to accommodate their lifeways to what the environment made possible.[32] Although it is uncertain when the people who call themselves the Pequots first arrived on the scene (and it is possible that they were simply there right from the Paleo-Indian start), they were successful in adapting their culture to the terrain.[33] Their traditional stories track the changes in the land as the earth warmed and the waters rose. According to their beliefs, it was the crow who first brought corn and beans to the region, a gift from their creator, Kyatan, and the world they inhabited, like all human worlds, was animated by forces that both helped and hindered their earthly endeavors, gave them medicines to overcome famine and illness, skill and agility to feed and clothe themselves, and stories around which to organize their spiritual beliefs and ceremonies, making them highly proficient interpreters of their particular environment.[34]

Seasonal subsistence cycles of the Pequots consisted of fishing, planting, harvesting, hunting, and, in the winter, among other things, storytelling and basket weaving. Although their boundaries were well understood and their settlements more or less fixed, they would relocate depending on the season to pursue their various occupations.[35] The Natives of New England had to be extremely attuned to their natural worlds and knowledgeable about changes in the environment. One early Dutch reporter, Nicholaes van Wassenaer, observed that the Pequot women in particular had a great store of star knowledge and that there "was scarcely one of them but can name all the stars; their rising, setting; the position of the *Arctos* . . . is as well known to them as to us."[36] This was a necessity for understanding the essential intricacies of when to plant and harvest.

The Pequots built their villages in the most fertile riverine valleys, not because "*instinct* had led them to it," as Bancroft suggested,[37] but rather because they were experienced cultivators who not only worked the land but tinkered with it, experimented and innovated with it, developing methods of agriculture that ultimately included crop rotation, pest control, fortifying the soil with nutrients to increase productivity, and exploiting the potential of raising their staple crops—corn, beans, and squash—in a symbiotic fashion, allowing for mutually favorable growth conditions that significantly reduced the amount of human labor required. These crops, when produced together in such a fashion, became known as the "three sisters," and this style of agriculture is still in use among Native people of New England today.[38]

Theirs was a village world, oriented more around clan and kinship networks than highly centralized forms of government or rigid nationalities. Nevertheless, it was a world of established customs and traditions that perpetuated order, ritual, community, sustenance, and stable relations for trade and diplomacy with neighboring peoples. While there were established leaders, called sachems or sagamores, who were involved in important decision-making processes, their power and influence was not through fiat but rather dispersed in councils and through the overall consensus of the community. Women were included in the decision making and, as the primary cultivators of food, held considerable sway in the body politic and were known to rise to the highest levels of leadership.[39] Colonists, however, tended to project their own linguistic frameworks of power, gender, and hierarchy upon the Native communities they encountered, and described "kings," "queens," and "monarchs" in their writings and diplomatic undertakings where no such equivalent existed.[40] English observers were often reduced to such rhetorical contortions and contradictions when describing Native communities simply because their own basis for understanding societal structure could not accurately reproduce the "curiously wrought" design of civic order with which they were confronted.

As European settlers first establishing themselves in the Northeast in the 1620s and 1630s asserted themselves into the local economy, it is safe to say that they radically transformed long-established patterns of diplomacy and exchange in the region. For the first few years of settlement, colonists required trade relations with the local Natives simply to stay alive. It was imperative, however, that they begin to turn a profit to meet the demands of their investors, and the most lucrative endeavor by far for Europeans was the fur trade. To succeed in this market, however, again required cooperation with indigenous hunters, who knew the region and had access to the inland routes where the most valuable pelts, including beaver, could be found. From the vantage of the Dutch and English, the Connecticut River provided the best route to these inland trade networks and, as a result, the mouth of the river, which stood as the western edge of the Pequots' sphere of influence, rapidly became a contested space for colonial control in the 1630s, disrupting the existing diplomatic infrastructure and resulting in the Pequots and Mohegans, originally one people, breaking into two separate nations.[41]

Exchange Rates: The Value of Wampum

The Dutch were the first major power to establish relations with the Pequot, beginning in 1614 with Adrian Block, who described them in his log as a fortified nation known as "Pequot or Pequatous."[42] Although the Pequots were initially willing to embrace the Dutch in their network of civil relations, the

Dutch quickly found that the Pequots lacked an appreciation for the basics of capitalist venture. As one Dutch observer noted, the Pequots had access to a great deal of valuable furs, "but they must get into the habit of trade, otherwise they are too indolent to hunt the beaver."[43] What he actually meant was that the Pequots, who had of course hunted and traded in the region for centuries, were not procuring enough furs to meet what would prove to be the inexhaustible demands of European commerce.

Trade, broadly interpreted, is a kind of universal language, but Native peoples of the Northeast did not pursue trade to gain economic advantage or increase their coffers, so to speak. As the historian Neal Salisbury argues in his book *Manitou and Providence,* their practice consisted of an ethos "in which relationships in the social, natural, and supernatural worlds were defined in terms of reciprocity rather than domination and submission."[44] While trade networks between various indigenous groups were established to meet the needs of the particular communities involved, trade also had a basic diplomatic element that was meant to maintain cultural equilibrium between two parties. The reception of goods created a social imbalance necessitating a reciprocal gesture. This ethos governed not only trade, but the use of resources and assistance sought of the spiritual world in occupations such as hunting, fishing, cultivating, and healing. Maintaining equilibrium with the various forces constituting one's environment was a means of keeping the world in balance. As the French Jesuit priest Paul Le Jeune observed in his dealings with the Algonquian peoples of New France in 1634, "To accept presents from the Savages is to bind oneself to return an equivalent."[45]

The Abenaki historian Lisa Brooks articulates this ethos as well when she refers to a term in common usage among Algonquian language speakers, *wlidôgawôgan,* which roughly translates to "thanks to all our relations." As Brooks explains, "The land, *aki,* is a self-sustaining vessel, but it requires participation from all its interwoven inhabitants. When humans deliberate on their relationships to other beings in their *wôlhana* [river valley landscapes], their thoughts lead to more conscientious action within their environment. Every community in the Northeast has a way of thinking through their relationships to others, and of acknowledging their dependence on nonhuman inhabitants through rituals of thanksgiving."[46] Offering thanks, particularly in a ritualized manner, was a way of restoring balance in relation to whatever forces contributed to the well-being of the community.

Once trade relations proceeded beyond the necessity for diplomatic exchange, however, the Natives of New England proved to be shrewd dealers, demanding exchanges of real, rather than symbolic, value and often frustrating the hopes of settlers who had persuaded themselves that Indians could simply be bought off with shiny glass beads and the like. As Roger Williams was prompted to observe, "They are marvelous subtle in their Bargaines to save a penny: And very suspicious that *English* men labour to deceive them." He noted that when Indians traded among themselves they exchanged "Corne, skins, Coates, Venison, Fish &c. and sometimes come ten or twenty in a Company to trade among the *English*. They have some who follow onley making of Bowes, some Arrowes, some Dishes, and (the Women make all their earthen Vessells) some follow fishing, some hunting: most on the Sea-side make Money, and store up shells in Summer against Winter thereof to make their money."[47]

When Williams spoke of "their money," he was actually referring to wampum. The function of wampum was not clearly understood by the English—apparently not even by Williams himself, though he was more intimate with Algonquian language and custom than were most other Europeans. In fact, the significance of wampum to indigenous peoples of the Northeast remains shrouded in historical and cultural misperceptions. Given that the Pequots and their neighboring nations were not organized around capitalist market structures, they did not recognize currency or money as a legitimate form of exchange. The function of wampum, like exchange itself among Native groups, was both diplomatic and ceremonial. European settlers, however, unschooled and largely uninterested in the ceremonial aspects of wampum, simply recognized the extent to which it was greatly valued by Native communities and could therefore be rendered a useful commodity. As such, its spiritual properties were thoroughly purged from colonial rhetorics.

Wampum consists of small beads, traditionally fashioned from the whelk and quahog shells, that when strung together in a particular order can be used to signify a number of ceremonial purposes. The use of wampum in some shape or form dates back at least four thousand years, although the ceremonial purposes to which it was put remained fluid and differed from one indigenous nation to the next over time.[48] Perhaps the best-documented ceremonial aspect of wampum exchange involves the foundational narrative of the Five Nations of the Iroquois, or Haudenosaunee. In that tradition, the spiritual seeker, Hiawatha, sought solace for himself after the death of his daughters by stringing together shells he found at the bottom of a lake and claiming, "Men boast of what they will do in extremity but they do not do what they say. If I should see anyone in deep grief I would remove these shell strings from the pole and console them. The strings would become words and lift away the darkness with which they are covered. Moreover what I say I would surely do."[49] It was the pure spirit often referred to as the Peacemaker, paddling into Haudenosaunee country on a canoe made of white stone, who first used wampum to console the grieving Hiawatha. Wampum was later used by the Peacemaker to bind together the Five Nations under one law.

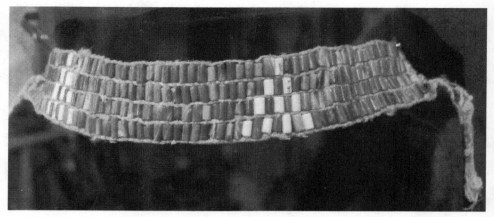

Seventeenth-century wampum representing split between the Pequot and Mohegan tribes. *Courtesy Tantaquidgeon Indian Museum.*

From this mysterious origin, wampum developed into the heart of diplomatic exchange ritual among the Haudenosaunees and came to signify a kind of formal structure through which healing from grief could occur.

This ritual was particularly significant when two nations were at war and grievances were nurtured on either side. The trauma of warfare leaves all parties concerned unable to reconcile both their grief and their desire for revenge. It twists natural reason, distorts the very senses with rage and hatred, rendering nations incapable of working through their differences and locking them in endless cycles of violence and war. Wampum exchange offers a structure allowing for a cleared ritual space where the darkness might be lifted and the grief ceremonially wiped away. Strings of wampum not only "lifted the darkness," as Hiawatha claimed, but would also "become words," representing what was spoken in condolences and treaties, the belts of wampum becoming records of what had passed. The ceremony itself was "sealed" by the wampum, and no diplomatic exchange could be regarded as legitimate without it. When successfully administered, it would lead to the burying of the weapons of war and an end to bloodshed.

For the colonist, however, wampum was understood strictly in terms of its trade value and as a source of power and control. Puritan leaders observed the exchange of wampum between indigenous nations with a mercantile fascination, understanding it to be a "tributary" system in which weaker nations "paid" stronger nations for protection in a large-scale geopolitical extortion racket. Historians have largely accepted this terminology, again influenced by a deep-rooted epistemological allegiance to colonial frameworks. If this understanding remains flawed, however, it perfectly pertains to the Puritan endeavor to position themselves within this system of exchange and play the role of alpha extortionists.[50] What had begun as a mutually beneficial relationship was now hitting up against unforeseen expectations and demands that in fact threatened to throw not just the Pequot world out of balance but all of the Native Northeast, humans and animals alike.

The Pequot War

As it happens, the shells from which wampum was produced tended to collect on the shores of Long Island Sound, which positioned the Pequots at the center of the wampum trade. Historians and anthropologists have wondered how an inland nation, the Haudenosaunee, centered their ritual life around materials from coastal sources, given that archeological sites demonstrate the presence of wampum, or "protowampum," in upstate New York going back well over four thousand years. But this merely speaks to the robust networks of trade that had long characterized indigenous life prior to European contact. Dutch explorers making their way along the Hudson Valley marveled at the extent of indigenous exchange networks, noting that the Pequots not only traveled upriver to trade with the Mohawks but that others regularly traveled south from as far as the Saint Lawrence River since, as one reporter noted, "our skippers assure us that the natives come to the fort from that river, and from Quebec and Tadoussac."[51] The Pequot had long stood at the source of the wampum trade, and this in part defined their regional influence, which transcended their own boundaries around the Connecticut River basin and spread over Long Island and much of the Connecticut River valley.[52]

When the English discovered the local significance accorded wampum, they too wanted to get in on the action. The Pequot, who had acted as good faith neighbors to both the Dutch and the English, suddenly found themselves caught in the middle of two larger forces competing for dominance in the region. Then, in 1633, disaster struck. Disease, in the form of small pox, swept through the Pequot villages, an evil wind taking countless lives, causing untold misery and heartbreak, and ripping apart the very fabric of what had been, until most recently, a thriving and prosperous nation. Mortality rates are estimated to have been anywhere between 55 and 95 percent of the population. As with other groups in the region who had suffered similar epidemics, it is impossible to imagine the personal and cultural trauma, the devastation to families and villages, the unspeakable grief, the stores of memory, tradition, and knowledge upset by such widespread havoc.

Even the colonists, who stood to benefit from this disaster and typically saw the hand of their vengeful God at work in such dire events, were stunned

by the magnitude of the destruction. William Bradford, then governor of
Plymouth Colony, described the epidemic, stating, "It pleased God, to visit
these Indians with a great sickness, and such a mortality that of a 1000, above
900 and a half of them died, and many of them did rot above ground for
want of burial." He noted of the smallpox that "they fear it more than the
plague; for usually they that have this disease, have them in abundance; and
for want of bedding, and linen, and other helps, they fall into a lamentable
condition as they lie on their hard mats, the pox breaking and mattering, and
running one into another; their skin cleaving (by reason thereof) to the mats
they lie on; when they turn them, a whole side will flay off, at once (as it were)
and they will be all of a gore blood, most fearful to behold." The Pequot fell
sick so quickly and in such great numbers that they could not bury their own
dead. There were none to care for those who were sick or provide comfort or
offer ceremony to properly send the dying on their way, and, as Bradford hor-
rifically observed, "They die like rotten sheep."[53] It was at this very moment
that the English and Dutch chose to finally press their advantage to secure
control of the wampum trade.

The event known as the Pequot War officially broke out in 1636. The catalyst for the war is often attributed to the 1633 death of Captain John Stone, an
English merchant who had been banished from Plymouth Colony due to his
unsavory conduct, and who was killed in an incident that remains more or less
obscured by the fog of war. What is clear, however, is that Stone was an early
English trafficker in wampum and, like the Dutch with whom he traded, was
in the practice of holding local Native leaders hostage in exchange for valuable wampum tributes. It was through just such a practice that the Pequot
sachem Tatobem had been killed a few years earlier. When the Puritans sent
John Oldham to the Block Island Natives to collect a tribute in retaliation for
Stone's death, he too was killed. Tatobem's death had given the Pequots just
cause to retaliate against the settlers, but even so, the Pequots sought a diplomatic resolution, arguing they were not responsible for the deaths of Oldham
or Stone. This mattered little to the English, however, and when the proposed
terms for peace proved too onerous, the Pequots withdrew from negotiations.
The English subsequently sent a war party against the Block Island Natives as
a reprisal and, in a foreshadowing of things to come, burned their village to
the ground. More deaths and reprisals ensued until the English objective of
domination or destruction of the Pequots came to its fiery climax.[54]

The major battle of the war took place at Mystic, where the Pequots maintained a village secured deep in the woods, two acres round and well fortified
with tall wooden stakes, or *palisadoes,* circling the perimeter. It was here they
hoped to safeguard their women and children in the event that the English
launched an all-out attack. Anticipating that the English force would come by

sea, as had happened in earlier engagements, they were taken unaware when, on May 26, 1637, the assault came from the opposite direction. The Pequots were wakened from their sleep by the cries of armed soldiers storming the gates. Captain John Mason led the attack from the northeast entrance to the fort, and Captain John Underhill entered with his army at the southwestern end. They met stiff resistance from Pequot defenders, however, and it wasn't until Mason determined to pull a firebrand from one of the wigwams and set the village altogether ablaze that the English were able to regroup outside the fort, forming a ring that prevented any from escaping the flames that all too rapidly engulfed the village in the stiff morning breeze.

As Mason reported, "Such a dreadful Terror did the Almighty let fall upon their Spirits, that they would fly from us and run into the very Flames, where many of them perished." More likely, the warriors, on seeing how quickly the flames spread, were doubling back to rescue their families—the women, children, and elders helplessly caught in the conflagration. The English, however, quickly shot down all who attempted to escape the fort. Although eyewitness participants disagreed on the numbers, anywhere between four hundred and seven hundred Pequot men, women, and children lost their lives in the terrible hour that ensued. When the slaughter was over, a party of Narragansetts who had accompanied the English troops and bore witness to the event, losing many of their own to friendly fire, were compelled to state of English warfare that "it is naught, it is naught, because it is too furious and slays too many men."[55] Even Puritan reporters of the incident would betray something of their anxiety about the slaying of so many innocents, with Bradford, himself noting, "It was a fearful sight to, to see them thus frying in the fire, and the streams of blood quenching the same, and horrible was the stink and scent thereof." Nevertheless he was able to conclude that "the victory seemed a sweet sacrifice," as though the few small skirmishes and trumped-up crimes attributed to the Pequots up to this point had suddenly risen to a level of egregiousness that warranted the annihilation of the tribe.[56] But in each case, the settlers found that God's hand had ordered events thusly, and the handful of English deaths that could safely be attributed to the Pequots were ranked among the highest of human blasphemies.[57]

In the months that followed, the remainder of the Pequots were rounded up and either killed or sold into slavery. In the 1638 Treaty of Hartford, it was determined that those surviving Pequot who had not been enslaved by the English, primarily women and children, would be divvied up among the Mohegans and Narragansetts. It was decreed that the Pequots would "never again inhabit their native Country, nor should any of them be called Pequots anymore." As Mason concluded, "Thus was God seen in the Mount, Crushing his proud enemies . . . burning them up in the fire of his Wrath, and dunging the Ground with their Flesh. It was the Lord's Doings, and it is marvelous in our Eyes! It is He that hath made his Work wonderful, and therefore ought to be remembered."[58]

But these were not, in fact, things that men wished to remember of themselves. Better by far to forget such obscenities—to forget the war and its consequences, to forget the Pequot and "to root their very name out of the Country" so that men would not have to dwell upon the acts of savagery by which they had claimed title to the land.[59] Mason would conclude, "The Face of God is set against them that do Evil, to cut off the Remembrance of them from the Earth . . . the Lord was pleased to smite our Enemies in the hinder Parts, and to give to us their Land for an Inheritance."[60] In fact, Mason himself would ultimately be granted the land where the Pequots' stronghold once stood at Mystic, now referred to as Pequot Hill, and his inheritors reside there to this day. But the Pequots did not disappear, nor were they utterly vanquished, and if God had intended for their name to be wiped from the history books, somehow they were soon to reconstitute themselves, to begin rebuilding, so that within a year, as Roger Williams remarked, "the Pequots are regathered into one, and plant their own fields."[61]

The Execution of Katherine Garret

The Pequot War of 1636–37 merely set the stage for the period of hardship and depredation to follow. Accounts of the war make a brave point of emphasizing how women and children were spared whenever possible in the "mop up" period after the battle at Mystic, but the men, including boys in many cases, were routinely "destroyed." Mason, whose determination it had been to set the Pequot fort afire, could still somehow boast later of the English "being loth to destroy women and children."[62] Increase Mather, however, in his history of the war, relates what seems to him a "pleasant" anecdote in which certain Pequot boys, upon seeing that the women were being preserved, cried out, "*I squaw, I squaw*, thereby thinking to escape with their lives."[63] The hilarious implication seems to be that many did not.

The first colonial laws regarding slavery in North America were penned as an a priori acknowledgment of the practices following the war. Perceived, by most colonists at least, as an indisputably "just" war, approved and prosecuted by the hand of God himself, it was therefore in accordance with certain biblical precedents to enslave the vanquished. With that understanding in mind, the 1641 "Massachusetts Body of Liberties" identified the Pequots as "lawfull Captives."[64] Although there was talk of some fourteen hundred Pequots being killed or captured, Winthrop indicates that only about two hundred could be accounted for by war's end, suggesting that a great majority were put to death, their heads brought in, and some put on pikes before the gates of the colonies.[65] Of those who lived, a portion were sold into slavery in the West Indies, roughly two thirds were given over to the Narragansetts and the Mohegans, and those remaining were retained by the English and were soon to be celebrated in promotional tracts as New England's "First Fruits," or the colony's first Indian converts to Christianity. Indian conversion had been one of the primary goals of the original colonial charter, and, as the 1643 publication by the name "New England's First Fruits" would boast, the Pequot children "received" into Puritan households "are long since civilized, and in subjection to us . . . divers of whom can read English, and begin to understand in their measure, the grounds of Christian Religion."[66]

In significant ways, these were the cultural forebears of William Apess—Pequot children living out a traumatic legacy in colonial "subjection" to the English and learning how to navigate not only English spirituality but Western literacy. Some would indeed prove successful at this and use these skills to, in some small way, promote the causes of their people.[67] It is nothing less than perverse, however, to submit to the blithe rhetoric that would suggest these unfortunate souls were happily assimilated to Puritan norms. Far from embracing Christianity, for the most part they led tormented lives at the beck and call of those who had massacred their families. Enduring traumatic loss and subject to rigid Puritan religious practices, many suffered psychic collapses, and others managed to escape, seeking shelter with neighboring tribes.[68] Runaways that could be apprehended were branded on the shoulder to prevent them from escaping again and melting back in with "free" Indians.[69] Such were the so-called First Fruits of English evangelism.

History has paid scant attention to this legacy of grief and, in fact, little can be known of these Pequot lives, as the Puritans were neither eager nor interested in recounting their individual fates. But an occasional glimpse surfaces in the archive, as when Roger Williams recounts in a letter dated November 10, 1637, that two escaped and almost starved "Pequot squaws" were handed over to him by the Narragansetts. Rather than return them to Boston, Williams kept them at his home in Providence and petitioned on their behalf, noting that one of them "complains that she of all natives in Boston is the worse used: is beaten with fire sticks" and forced to "lay" with her master.[70] While we cannot project the fate of all Pequot women captives from this one incident, her rare and unofficial testimony stands witness to the fate of generations of Native women.

Past cultural mores requiring a constrained delicacy regarding such matters has kept a great deal of this history in check. The sexual abuse of Native women is an issue, however, that strains at the margins of Apess's memoirs. He writes of the "intense and heart-corroding affliction" Native peoples suffered, of having "their daughters claimed by the conquerors."[71] Employing perhaps the harshest language possible to address this issue, he asserted that Europeans "committed violence of the most revolting kind upon the persons of the female portion of the tribe."[72] Native women, who formerly held considerable power and sway in their own communities, were, of course, doubly marginalized within this new milieu, and the English acted quickly to impose restrictions on Natives who now fell within their sphere of influence.

These restrictions pierced to the heart of traditional mores, broaching matters as foundational to a culture as marital relations and spiritual beliefs, and as seemingly arbitrary as how to wear one's hair or whether or not a woman might go about with her breasts exposed.[73] Puritan magistrates also moved quickly to curtail women's speech. The Puritan minister John Eliot, tasked with instructing the local Natives on the practices and beliefs of the English colonists, commented that "because we knew how unfit it was for women so much as to aske questions publiquely . . . we did therefore desire them to propound any questions they would be resolved about by first acquainting either their Husbands, or the [Indian] Interpreter privately therewith."[74] The intent was, of course, to restrict the practice of women's speech in the public sphere and entrench the patriarchal gender hierarchies normative to seventeenth-century Christian values. This was yet one more way that the Pequot world was kept out of balance.

Formerly situated in empowering domestic structures that facilitated their routines and bore the strength of tradition, indigenous women now found themselves in a precarious situation. Polygamous marriage practices had stabilized the indigenous household, serving to divide the labor that structured daily life, and formed tight kinship bonds that rippled through multiple families, clans, and villages. The Puritans forcefully broke up these marriages, compelling men to abandon their second and third wives, which presumably alienated these women from the protections and entitlements the institution afforded. We can safely assume that, even after the pandemic diseases that shredded populations, a still larger percentage of Native men were killed in warfare with the English, thereby leaving a significant number of Native women out in the cold under the new colonial order. Eliot signals to us that this is already the case as early as 1647 when he comments upon a woman from the Massachusett tribe whom he counted among his converts that "she was industrious, and did not go about to *English* houses a begging, as sundry doe . . . but kept home, kept her children to labour, making baskets to sell." Most noteworthy in this passage, perhaps, is not the exemplary example this women set but the "sundry" Indian women forced to beg at the doors of the English and the unspoken fate of their children, whom the English were eager to scoop up and place in servitude.[75] It does, however, suggest that the proper course for Native women to pursue was basket making on a commercial level, presumably so these wares might be pedaled to New England households.

If we can never adequately know the details of the life of Apess's grandmother, we can perhaps apprehend something of her experience through the lives of other Native women of her time who manifest a sort of shadow presence in the archive.[76] One such woman of the Pequot Nation was Katherine Garret. The Pequots, sent to live with their traditional "enemies" the Mohegans and the Narragansetts in 1638, either married into those tribes or were soon granted autonomy and, as mentioned earlier, quickly began to reorganize on their former lands. Cushawahet, or Harmon Garret, was one of the Pequot leaders who emerged at this time and who, in 1650, was able to gain a colonial appointment as "governor" of the newly established Eastern Pequot reservation eventually situated at Lantern Hill in the area of what is today North Stonington, Connecticut.[77]

The Pequot struggled to stabilize themselves in these years and continued to lead lives shaped by their own traditional beliefs despite continued hardships and upheavals. Weunquesh, a cousin of Harmon Garret's, served as squaw sachem for the tribe in the 1670s and 1680s, attesting to the continued ability of Pequot women to hold positions of power. But by the 1730s, even a direct descendant of this once powerful family found it necessary to live out a life of servitude in English homes in order to scrape out an existence. If Katherine Garret, or "Indian Kate," as the colonists referred to her, could claim the blood of former female sachems in her veins, it could not protect her from the abuses of a patriarchal system nor of being accused of infanticide in 1737, precisely one hundred years after the massacre at Mystic.[78] Her transgression of "destroying the fruit of my own Body" led not only to her attracting notice in the colonial archive as one more disenfranchised Indian woman but resulted in the publication of her confessional tract, which she penned herself, making Katherine Garret the first Native in all of New England to have her own writing disseminated in print form.

As with so many other unfortunate women of this era, Garret labored to conceal her pregnancy from prying eyes in the home of the man for whom she worked, the Reverend William Worthington of Saybrook. In her moment of crisis, she excused herself from her mistress complaining of stomach illness and retreated to the barn to live out an intense private battle that was undoubtedly still written upon her features when she returned to her chores shortly thereafter. Garret was in her late twenties. It would have been highly unusual had she not been sexually active at this age, but her subaltern station in the home of an influential white family to whom she had been bonded out since childhood would have left her few opportunities to legitimately consummate a relationship. A woman in her situation had no guaranteed rights, no presence or power in a court of law, no domestic structure designed to protect her or provide for her descendants. If the child of such a woman was indeed brought to term, as bastard or ward of the state, that child was almost surely consigned to a life of forced labor. Ann Marie Plane notes in her book *Colonial Intimacies* that "an English system of indentured servitude that had once functioned as a temporary stage in a young person's life now became the end of the road for many, especially those of non-European descent."[79] Needless to say, such an arrangement left Native women extremely vulnerable to acts of sexual predation. Whatever the circumstances leading to its birth, the Reverend William Worthington promptly discovered Garret's child in the barn buried under some hay a few hours later after reportedly hearing a child's cry.

Garret maintained her innocence throughout the court trial that followed, admitting to bearing the child and, eventually, even striking it, but refusing to say that she had murdered it, and there are some discrepancies in her case to support her claim. For one, if she had murdered the child, as the Worthingtons testified, it seems odd that the reverend would have heard the child still crying some "hours" later. And if Worthington was the last to actually see the child alive, this fact conveniently slips through the cracks of the court transcripts, despite the fact that it would seem to make him a suspect. Garret's original testimony was that she had simply tried to conceal the child and had even come back to the barn once to check on it and perhaps feed it. But it was unlikely that a colonial court would question the sworn testimony of the community's religious leader or take into account the levels of coercion that might persuade a powerless Indian woman to claim responsibility for acts she did not commit. Notably, it was the reverend's wife who, according to the testimony, ultimately compelled Garret to admit that she had not simply sought to conceal the child but had struck it on the head twice with a wooden block. And only the Reverend Worthington himself claimed to know the identity of the father, although this identity was not considered relevant enough to be mentioned at any time during the hearings or in the document trail that follows.

Garret was ultimately executed for her alleged crime in 1738. Her written account follows what most scholars of the period recognize as a generic formula for prison confessions of this time. The community, spearheaded by the ministry, placed a great deal of pressure on prisoners to conform to a preapproved script designed to reassure the public of the infallibility of both church and state in these matters. The convicted were pressed to admit their crimes, accept the justness of their sentence, and offer up their souls to God in a contrite manner. Particularly for a Native woman, such a textual expression can only be considered as an indigenous "x-mark"—or "a sign of consent in a context of coercion."[80]

Katherine Garret was a proud and intelligent woman who clearly defied the low expectations generally assigned someone of her ethnicity and station. The Reverend Eliphalet Adams, who attended to Garret during her incarceration, was apparently struck by her demeanor. He remarked that "she was of a proper Stature & goodly Countenance and seemed to be Naturally of an Ingenious Disposition." He further noted that she "generally gain'd the Esteem and good will of those that Came about her" and that "many of her expressions from time to time were valuable and worth the preserving." In her final days she agreed to be baptized but refused to fully submit to her accusers, insisting that many had "reported of her things that were false." Adams may also have been struck by "Indian Kate's" flashes of defiance, as when, at the reading of her guilty verdict, her expressions "became rash and unguarded and she scarce forebore throwing blame on all sorts of persons."

The white colonial power structure was, perhaps, unaccustomed at this time to hearing Indians speak in an "unguarded" manner. Such free and unconstrained Indian discourse could never be allowed entrance into the archive and, as such, Katherine Garret's unguarded thoughts and accusations are elided from the narrative. If she had a separate account to tell regarding what happened in that barn on the fateful day she gave birth, Adams knew better than to commit it to print. And if her proud bearing bespoke an identity that confounded Adams's preconceptions of what an Indian should be, he could only hint at it, remarking upon her dignified departure from this world that "she added many Other Warnings and Counsels by word of mouth, Lifting up her Voice as she could that she might be farther heard; We took our leave of her and she of us in an Affecting Manner."

In the final analysis, regardless of what Katherine Garret may have wished to communicate to whoever might read her short narrative or hear her last words spoken at the gallows (and so rare is it for a Native woman's voice to appear at all in the archive at this time that it behooves us to pay close attention), it is the silences that strike us, the rash and unguarded words left off the page that still stand out somehow, as opposed to the heavily guarded and mediated words that appear in print. We are told that Garret spoke very affectingly from the gallows and with great strength, but we are also told by Adams that sometimes her "expressions were more broken and incoherent." But in neither case do we get to listen in on these "expressions." They serve as an archival vanishing point. Was she simply babbling in these "incoherent" moments, thrown into agitation by her mortal predicament, or did she once more speak of things that did not fit the colonial script? Or perhaps even more tantalizing, did she shift into the Algonquian language at some point to speak intimately to her Pequot relations, who undoubtedly stood in the crowd? One wonders if her so-called moments of incoherence were, perhaps, her most lucid utterances. Whatever we might apprehend from these silences, her narrative was used to forward a colonial agenda of coercion and conversion. Leaving nothing to chance, Adams reminds us of the take-home message when he concludes, "May all her Country people, in their several Tribes . . . hearken diligently to the Offers & Proposals of the Gospel that are made to them! Let there be Nothing to Obstruct & Discourage so good a work." In a sense, Garret's very public execution was yet one more Pequot head on a pike set as an example for all to see what happens when the colonial order is defied.

Regardless of her determination to face death with dignity, Katherine Garret could not protect herself from the colonial power structure that had consigned her to a life of servitude from the start. As an Indian woman in the eighteenth century, she was left with precious few choices. She could maintain her innocence and be lead to the gallows with a rope around her neck; she could admit her guilt and be offered the same fate; or she could have submitted the child immediately to her colonial masters, consigning her progeny to a life of servitude while gaining for herself the label of Indian whore.

We might readily imagine that Apess's grandmother faced many of the same questions and choices in her lifetime. Apess would relate in his 1833 sermon "An Indian's Looking-Glass for the White Man" that should a "gentleman and lady of integrity and respectability visit these places" they would be surprised to see "females who are left alone, children half-starved and some almost as naked as they came into the world. And it is a fact that I have seen them as much so—while the females are left without protection, and are seduced by white men, and are finally left to be common prostitutes for them and to be destroyed by that burning fiery curse, that has swept millions, both of red and white men, into the grave with sorrow and disgrace—rum."[81] He might have been describing his own grandmother here. He might also have been describing Anne Wampy, an elder of the Pequot community in Apess's own lifetime, who, in her final days, was converted to Christian spirituality. Apess wrote of Wampy in his 1833 tract *The Experiences of Five Christian Indians of the Pequot Tribe,* describing her as "an old veteran of the woods, who despised all that was said to her upon the subject of salvation and would use very bad language in her way, being not able to speak plain English."[82] Wampy was also remembered in colonial lore as the women who would

> make an annual trip in the early spring . . . up through Preston City, Griswold and Jewett City, selling the baskets she had made the previous winter. When she started from her home she carried upon her shoulders a bundle of baskets so large as almost to hide her from view. In the bundle would be baskets varying in size from a half-pint up to five or six quarts, some made of very fine splints, some of coarse, and many skillfully ornamented in various colors. Her baskets were so good that she would find customers at

"The Indian Basket Seller," from an oil painting by Cornelius Krieghoff, copied 1865. *McCord Museum, Montreal, I-14905.1.*

almost every house. And after traveling a dozen or twenty miles and spending two or three days in doing it her load would be all gone. Then she would start on her homeward journey, and, sad to relate, before she had reached her home a large part of what she had received for her baskets would have been expended on strong drink.[83]

Anne Wampy's story is the story of Apess's grandmother, who made and carried baskets to sell to her white oppressors, both of them carrying the legacy of a century and a half of violence against their people, their children, their traditions, their livelihoods, their bodies, upon their backs. Colonial literature and lore is, in fact, redolent with tales of the wizened Indian squaw, widow, and medicine women living on the outskirts of the community, remnant of a vanquished people and repository of ancient arts, making potions, dark wares, and "curiously wrought" baskets for purchase. Like many survivors of trauma, they self-medicated with alcohol and acted out at times in a manner that reflected the unspeakable anguish of their situations. "At least some portion of my sufferings" were justly chargeable to the whites, Apess reminded us. But it was not a simple charge to make. The history was long and complicated, and who really wanted to hear it? To blame it all on the introduction of rum to the Indians became convenient shorthand for other longer stories too complex, too painful, to relate. But the baskets carried those stories, traveled the long roads on the backs of Native women, inscribed with details of Pequot experience, hardship, tradition. The baskets carried those stories. "Do you hate me?" Apess's grandmother had asked. In Apess's memory he answered yes, although I wonder if, as with Anne Wampy, Apess's grandmother had difficulty speaking "plain English." Perhaps she spoke Algonquian. Perhaps the younger Apess simply misunderstood the question.

CHAPTER TWO
Birthright, Bondage, and Beyond

He pitched his tent in the woods of a town called Colrain.
—WILLIAM APESS, *A Son of the Forest*

"William Apess Was Born Here"

Colrain, Massachusetts, where William Apess was born in 1798, sits on the border of Massachusetts and Vermont, closer to the western end of Massachusetts, where the soft rolling Berkshire Hills begin to merge into the sturdier Green Mountain range. As the Abenaki scholar Lisa Brooks observes, this is an "ancient crossroads," Native space, where Ktsi Amiskw, the Great Beaver, still watches over Kwinitekw, reminding us of the shared responsibilities of maintaining communities and resources.[1] The land had long been both fishing and hunting grounds for the Pocumtuck, Mohican, Nipmuck, and Abenaki tribes, who came together in the spring season at the various fishing holes to trade, exchange news, and catch salmon, shad, and other fish. The large meadows and swamps in the region were a cornucopia of wildlife, edible plants, medicinal herbs, and other necessary materials of Algonquian life.

As with the Pequots and other coastal New England nations, however, a long century of colonial warfare had forced these peoples to either withdraw or lay low, making room for Europeans to wedge their way in and lay claim to the land. When many of the deeds to these lands were drawn up in the wake of the 1735 Conference at Deerfield, there was a tacit understanding that the territorial "needs of both groups" would be accommodated. Native leaders put their x-marks to this treaty, as Brooks observes, believing "that they were granting settlers the right to occupy land in common . . . rather than relinquishing their own right to inhabit it."[2] But the English leveraged the perceived ambiguity of such claims to override the original spirit of the Deerfield Treaty and ultimately claim the land as their own.[3]

Lodged in a narrow valley between twin river branches that spill into the Deerfield before draining into the Connecticut, the town itself seems precariously pitched between hill and water, its old churches, barns, and homesteads dug into the sloping hillside with only the smallest available margin for flatland farming. This bottomland was quickly bought up by the wealthiest pioneers in the 1740s, when Colrain was simply Boston Township Number Two. These speculators, joined by a handful of other mostly Scotch-Irish immigrants driven out of the eastern part of the state by economic and cultural forces, staked their claim in this rugged country. As one of the early town historians intones, "Granted, this Colrain was a wilderness haunted by wild beasts and menaced by savage Indians, but I tell you that its [first inhabitants] felt themselves to be kings and lords of all creation, for was not this land on which they trod their own and no landlord, as in the land from which they had come, could dispute their right to the possession and improvement of it?"[4]

Such rhetoric, with its claims to a first occupancy that none "could dispute," is in keeping with what the Anishinaabe historian Jean O'Brien refers to as "firsting" in her impressive study of New England town histories titled *Firsting and Lasting: Writing Indians out of Existence in New England.* O'Brien argues that nineteenth-century town histories (and no New England town is without one) made a habit of cataloguing "firsts" in the New World, as though every time colonists accomplished any particular thing—be it poking a flag in the ground, establishing a township, erecting a temple for spiritual worship, getting married, giving birth, taking in a harvest, etc.—it was the absolute first time such an event had ever been noted to occur in that spot under the roof of Heaven. As O'Brien observes, this practice "implicitly argues that Indian peoples never participated in social, cultural, or political practices worthy of note, and that history began only with the gathering of English people in a place."[5] The honorific of "firsting" helped to erase Native title to the land and enabled later generations to forward such bold claims regarding "possession and improvement."

Colrain history is redolent with such "firsts." It was unable to fully prosper as a settlement, however, until the conclusion of the French and Indian War when, in the relative peace that followed, poorer settlers began to buy or lease the cheaper lots carved out along the town's hillsides. These immigrants began to clear-cut the forests, harness the swift roiling waters for small-scale industrial mills, and bring sheep and cattle into the region, so that by the turn of the nineteenth century a thriving township had begun to take hold.

Colrain's most recently penned histories still relish the flavor of these pioneer exploits and follow a long local tradition of crafting carefully metered poems to cast past events in a gauzy romanticized light. The town library holds any number of books and manuscripts that relate in verse how "The dusky Indians one by one, / Have onward passed toward the setting sun."[6] Or how the first settlers encountered a "wilderness" that "Fence and Furrow as you will / It stretches vast and limitless, / Unexplored and savage still. // One misstep and a man is dead, / Look away and a child is gone, / Turn your back or turn your head, / The knife is fleshed and the bowstring drawn."[7] Such thrilling doggerel heightened the perceived valor of the early white settlers by placing it against an ever-present and largely exaggerated Indian threat. In these texts, the word "savage" is used interchangeably with "Indian," suggesting the extent to which the overall authority of these tales, even in recent times, rests somewhat callously upon a denigration of Native culture and agency. And yet it was here that William Apess's father determined to "pitch his tent," and the question remains, why Colrain?[8]

There is an old story that remains in circulation throughout certain parts of New England concerning a man named Joseph Griswold, who immigrated to America from southern England in the 1750s and was rescued from drowning in the Connecticut River by a Pequot maiden, daughter of a "medicine man" who was reputedly the brother of a "powerful sachem." It is a story that retains currency in northern New England and has recently even been made the subject of a children's book.[9]

According to the tale, Griswold fell in love with his Indian rescuer, they were married and eventually moved to Randolph, Vermont, due north of Colrain, where they had many children and lived more or less happily ever after. If so, such a fate for a Pequot woman was radically different from the kind of life mapped out for other Pequot women, such as Katherine Garret, the Native woman hung for alleged infanticide some twenty years earlier. The father of *this* Pequot "princess," referred to in the tale as Dogerill (perhaps because the cadence of his "naturally" poetic Indian speech was comically denigrated as "doggerel"), was said to have become sachem of the tribe upon his brother's death, although, according to the story, the title of sachem was "only a sinecure—the glory of the once powerful tribe had departed, and the few feeble remnants soon dispersed." In the fall of 1798 (year of Apess's birth), mournful for his lost estate and having no reason to stay put, this "chief" decided to travel to Vermont to visit his wayward daughter. He reached their home in a "dispirited and sick" condition, and a week later was carried out in full regalia, tomahawk in hand, to be laid down in a field beyond the house. It is said that two large stones still stand there to mark his resting place.[10]

The Griswolds were a large and influential family in early Connecticut history. Several books have been published with no other objective than to trace their voluminous family lineage. Interestingly enough, the one book that mentions the story of Joseph and his Indian princess wife also makes a point of disclaiming the tale, characterizing it as apocryphal.[11] True or not, however, the story exists to both perpetuate and bury something in the memory of the settler culture. If the Griswold family disowns their relation to the tale, still it remains in circulation to enshrine the loss of power and prestige of the Pequots. The Pequot "princess" is disenfranchised by the family historians in an attempt to keep bloodlines clean of interracial muddying, and her father, the chief, is disenfranchised of land and power, to become but a "feeble remnant" of a "dispersed" race, buried without so much as a line of inscription on his tomb.

When writing biographies of established historical figures, convention dictates that something of the individual's family lines be summarized. The Griswolds apparently require several publications to perform this obligation, tracing their roots back through the *Mayflower* to William the Conqueror and beyond (one of the family histories remarkably traces its line eighty-two generations back, to Adam and Eve).[12] But for Native peoples the records are less yielding. The births and deaths of Natives in New England often went unrecorded, and their domestic liaisons were typically not officiated over by the church. The settler culture was more invested in breaking apart and obscuring the historical presence of such lines than in carefully preserving their continuity in books and records. O'Brien notes that "by the end of the eighteenth century neither the English minister nor the English town clerk took care to record the beginnings and ends of Indian lives." Early New England census data, rather than documenting the presence of Native people and communities, worked instead to "narrate the gradual erasure of Indians from their own place."[13] This archival erasure is, in and of itself, another painful legacy of colonialism and poses challenges for conventional biography.

In the case of William Apess, we have little more than what he chooses to reveal in his writings with which to construct a more comprehensive picture of the lives he and his family members led. No birth announcement has turned up for Apess himself as of yet, and it is difficult to find records tracing his ancestral line, rendering the act of biographical recovery almost completely conjectural. Nevertheless, we can trace the presence of the Apes family in Pequot space going back at least as far as 1730, when Samuel Apes was born. As was often the case, the archive took notice of Samuel because the colonies required his services in war—in this case the French and Indian Wars. (Here it is important to note that, although the subject of this biography, William Apess, for whatever reason, took to spelling his name with two *s*'s later in life, the family name originally had only the one *s*. Therefore, when referring to members of Apess's family, I will always use Apes, such as when referring to Apess's father, William Apes.)

Samuel Apes would have been roughly twenty-eight years old when he enlisted under Captain John Denison with the Twelfth Company from Stonington, Connecticut, in 1758. Although there is no record of his activity in 1759, his name shows up again on the rolls in 1760 with the Eleventh Company under Captain Christopher Palmer.[14] Samuel Apes's name stands alongside that of Joseph Garret in the military rolls, suggesting that he served with this descendant of Katherine Garret. Little else is known of Samuel beyond his military service, but when he died in 1773, some sixty "Indian hearers" came to mourn his passing, suggesting that the local Native community held him in some esteem. The white minister, Joseph Fish, who made a note of this incident in his diary, presided over the funeral and spoke from Colossians on the hope of God's glory.[15] By 1792 the town of Stonington was still trying to collect on the balance of Apes's debts following the liquidation of his meager estate.[16]

The records show that Samuel Apes also served alongside a William Apes in Captain Stanton's Company in 1761. As with Samuel, most of what we know of this William Apes is a result of his military service. Listed as a Pequot, he served with Colonel Lyman's regiment from Connecticut in 1756–57 and again with the Fifth Company in 1762. By 1791 he was still living, a resident of Stonington. He was almost certainly too old to have been Apess's father and was unlikely to have been his grandfather either, since Apess himself claims that his paternal grandfather was "a white man."[17] Therefore he must surely have been a great uncle from whom Apess's father received his name. A Peter Apes of Stonington is also listed among the Native men who fought in the Revolutionary War. These Pequot men served alongside other leading Native New Englanders, with names such as Uncas, Occom, Ashpo, and Johnson. Given the economic fragility of their lives, it was difficult for Native men of this and other periods (regardless of their traditional standing in the community) to pass up military service in the armed forces of the colonizer, assuming this was even a choice.[18]

If the lives of the men are difficult to trace, Native women remain even less visible in the dominant archive. However, on Christmas Day of 1798, a Polly Apes is noted to have married "Peter Gorge" in the nearby village of Preston. The Georges would prove to be an influential family in the Pequot community, and Apess would develop strong emotional and spiritual ties to his Aunt Sally George in coming years. The timing of Polly Apes's marriage suggests she may have been a sister to Apess's father. She and Peter George were married by what was known as the Separatist Church in Preston by a Reverend Paul Park.[19] The Park family had long-established ties with the local indigenous community. A generation earlier, the Mohegan preacher Samson Occom recorded in his journals many a warm visit with the Park family of Preston, at times preaching back to back meetings with Deacon Park, where, as he writes, it proved "a comfortable season to the children of God." It seems that Sally George was herself a bondservant with the Park family in her youth, and it is possible she would have recalled Occom's visits.[20] There was also a Tyra Apes in the area of Groton at this time who married James Nedson in 1787 and had eleven children.[21] Certainly there were many other family members who simply do not appear in the records.[22]

On Apess's mother's side even less can be said. As Barry O'Connell has surmised, she was quite likely the same Candace Apes who was listed as a "Negro Woman" in the possession of a Captain Joseph Taylor of Colchester. Although we assume from Apess's birth in 1798 that his father and mother were "married" sometime previous to this, we know that Candace was not officially freed until 1805 with a certificate granted by the state assuring she was in "good health" and would not be a burden on the community now that she was no longer under the "care" of her owner. According to Connecticut law at the time, slaves had to be at least twenty-five years of age and given a clean bill of health before they could be released into the world. The documents assert that Candace was twenty-eight when she was emancipated, meaning she was roughly twenty-one when her son William was born.[23]

Critics have been baffled by the classification of Candace Apes as a "negro" because it seems to contradict Apess's own claim in *A Son of the Forest* that his father "married a female of the tribe, in whose veins a single drop of the white man's blood never flowed."[24] This has led to the persistent and mistaken impression that Apess's mother was "a full-blooded Pequot woman," when in fact it merely states that Apess's mother was not white.[25] O'Connell observes that census information regarding race was extremely unreliable at the time, and the terms "Indian" and "Negro" might often be interchangeable depending on the whim of the census taker.

The fact that Native and black communities had formed tight cultural and familial bonds in nineteenth-century New England only further complicates the matter. Barbara W. Brown and James M. Rose, whose book *Black Roots in Southern Connecticut* meticulously traces the lineages of African American families in this region from 1650 to 1900, write in their introduction that "the regularity with which intermarriage between blacks and Native Americans occurred has necessitated the inclusion . . . of many Indian genealogical records. William Apes, for example, was of Indian origin and was a servant of Captain Joseph Taylor of Colchester just prior to 1800. Taylor also had a black slave named Candace, who became Apes' wife . . . The grandchildren of William and Candace Apes were recorded as black."[26]

Apess doesn't explicitly claim or disavow any of this, but close attention to his language reveals his own consciousness of just how slippery racial discourse could be in nineteenth-century New England, particularly as it was construed through "bloodlines." If the blood of the white man never flowed through his mother's veins, all it took was a "single drop" of so-called black blood to transform this Pequot woman into a Negro. As we will see, Apess was careful throughout his career to deconstruct or problematize the rhetoric of race, and yet, given the social mores of his time, it mattered a great deal whether he posited himself as "Indian" or "Negro," and this may, in part, account for his partial obfuscation of his mother's background. As for Candace's parentage, it is as of yet unknown, although we understand it to be Candace's mother, the basket seller, who so cruelly beat young Apess, as noted in the first chapter.

Apess writes in *A Son of the Forest* that, upon coming of age, his father, William Apes, married and then "removed to what was then called the back settlements, directing his course first to the west and afterward to the northeast, where he pitched his tent in the woods of a town called Colrain."[27] A number of Pequot were looking for new homes in the latter part of the eighteenth century, and it might be useful to connect Apess's father to this overall movement. The Pequot had struggled to maintain their land base ever since their decisive defeat in the 1636–37 Pequot War. Although they were able to reestablish holdings at Mashantucket and Lantern Hill in the late seventeenth century, they faced a long battle of continued colonial encroachment upon their lands, resulting in a series of legal struggles that, by 1785, had resulted in the loss of well over half the land originally returned to them by the Connecticut authorities in the previous century.

As one white overseer noted in 1804, the Pequots "say that the People of Groton have wronged them . . . out of all the benefit of their land," not only through court decisions but by "neighboring proprietors" who would habitually trespass on Pequot land, "destroying the wood timber," or, in other words, hauling off the resources of the land for their own benefit.[28] A 1922 town history of Groton, Connecticut, noted of the Pequots that they "were robbed of their possessions. . . . The settlers justified their action on the ground that the Indians were not fee-simple owners of the land but only life tenants, and as they made no use of the land, it was a pity to see it running to waste."[29]

Similar dynamics occurring throughout Native New England persuaded a number of Natives to try their luck elsewhere, and in 1784, the Mohegan minister Samson Occom, accompanied a group of Mohegan, Pequot, Narragansett, Niantic, Montaukett, and Tunxis emigrants to the newly formed Indian settlement of Brothertown, or Eeyawquittoowaucinnuck, in what was then considered the "back settlements" of upstate New York. The Brothertown movement offers a singular instance in early American history of Native peoples attempting to resist the violence of land cession and forced removal by forging their own frontier community on what was then the precise edge of English expansion. The town was established on lands granted by the

Mohegan church portrait of Samson Occom by Doug Henry, 1996.
Courtesy Tantaquidgeon Indian Museum.

Oneidas, who were, perhaps, interested in strategically creating a buffer zone of their own to protect against aggressive settler encroachments.[30]

Consisting mostly of self-professed Christian Indians, the Brothertowners and their counterparts, the Stockbridge Indians (a group of Mahicans from western Massachusetts who would go on to form a neighboring settlement), cleared new ground, apportioned lots, built clapboard houses, and on November 7, 1785, established themselves as a "body politic." As Occom recorded in his journal for that day, they compounded together to "live in Peace, and in Friendship and to go on in all their Public Concerns in Harmony."[31] While the Brothertown movement as a whole has very little purchase in the American imagination, it nevertheless offers a crucial counterweight to the staple image of the "noble savage" offered up by nineteenth-century discourse. James Fenimore Cooper, who played such a significant role in immortalizing the trope of the vanishing Indian, lived in Cooperstown, New York, and could practically see Brothertown from his back door. This did not prevent him, however, from unwitnessing the thoroughly modernized Christian Indians who were his neighbors and inventing another kind of romanticized Indian with which to replace them in his popular fictions.[32]

While other explanations might serve, it makes sense that the newly married William Apes would determine in the early 1790s to try his luck at Brothertown. As Apess notes, his father directed his course "first to the west" before retracing his steps back east toward Colrain. In his more truncated autobiographical tract, *The Experiences of Five Christian Indians of the Pequot Tribe,* Apess says of his parents that they "were of the same disposition of the Indians, that is, to wander to and fro. And, although my father was partly white, yet he had so much of the Native blood that he fashioned after them in traveling from river to river, and from mountain to mountain, and plain to plain on their journey."[33] A 1795 census suggests that, of the 135 immigrants living in the Brothertown community, at least ten were originally from Mashantucket. The census also shows that the largest demographic of Brothertown residents were children under ten years of age, suggesting that many of the immigrants in the settlement's first ten years of existence were young families just starting out, as the Apeses were at this time. Undoubtedly the Apeses would have shared familial ties with those who relocated to this spot, and there was the chance that Apes might be granted land there as well, where he could start a family of his own without fear of white settlers edging him off his stake at any moment.[34]

The identity politics of the era were such, however, that Brothertown might not have proved an ideal home for William and Candace. Part of the original agreement the Brothertown immigrants worked out with the Oneidas was that no land in the community could be owned by tribal members known to be "descended from, or [to] have intermixed with Negroes, or Mulattoes."[35] This provision proves a stain on what was otherwise a worthy enterprise, particularly when one takes into account the extent to which black and Native communities had already bonded together in this time in the Northeast as a result of their mutual marginalization from dominant economic structures.

The best way to understand this unfortunate caveat is to consider the various ways in which Native peoples could be disenfranchised from their lands. All of the New England Natives at Brothertown had seen their tribal holdings decimated through the legal processes of the dominant culture's nominal justice system. As the historian Brad D. E. Jarvis explains, "Colonists generally deemed those of 'intermixt' Indian-African ancestry as being 'black,' 'negro,' or 'Mulattoe' and not as being Indian. . . . Increasingly colonial officials viewed Native populations as disappearing and communities as becoming populated by non-Indians. For Native communities seeking to protect their lands from encroachment, this development was troubling, and many accordingly distinguished themselves from those of African American descent."[36] In other words, if an individual of tribal descent could be classified as non-Indian (which any amount of "Negro blood" might theoretically accomplish), one could be readily displaced from lands specifically designated for "Indian" use.

A great deal of the correspondence between white overseers and governing authorities in the late eighteenth and early nineteenth centuries would seamlessly join these motifs together, as when overseer Samuel Mott observed to the Connecticut General Assembly that "difficulty has arisen from the mixing of Negroes with the females of the tribes, a considerable part of the Tribe has, within this Ten years Remov'd to the Oneida Country and still claim their Right of the Avails of Sequestered Land where their fathers have cultivated."[37] Of what this "difficulty" consisted goes unstated, but from a tribal perspective, this language threatened continued cultural and economic disenfranchisement. Such complexities of nineteenth-century racial designation would figure heavily throughout Apess's life and would ultimately inspire him to craft some of the most poignant rhetorical arguments of his day against the utter fallacy of racial construction. But the practical consequences of these imposed racial distinctions could not simply be shrugged off or dismissed.[38]

If the Apeses did try to make a go of it in Brothertown, this provision conspired against their prolonged occupancy. This may explain why William and Candace Apes turned back east. But again, why Colrain? The best answer may be that affordable land was opening up in Colrain in the 1780s and 1790s. Much of the new development was occurring along the ridges of Catamount Hill, which forms much of the western border of the town. Hilltop settlements were at a peak in late eighteenth-century New England, as poor immigrants sought affordable land upon which they could eke out a subsistence living. In 1793, a 150-acre lot on Catamount Hill went for £52.10, and certainly smaller 50-acre lots were available as well.[39] While Apes himself may not have been in a position to purchase his own lot, there were additional opportunities throughout Colrain for hired hands and squatters. The first order of business in these backwoods settlements was to clear the forests to allow sunlight in for planting potatoes and Indian corn, create pasture land for sheep and cattle, and provide lumber for building homesteads. The excess lumber could easily be sold, and there was probably steady work in the early years of settlement. As a result, by 1800 the hills surrounding the town were almost completely harvested of wood.[40]

The Catamount Hill settlement consisted of thirty-five documented households in 1790, around the time that William Apes first "pitched his tent in the woods" of Colrain. The "tent" of which Apess writes may well have been a traditional wigwam, or, if not, probably resembled other crude wooden cabins in the area consisting of stripped logs caulked with mud, often with no more than an earthen floor and a root cellar in place of a foundation. Until the forest was cleared for cultivation, residents relied on hunting and salmon fishing, which could be performed without a license in the North River that spilled through the valley below. Most of these families, once again, consisted of young, newly married couples. A good many of them were Methodists, although some were of Baptist persuasion as well. Many of the men had served in the Revolutionary War, and some of these had accepted land instead of pay for their service, as was customary. The typical household in the hilltop settlements had only a few acres for tillage. The rest of the land was used for pasture or mowing or was set aside as woodlots. Residents may have boasted a team of oxen, a few cows, and a pig. Some had sheep, and the women spun both wool and flax for clothing.[41]

Apess's father would always return to Colrain throughout his life and, we can infer from the first edition of *A Son of the Forest,* published in 1829, that he and Candace had in fact "continued there for some time" prior to Apess's birth.[42] I suspect that Colrain not only offered certain economic opportunities but that William Apes's own white father and Pequot mother lived somewhere in the vicinity, and so (as would later prove the case for his son as well), there were kinship ties that drew him there. In his biographical narratives Apess offers only the most ambiguous sketch of his paternal grandparents. In the 1829 edition of *A Son of the Forest* he writes, "My grandfather was a white, and married a female attached to the royal family: she was fair and beautiful. How nearly she was connected with the king I cannot tell; but without doubt some degree of affinity subsisted between them."[43] In the revised 1831 edition, he went a step further by suggesting his grandmother was a direct descendant of King Philip, the Wampanoag leader also known as Metacom, "so well known in that part of American history which relates to the wars between the whites and the natives."[44] Apess, a tireless self-promoter, may have added the King Philip connection to lend his story more cultural cachet. Philip, although dead for more than 150 years, was the most storied Native of that era, and his name would have immediately been recognized by Apess's audience.

Whatever the case, we learn little of Apess's grandparents, how they were married, what troubles they would have faced as a mixed-race couple, and why it was that the men in Apess's family retained their grandmother's name rather than adopting that of their grandfather. While the Pequot themselves were traditionally matrilineal, it had become common practice among them after two centuries of colonization to take one's father's surname, in the European fashion. Certainly Apess took the name of his father, and Apess's own children would take his surname and not the name of his wife. Apess reports that both his grandparents were Christians who "lived and died happy in the love of God," but he never references his paternal grandfather again. In the 1829 edition of *A Son of the Forest,* however, he reveals that he had "frequently heard my grandmother talk about" their royal Pequot lineage.[45] In the end, it is difficult to know what to make of all these implied connections. If nothing else, they suggest that Apess had an intimate relationship with his paternal grandmother, who may have resided in Colrain with Apess's father. Apess himself would spend many a season in Colrain in later years, and perhaps it was here he had opportunity to listen to his grandmother's stories before she died.

Apess may have been born on Catamount Hill. The *New England Historical and Genealogical Register* for 1942 includes a report cataloguing all of the private lots on Catamount Hill in the 1790s, matching each with its original owners. Many local notables of Colrain's town history are represented here, but one lot in particular, Lot 78, remained unidentified and was known simply as "the Savage place." Whereas all of the other lots on the hill could be connected to known families in the community, "all traces" of this one family were lost, "and nothing is left to mark the site."[46] "Savage" may simply have been the surname of a family that lived at this spot, but such a definitive erasure wraps itself around the tale that it suggests these "Savages" may have been of Native descent and perhaps even the Apes family. A later town historian, Elmer F. Davenport, records that a "Barnard McNitt of Buckland made his pitch here in the 1780's," served for three years in the Revolutionary War, and then moved on in 1794, leaving his lot (Lot 78) vacant.[47] Given that all the new settlement in Colrain was happening on Catamount Hill in the 1790s and that this lot is the only one left unclaimed—save, of course, for the family of "Savages" who took it over—a strong argument can be made that this was the actual birthplace of William Apess.

The general vicinity of the site can be located today with a certain amount of accuracy. The cellar hole of the neighboring Farnsworth estate still retains its footprint on the hill, and if you travel half a mile through the brush from there, where a row of tall oaks still mark the old roadside, bypass the small settlement of beaver that have repatriated the hillside, and follow the stone wall boundary line to the top of the knoll overlooking what is now McCleod Pond (but in 1790 was known as the Beaver Meadow, and may well be the swamp where Apess nearly perished twenty years later on his return home), you will come upon the spot staked off as Lot 78. It sits on a grassy patch of hillside, alongside a ridge trail that would have led directly to important sites in the Catamount community, such as Owen's General Store and "The Oven," where Methodist meetings were regularly held in the 1820s and 1830s and where Apess almost certainly preached. No structure of substance was built on Lot 78, although there are a few depressions and pieces of stonework on the hilltop that may indicate where a family "made their pitch." And it may be here, on what is now an overgrown thickly forested hillside high above Colrain proper, that William Apess first came into the world in late January of 1798.

An alternative possibility is that the Apeses lived across town in East Colrain, on the border of what is now Leyden Township along the banks of the Green River, where a small black community had planted itself at that time. No concrete evidence exists to support this claim either. However, a number of families from Stonington, Connecticut, relocated to East Colrain in the 1780s, and local historians claim that here an Edward Denison married "an Indian maiden of high birth" and that "a number of similar marriages" were known to have taken place in the Leyden area.[48] As with the story of Joseph Griswold, such claims were most often highly romanticized attempts by white settlers to bestow upon themselves a blood connection to the land. Unions between white and indigenous couples obviously occurred. Apess himself would note, "I can assure you that I know a great many that have intermarried, both of the whites and Indians—and many are their sons and daughters . . . people, too, of the first respectability." As Apess is quick to note, however, such marriages were illegal in the state of Massachusetts and were severely discouraged everywhere else in New England.[49]

The need for local lore to attach a rank to the Indian "maidens" in question, fashioning them as "princesses" or of "high birth," speaks to the layers of racial anxiety and complicated acts of erasure that continue to attend such tales. For these stories to circulate at all required that any adherence to tribal specificity or retention of traditional practice or belief be stripped clean from the narrative. Nevertheless, Apess himself claimed his grandmother to be of "royal blood," and one wonders if any of these gauzy town stories connect back in any way to the Apes family.[50] The Denisons in particular had direct dealings with the Pequots. As mentioned earlier, Samuel Apes had served under a Captain John Denison in the French and Indian War, and a Reverend Frederick Denison had at one time made his rounds among the Pequot in Groton.[51]

Whatever the case, Abenaki anthropologist Margaret Bruchac maintains that Colrain remained a "key touchstone" in Apess's life. "Whenever he was most in need of refuge, he returned to [this] place that restored his spirit."[52]

Many of Apess's own children would be born in Colrain, his career as a Methodist minister was launched there, and, of course, he himself was born there.[53] Nevertheless, the Apes name appears nowhere in the town's voluminous self-narrated history. Nor is it highlighted in any of Colrain's contemporary promotional literature. Given that the town's public identity is so squarely rooted in a binary of savagery and civilization, it is small wonder that William Apess does not fit comfortably into its autobiographical narrative, despite the fact that he is arguably Colrain's most famous native son. Certainly he is the only Colrain Native whose life and works are studied in literature and history classes across the country. To mark his contribution, however, would powerfully resist the grain of national history making. And so Apess remains an unwitnessed presence in Colrain's self-historicizing, his life at once the most widely documented and the least visible.

The name Griswold, however, remains highly visible, as from the 1830s on the Griswold family operated the textile mill that became the most lucrative industry in town—a distinction that would hardly be worth mentioning here except for the fact that Griswold was also the name of Apess's younger brother, Griswold Apes, born in 1812, thus linking the two names together. Griswold was by no means a common first name, nor do any Griswolds show up in the Pequot community prior to Griswold Apes. Was Apess's grandfather a member of the Griswold family? Was he a Denison? Or was he one of the many other leading families that could trace back their lineage "proudly to Indian ancestry?" Although these questions remain unanswered, according to local legend, the Indian maiden betrothed to Edward Denison was laid to rest in a "mysterious burying place" in a "walled enclosure with a single unmarked stone . . . because of her Indian stature." The tale is likely apocryphal, but as is typical, even in the same breath that "Indian ancestry" is proudly claimed, it is simultaneously buried and erased, contained in its own unmarked grave and segregated from white family members—a dubious honor that speaks powerfully to the manner in which indigenous identity was systematically written out of New England history.[54]

Childhood in Colchester

Whatever opportunities Colrain offered , sometime not long after William's birth the Apes family determined to move back to the area of Colchester, Connecticut, where, Apess claims, "our little family lived for nearly three years in comparative comfort."[55] Perhaps greater opportunities for work emerged that year in the more established economy of Colchester. A new road to the local hub of New London was in the process of being built that spring, and Natives may have formed part of the work crew. Apess was too young to remember this time with any clarity, and his narrative must surely be stitched together through inference, family stories, and narrative necessity, but this latest move hardly proved smooth sailing for the young family. If it began in "comparative comfort," Apess cryptically adds that it wasn't long before "circumstances . . . changed with us."[56]

For one thing, it may be that Candace's owner, Joseph Taylor, demanded her services once more given that there were still four or five years to go until her actual manumission. According to Connecticut law, Taylor would also have legitimate claim to Candace's children as free labor until they reached the age of twenty-five. Quite possibly the only thing that exempted Apess from this statute was that his parents, either purposefully or by chance, gave birth to him in a different state. According to Colchester church records, William and Candace had a second child that died in April of 1802 from unspecified causes, creating further emotional strains on the family.[57] The Apeses' most uncertain circumstances were forged by liminality, economic fragility, and personal hardship, so that, whatever the catalyst, they were forced to move in with William's maternal grandparents.

Evidence suggests that Apess's grandparents lived in what today is the town of Salem, Connecticut, which in 1802 was still within the bounds of Colchester. Their hut stood in the vicinity of Gardiner Lake (known as Mason's Lake at the turn of the nineteenth century, after John Mason who was responsible for setting the Pequot Fort on fire in 1636), most likely in a spot that today is known as Indian Fields. Apess writes in *The Experiences of Five Christian Indians* that his grandparents' hut was no more than "about a mile off" from the white man, later identified as Mr. Furman, who would at times bring milk to the indigent family.[58] By examining property transactions from the period in the Colchester town records and matching up specific details listed in each deed with names scrawled on old town maps, it can be determined that the Furmans owned property bordering on Welch's Farm in New Salem Parish, along what was then referred to as the New London Road. Their house was almost directly across from the Baptist church and about a half mile from the lakeshore.[59]

Apess recalls the entire family living together at this time, with two brothers and two sisters, although according to census data, Apess's other siblings had yet to be born.[60] Certainly there had been little time for William and Candace to have had four other children, although it is possible that Apess had at least one sibling, a younger sister, whose birth, like his own, went unrecorded. The others may well have been stepsiblings belonging to Apess's unnamed uncle, who lived in the apartment adjoining his grandparents' cabin. Like most other New England Natives of the time, it is clear that Apess's family was hard-pressed to sustain a living. Of the few memories Apess is able to cobble together, he recalls how his mother would make porridge from frozen milk brought over by a kindly white neighbor, and this they would all lap up "like so many hungry dogs." He also remembers that "my father and mother made baskets which they would sell to the whites."[61] But such activities proved insufficient to keep the family in a state of unity, and Apess relates that in the end his parents "quarreled, parted, and went off a great distance, leaving their helpless children to the care of their grandparents." Twenty years would pass before Apess saw his mother's face again.[62]

Although Apess had no way of knowing where his parents had disappeared to, the records indicate that his father, at least for a brief while, returned to Colrain. Town documents from Buckland County (the county seat for Colrain at the turn of the century) list all pertinent births, deaths, and marriages in the settlement's early years. It would be easy to miss any vital information concerning the Apeses here unless you continued to the back section of the old record book, where, under the heading "Negroes" one finds that a son to William Apes, "an Indian," died of dysentery between July 24 and September 7, 1803.[63] Dysentery swept through the town of Colrain that summer, taking some twenty-six lives, mostly those of children under the age of four.[64] This suggests that William Apes, having lost one child already and compelled to abandon his firstborn son to the care of Candace's parents, returned to Colrain only to experience more grief at the death of yet another child. The records, of course, do not make it clear if it was Candace or some other who was mother to this child. Given Candace's continued ambiguous status as a slave and the frayed social structures that bound the couple together, it would be easy enough to imagine that the two had in fact "parted," as Apess claims in A Son of the Forest (after all, he knew full well the details of the relationship between his mother and father at the point when he was writing his memoir), and that his father had taken up with another woman in Colrain.

Back in Colchester, Apess recalls, "our fare was of the poorest kind, and even of this we had not enough. Our clothing also was of the worst description. Literally speaking, we were clothed with rags, so far only as rags would suffice to cover our nakedness. We were always happy and contented to get a cold potato for our dinners—of this at times we were denied, and many a night have we gone supperless to rest."[65] He recalls living in a state of constant hunger, reduced to begging food from neighboring families and being forced by his grandmother into the cellar, where she "unfeelingly bid us dance" to ward off the rain and cold. He reports of the near death of his younger "sister," who was slowly wasting away from hunger.[66] "Young as I was," he recalls, "my heart bled for her."[67] And then, of course, came the terrible beating Apess endured at the hand of his grandmother, who came in one evening from selling her baskets, embittered and intoxicated, only to vent her fury on the defenseless four-year-old while Apess's grandfather apparently looked on in indifference.

It was Apess's uncle who ultimately interceded for him, extracted him from the home of his grandparents, and hid him away until a white neighbor, Mr. Furman, could be enlisted in applying to the town selectmen for relief. The town apparently determined that all of the children in the household (there being four others besides Apess) should be bound out to local white families for their own protection and further well-being. Apess was brought to the Furman household, and there his mangled arm was looked over by a pair of surgeons. Apparently the injuries had gone unattended for such a period of time that they had begun to heal improperly, and the surgeons were required to reset the bones to put them back in their proper place. Apess recalls that he "scarcely murmured" throughout the painful operation, perhaps signaling his extraordinary anxiety at having arrived at this unfamiliar and seemingly precarious sanctuary. He didn't have the luxury of crying out in pain and thereby threatening his place among white strangers, although the pain caused by rebreaking and then resetting the bone must have been excruciating.

Over the course of the ensuing year, Apess was allowed to recuperate as a ward of the state. The town treasurer at the time made a number of entries noting how he compensated himself for the "disposal" or "selling of the town poor." Most of these poor were either former black slaves or indigent whites, but in 1802, the treasurer awarded himself two dollars for a day spent "taking care of two Indian children" and "making indentures of two Indian children." One of the "Indian" children was probably Apess's younger sister, although no name is given her and she appears nowhere else in the records. There are repeated references, however, to William Apes, an Indian boy, who is identified by name in regard to his medical care. Doctors made multiple visits to Apess in 1802, applying unguents and plasters to his "fractured arm." At one point Apess was prescribed a pint of rum, apparently for medicinal purposes (perhaps for when they reset the broken bones).

It was the Furmans who took care of Apess during this time, although the town records show that he also spent at least ten days recuperating at the home of one "Lemuel Ashbo, Indian." Apess makes no mention of this stay in any of his autobiographical writings, but the Ashpos were an influential Mohegan family in the area. Given that it was highly unusual, if not unheard of, to board an indigent child with a Native family, a very plausible explanation is that Lemuel Ashbo was Apess's "uncle" who had saved him from the hand of his grandmother. No other evidence exists, however, connecting Apess with the Ashpo family at present, and when Apess was considered well enough to work, he was officially bound out to the Furman family, to be their servant until he should reach the age of twenty-one.[68]

It is difficult to know how to read Apess's time with the Furmans. David Furman (in the town records his name appears as Ferman, Firman, Farmen, and Fairmen, but never Furman) was a cooper and a laborer who kept some livestock and farmed his own land. Although Apess describes him as being poor, the Furmans apparently had financial resources enough to take on additional help. Apess describes multiple encounters with other servants and at one point refers to "all the children" who labored for the household, the majority of them probably serving as seasonal labor but also, possibly, as slaves. In the time that Apess came to live with him, town records show Furman buying and selling land in the section of Colchester then known as New Salem (it would incorporate into the township of Salem in 1819).[69]

The Furmans had no children of their own when Apess was brought to them, and to some extent Apess seems to have bonded with the Furmans as surrogate parents. He attributes the very survival of his childhood abuse to Mrs. Furman, whom he describes as a "kind, benevolent, and tenderhearted lady."[70] And he praises Mr. Furman for keeping him on during his year of convalescence, despite concerns that, broken as he was, he could be of little service to the household. "Such was the attachment of the family toward me that he [Mr. Furman] came to the conclusion to keep me until I was of age, and he further agreed to give me some instruction as would enable me to read and write."[71] If prior to living with the Furmans Apess was "almost always naked, or cold, or hungry," he now found he was "comfortable, with the exception of my wounds."[72]

In the 1829 edition of *A Son of the Forest,* Apess characterizes his affection for the Furmans as having the "strength of filial love," and elsewhere he notes that they "became more fond of me than is usual for people to be of *adopted* children."[73] Despite his obvious gratitude to the Furmans for sheltering him in his time of trial, however, there are moments when we are allowed to see the chinks in the foundation and understand that Apess's relationship with them was not one of adoption but was instead contractual and dependent upon considerations of strained racial tensions and crude economics. Mrs. Furman comes across as tender toward Apess in her early ministrations to him, but her presence grows faint as the narrative progresses, and she seems to surface at times merely as a foil to Mr. Furman, with whom Apess's relationship becomes much more troubled. The most he can say of his surrogate mother in the latter half of this chapter of his life is that she was "ever ready to give me good advice" when he misbehaved, whereas Mr. Furman was quicker to resort to the whip.[74]

The most prominent example of such advice occurs when Apess finds himself, as a six-year-old child, unacceptably complacent regarding the future state of his soul. Apess, having received little or no religious instruction in his life, and being too sickly in his time with the Furmans to attend church services, had probably picked up only bits and pieces of Christian orthodoxy. When he informs Mrs. Furman that he is too young to worry about death or future states of existence, the good woman takes him to the nearby Baptist graveyard, which one can still visit today on Colchester Road along Route 345 in Salem. Mrs. Furman impressed upon Apess how many tombstones proclaimed the brief lives of children his age and younger "laid there to molder in the earth." Such instruction was perhaps not contrary to the temperament of the times, and Apess seems appreciative of the lesson itself, but its effect on him is noteworthy. He recalls that, upon receiving this news, he felt "an indescribable sensation pass through my frame; I trembled and was sore afraid and for some time endeavored to hide myself from the destroying monster, but I could find no place of refuge."[75]

Apess's narrative is nothing if not a spiritual autobiography meant to put on display his profound journey from squalid beginnings to an exemplary spiritual state. The nature of spiritual autobiography is to track the incremental advances and frequent backslidings of the individual's journey toward faith, with the added awareness that God's presence is always there, a gentle urging of the soul toward right choices even while man's fallen condition compels one to stumble headlong down false paths and blind alleyways. As such, *A Son of the Forest* recasts John Bunyan's *Pilgrim's Progress* as the narrative of a Christian soul on the long and winding road to redemption. But Apess's language also speaks to the layers of trauma that constantly undergird his experience, quite possibly in ways he could not easily acknowledge or express. Although he presents his response to Mrs. Furman's grim tutorial as a pious consideration of spiritual states, Apess's frail psyche still bears the scars of his recent near-death experience, and such a confrontation with his own mortality may have exposed the vital terror of betrayal and bodily harm lurking just beneath the surface. Apess looked to the Furmans as a "place of refuge," but even here "the destroying monster" sought him out, and this sense of dread resurfaces throughout his childhood.

It may be small wonder then that, even at a very early age, Apess began to actively seek additional refuge in the church. For Apess, the church held out the promise of a spiritual power and protection he could not offer himself as a child. It promised peace to a heart in chaos. But the price of the ticket seemed to be that he must disavow his own heritage, and therefore he was thrust into a precise postcolonial state in which he could never shed the reviled skin placed before him in the mirror. It was not uncommon for preachers of the day to denigrate the lowly Indian "savage" or to construct a sermon around the perilous contrasts between savagery and civilization. As Apess informs us, he was thoroughly conditioned to hate and fear his own people so that the "mere threat of being sent away among the Indians . . . had a much better effect in making me obedient to the commands of my superiors than any corporeal punishment that they ever inflicted."[76]

At the age of eight, however, Apess came into contact with an itinerant sect he identifies only as "the Christians," which held great outdoor camp meetings, was welcoming to people of color, and seems to have encouraged freelance vocal participation from the congregation. Attending services, Apess "could not avoid giving vent to my feelings," and he claims that he would often break out in uncontrollable weeping. These gatherings probably provided a sanctioned environment for Apess to express emotions that had no other outlet, or were perhaps too complicated for conventional forms of communication. The Furmans, however, became distressed by Apess's enthusiasm, thus compelling them to put an end to his attendance at the meetings. Apess writes that he was "tried and tempted" by these prohibitions. "I would be overcome by the fear of death. By day and night I was in a continual ferment."[77]

In his own writings, Apess comes across as an odd child, precocious, anxious, at turns overly compliant and openly rebellious, difficult in the ways his fears continuously manifest themselves both physically and psychically. He was a handful for the Furmans and taxed them as much with his fierce devotions as with his intermittent bouts of inexplicable illnesses and wayward disobedience. He was also keen to the slights he received as a Native child among whites. He observes at one point that nothing grieved him so much "as to be called by a nickname. If I was spoken to in the spirit of kindness, I would be instantly disarmed of my stubbornness and ready to perform anything required of me." But he recalls finding it disgraceful that he was frequently referred to as an "Indian," which was "considered as a slur upon an oppressed and scattered nation," and he wonders from whence the term came given that it was so frequently thrown "as an opprobrious epithet at the sons of the forest." The older and wiser Apess displays his wit by noting he could never find this word "Indian" in the bible. He wonders if it was a word devised "for the special purpose of degrading us. At other times I thought it was derived from the term *in-gen-uity* [a play on the more colloquial and perhaps more frequently heard "injun"]." But, as Apess declares, "the proper term which ought to be applied to our nation . . . is that of '*Natives*'—and I humbly conceive that the natives of this country are the only people under heaven who have a just title to the name."[78]

When Apess would occasionally lapse into bad behavior, his master, Mr. Furman, flogged him. He became an easy mark for the other servants in the household as well, who would persecute and tell lies about him, causing him to be further punished. Apess concedes that he was, at times, justified in receiving these punishments, as he had told lies once or twice himself and therefore could not expect to be believed at other times. In keeping with the demands of spiritual autobiography, there is an exacting message of moral piety to be taken from his account. But the implications of racial discrimination are made apparent as well. Mr. Furman, in doling out punishment, was apparently in the habit of hurling epithets at Apess, calling out, "I'll learn you, you Indian dog." When he refused to let Apess attend church services, it was because he viewed it as one more attempt by Apess to meet up with other boys and misbehave. Apess, however, insists upon his affection for religious communion and suggests that his being kept from service caused him a great deal of "mental agony."[79]

This tortured state of mind, twisted and made crooked by colonial constraints, helps to explain a strange anecdote Apess relates of his time with the Furmans. One day he accompanied the family into the woods on a berry-picking expedition where, after a short time, he encountered a small group of women on a similar errand. Although it is difficult to imagine what could be more nonthreatening than to run up against a group of women picking berries in the forest, the young Apess fled from the scene in abject terror, racing all the way back home, not once daring to look back. At the house he encountered Mr. Furman (whom he describes here as "my master") and conveyed his dire apprehensions about having come across a threatening band of Natives, picturing out "a tale of blood." Apess makes it a point in his narration to note that the women from whom he ran were, in fact, white, but adds that their "complexion was, to say the least, as dark as that of the natives." When the men of the household rushed back into the woods to investigate the scene, they found Mrs. Furman and the others to be perfectly safe, if now preoccupied with the task of looking for the runaway child.

The story seems to suggest a multilayered account of mistaken identities, forcing the reader to wonder why Apess would misapprehend white women for Indians and why, if he thought they were Native like himself, he would flee from them in terror. Apess remarks, "The great fear I entertained of my brethren was occasioned by the many stories I had heard of their cruelty toward the whites—how they were in the habit of killing and scalping men, women, and children. But the whites did not tell me that they were in a great majority of instances the aggressors—that they had imbrued their hands in the lifeblood of my brethren, driven them from their once peaceful and happy homes—that they introduced among them the fatal and exterminating diseases of civilized life."[80] This sort of rhetorical reversal is a useful strategy Apess employs and perfects in his writings as he offers stories that implode on themselves or reflect conclusions that drastically diverge from their initial trajectory. It is one of the earliest examples of Apess's use of what I call his "negative work." He perceives himself to be in a world in which meanings do not properly cohere and nothing is quite what it appears to be.

The stories informing Apess's childhood portrayed Native people as blood-thirsty savages, indiscriminate killers, and a threat to civilization. Before Apess was even old enough to read or write, he had already internalized this image of Native identity, which was at least partially confirmed by his own troubled past. And yet, the older Apess, in the act of writing, exposes the cultural forces that have firmed up these narratives, tracing their roots back to the violence of colonization and the white culture that had "imbrued" its hands in "the life-blood of my brethren." In a sense, the young Apess was right to run from the white women in the forest. As members of the dominant culture, they posed a threat more immediate to his well-being than any "poor Indian" ever could. But in his childhood world of negative reflections, race becomes confused, white complexions become dark, victims become aggressors, and the young Apess is found fleeing toward the very thing he might rightly fear.

Apess's childhood traumas, which I do not believe can or should be over-looked, ultimately led to states of bodily distress. He reports of a strange sickness that none around him, including the physician, had ever before witnessed. He recollects, "I felt continually as if I was about being suffocated and was consequently a great deal of trouble to the family" as he apparently could not be left alone in this condition. He notes that "whenever I would try to lay down, it would seem as if something was choking me to death, and if I attempted to sit up, the wind would rise in my throat and nearly strangle me."[81] His sickness, not surprisingly, manifests itself as an almost perfect metaphor for his existential crisis. His frequent night terrors, experiences of betrayal by his surrogate family, absence of personal security, and a lack of access to any outlets or expression for his anxieties result in a sense of being asphyxiated or having an obstruction to the throat.

Trauma experts observe how one of the great obstacles in overcoming trauma is the extreme difficulty of communicating it. As the psychiatrist Judith Herman observes, "Certain violations of the social compact are too terrible to utter aloud: this is the meaning of the word *unspeakable*."[82] Apess's traumas are unspeakable. There is no one to speak them to. He is disassociated from his parents, his kin, and his community. He is denigrated and abused. Quite likely, his floggings at the hands of Mr. Furman brought back recollections of being beaten nearly to death by his grandmother. The question "Do you hate me?" must have resonated even more deeply, as Mr. Furman mixed racial epithets with his corporeal punishment, the signifier of hate blurring in the onrush of physical violence, transforming from "Do you hate me?" to "I hate you!" and back again.

Herman writes, "The pathological environment of childhood abuse forces the development of extraordinary capacities, both creative and destructive. It fosters the development of abnormal states of consciousness . . . [and] the elaboration of a prodigious array of symptoms, both somatic and psychological. And these symptoms simultaneously conceal and reveal their origins; *they speak in disguised language* of secrets too terrible for words."[83] Consequently, Apess writes about how, in this continued distressed condition, he went out one day with Mrs. Furman and began to feel himself in an altered state. "I felt very singular and began to make a strange noise. I believed I was going to die and ran up to the house; she followed me immediately, expecting me to breathe my last. Every effort to breathe was accompanied by this strange noise, which was so loud as to be heard a considerable distance."[84]

Mr. Furman interpreted Apess's inexplicable behavior as demonic possession. This, too, has historically been a typical response to traumatic symptoms, and it demonstrates the manner in which the responses to trauma not only contribute to and exacerbate its condition but also continue to contain it within a sphere of unspeakability. Mr. Furman, apparently hoping to frighten the ailing child back into health, told Apess that the devil had taken possession of him "and that he was determined to flog him out." Apess recalls that one night "I got up and went out, although I was afraid to be alone, and continued out by the door. . . . Mr. F. got up and gave me a dreadful whipping. He really thought, I believe, that the devil was in me and supposed that the birch was the best mode of rejecting him."[85]

Although Apess ultimately recovered from his strange disease, he would continue to exhibit similar symptoms of trauma throughout his childhood— what he refers to as "the disease of my heart."[86] On one occasion he writes of how "I fancied that evil spirits stood around my bed—my condition was deplorably awful—and I longed for the day to break, as much as the tempest-tossed mariner who expects every moment to be washed from the wreck to which he fondly clings. So it was with me upon the wreck of the world." Once again, Apess frames his trauma within a discourse of piety, noting, "Sin was the cause of this, and no wonder I groaned and wept. I had often sinned, and my accumulated transgressions had piled themselves as a rocky mountain upon my heart." But he had also been grievously sinned against, and his disproportionate sufferings were enough to "crush me down. In the night season I had frightful visions and would often start from my sleep and gaze round the room, as I was ever in dread of seeing the evil one ready to carry me off."[87]

If this is ostensibly the testimony of a self-confessed sinner attempting to shrug off the weight of sin, it is also, once again, a textbook description of the symptoms of trauma, which, according to Herman and other trauma experts, include sleeplessness, startle reactions, hyperalertness, vigilance for the return of danger, nightmares, and psychosomatic complaints.[88] Apess would write of periods when "sleep departed me" and he would lie in bed, fearful that if he dozed, he would "wake up in hell." He had dreams of a "world of fire . . . no tongue can possibly describe the agony of my soul, for now I was greatly in fear of dropping into that awful place."[89] Conversion to Methodism was supposed to involve soul searching, debilitating doubt, and even altered states of consciousness, but Apess locates within these conventions outlets for other aspects of his tortured emotional experience that, in terms of mental anguish, far outstrip conventional narratives of spiritual growth.[90]

Apess, it seems, was ever vacillating between the faith of an absolute convert and the soul of a rebel, caught between struggles of sin and redemption, compliance and resistance. His identity was in a constant state of flux as he grappled for a foothold in whatever community might offer itself up to him, or was spontaneously repulsed by the constant affronts to justice that defined his status. He was able to acquire six stray years of schooling during this period, in which he learned to read and write sufficiently. But like most bonded servants of the day, the education provided him was the barest minimum, and was undoubtedly broken up by the demands of seasonal labor. Noting that it was fashionable at this time for boys to run away from home, Apess was persuaded to do just that by one of the older boys working on the Furmans' farm. Dreaming of riches in the big city of New London and of "becoming a person of consequence," Apess packed his bags and prepared to flee but was apparently betrayed by the very same boy who tempted him to leave in the first place, and was caught before he ever made it out the door. Mr. Furman determined at this point that it would be best if Apess were to have another master. This decision apparently came as a crushing blow to the young boy. He implored Furman, saying that he was "as unwilling to go now as I had been anxious to run away before," but the Furmans had apparently reached the breaking point with Apess, and the familial relation they ostensibly bore him was about to suddenly terminate.[91]

"I Was Greatly Mortified to Think That I Was Sold in This Way"

Apess's indenture was transferred for the sum of twenty dollars to one William Hillhouse, a wealthy landowner, judge, and politician of New London who had served as a major with Connecticut's Second Cavalry Regiment during the Revolution and as Connecticut delegate to the Continental Congress from 1783 to 1786. Hillhouse was the great-grandson of none other than John Mason, the Puritan who had claimed responsibility in 1637 for setting fire to the Pequot Fort at Mystic in which roughly seven hundred women, children, and elders were killed, along with many Pequot warriors. Hillhouse served at various times as colonial overseer of the Mohegan and Pequot nations. In certain circles he was known as "the Sachem" and was said to have kept a hatchet on his judicial bench that he casually displayed during contentious arguments as an ostensible reminder for competing parties to "bury the hatchet."[92] His brother, James Hillhouse, held the position of "king's attorney" for the colony and, among other things, served as prosecutor in the trial of Moses Paul, a Wampanoag who was convicted of murdering a white man and hung for the crime in 1772.

The connection to the Moses Paul trial might be of little interest (in fact none of the published historical material I have uncovered concerning the Hillhouse family bothers to mention it) save for the fact that Paul's final moments were presided over by Samson Occom, the prominent Mohegan minister and one of the founders of the Brothertown settlement. The execution sermon Occom delivered at Paul's death was a cultural event, drawing the largest crowd Connecticut had ever seen at that time, and was subsequently published, becoming a popular success that would go through at least twenty-two different printings in the eighteenth and early nineteenth centuries. Occom's *Sermon at the Execution of Moses Paul* (1772) is generally regarded as the first published text to be authored by a Native American in the English language.[93] Some years later, a descendant of this Moses Paul (also named Moses Paul) would put his name to a Mohegan petition penned by Apess.

Although I can find no mention of it in the records, Judge Hillhouse likely presided over the Moses Paul case. He was personally acquainted with Occom and had been present in 1769 at the burial of the white-appointed Mohegan sachem Ben Uncas III. Uncas was unpopular among much of the Mohegan tribe, and in a letter to the governor of Connecticut, Hillhouse reported with a note of alarm that in the middle of the sermon, "before divine service was over, Sampson Occom withdrew and went off and [was] very soon followed by others of the Tribe" so that there were none left to assist in carrying the corpse (which Hillhouse described as "being very heavy" and left in state too long) to the graveyard. Hillhouse certainly recognized this act of civil disobedience for what it was, but his letter strives to reframe the incident to a degree, noting that "the tempers of a number of Indians is worked up to the highest pitch of jealousies."[94]

Occom's execution sermon must surely have been on the bookshelves at Judge Hillhouse's estate. But Apess somehow never mentions Occom in any of his writings. Although we hear traces of Occom's language in Apess's authorial voice, this connection remains yet another peculiar silence with which we must grapple. In his 1768 autobiographical narrative, Occom's most widely anthologized piece, he offers an anecdote concerning the "constrained" state within which Native peoples were forced to exist in colonial New England.

He compares his own estate with that of a "Poor Indian Boy" bound out to an English family who was "Whipt and Beat" most every day. When asked why he was treated so, the boy replied that he supposed it was because he could not drive the plow any better, but at other times he assumes he is beat because his master "is of mind to beat me," but, the boy continued, "I believe he Beats me for the most of the Time, because I am an Indian."[95] This anecdote speaks not only to the racial violence around which colonial culture was structured but also to just how common it was for Native children to be bound out to white families. Apess's condition, far from being unusual, was precisely the norm for Native children growing up in New England in the late eighteenth and early nineteenth centuries. As Apess, too, attests, when he was beaten, it often wasn't so much for something he had done but because he was an "Indian dog."

The historian Margaret Ellen Newell has referred to the common practice of bonding out Native children as "judicial enslavement." The economic dominance of the colonial culture ensured that Native peoples were forced into long periods of involuntary servitude to settle debts, escape criminal sentencing, or avoid becoming wards of the state. With no representation and little recourse to the justice system, Native communities found themselves thus marginalized and exploited. If, formally speaking, their collective rights as free Indians were recognized, Newell concludes, "New England governments crafted new racially-based tax and legal codes that further eroded the status of Indian servants." She continues, "Once indentured, Indians could find themselves bought and sold, separated from their families and taken from the region. Running away, stealing from one's master, and a host of other violations could double or triple the length of a servant's time obligation."[96] Binding out entire generations of Native children proved a violent destabilizing agent for an indigenous community, breaking familial chords, and forcing children into often-traumatic situations of violence, sexual exploitation, and servitude, as well as divorcing them from their cultural moorings. Apess, always an astute observer of the rationale behind colonial practices, would write, "So completely was I weaned from the interests and affections of my brethren" that he feared rather than revered his own people.[97]

Ruth Wallis Herndon and Ella Wilcox Sekatau, in examining the bonding practices of Rhode Island at this time, offer a portrait that precisely follows the experiences of William Apess. They write, "Town leaders usually bound out a child in response to a 'complaint' lodged by a respectable person in the community concerning perceived poverty or disorder in the child's family. . . . Oral tradition asserts that such contracts were less concerned with real payment of the supposed costs of maintenance than they were an opportunity for masters to coopt labor."[98] Seen in this light, one might cynically question the original motives of the Furman family for expressing interest in the Apess children by bringing them milk and giving them food when they came begging. Apess essentially spent his childhood providing free labor for white families and might have gone on doing so indefinitely had he not eventually taken matters into his own hands. Perhaps this complaint seems negligible, given that Native communities of New England were far too poor to care for their own. But these circumstances were, in fact, the direct consequences of a colonialism in which Natives were systematically robbed of their own land and resources, leaving white people the assumed "right to manage the lives of Indian and African American children."[99] If, from a distance, the practice appears benevolent, it is in fact part and parcel of a coercive system of white hegemony.

Apess's own situation was further complicated by the fact that his mother, Candace, was likely of African American origin. Connecticut law, and in particular the Gradual Abolition Act of 1784, provided that no "Negro or Mulatto Child, that shall, after the first day of March, *One thousand seven hundred and eighty-four,* be born within this State, shall be held in Servitude, longer than until they arrive to the Age of twenty-five Years, notwithstanding the Mother or Parent of such Child was held in Servitude at the Time of its Birth; but such Child, at the age aforesaid, shall be free; any Law, Usage or Custom to the contrary notwithstanding."[100] The law may sound progressive in its language—abolition generally being considered a good thing—but it didn't free a single soul from slavery. At least not right away. It did ensure, however, that another generation of black and Native children would toil under bondage for a good part of their lives, and depart that condition with little or no hope of upward mobility. Although the law promised to liberate individuals born after the passing of the act in their twenty-fifth year, it was organized in such a manner that Connecticut would not completely rid itself of the institution of slavery until the late 1840s.[101] The only reason, it seems, that Apess was not himself legally bound out to Joseph Taylor, Candace's owner, was because he was born in Massachusetts instead of Connecticut. Nevertheless, Colchester retained a healthy slave population in the last quarter of the eighteenth century, and one out of every fifteen persons there was a slave.[102]

The distinction between bondsman and slave could hardly have meant much to Apess, however, when the Furmans sent him to live with Judge Hillhouse. Apess seems to have originally been told that the arrangement would last only a fortnight, and that, if he so chose, he might return to the Furmans at the end of this period. He writes that he was "homesick" throughout this trial, and as soon as the fortnight ended he packed his things and, without notifying the judge, promptly went back to the Furmans. But he was in for a sad surprise. He recalls, "The joy I felt on returning home, as I hoped, was turned to sorrow on being informed that I had been *sold* to the judge and must instantly return."[103]

Apess's language is deliberately meant to invoke the conditions of slavery, and his narrative at times feels very much like the slave narratives of a few decades later. Hillhouse kept slaves on his estate, and Apess would have been in frequent company with them, worked alongside them, and felt his station in life little removed from theirs. In fact, the differences between them were mostly negligible. Apess says of his time on the Hillhouse plantation that there was never a shortage of work. The education he had been promised, and which he had begun, however haltingly, with the Furmans, was now withheld. "To be sure, I had enough to eat, such as it was," but he had few freedoms, he was clothed in rags, he was forbidden once again from attending church meetings, and he was flogged when he frequently disobeyed this injunction.

Ultimately, Apess decided that the old judge was too feeble to maintain control over him and he ran away again. Apparently there was a strong enough network of communicants in Apess's social sphere for the young boy to catch word that his father had returned to the region and was about twenty-five miles off, in the vicinity of Waterford. Records indicate that Apess's father remained in the area over the next few years, living, perhaps, off money he made selling his land to the Taylor family in Colchester in 1811 (these were the same Taylors who had been Candace's owners). He was busy raising a new family, as Apess's brothers Gilbert and Griswold were born at this time, in 1809 and 1812 respectively. Apess probably sorely craved some measure of contact with his father and, in all likelihood, entertained complex feelings about his father's new domestic arrangements. His father remained an intermittent presence in his life, and Apess practices a great deal of restraint when it comes to detailing the particulars of their relationship. Upon running away from Hillhouse, the ten-year-old boy arrived safely at his father's place, promptly informing him that "I had come on a visit and that I should stay one week. At the expiration of the week he bid me go home, and I obeyed him."[104] What hidden world of mixed emotion and familial devotion lies concealed in such passages, it is difficult to say.

Left with no option but to return to the Hillhouse estate, Apess retraced his steps but continued his rebellious ways, running away repeatedly until once again he was sold without his consent or knowledge "as a farmer would sell his sheep for the slaughter."[105] He writes, "I was greatly mortified to think that I was sold in this way. If my consent had been solicited as a matter of form, I should not have felt so bad. But to be sold to and treated unkindly by those who had got our fathers' lands for nothing was too much to bear."[106] This was no idle claim. As Apess surely knew, the Hillhouse estate in Montville, Connecticut, was affectionately known by its owners and the larger community as Sachem's Wood, which is suggestive of its former Mohegan/Pequot proprietorship. The Hillhouses stood at the end of a long lineage of powerful colonial families that had worked to destroy, dislocate, and divest Pequot people of their holdings, and they now claimed the privilege of trafficking in the lives and labor of Pequot children.

The next and final stop for Apess in his life as indentured servant was with the Williamses, yet another old and powerful New England family residing in New London. General William Williams was descended from the Reverend John Williams, who a century earlier had been taken captive during the French, Mohawk, and Abenaki raid on Deerfield, Massachusetts, and who had penned a famous captivity narrative about his experiences in 1707. John Williams's daughter, Eunice, who was also captured, would remain with the Mohawks at Kahnawake and would ultimately marry into the tribe, leaving a bitter legacy for this diehard Puritan dynasty. The Williamses continued on as influential powerbrokers in the region, their lands, lives, and fortunes often intricately entangled with Indian affairs. Williams's father had been a signer of the Declaration of Independence, and William Williams himself would become "overseer" of the Mashantucket Pequot tribe at about the same time that he took in young Apess as a bondservant. If Apess, for various reasons, felt this to be a much-improved situation, it was still one fraught with tension, and Williams informed Apess in no uncertain terms that if he were ever to run away, "he would follow me to the uttermost parts of the earth."[107]

With the Williamses, Apess was given good new clothes and never went hungry. His workload was light, but as before he would somehow run afoul of the other servants, who, according to Apess, told lies about him that often resulted in his being flogged. A chambermaid even went so far as to push him down a flight of stairs, resulting in a head injury that, Apess relates, disabled him for a long period of time. Once again, such vicious treatment must have triggered many of Apess's traumatic childhood memories. Although he never explicitly connects his physical and mental anguish to the acts of violence perpetrated against him, he nevertheless recounts the recurrence of night terrors at this time, accompanied by feelings of powerlessness and anxiety dreams of death and damnation. He writes of lying in bed in a fearful state, "mourning like a dove." He would have no way of equating his distressed mental state with a diagnosis of trauma, as no such diagnosis existed in Apess's time, and so he relates these experiences instead as his soul's struggle for redemption. In fact, many of his difficulties are tied to this struggle, and he concluded, "The abuse heaped on me was in consequence of my being a Methodist."[108]

"Like an Overwhelming Flood": Apess Meets Methodism

The Methodists began to "'hold meetings in the neighborhood" of New London sometime around 1812, creating a stir with their "noisy" devotions and unconventional doctrine.[109] If we are to take Apess at his word, even as a child he was extremely particular about where he worshipped. Such determinations may have had more to do with community and even politics than with denominational ritual or doctrine, although perhaps all four factors came together. Apess makes a note of the fact in his autobiography that both Hillhouse and Williams, when leading the family in prayer, would offer rote recitations. He repeatedly refers to such prayer as "an empty sound and a tinkling symbol," invoking the famous biblical passage taken from Paul's letter to the Corinthians in which we are reminded that the world only appears to us on this human sphere as though "through a glass darkly."

Part of the appeal of the Methodist and New Light movements for disenfranchised communities was that they placed less emphasis on prepared performances and the rote recital of scripture, preferring instead the effluent spontaneous responses of the heart. This is what led some to characterize their meetings as "noisy." Congregants might vocalize, testify, weep, and perhaps even speak in tongues in some instances, depending, as Apess remarks, on "the Holy Spirit's influence entirely."[110] Apess found himself swept up in this movement that was responsive to his emotional needs and offered a sympathetic space for people of color. He apparently became convinced at this time "that Christ died for all mankind—that age, sect, color, country, or situation made no difference. I felt an assurance that I was included in the plan of redemption with all my brethren. No one can conceive with what joy I hailed this *new* doctrine, as it was called."[111]

It is not difficult to see how such a message might have social and political implications, as it ran counter to the well-established hierarchies—racial, economic, and spiritual—to which the region remained bound. The movement threatened to empower marginalized populations and bring them together under a separate roof and a separate calling, releasing them from the prescribed dictates and moral coordinates of the privileged classes. Apess recalls that "all denominations were up in arms against" the Methodists "because the Lord was blessing their labors and making them (a poor, despised people) his instruments in the conversion of sinners."[112] Rumors about the Methodists flew throughout the community, and "respectable" people were greatly discouraged from appearing in their company. If the unconventional methods used by the Methodists sent ripples of discontent through the community, however, it was of little concern to Apess. He determined that he need not worry if his character was besmirched through his association with the sect, for he "had no character to lose in the estimation of those who were accounted great. For what cared they for me? They had possession of the red man's inheritance and had deprived me of liberty; with this they were satisfied and could do as they pleased; therefore, I thought I could do as I pleased" when it came to choosing his form of spiritual devotion.[113]

This was the religious climate in New London in 1813, which swept over young Apess "like a flood," so that on the fifteenth day of March of that same year he records his own conversion. Joseph Snelling, a Methodist circuit rider for the region, reminisces about visiting the Pequot tribe in his 1847 narrative, recalling, "A lad about twelve or fourteen years of age, who had been in the enjoyment of religion for some time, arose and exhorted sinners to repentance, in a most pathetic manner, with tears flowing from his eyes, and his soul filled with the love of God. Much good I believe was done."[114] This young boy was almost certainly William Apess.

Although Apess's tale will afford many instances of backsliding and continued interdenominational conflict even among his beloved Methodists, for the moment at least Apess felt his heart lifted up to God, and an altered state come over him, a "peace of mind, which flowed as a river," erasing all his "burdens and fears." It is difficult in the ensuing passage to know if he is speaking of Methodists in general or more particularly of his own Pequot community when he writes, "The children of God I loved most affectionately. Oh how I longed to be with them, and when any of them passed by me, I would gaze at them until they were lost in the distance. I could have pressed them to my bosom, as they were more precious to me than gold, and I was always loath to part with them whenever we met together. . . . I continued in this happy frame of mind for some months. It was very pleasant to live in the enjoyment of pure and undefiled religion."[115]

The Williamses apparently could not allow their family name to be associated with the Methodists, even through one of their servants, and so Apess was once again forbidden to attend services. The pattern begins to become familiar. Prohibitions led to disobedience, which led to recrimination in the form of flogging. Severed from his sole source of communal comfort, Apess felt friendless, unpitied, and alone. He confesses that at times he "wished to become a dweller in the wilderness."[116] And so, when the situation became intolerable for Apess, he once again, at "an evil hour," listened to "the voice of the devil" in the form of another young companion and began plotting his next escape.

I suppose Apess equates his "escape" with evil because the Bible is clear on the doctrine of servants obeying their masters. But he absorbs this blame rather painlessly, and it is doubtful that he looks back in any meaningful way on this "devil's" work. Nevertheless, as he put his life of bondage behind him, he also "began to lose sight of religion and of God."[117] He sets out on a rainy night with his companion and a bottle of rum, which they would finish before daybreak. If his escape was the consequence of listening to the devil, then, just this once, the devil had served him well. He may have awoken with a hangover the next morning, but he had set his life on a new path. Apess did not know where he would go or what the future held for him, but his choices were clear: he could either claim agency by seeking out a new destiny, suffering whatever consequences such action might entail, or remain in the bondage of those who had destroyed his people and stolen the lands of his fathers only to have his spirit continuously and deliberately broken.

CHAPTER THREE
The Broad Theater of the World

Here ended all hopes of our remaining at peace—having been
forced into WAR by being DECEIVED.

    —BLACK HAWK (MA-KA-TAI-ME-SHE-KIA-KIAK)

O, that God would be pleased to put an end to all wars.

    —ELEAZAR WILLIAMS

What a fine thing it was to be a soldier.

    —WILLIAM APESS

Worldly Affairs

In 1813, an ad placed in the *Connecticut Gazette* by William Williams notified
readers of a runaway "Indian Boy named William Apes, aged 15 years." It
asked that "all persons forbid harboring or trusting him on penalty of the
law." A one-cent reward was offered to anyone who might return Apes to
his rightful owner.[1] Williams had warned Apess that he would follow him
to the "uttermost parts of the earth" should he try to run away, and that was
precisely where Apess was headed—or at least as far as the uttermost boundaries of the continental United States. But before tracking Apess's sojourn in
the Canadian borderlands, it is important to know something of the events
unfolding in the years of his short life up to this point, and how such events
would shape and influence the lives of Native peoples in the Northeast as well
as the fate of the young runaway.[2]

    Sometime late in 1791, the Mohegan preacher Samson Occom, having
moved his family to New Stockbridge in what was now, officially, the state of
New York, picked up the November 3 edition of the *Albany Gazette* and read,
among other things, of events taking place in Philadelphia, the current seat of

the newly formed U.S. government. Occom was sixty-seven years old. Having traveled a long and arduous path in life—traversing old wampum trails, crossing the Atlantic and back again to raise money for Indian education, advocating for Native causes, helping to organize an unprecedented exodus of New England Natives to Oneida territory, and having sought a form of spirituality within colonial Christian frameworks that might somehow sustain Native community—Occom was finally showing signs of wear. He would not live to see another year through, though his battles were ongoing.

Occom watched helplessly as more and more whites streamed westward, pressing onto lands that had been set aside for the Brothertown and New Stockbridge Natives. Some in his community welcomed this influx, hoping to enter into the white capitalist economy and profit from land leases. Occom, however, intuited that it portended disaster for the dream of Native autonomy that had instigated the move to Oneida territory in the first place. In his final weeks and days, he continued to lobby to halt the flow of white settlement while simultaneously seeking assistance for a community that was, he acknowledged, in dire economic straits. In one of the last letters he ever wrote, he reflected on how his people suffered for lack of good clothes and farm implements. He was mostly concerned, however, that there was a need for new books for the education of Indian children, and he insisted that, rather than send white educators or missionaries, it was necessary "that the Indians must have Teachers of their own Coular or nation," for having been wronged and imposed upon too often, they had developed a distrust of the white people, "and good reason for it."[3]

Occom's tone in this letter was uncharacteristically bleak, and his understanding of worldly affairs had persuaded him that there was only more conflict and trouble yet ahead. He remarked that, as had been the case for too long, Native people found themselves positioned "between Contending Nations" and "imposed upon too much." Both the British and the Spanish were now pressuring indigenous powers to combine against the newly minted American nation, and he seemed to reluctantly resign himself to the fact that these imperial powers would have their way. In fact, his thoughts on the matter would prove prophetic. The War of 1812 would effectively shatter the Haudenosaunee power base in western New York and leave no protection for the fledgling Brothertown and New Stockbridge settlements. Within a matter of a few years, these immigrants, having risked so much to make a new start, would find themselves pushed still further west of their ancestral homes. Even as Occom was writing, Hendrick Aupaumut, a Stockbridge Mohican who had been instrumental in forging Native community in the new settlement, was meeting with other indigenous groups along the White River in Indian Territory, seeking to seal old alliances and scout out new lands. In a postscript to his letter, however, Occom observed there was one item in the newspaper that had given him encouragement. He wrote that he rejoiced to see how "at the opening of Congress the President Deliverd a Speech" (it was printed in its entirety in the Albany paper), which Occom apparently read with special attention to what it meant for him and for indigenous people in general.

It may be difficult, at first glance, to understand why Occom "Rejoiced" at George Washington's October 25, 1791, address to Congress. Unfortunately, Occom's surviving letter is torn and faded in places so that his further sentiments are illegible. But the speech contained little that could be viewed as positive for Native Americans. Washington declared that the most pressing issue facing the nation remained "the defense and security of the Western Frontiers," which he hoped to pacify under the most humane principles employing "moderation and justice." If this sounded encouraging (and I'm not saying it did), it was nevertheless followed by the announcement that "offensive operations have therefore been directed" at "deluded" and "hostile" Indian nations to make them "sensible that a pacification was desired." The stated goal, as ever, was to instill a system of "Religion and Philanthropy towards an unenlightened race of Men, whose happiness materially depends on the conduct of the United States." Washington noted that the United States had already provisionally concluded treaties with the more tractable tribes, such as the Cherokee and the Six Nations of Indians, and these only awaited congressional ratification.[4]

Perhaps Occom was encouraged by the initiation of the treaty-making process indicated here and saw it as a tacit recognition of continued Native sovereignty. Washington had maintained that all Native peoples "should experience the benefits of an impartial administration of justice. That the mode of alienating their lands, the main source of discontent and war, should be so defined and regulated, as to obviate imposition."[5] Reading between the lines, Occom understood this to mean that the federal government would take control of all negotiations with indigenous peoples, treating them as sovereign nations and putting a stop to the coercive land transactions that the separate states, and New York in particular, were relentlessly pursuing to the great detriment of Native communities. Washington was, in fact, asserting federal authority under the newly forged Constitution, taking power away from the states that had basically been acting as independent agents under the Articles of Confederation.

If one were to take a cynical view of matters, one might entertain the notion that Washington's Indian policy, otherwise known as the Non-Intercourse Act, was simply designed to keep the fast-acting states of New York, Connecticut, Pennsylvania, and Massachusetts from laying claim to

the Ohio Territory, which Washington had long coveted for Virginia planters. But his policy proved popular with eastern Native nations and would
have long-lasting ramifications for treaty law. As the early twentieth-century
Seneca historian Arthur Parker would observe, "Washington's magnanimity
is little less than astonishing, and his gentle firmness and diplomacy make
his policy one of the triumphs of statesmanship."[6] Parker was laying it on
thick, cognizant as he was that he was writing for a largely white audience.
Rightly or wrongly, however, Washington's reputation among many Native
peoples was somewhat recuperated by his decree. Up until this moment,
Washington had been reviled among the Haudenosaunee as Hanadahguyus,
or Town Destroyer, for his scorched-earth policies directed at the People of
the Longhouse. If Washington redeemed himself in the eyes of many Natives
by initiating this more judicious policy, nevertheless, the name stuck. American presidents are still greeted by the Haudenosaunee to this day by their
traditional title of Hanadahguyus or "town destroyer."[7]

Control of the Ohio Valley had been a long-standing goal of the nation,
stretching all the way back to colonial times, when a young George Washington and others of the Virginian planting class attempted to lay claim to
the territory through the machinations of the Ohio Company. Washington
and his wealthy cohorts became involved in land investment schemes that
aimed at purchasing huge swaths of territory from the Iroquois, ranging from
Kentucky to Minnesota, at a price of roughly four hundred pounds.[8] Such a
sale, even if the Iroquois themselves had truly been amenable to the terms,
simply ignored the existence of other indigenous nations who occupied these
regions.

Washington's early military career involved frontier "surveying" expeditions
that had the ulterior motive of seeking out diplomatic relations with western
Natives in this "empty" space in an attempt to dismantle French fortifications
and open access to these lands supposedly now in the colonial domain. In
November of 1754, Major Washington personally exchanged wampum before
an audience of Lenape and Haudenosaunee leaders, involving himself in the
diplomatic bonds of the condolence ritual and seeking advice and assistance
of his indigenous "Brothers."[9] Even so, he was unable to persuade Native
leaders of his nation's sincerity. His diplomatic forays erupted into tactical
blunders, an ill-considered raid, and ultimately a desperate stand at Fort
Necessity in 1754 that led to his surrender to the French and Lenape. Washington's frontier campaigns were capped off by his participation in General
Edward Braddock's infamous offensive on Fort Duquesne a year later, in
which British troops were ambushed by a patrol of French and Lenape scouts
and almost entirely wiped out. Washington was fortunate to escape with his
life. The so-called French and Indian Wars that ensued ultimately did secure

British dominance of the Eastern Seaboard, but still failed to win the Ohio Valley for British colonial settlement.

During the Revolutionary War some twenty years later, Washington would make yet another attempt to secure the western territories for colonial power through a series of offensives that first earned him the sobriquet "Town Destroyer" among the Seneca.[10] Three separate colonial invasions in 1779 were designed to pursue the type of scorched-earth campaign that had proven so effective against Pequot resistance some one hundred and fifty years earlier. The Sullivan, Clinton, and Broadhead invasions ostensibly targeted those Haudenosaunee communities siding with the English in the war, despite the fact that such alliances were only partial at best, and the real victims of these assaults were typically the women, children, and elderly who were left without shelter or food regardless of their political allegiances. Sullivan's invasion alone ravaged some forty villages of the Seneca, Cayuga, and Onondaga. The colonial army reported destroying 160,000 bushels of corn and, according to Sullivan, left not "a single settlement or a cornfield in the country."[11]

Arthur Parker, detailing the destruction of Iroquois maize in the wars, summarized his findings as such: "Bent upon wreaking revenge upon a tribe of ignorant savages, [the colonial armies] entered the Genesee valley with feelings of utmost surprise for they found the land of the savages to be, not a tangled wilderness but a shining blooming valley, and the savages domiciled in permanent houses and settled in towns."[12] Revolutionary soldiers engaged in this wanton destruction, many of them former farmers themselves, marveled at the "goodness" of the crops, with one observing it to be "unequaled by any I ever yet saw."[13] And yet all of it was ordered destroyed. Parker, writing in 1926, referred to Sullivan's campaign as "the Holocaust," as it proved unspeakably devastating to the Haudenosaunee community in terms of lives lost, communities displaced, and property devastated. Although the Mohawk leader Joseph Brant, along with a coalition of British and Native forces, staged effective counterattacks in response to these campaigns, Haudenosuanee control over the Longhouse was severely shaken. But even after all of this, the colonists still could not declare a decisive victory, as they had failed to punch through to the coveted Ohio Valley.[14]

Following the surrender of the British in the Revolutionary War, the 1783 Treaty of Paris reconfigured the lines of empire in the Northeast. The British, who had been allies with much of the Five Nations during the Revolutionary War, held on to the regions north of what is today the U.S.-Canadian border. The newly formed United States acquired all the lands south of that border, including, according to the terms of the treaty, everything east of the Mississippi and north of Florida. It once again escaped the attention of those who framed the treaty that this expansive domain had never been in British control to begin with, but was instead homeland to a large number of sovereign indigenous nations. As the Haudenosaunee historian John C. Mohawk observes, "The United States' claim to these lands continued to be based on the theory that the Indians who occupied these lands had been conquered along with the British during the American Revolution—a theory the Indians hotly contested."[15]

Exhausted by warfare on all sides, the Iroquois, under the leadership of the Seneca chief Cornplanter, signed the 1784 Treaty of Fort Stanwix with the United States, the first treaty forged between the United States and a Native nation. This treaty, in which the United States insisted on characterizing the Iroquois as a "conquered" people, forcing them to give up huge chunks of land, was not agreed to by a large portion of the Six Nations, and remained a point of contention for at least the next decade. To maintain Native control of the Ohio, the Mohawk leader Joseph Brant labored to hold together a United Indian Confederacy consisting of Haudenosuanee, Miami, Lenape, Sauk, Ojibwe, Wyandot, Potawatomi, Missassaugua, Shawnee, and other nations claiming territory from Grand River all the way west through Minnesota and the Great Lakes region. This confederacy rejected the terms of the Treaty at Fort Stanwix and was prepared to fight if necessary to maintain sovereignty over territories these nations had neither lost in battle nor peacefully ceded.

Worth emphasizing is that indigenous peoples responded to the events of the American Revolution as sovereign nations, engaging in hard-edged diplomacy, negotiating over land and resources, forging intertribal alliances, and threatening coordinated military resistance. But this fact remains just one more casualty of U.S. history making. The Revolutionary War is typically painted as a precise engagement between red and blue coats (with perhaps a smattering of French and German participation), but the high-stakes battle over who would maintain control of the land affected Native nations at least as much as it did the colonial armies lining up against one another on the Eastern Seaboard. Native actions to protect their interests are often relegated to the status of frontier skirmishes, Daniel Boone captivity stories, or, worse yet, unprovoked Indian massacres, but the so-called frontier was more accurately yet another *front* in a multifaceted war for dominance in the region. Although the United States defeated the British, they did not defeat the western Native alliances, and although they felt they held the upper hand after the war, the very fact that they were willing to negotiate peace treaties under Washington's new policies was a tacit recognition that Native nations maintained sovereignty over their lands. Facing internal disorder, fatigue, economic insolvency, and disunion in the immediate aftermath of the war, the United States was eager to call a cessation of hostilities even if it was ultimately just biding its time to fight another day. The Native groups involved needed time to recover their strength as well.

As Samson Occom predicted in 1791, the reprieve was not destined to last long. The Shawnee remained at perpetual war with white settlers, who, ignoring boundary lines drawn up in various treaties, made of Kentucky a "bloody ground." And the United States was already preparing to send more troops into the Ohio Valley to pacify those "deluded" Indians who didn't view settler expansion with an approving eye. This initially led to the humiliating rout of Arthur St. Clair's troops at Fort Recovery only days after Washington delivered his 1791 address to Congress. Some nine hundred colonials were killed in this engagement, championed on the Native side by the Miami leader Little Turtle, who could count among his number a young Shawnee warrior named Tecumseh. Another attack on Fort Recovery in 1794, consisting of both British troops and warriors of the Western Confederacy, proved indecisive, but later that year General Anthony Wayne launched an offensive resulting in the Battle of Fallen Timbers that proved a decisive victory for the United States, causing disruptions in the balance of power throughout the region.

Ironically, as Natives of the Northeast were increasingly pressured to adopt the agricultural practices of the settler state, they found themselves pinched by crop failures and hunger where before they had enjoyed seasons of surplus crops. A religious revival movement spearheaded by the Seneca prophet Handsome Lake attempted to restore some sense of cultural vitality for the Haudenosuanee through newly interpreted traditions built around the political and spiritual structure of the longhouse. Within a decade, the Shawnee prophet Tenskwatawa was also envisioning a new spiritual order for the people of the Ohio Valley. But another path to regenerating tradition, land, and sovereignty lay in allying with the British, who remained interested in recouping their colonial losses. Leaders such as Blue Turtle, Black Hawk, and Tecumseh (brother of Tenskwatawa) began to see armed conflict as the only way to maintain a permanent home in the lands of their fathers.

Like the American Revolution, the War of 1812 is typically regarded as a dispute between the British and the colonists, a continuation, in fact, of the earlier war. But despite tensions in the Atlantic world, where the British were having their way with America's unprotected commercial shipping interests, confiscating goods and impressing American sailors into the British Navy, the War of 1812 was truly one of opportunistic expansion on the part of the United States under the Monroe administration. As the historian Alan Taylor has recently written, it is a war that "looms small in American memory."[16] Popular culture memorializes it through songs such as "The Star Spangled Banner," written by Francis Scott Key during a naval engagement at Chesapeake Bay, or "The Battle of New Orleans," which immortalized Andrew Jackson's 1814 victory in a negligible engagement (for the British and the Americans at least) fought after the war had already officially ended. We also tend to recollect that the White House was burned down at some point during the conflict. But, as Taylor reminds us, "most of the war's fighting and destruction" occurred on the long borderline between the United States and Canada. It was an offensive war launched by the United States in a brazen attempt not only to expand its boundaries northward but to secure a dream of continental dominance stretching from one ocean to another, best understood in terms of the ideology of Manifest Destiny.

Britain, otherwise engaged in the ongoing Napoleonic Wars, had few troops or resources to spare in the Canadian colonies, leaving them unprotected and apparently vulnerable. Sensing this weakness, U.S. warmongers saw an opportunity to cut off supplies of British arms and goods to the western Native nations. Thomas Jefferson, nobody's idea of a military strategist, provoked President James Madison by insisting the conquest of Canada would be a simple "matter of marching."[17] Others disagreed. As Colrain minister and Massachusetts representative to Congress Samuel Taggert would assert,

> The conquest of Canada has been represented as so easy as to be little more than a party of pleasure . . . it has been suggested that they are a debased race of poltroons, incapable of making anything like a stand in their own defense, that the mere sight of an army of the United States would immediately put an end to all thoughts of resistance, that we had little more to do than march and that in the course of a few weeks, one of our valiant commanders . . . might adopt the phraseology of Julius Caesar: veni, vedi, vici.[18]

As Taggert predicted, such assurances of easy and painless victory proved false. One thing U.S. officials had somehow failed to consider was the staunch resistance Native tribes would put forward in their alliance with the British to protect their homelands and possibly recoup their losses from previous wars.

Devil in a Stone Canoe

Back in Connecticut, before leaving the environs of New London behind him, William Apess decided to pay a final visit to his father. He and his companion, John Miner, unconcerned about the events of the world closing in around them, spent their first night as runaways in a barn they had stumbled across in their flight, burying themselves within the hay so as not to be spotted when the proprietors came in to feed and milk their cows in the morning. The next day, managing to extract themselves from the barn unseen, the two boys breakfasted on rum, bread, and cheese, and then traveled ten miles with enough money still in their pockets that they were able to put up at a tavern come nightfall. On the second morning, they traversed the final four miles to the house of Apess's father in Colchester.

As with earlier visits, Apess describes this family reunion in the most clipped terms. He told his father he "had come to stay only one week, and when that week had expired he wished me to redeem my promise and return home"—"home" in this case being the Williamses' estate in New London.[19] Nothing else by way of enlargement or characterization is offered to describe this ambiguous reunion. Apess's father, probably remarried at this point or at least living with a woman other than Apess's mother, had four young children to raise: Elias, Mary Ann, Gilbert, and Griswold. Quite possibly the two older children were already bound out and working for white families in the area. But the two youngest, Gilbert (who was four years old) and Griswold (who was only one), would still have been living under Apess's father's roof. Was it difficult for the fifteen-year-old William to see his half-siblings dwelling in the presence of family connections while he endured profound loneliness, beatings, and abuse as an indentured servant? Or were these just facts of life that an Indian boy learned to quietly accept in nineteenth-century New England?

When it came time to part ways, Apess's father, suspecting his son might have ideas other than promptly returning to New London as promised, placed the two boys on the proper path and then sat himself down by the roadside, keeping a determined eye on them until they had fallen completely out of sight. Perhaps this was a sign of his concern and devotion. Perhaps it was the only gesture of fatherly care and guidance a man in his situation was capable of offering. Perhaps it was more difficult than we can ever know for William Apess's father to watch his fifteen-year-old son depart, with no parental guidance or protection, into a very uncertain future in a time of war and deprivation. Whatever the case, when the two boys felt sure they could no longer be spied, they quickly doubled back through the woods and placed themselves on the road headed in the opposite direction, toward Hartford. As Apess would later relate, he was now "without father, mother, or friends as he stepped out into the broad theater of the world."[20]

To be a runaway in this era was not simply seen as the romantic caprice of a slighted child; it had financial implications wrapped up in the institutions of slavery and indenture. Both custom and law required that such fugitives be promptly returned to their masters, and rewards were typically offered. Apess and Miner, understanding the precariousness of their situation, invented a string of elaborate lies to provide cover for themselves. With the War of 1812 well under way, the British had formed a blockade around Long Island Sound to close off shipping interests. This provided the materials for a serviceable cover story in which the two youths claimed to be sailors on a privateer that had been captured by the British. Set ashore at New London on account of their youth, they claimed they were now attempting to make their way back home to New York City.

With this tale as protection, the two continued north to Hartford hoping to secure positions on a brig and work their way south toward Manhattan. Thanks to Miner's confident manner, their story was not challenged. Unfortunately, all shipping traffic was halted due to the British blockade, and so the two boys were forced, instead, to make their way to the big city on foot, at least as far as Kingsbridge, New York, just north of Manhattan. There Apess and his companion finally managed to secure passage on a vessel headed into the city. Once on ship, however, they were questioned by the captain, who found gaping holes in their story and began to suspect them for runaways. As they came in view of the city, the captain told them "we were very near to Hellgate (Hurl-gate)—that when we reached it the devil would come on board in a stone canoe, with an iron paddle, and make a terrible noise, and that he intended to give us to him. I thought all he said was so. I therefore confessed that we were runaways."[21]

Their boat was, in fact, headed through the turbulent gap where Long Island Sound converges with the East River. Here was the notorious set of rapids known as Hell Gate, or, in the early nineteenth century, "Hurl-gate," a difficult channel in which many a mariner had met his end on the shifting currents and hidden rocks. Interestingly, this stretch of river had been given its name by the early Dutch explorer Adrian Block, who was also the first person to record the name Pequod in the colonial archive.[22] In 1670, an English explorer, Daniel Denton, commented that "the Current sets so violently" in these rapids "that it threatens present shipwreck; and upon the flood is a large whirlpool, which continually sends forth a hideous roaring, enough to affright any stranger from passing further, and to wait for some Charon to conduct him through."[23]

Washington Irving, in his *Knickerbocker's History of New York,* also made note of the many deaths that had occurred there. He intimated that it was a haunted space, and spoke of "the black man in a three-cornered hat seated in the stern of a jolly-boat who used to be seen about Hell-gate in stormy weather and went by the name of the pirate's spuke (meaning pirate's ghost), and whom it is said old Governor Stuyvesant once shot with a silver bullet." Irving was apparently fond of this tale, and offered a separate version of the Dutch governor's exploits, noting that "not an individual but verily believed the old governor was a match for Beezelbub himself; and there was even a story told, with great mystery . . . of his having shot the devil with a silver bullet one dark stormy night as he was sailing in a canoe through Hell-gate; but this I do not record as absolute fact."[24]

The idea that the devil patrolled these waters in a canoe or jolly boat, hunting down careless souls, was clearly part of the folklore surrounding Hell Gate in the first decades of the nineteenth century. Apess's story remains curious, however, for its characterization of the devil's "bark" as a "stone canoe." The stone canoe is a fixture of both Iroquoian and Algonquian Native narrative tradition. According to Haudenosuanee stories, it was in just such a canoe of white stone that the Peacemaker first appeared on the shores of Lake Ontario, setting in motion the organization of the original Five Nations of the Longhouse. The Peacemaker, alongside his counterpart Ayowentha, or Hiawatha, would eventually unite the warring tribes of the Northeast with a message of peace and reconciliation and, through the rituals of the condolence ceremony and the use of wampum, help to heal the historical traumas of the people, putting an end to their cycles of violence. As such, the stone canoe, which according to the Peacemaker would "be a sign that my words are true," has important symbolic significance in Haudenosaunee culture.[25]

Algonquian stories also incorporated the motif of the stone canoe as a kind of wonderwork associated with culture heroes and their epic adventures. In one Passamaquoddy legend recounted by the nineteenth-century ethnographer Charles Leland, the culture hero of Algonquian narrative, Glooskap, fashions a canoe out of stone and travels to Europe in a time "before the white people ever heard of America." While in Europe, the French take him prisoner and endeavor to shoot him out of a canon. But when they go to seek his remains, Glooskap pops his head out of the canon, knocks the ash from his stone pipe, and resumes smoking, unfazed by the experience. The king of France acknowledges his power, and Glooskap returns home in his unsinkable canoe. The story not only represents the kind of chaotic energy invested in certain "trickster" tales but it reverses the direction of the discourse of discovery, depicting Native peoples as first traveling to Europe rather than the other way around.[26]

If the stone canoe is a common feature of indigenous myth and history, it had very little purchase in the new-sprung lore of the colonist in the first half of the nineteenth century. Henry Rowe Schoolcraft's *Algic Researches,* which would first bring the story of Hiawatha into the public domain, however inaccurately, was yet to be published in 1829 when Apess first tells his story. The "stone canoe" seems to have surfaced in stories circulated by whalers, who claimed that upon crossing the equator, "old King Neptune would arrive on a stone canoe with paddles of whalebone and demand a tribute of the mariners." Such stories probably had their roots in the oral tradition of Algonquian whalers.[27] But the embellishment of the devil riding in on a stone canoe at Hell Gate appears nowhere else in the literature and seems to have been Apess's own innovation, a place where not only do the currents of two rivers come together but narrative currents converge as well, creating a turbulent swirling force of competing cultural contexts that Apess, as a kind of literary trickster himself, allows to occupy the same textual space.

Although Apess, as a child, had mostly been kept alienated from the cultural narratives that bound Native communities together, we will see that by 1829, as he was writing his memoir, he was likely to have understood the significance of the "stone canoe" to indigenous belief structures, and it is typical of Apess to insert such knowledge into his narrative in a manner that would elude the surveillance of his white evangelical audiences. He had stated earlier that it was the "devil" that had persuaded him to resist his indenture and "pursue a course directly at variance with the gospel."[28] And here again, in the Hell Gate passage, he notes how "the devil prompted me to tell a lie" to persuade the ship's captain that the reward for returning him to his indenture was too small to be worth the trouble of collecting.[29] Apess's life would forever be bound up in such contradictions, wherein the path to righteousness, from the dominant cultural perspective, stood at variance with his own rights, needs, and spiritual concerns as an indigenous person.

If to tell a lie was sinful, there were few outlets for a Native in Apess's position to voice truth. From the vantage point of Christian culture, any projection of indigenous spirituality was equated with devil worship. Locations of cultural or spiritual import to indigenous communities were often pejoratively referred to as haunts of the devil, and maps of the Northeast are sprinkled with locales bearing names such as Satan's Kingdom, Spuyten Duyvil, the Devil's Hopyard, the Devil's Wishbone, and others that were, and in many cases remain, loci of power for traditional Native belief.[30] To embrace Christian rhetoric apparently necessitated, at the very least, a rhetorical denigration of indigenous tradition. Apess often found himself negotiating a careful path between these two competing narratives of power. But he was adept at performing this kind of negative work, orchestrating subtle inversions that divested language of its purposed signification and punctured its implied meanings. In this case, for Apess to listen to the devil at Hell Gate was to claim his own spiritual freedom, as an individual, an Indian son of the forest, and as a Christian minister. At this important passage, Apess negotiates these dual currents and appears to signal his first youthful intimation that his life will be dedicated to pursuing his own path of peace within competing cultural frameworks.

A Hell on Earth

Upon slipping from their vessel, Apess and Miner took a room together at two dollars a week in a boarding house on Cherry Street, which ran parallel to the docks on Manhattan's lower east shore. Manhattan had long served as an ideal crossroads of commerce and culture. By 1813, most of its twenty-five thousand residents were packed into the portion of the island south of 14th Street. There were no buildings over a few stories in height and everything north of 14th

Street was either farmland, marsh, or wooded grove. DeWitt Clinton, who had experienced great success as a surveyor and purchaser of Indian lands in the previous decade, was now mayor. One of his major accomplishments was his effort to fortify the city's ramparts against invasion. This proved a timely expenditure, as the second war with Great Britain was just getting under way. Clinton's measures were ineffective, however, in preventing the onset of severe hardship for New York once the British blockaded the harbor, resulting in the loss of labor, goods, and income. When Apess arrived in late May or early June of that year, merchant ships were apparently rotting in every cove as they sought to conceal themselves from British man-of-wars. Goods were spoiling in their warehouses, and lines of communication were virtually shut down.[31]

Despite all this, Apess and his companion quickly found work at sixty-two and a half cents per day and therefore had no trouble paying their board. The world somehow never seems too big for Apess in his telling of it, and he says of this time, "My mind now became tolerably calm." If the city was a hard-scrabble place of bad habits and loose morals, he apparently blended right in, confessing that "by this time I had acquired many bad practices."[32] Within a very short time, however, Apess learned that Miner had procured work on a privateer. He suddenly found himself abandoned again, "left entirely alone in a strange city" to wander aimlessly among the street peddlers and oyster stand criers.

It didn't take long before Apess "fell in company" with a group of men looking to enlist soldiers into the U.S. Army, and, after being plied with the proper amount of "spirits" and regaled with romantic stories of war, Apess cheerfully agreed to join. "I was pleased with the idea of being a soldier," he writes. He "took some more liquor and some money, had a cockade fastened on my hat, and was off in high spirits for my uniform." In retrospect, he would conclude, "I could not think why I should risk my life and limbs for fighting for the white man, who had cheated my forefathers out of their land," but this objection seems not to have dawned on him until some short time later, once sobriety had set in.[33] "Too much liquor was dealt out to the soldiers," Apess admits. "I have known sober men to enlist, who afterward became complete drunkards, and appear like fools upon the earth. So it was among the soldiers, and what should a child do who was entangled in their net?" Indeed, Apess was only fifteen years old when he became "entangled" in the military adventures of the U.S. Army. If he was too young to legally serve, this was a fact that his recruiters were all too willing to overlook.[34]

Apess's official army record gives him as being seventeen years of age at the time of his enlistment. He was described as five feet two inches tall, with hazel eyes, black hair, and a complexion listed as "dark." His occupation was given as that of "laborer." He had signed into John McKeon's 3rd Artillery Regiment and was promptly ferried over to Governors Island, a small patch of land that stands watch over the opening of New York Harbor and that had recently been fortified under Clinton's plan to build up the city's defenses. Because of his age (even his falsified age of seventeen was too young for proper enlistment), Apess was assigned the role of company drummer, and claimed to have taken a great deal of satisfaction "in beating on an old drum."[35] He described the base itself, however, as "hell on earth," a place of drinking, profanity, gambling, and other soldierly vices. Nevertheless, the impressionable young Apess quickly became a full participant in these activities, "almost as bad as any of them," as he lets on.[36]

Apess's most memorable experience on Governors Island, however, was when he was made to witness the execution of a deserter, an event he renders in vivid detail in his memoir. Executions were meant not only as punishment, of course, but as a visible deterrent to desertion. The protocol at Governors Island was for the regular soldiers to march through the parade grounds and

"Scenes at La Prairie, 1812–13," pen-and-ink illustration by unknown artist of a military execution by firing squad carried out at La Prairie in Lower Canada in 1813, with deserter positioned on his own coffin. *Courtesy Library and Archives Canada / Historical Photographs of Individuals and Groups, Events and Activities from across Canada Collection / C-03759.*

then line up in a large "U" formation, or "hollow square" as one soldier called it, leaving one end open for the grim purpose at hand. Apess does not say whether he was part of the fife-and-drum corps brought forward that day to play its round of "Rosalyn Castle," as was the tradition. He does, however, place his account of the execution directly following his relation that he had been made a regimental musician, suggesting that the two events were linked in his memory.

Apess recalls how, next, two men were led out onto the parade grounds, clothed in white with white caps placed on their heads and Bibles in hand. "The band struck up the dead march, and the procession moved with a mournful and measured tread to the place of execution, where the poor creatures were made to kneel on the coffins, which were alongside two newly dug graves." Twelve privates and a sergeant were chosen to perform the execution, their rifles loaded by officers so that no one soldier knew if his piece were truly loaded or not. After a short council with the chaplain, the two men's caps were pulled down over their eyes. It was customary to pin red targets over the hearts of the deserters to direct the aim of the riflemen. Apess recounts how one of the condemned was suddenly pulled off to the side. The provost marshal signaled for the music to stop, a handkerchief was raised, preparing the platoon to fire, and then a final signal given, at which point the platoon emptied their charges "and the immortal essence of the offender in an instant was in the spirit land." The man whose life had been spared broke down weeping, and Apess reflected that his own heart "seemed to leap in my throat. Death never appeared so awful."[37] But it was, in fact, just a pale intimation of horrors to come.

All's Not Quiet on the Northern Front

Shortly after the deserter's execution, Apess was sent to Staten Island for two months, where the accelerated drilling of the soldiers continued. Although they didn't yet know it, the new recruits were to be marched up to the Canadian border, where the war was ultimately to be decided in all of its glorious indecisiveness. Like soldiers at all times, Apess's regiment had quickly grown bored and restive, and craved a change of scenery. When they received their marching orders, the troops were excited to be headed for the front, little realizing or caring what lay in store for them. Apess remarks with no small amount of irony that "they thought it a great thing to march through the country and assist in taking the enemy's land."[38] But Apess found it difficult, now, to share in the sentiments of his fellow recruits. He could not help but view events through an inverted glass, where what appeared right, noble, brave, or, at the very least, thrilling to those in his company was for him laced with bitter realities of not-so-glorious tales of conquest and an ever-present sense of the unacknowledged history of his own people.

In late July or early August of 1813, Apess's artillery regiment was carried by sloop to Albany and from there marched some ten or fifteen miles to their barracks at Greenbush, New York. Apess apparently discovered only once the mobilization was well under way that he had been shifted to the ranks, despite his age, and would be expected to perform all of the duties of a regular foot soldier, including carrying a musket and pulling guard shift. Considering this a breach of contract, and having grown "heartily tired of a soldier's life," he sought out the opportunity to escape, planning once more to seek sanctuary with his father. He was quickly apprehended in his attempt, however, and was fortunate to escape the fate of the deserter whose death he had earlier witnessed.

Nevertheless, his sense of alienation persisted, and on the long march to the Canadian frontier he was reminded constantly of his status as "other." He recounts how the officers tormented him, threatening to hold "powwow" over him, stick him full of pine splinters, and burn him at the stake.[39] If in the popular imagination this was the way savage Indians treated white prisoners, Apess was once again caught in what appeared to be a fun house distortion of reality—an Indian prisoner threatened with brutal torture at the hands of his white captors. Such taunting must have represented a severe trial for the young boy, forced to take on the role of a man in the most demanding of circumstances, and yet as a complete outsider with no secure sense of belonging or shared patriotism. The racial taunts he suffered also speak directly to certain powerful rhetorical currents regarding presumed Indian massacres of troops and civilians—rhetoric that served to horrify and inflame popular American sentiment against Natives at the time.

According to Alan Taylor, American troops lived in dread of their Native opponents, spoon-fed as they had been on their own tales of frontier outrages. Such narratives invoke a difficult history. Without a doubt, atrocities are committed on all sides in wartime, but while there is a tendency to view atrocities committed by Natives as an essential component of a savage identity, atrocities committed by whites are typically viewed as aberrations or, more precisely, justifiable acts of wartime vengeance. It became something of an unspoken truism that war with savage peoples requires retaliatory acts of savagery, a disturbingly persuasive calculation that has continued to hold currency over the centuries. Rarely is the idea entertained that perhaps Native people, too, were driven to acts of retribution by the traumatic experiences of grief and loss provoked by colonial violence. Rarer still is the account that emphasizes indigenous forbearance and restraint, or invokes a Native cultural foundation based on peaceful resolution.

Taylor recounts the testimony of one New Yorker during the war who confessed that not a single child "was allowed to grow up in that region, without imbibing . . . hatred and horror of the Indians."[40] Such lore proved a necessary cultural primer that ostensibly justified every appropriation of Native land by colonial power, and it was imbibed by Americans of every station, gender, and class distinction. Ironically, Apess himself had been bred on such tales, as was made clear in the account of his childhood berry-picking debacle when he fled in terror from a group of white women whom he mistook for a party of "savages." But, as Apess clearly meant to suggest in his anecdote, the reality of Native identity, in warfare or otherwise, was much more complex than such one-sided tales of blood and torture would allow.

Another "writing Indian" siding with the British in the War of 1812 was the Cherokee John Norton. Norton's story is every bit as fascinating, far-reaching, and strewn with paradox as is Apess's. He was yet another child of colonial violence, born of a white Scottish mother and a Cherokee father whose village was raided and burned to the ground by the British in the 1750s. Norton's father, while still a boy, was one of the few spared in the raid and was brought to Great Britain, where he was raised into a military life. He married, had a child, and then shipped off to Canada in the 1780s, only to dessert and eventually find his way back to his Cherokee homelands. John Norton, the son, was raised by his Scottish mother, but as soon as he could he followed in his father's footsteps, enlisting in a regiment as a drummer boy at roughly the age of sixteen and shipping off to Canada in 1786.[41] He seems to have carried with him a powerful sense of his indigenous heritage, for he too soon left the army and made his way to the newly formed Tyendinaga reserve on Lake Ontario, where in a short time he became a teacher to Mohawk children.

Norton must have been a fairly talented and charismatic young man. He quickly learned the Iroquois language and won the trust of both Native communities and the British authorities who frequently employed him as a translator. He traveled extensively, eventually making his way to Detroit as a fur trader and establishing himself with the Mohawk leader Joseph Brant, who would ultimately adopt Norton into the tribe and groom him as a future chief. Under Brant's tutelage, Norton developed into an advocate for indigenous unity, nationalism, and sovereignty, dedicating himself to what he saw as indigenous codes of peace and justice. He took on the name Teyoninho-karawen, or It Keeps the Door Open, but when the War of 1812 broke out, he found himself compelled to fight alongside the British, recognizing the United States as "the common enemy of all the Aboriginal Race."[42]

Norton's journal, not published until well over a century after his death, is a long and sprawling text covering decades of travel, from Grand River in Upper Canada to Cherokee lands in Georgia, relating Native history and lore, and offering a detailed account of his engagements as a leader of Mohawk scouts in the War of 1812. But the journal also seems to have been constructed with a keen eye toward shielding Native peoples from persistent accusations of savagery and wartime atrocities. Norton understood that he was a rare and able witness not only to the cultural complexity and efficacy of Native culture and tradition, but to the extremes of warfare in which both Native and colonist were driven to acts of violence and desperation. At every turn, he is careful to offer an equipoised view of geopolitical events while forwarding positive representations of Native peoples.

In keeping with this aim, Norton reports on his travels to the western indigenous nations, which he undertook at the precise time that Tecumseh and his brother, Tenskwatawa, the Shawnee prophet, were spreading their message of Native sovereignty and resistance throughout the Ohio Valley. Because Norton is writing for a British audience and has certain rhetorical objectives he must keep in sight, he makes his visit sound something like a chance encounter, but in fact he must have quite purposefully journeyed west to witness these proceedings as a representative of Joseph Brant's Indian Confederacy. The Mohawks, as well as other members of the Six Nations, would have to decide where they stood in the conflict that was clearly brewing.

Although it doesn't appear as though Norton met Tecumseh personally, he was on hand for a Shawnee council in which Tecumseh's vision of a unified indigenous front was the topic of discussion. His understanding of Tecumseh (or Tecumthi, as Norton refers to him) was that he was "a very sensible man, and brave Warrior, of an independent spirit, and enthusiastic to preserve the territory and independence of his brethren." Norton adds that Tecumseh was "quite an enthusiast on the score of territory, denying the validity of all Treaties, and insisting that the right the Great Spirit had given the Aboriginal Natives to the soil they possess, should be defended even at the expense of their lives." Despite what might seem to the casual reader to be some tough talk coming from "hostile Indians," however, Norton left the council concluding, "I could not think any violent measures would be adopted by them, unless the avidity of some people for land, should oblige them to fight *in defense* of their country."[43]

Norton was on hand once again for a June 1812 meeting that took place between the Haudenosaunee at Grand River and a number of "young chiefs" of the "Ondowaga, Onondague and Cayagwas" from the U.S. side of the border. The visiting chiefs argued, in traditional diplomatic language, that if the United States and Britain were, in fact, on the eve of war over "some rights on the Sea," and if it should end in contest, then "let us keep aloof;—why should we again fight . . . ? We know that neither of these powers have any regard for us. In the former War, we espoused the cause of the King, we thought it the most honorable,—all our former Treaties having been made with his Representatives. After contending for seven years . . . we found that Peace was concluded across the Sea, and that our Enemy claimed our Territory in consequence of the boundary Line then acceded to. We found none to assist us to obtain Justice." The orator was of course referring to the 1783 Treaty of Paris, in which the British ceded away Native lands despite the fact that the Native groups in question had never surrendered or forfeited those lands, nor had been offered a place at the treaty table. The speech was sealed with the exchange of wampum "in token of our sincerity."[44]

When his turn came to speak, Norton reminded the visiting diplomats of white atrocities such as General Sullivan's raids on Haudenosaunee villages in

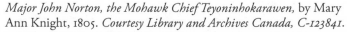

Major John Norton, the Mohawk Chief Teyoninhokarawen, by Mary Ann Knight, 1805. *Courtesy Library and Archives Canada, C-123841.*

1779, the slaughter of peaceful Christian Natives at Gnaddenhutten in 1782, and the unprovoked assault that had more recently occurred at Tippecanoe, where Tenskwatawa's village, Prophetstown, was destroyed by General William Henry Harrison's troops a year earlier.[45] Norton wondered, given this past record, how the Six Nations could expect any compassion to be shown their women and children if they sat idly by. No final accord could be reached in this meeting, but it accurately recorded the concerns and protocols of the indigenous communities that would soon be thrust into the center of a border war between the United States and Canada.[46]

The early battles of the War of 1812 were fought along the Great Lakes settlements of Chicago, Detroit, and Amherstburg before spreading east across the border and into other coastal theaters. The United States marched its troops into Canada under the leadership of General William Hull, then governor of Michigan Territory, in the midsummer of 1812 and met stiff unexpected resistance from Tecumseh and his coalition of Shawnee, Chippewa, Pottawatomie, Huron, Miami, and Delaware warriors who had allied themselves with the British under General Henry Proctor. Americans complained bitterly about the inability of the Indians to abide by humane conventions of warfare. President Madison, pronouncing before Congress the "spectacle of injuries and indignities" Great Britain had "heaped upon our Country," particularly called out their continued intercourse with the "Savages," who were known in their warfare "to spare neither age nor sex, and to be distinguished by features particularly shocking to humanity" (we might recall that this language closely echoes that used in describing Indians in the Declaration of Independence).[47] But, according to Taylor, it was the United States, in the person of a Captain William McCullough, that took the first war scalp, from a Menomonee warrior.[48] In fact, there were long-standing blood feuds between many of the white frontiersmen—particularly Kentuckians—and their Native rivals, and these feuds would angrily play themselves out in the course of the conflict.

In an August 1812 letter to the secretary of war, Harrison wrote, "You may rely upon it, Sir, that the western country was never so agitated by alarm and mortification as at the present moment."[49] Harrison, who now served as major general by brevet of the Kentucky militia, and whose troops had defiled Native graves in their unprovoked sacking of Prophetstown, continued to prosecute his offensive scorched-earth campaigns, burning every Native village in his path and destroying agricultural stores as he advanced toward the Canadian border to join the fray.[50] In one of the early battles of the war, at Frenchtown, on the Raisin River, Native warriors also burned and looted, in part to retaliate for Harrison's previous offenses. Nevertheless, "Remember Raisin River!" became the battle cry of the Kentuckians who were experienced in fighting Indians and knew the value of ginning up a strong motive for bloodlust. In their righteous fury they sang, "Arouse and fight the faithless foe, / Scalps are bought at stated prices, / Malden pays the price in Gold," unambiguously acknowledging the monetary incentive to take Indian scalps.[51]

The Sauk leader Black Hawk, whose 1833 narrative appeared close on the heels of Apess's *A Son of the Forest,* was present at the sacking of Detroit in August of 1812 and voiced concerns about how Natives were represented. His testimony is clouded somewhat by the intervention of his amanuensis, a white newspaper editor, John B. Patterson, but Black Hawk is said to have noted how "the British had taken many prisoners, and the Indians were killing them! I immediately put a stop to it, as I never thought it brave, but cowardly, to kill an unarmed and helpless enemy."[52] British participants at the scene, in fact, did not report any Indian atrocities, although one British officer, Charles Askin, actually affirmed in his journal that some Sauks who "had begun to plunder were stopped . . . and they even retur'd some things they had taken."[53]

The taking of plunder was, of course, common enough practice among British and American colonials as well, if officially frowned upon. But if Harrison kept busy not only plundering but burning entire Indian villages to the ground, the Sauk were seen returning their plunder. Detroit was a border town in 1812, with sympathies and loyalties that traversed the national dividing line upon which it sat. Both the British and the Americans were eager to retain the fort's loyalty, and so whatever plundering took place was largely blamed on the Natives. Interestingly, Askin reports that the members of one particular British brigade joining in the battle "were most all painted as Indians," suggesting the difficulty of actually knowing who was plundering whom.[54] Neither Black Hawk nor Norton denied that depredations took place at these events, but they viewed them as aberrations, departures from the warrior's code, and not representative behavior.

Following the fall of Frenchtown, John Norton observed that American prisoners "fabricated many stories of the cruelties exercised by Indians."[55] Norton readily admits that individual acts of violation may have occurred, but, relying on the testimony of several captured American officers, he concludes, "It would be useless as well as endless to repeat the number of cruelties that had been asserted, & as bluntly contradicted,—without proofs to substantiate either on one Side or the other,—and as the Americans are fond of complaining of cruelty, without just cause,—I should be more inclined to believe the contradiction than the assertion."[56] Norton had good reason to suspect Americans of equal or worse atrocities given his own witness of events alongside the fact that General Hull had placed a forty-dollar bounty for every Indian scalp American troops might bring in—a reward that distinguished not over niceties of age or sex.[57] When Native encampments were marauded by American forces in the evacuation of the Christian Indian mission village of Moraviantown in October of 1813, Norton observed that although "few of the Women or Children fell into the hands of the Enemy . . . some of these which they [the American forces] took they inhumanely butchered,—and they barbarously skinned the body of the gallant Tecumthi [Tecumseh]."[58]

Tecumseh continues to strike a stirring romantic image in the American imaginary, becoming the subject of movies, books, and paintings. The British commander, Major General Isaac Brock, observed at an August 1812 council with the Natives at Amherstburg that, "among some extraordinary characters," the one who "attracted most my attention was a Shawnee chief, Tecumset . . . who for the last two years has carried on (contrary to our remonstrances) an Active Warfare against the United States—a more sagacious or more a gallant warrior does not I believe exist. He was the admiration of everyone who conversed with him."[59] British commander Henry Proctor would similarly say of Tecumseh that he had "that natural superiority of genius which, sometimes in civilized communities and almost always in a rude society challenge deference from common minds. . . . He was above the middle stature, the general expressions of his features pleasing and his eyes full of fire and intelligence."[60]

When Tecumseh learned of the sacking of Prophetstown in his absence in 1811, he is said to have remarked, "Had I been at home and heard of the advance of the American Troops towards our Village, I should have gone to meet them and shaking them by the hand, have asked them the reason of their appearance in such hostile guise."[61] By the time of his death at Moraviantown in October of 1813, however, the prospect for peace had certainly vanished. As the tide turned against the British army and Harrison's troops stormed through Moraviantown, a Colonel Richard Johnson, leading his division of Kentuckians, claimed the privilege of having personally killed Tecumseh, who had kept at the rear to guard the retreat. Some dispute whether it was Tecumseh that Johnson killed that day, and instead claim that it was some other high-ranking Native individual. Nevertheless, Tecumseh's alleged death scene at the hands of Johnson would become a popular subject for nineteenth-century canvases, offering a study in noble savagery. His warrior's death, as depicted, endeared him to the American populace, making of him the exemplary Indian, fierce in protecting his homelands but prepared to conveniently vanish when finally called upon to do so.

John Norton, though not present at the battle that took Tecumseh's life, had reliable Native intelligence networks informing him that it was, in fact, Tecumseh who had been killed and subsequently "skinned" by American troops that day. Whoever it was that Colonel Johnson killed, this unfortunate soul became the target for the collective war rage of the Kentuckians. They defiled the corpse, stripping the flesh from the dead warrior's thighs, each, to keep as mementos, fashion into bridle reins, or use as personal razor strops. As horrific as this may sound, it was a practice that became virtually commonplace, particularly during General Jackson's later campaigns against the Creek.

Tecumseh holds an exalted, if murky, place in American memory, but is mostly a figment of the dominant imagination, a name that might be easily supplanted by any other serviceable Indian name from the noble savage genre ranging, from King Philip to Pontiac to Crazy Horse. John Norton, however, has faded behind even thicker layers of historical obscurity. As a writing Indian whose very skill at literacy should have assured him some level of scrutiny, he instead seems to have written himself out of the all-too-narrow cultural roles typically prescribed for Indians of the nineteenth century. The historian Sandy Antal, in an otherwise evenhanded account of the border conflicts of the War of 1812, observes that Norton, although perhaps a restraining influence on the Indians, was nevertheless "adept in the use of the scalping knife."[62] There does not appear to be any evidence on which to base such a conclusion. As a man of the frontier who spent time in the fur trade and fought in many battles, Norton was no doubt handy with a knife. But the impulse to render the taking of scalps as one of his defining characteristics is unfounded by any actual evidence and suggests the extent to which modern discourse is still shrouded in this assumption of Indian savagery. Despite his repeated denunciations of wartime mutilations and depredations, Norton himself must still in some manner be slotted into the only role imagined for Native warriors. No one ever says the same of, for instance, future U.S. presidents Andrew Jackson or William Henry Harrison, although they just as well might.

We should not be surprised, then, that what were deep matters of concern for a Native writer such as Norton were also of concern for William Apess, who would write of white European colonists in his *A Son of the Forest*, "These invaders of a country . . . made war upon them [the Natives] with all the advantage of fire arms and the military knowledge of Europe, in the most barbarous manner—not observing any rules of nations, or the principles of modern warfare, much less benign injunctions of the Gospel."[63] Given the history of his people, the Pequot, Apess was well-positioned to make such a claim, and he concludes in his 1836 address, *Eulogy on King Philip,* that whatever we might assert about the differences between "civilized and uncivilized" nations, "we cannot but see that one mode of warfare is as just as the other."[64]

"The Work of Death Paused Not"

William Apess found himself near the Canadian border, in the town of Plattsburgh, New York, in the late summer of 1813. He arrived at a scene of low morale among troops that had already suffered greatly from poor leadership and a harsh winter encampment the previous season. Nevertheless, he was settling into military life, however reluctantly, and occupied himself in playing cards, drinking rum, and "other acts of wickedness." He notes that he also added the habit of taking the Lord's name in vain to his growing repertoire of worldly sins, and perhaps with good reason, given that sometime around mid-October of that year Apess's regiment joined up with the main army to partake in one of the more inept military offensives in American history.[65]

One of the primary objectives of the U.S. invasion of Canada had necessarily been to take Montreal. Only by dealing a deathblow to the British occupation of Canada could the United States halt the supply of guns and trade goods to the western Indian nations and thereby achieve its dream of westward expansion. This had always been conceived as occurring on two fronts, with one force working its way northeast from Michigan through the corridor of Upper Canada to the capital city, and the other heading due north from the Lake Champlain region. In the fall of 1813, General James Wilkinson, head of the northern armies, perceived an opportunity to strike directly at Montreal despite failing to have achieved naval supremacy on Lake Ontario or success in punching through Upper Canada. He launched a two-pronged attack, his own troops embarking from Sacketts Harbor, New York, and General Wade Hampton's troops pressing north to Montreal from Chateaugay, a small fort town due west of Plattsburgh.

Thrown in with Hampton's army of four thousand infantryman, "a squadron of horse and a well-appointed train of artillery," Apess recalls the hardships his regiment faced, noting that "it was now very cold and we had nothing but straw to lay on. There was also a scarcity of provisions, and we were not allowed to draw our full rations. Money would not procure food—and when anything was to be obtained the officers always had the preference, and they, poor souls, always wanted the whole for themselves."[66] Forced to feed on raw corn pillaged from neighboring farms or Indian villages, the hungry soldiers pressed forward alongside the Chateaugay River into Canada. The enemy retreating before them made sure to burn everything in their path, destroying all forage for man and horse. Apess must have had skill in handling horses from his experience as an indentured farmhand (he speaks of this briefly during his indenture with Judge Hillhouse), and he counted himself lucky that he was placed in charge of a team, allowing him the privilege of riding. As for the majority of foot soldiers, he reports, "They were badly off, as the officers were very cruel to them, and for every little offense they would have them flogged." Apess, too, found himself "pricked" in the ear by an officer's sword for some unspoken offense.[67]

One of the flaws of Hampton's strategy was that the Chateaugay corridor through which he advanced was thickly wooded, making it extremely difficult for a large army to pass through. Nor, by all reports, had it been adequately scouted, and Apess notes that "the pioneers" tasked with creating a route through this wilderness "had great difficulty in clearing the way." To make matters worse, according to a Captain Robert Purdy, the men were, like Apess, mostly raw recruits with no experience in combat and no military discipline. Without any knowledge of the terrain, Purdy was ordered to circle around the enemy through thick forests and swamps in the dark of night and ambush the enemy's rear. He quickly became lost, however, his line stumbling over itself in the night and men mistaking one another for British troops or, worse yet as he saw it, Indians. Hopelessly disoriented, the ambushers suddenly became the ambushees when there came "a great discharge of musketry, accompanied by the yells of the savages." The far-outnumbered British, accompanied by a small number of Abenaki warriors, used their knowledge of the terrain to seize the advantage, and they set up trumpeters at various points around the main American force to give the impression of being outflanked by superior numbers.[68] An adequate sense of the series of blunders that ensued is given by Apess, who reports,

> After we had proceeded about thirty miles, we fell in with a body of Canadians and Indians—the woods fairly resounded with their yells. Our "brave and chivalrous" general ordered a picked troop to disperse them; we fired but one cannon, and a retreat was sounded to the great mortification of the soldiers, who were ready and willing to fight. But as our General did not fancy the smell of gunpowder, he thought it best to close the campaign by retreating with seven thousand men, before a "host" of seven hundred. Thus were many a poor fellow's hopes of conquest and glory blasted by the timidity of one man.[69]

Apess's account of the war is almost unique in the genre of this period for its consistently ironic tone. Although acutely aware of the hardship and suffering endured by the men, himself included, in these campaigns, his account is a surprisingly modern critique of military absurdity and inefficiency, in line with what Paul Fussell has referred to as the inherently ironic attitude of the modern foot soldier.[70] Both Generals Hampton and Wilkinson were roundly perceived to be ludicrously inept, difficult to deal with, and reviled by their men. And both would soon be removed from their commands. Nevertheless, Apess's sense of these proceedings is marked by his position as an outsider, his lack of investment in the cause leading him to his bitingly satirical portrait of Hampton as a coward and a bungler. He wryly concludes, "This little brush with an enemy that we could have crushed in a single moment cost us several men in killed or wounded."[71]

But Apess also remonstrates, "People generally have no idea of the extreme suffering of the soldiers on the frontiers during the last war. They were indescribable."[72] The previous winter at Plattsburgh had gone down in the record books as one of the most brutally cold in memory, making life extremely dangerous for the poorly nourished American forces stationed there. Disease ran through the winter camps, and men died at alarming rates.[73] Apess would describe similar conditions for his winter campaigns in 1813–14. Although his constitution was surprisingly hearty and he claims not to have had a single day of illness, he writes that the troops "suffered greatly for want of barracks" (which had been burned down the previous year when the British sacked Plattsburgh) and that "many of the poor soldiers sickened and died. So fast did they go off that it appeared to me as if the plague was raging among them."[74]

On March 30 of 1814, under the command of General Wilkinson, Apess was again marched, along with four thousand other men, over the Canadian border, this time toward Odeltown and La Colle Mill. Apess resumes his satiric voice as he describes this engagement, noting that "with a noble commander at our head and the splendid city of Montreal in our view . . . we moved on with all the pomp and glory of an army flushed with many victories." The affair began promisingly in its initial skirmishes, with "our feminine general with his nightcap on his head and a dishcloth round his precious body, crying out to his men, 'Come on, my brave boys, we will give John Bull a bloody nose.'" But things quickly went south, and Apess's tone shifts as well to acknowledge the fearsome carnage that ensued. As an artilleryman, Apess manned one of the twelve-pounders that had been hauled along with the army in place of the more destructive twenty-pound cannons, which had become mired in the spring mud and were left behind on the road. U.S. forces met the significantly smaller British force at the blockhouse at La Colle Mill, the site of a previous failed thrust the year before. The twelve-pound cannons proved ineffective in breaching the walls of the blockhouse, but they nevertheless provided a strategic target at which the British could direct their own aim. As a result, Apess found himself under a steady barrage of artillery fire. The scene was one that he would never forget.

Apess writes that "their balls whistled around us and hurried a good many of the soldiers into the eternal world, while others were most horribly mangled." His fellow soldiers fell so quickly around him that there was no time to remove them, and "the horribly disfigured bodies of the dead—the piercing groans of the wounded and the dying—the cries for help and succor from those who could not help themselves—were most appalling . . . oh, it was a dreadful sight to behold so many brave men sacrificed in this manner." Colonel George McFeely, in his journal, confirms Apess's recollections, noting that at La Colle "our artillery men suffered severely . . . the place could have easily been taken had the heavy cannon been brought up, but this was impossible without a great deal of trouble and time" given the condition of the roads. After a two-hour engagement, Wilkinson ordered his forces to retreat, resulting in his being immediately stripped of command and ultimately court-martialed. Apess returned to the encampments at Plattsburgh, where he spent the remainder of the spring building a number of redoubts, or small forts, in preparation for what would prove to be his most significant battle as a soldier in the U.S. Army.[75]

Before discussing that engagement, however, there is one more detour to be made. Prior to the battle at La Colle Mill, in late January of 1814, Wilkinson had sent a special detachment of Mohawk scouts to reconnoiter the area and ascertain the number of British troops present. Leading that expedition was the Caughnawaga Mohawk Eleazar Williams. Williams's life would become the subject of sordid historical speculation in later years when he gained notoriety by promoting himself as the Lost Prince of France. Aside from this bit of cultural burlesque, Williams's name was also attached to colonial lore by his being descended from Eunice Williams, daughter of the Puritan reverend John Williams, also known as the Unredeemed Captive. As noted earlier,

The Block House at La Colle Mill, Canada, where Apess fought under General Wilkinson in the spring of 1814. *Photo by the author, 2014.*

Eunice had been taken captive by the Mohawk during Queen Anne's War at the turn of the eighteenth century. Despite persistent efforts by her reverend father to secure her release, she ultimately married into the Mohawks and became, by all accounts, and much to the dismay of her Puritan family, contented with her adopted identity.

Eleazar was the great-grandson of Eunice, raised by the Mohawk side of his family. By the most coincidental of flukes, he was also directly related to William Williams, another member of the prestigious old Williams clan, and the man who still owned Apess's indenture. When Eleazar came of age, he was brought by his father to be educated in white schools in Massachusetts to become a Christian missionary to the Indians. When Williams finished his schooling, he was assigned by the American Board of Congregational Missionaries in 1812 to serve as missionary to the Mohawk community at Saint Regis. His ability to tend to his newly assigned flock was quickly disrupted, however, by the breaking out of war along the border.

At the start of the war Williams was deployed to persuade the Haudenosaunee on the American side to remain neutral. Much like Norton on the Canadian side of the border, Williams was asked to perform as cultural intermediary, often caught on uncertain ground amid shifting allegiances. Also like Norton, he was concerned about the justness of colonial warfare, observing at a later point that "every soldier ought to be impressed with the idea that offensive war is murderous; and that no government on earth has any right to compel him to shed blood in a wanton and aggressive war." But as a young man occupying a liminal position with no authority or power on his side, Williams was fully drawn into the aggressive ambitions of the U.S. government in 1812.[76] Come summer, he was appointed by General Dearborne to lead a secret corps of "Indian rangers and scouts of the army" and apparently performed this role admirably, although leading him to bemoan, "I am in distress for my sins—they are great." He helped direct an attack on Saint Regis in October of that year during which his allegiances were certainly placed on trial though he labored to warn all "friendly" Indians of the impending attack. As he points out in his journal, Saint Regis's was the first flag to switch from British to American in the war.[77]

Like Apess, Williams was horrified by the sickness in the camps. Stationed at Plattsburgh during the first brutal winter of the war, he commented on the dysentery and diarrhea, noting that men were being buried at rates of ten to twelve a day. He, too, found both Wilkinson and Hampton to be incompetent, and often comments on their unfortunate tendency to ignore his scouting reports. Williams referred to Hampton as "the most unpleasant commander of the American army" and was repelled by his "rough language," which no doubt contained some choice characterizations in regard to indigenous peoples.[78] Having previously scouted the route, Williams advised strongly against sending Hampton's army up through the Chateaugay corridor during the 1813 attempt on Montreal, and was dumbfounded by Wilkinson's decision to try to take La Colle without the eighteen- or twenty-four pounders needed to blast through the heavily reinforced walls of the blockhouse and mill.[79] Although Williams was not present at the actual battle at La Colle Mill, he was back in Plattsburgh with Apess in the summer of 1814 as the town braced itself for a full-on assault by the British.

The Napoleonic Wars in Europe had come to an end by the summer of 1814, and Great Britain was now able to turn its full attention to the conflict taking place in the colonies. General George Prevost, directing the British forces at Montreal, was reinforced with battle-ready troops from England and set his sights on Plattsburgh with the idea of launching a decisive strike. A previous feint westward by the British had drawn off most of the American troops to Sacketts Harbor on Lake Ontario, leaving Plattsburgh with a much-diminished force of fifteen hundred men, now under the command of General Alexander Macomb, to face off against Prevost's army of roughly eight thousand regulars, two thousand Canadians, and two hundred Natives.[80] Unlike the other American generals, Macomb exuded a confidence and courage respected by the men serving under him. Even Apess would remark that "fortunately for us and for the country, a brave and noble commander was placed at the head of the army."[81] Williams, returning from a scouting expedition to determine the strength and intentions of the enemy troops amassing at the border, was pleased to find defense preparations well under way in Plattsburgh, and sketches a striking picture of Macomb, himself, leading a team of men with a pine stake pitched over his shoulder to add to the abatis being constructed along the roadways to obstruct access into town.

Apess spent these late August days in artillery drills and helping to fortify the "several redoubts that have been raised as batteries."[82] High pickets were placed all around "the Oval," as the barracks and parade grounds were called, except where it bordered Lake Champlain, and deep trenches were dug around the forts. Most of the residents, aware of the coming attack, were fleeing the city, and the scene was surely one of chaos and frantic activity. Amid all this, news arrived that Washington, DC, had been captured on August 24 and the Capitol had been burned to the ground. Speculation ran through the camps that official enlistment papers had been destroyed in the fire, and this might have presented itself as an ideal moment to desert. By September 2, Williams's scouts reported that the enemy had now crossed "the great territorial line and are encamped at Champlain." In his journal, Williams mulls over his own decision to engage in the battle, noting, "I am not strictly bound, according to my office, to take the carnal weapon into my hand." His actual "office" is somewhat difficult to ascertain, but as a Mohawk, a preacher, and an American spy, he probably crossed over various lines of loyalty and identity. He concludes that given "the feeble state of the American force" and the general "distress of the inhabitants," he was under obligation of "putting on my armor and buckler, to sustain the honor of the American government."[83]

The Battle of Plattsburgh began in earnest on September 6, 1814, and would rage on for six full days, with both Apess and Williams caught directly in its fury. Apess served under Captain Alexander Brooks's Corps of Artillery, which held Fort Brown, one of the three hastily constructed redoubts (the other two being Fort Moreau and Fort Scott) on the banks of the Saranac River where it empties into Lake Champlain.[84] From the makeshift fort, Apess could look out over the lake and spy the British fleet coming down from the north, with their sails and streamers fluttering in the wind. Facing in the other direction, he could see the British army and General Prevost himself, in all his finery, stationed atop a nearby hill. Through a set of field glasses it was possible to spy the captain general gazing back at them from his command post in the abandoned home of a prominent Plattsburgh resident, and Apess recalled that it presented an imposing aspect. He could see the red uniforms of the troops "and the instruments of death which they bore in their hands [which] glittered in the sunbeams of heaven, like so many sparkling diamonds."[85]

Now within range, the two armies began bombarding each other with Congreve rockets, cannonballs, and bombshells that "poured upon us like a hailstorm" without intermission for six days and nights. Apess took charge of a small magazine and lived amid its constant brimstone reek, heat, and thunder for the remainder of the engagement. Williams does not specify which of the redoubts he occupied, but he does note that he stationed himself with the artillery and that his position was strategically placed to oppose the enemy with cannon fire should they attempt to ford the river. This makes it reasonable to conclude that Williams and Apess were thrust together in the very same fort (Fort Brown being the only fort built directly on the river bank) and that they came to know one another, in whatever ways such intimacies were possible, in the course of the battle. Williams was in close proximity to the cannons and reported in his brief journal entry on September 9, the fourth day of ceaseless battle, "I am quite deaf this evening."[86]

September 11, day six of the battle, opened with a heavy bombardment on Fort Brown. Williams's journal provides a likely report of what Apess experienced. He writes, "A tremendous cannonade ensued—terrific was the noise of more than two hundred pieces of cannon; bomb-shells, shaapnells, balls, and Congreve rockets, were thrown into the American lines during the whole day." The British attempted repeatedly to ford the Saranac River, but, as Williams reports, they were

Remains of Fort Brown earthworks, where Apess was stationed during the 1814 Battle of Plattsburgh. *Photo by the author, 2015.*

saluted with such a storm of shot and grape from our battery, as to compel them to fall back, and to make their way into the houses, shops, farms, and ditches. Thence they kept up a heavy fire and contended with our riflemen, who were in two mills near the bridge. While the cannonading went on, we either answered the enemy's fire, or poured shot into every body of their troops, that presented a tolerable mark. Never, perhaps, were skirmishes, if such they deserved to be called, conducted with more bravery on both sides. If our troops, in this quarter, lacked skill, they more than made up by their daring.[87]

The battle at Plattsburgh was ultimately decided by the concurrent Battle of Lake Champlain in which the American captain, Thomas MacDonough, with but two boats at his command, outmaneuvered the British fleet and gained a stunning victory. Apess appears to have been able to witness some of the naval engagement from his prospect, and was more than likely drawn into the coordinated land and sea assault that he next describes. He recalls that as "the British commander bore down on our vessels in gallant style . . . our men flew to their guns. Then the work of death and carnage commenced. The adjacent shores resounded with the alternate shouts of the sons of liberty and the groans of their parting spirits. A cloud of smoke mantled the heavens, shutting out the light of day—while the continual roar of artillery added to the sublime horrors of the scene," and all the while "on land the battle raged pretty fiercely."[88]

In the end, Williams reports, it was "the result of the battle between the two naval armaments, which continued upwards of two hours, [that] ultimately determined the action on land . . . the annihilation of his fleet being announced to Sir George, he immediately withdrew his forces from the assault of the American works." With nightfall on September 11, the British troops began their retreat in earnest, leaving behind their sick and wounded. Williams was shot sometime during this final round of action in a last-ditch cannonade. Nevertheless he notes that his corps was ordered to pursue the enemy, and so he, and most likely Apess as well, marched through a pouring rain over roads that had been hammered by the boots of thousands of men, horses, cattle, and cart wheels, under deadly rear-action fire from the British, until the men, already pushed beyond the limits of human stamina, were finally ordered to fall back, "shivering under the north-westerly wind, fatigued, and hungry."[89]

After the battle, Williams was put under the care of his father, who used his indigenous medicinal knowledge to heal his son rather than leave him to the mercies of the squalid disease-ridden camp hospitals. Reflecting in his journal a few days later, Williams would write, "The cause of great anxiety had now passed—the enemy had retreated—and, although victory was on our side, yet in sober and serious reflections, there were grounds and reasons not only for painful sensations, but sorrow. Many promising young men had met an untimely death. Among them were our friends, and acquaintances, whom we loved and esteemed, whose exit we greatly lamented, and whose dead bodies were still in an exposed state. Is this the fate of war? Were they prepared to die thus?"[90]

The fact that two writing Indians, one Pequot and one Mohawk, were present to record this significant battle and offer two of its most stirring personal accounts might seem to defy all odds. Certainly their writings have been little regarded, and to my knowledge not a single historical account of the war draws from Apess's firsthand witness. But literacy among Natives was far more common than people imagine in the nineteenth century, and it is quite possible, given the level of Native involvement in the war, that additional accounts exist of which we remain unaware. David Cusick, a Tuscarora, who would write and publish a short history of the Six Nations in 1828, also served in the war, as did hundreds of others from the combined Seneca, Cattaraugus, Onondaga, Oneida, and Tuscarora reservations. Typically the reward for their service was no pay and a subsequent loss of land.

The extent to which Native men fought and died for colonial, and later national, causes is one of the great casualties of American memory keeping. Native men have fought alongside their colonial counterparts in every war in our collective history, including the Pequot War, which enlisted the aid of the Narragansetts in subduing their powerful neighbors. Eastern Native communities, such as the Pequots, Mohegans, Wampanoags, and Mohicans suffered devastating losses fighting alongside the Continental Army in the French and Indian War, as well as in the Revolutionary War. Some lost as much as a quarter of their male populations in these conflicts. And, of course, William Apess himself fought as a foot soldier in the U.S. Army, participating in some of the most heated battles of the War of 1812. As Apess reflected on his own wartime experience, his thoughts would quickly turn to the political repercussions for Native people like himself, Norton, Williams, Cusick, and countless others, who sacrificed so much for so dubious a cause and were denied arguably the one thing that soldiers in combat crave above all else—public recognition of their sacrifice. Instead, they were typically degraded as savages.

CHAPTER FOUR

"And They Held All Things in Common"

I then turned my eyes to the forest, and it seemed alive with its sons and daughters.

—WILLIAM APESS

A Son of the Border

Apess's activities directly following the War of 1812 are shrouded in a series of silences that can be attributed to a number of factors. But it is always worth considering that wherever we encounter silences in nineteenth-century Native authored texts, we are very likely brushing up against the narrative borders of speech itself, the regions of indigenous identity that have no articulation in the written discourse communities in which Apess moved.

It might also be considered how Apess, already a child of trauma, had compounded his psychic anguish in combat. If the War of 1812 is a vague and largely meaningless blip in the cultural memories of most Americans, it almost certainly ripped through every other impression in Apess's young life, forging a flickering panorama of adrenaline, fear, tedium, and horror with which all his other memories would, from thereon out, contend. This suggests that there will be gaps in his narrative, a shattered emotional state difficult if not impossible to articulate, and experiences beyond the pale of what Western audiences were capable of hearing and what he himself was capable of telling. Both physically and emotionally Apess found himself, after the war, in a borderline state, in search of an identity that might hold him together, and the wonder really is, after all he had experienced, that he could still even stand on his own two feet.

But the silences also stem from prolonged historical disinterest in Apess's story, an archival negligence that runs through the field of early Native studies. Literary critics tend to bypass this portion of Apess's life, and historians have failed to locate Apess within the nexus of firsthand witnesses who reported on the war and its aftermath. Alan Taylor's 2010 "border history," *The Civil War of 1812,* offers a more than competent account of "American Citizens, British Subjects, Irish Rebels, and Indian Allies," and yet Apess appears nowhere among the large catalogue of firsthand reporters Taylor names. Keith A. Herkalo, who trains his eye on the Battle of Plattsburgh, writes of the Mohawk Eleazar Williams that "his is the only known first-hand chronicle of Plattsburgh's and the North Country's involvement in the War of 1812" written by an "Indian."[1] To which I can only say, not so. Apess not only fought in these battles, but, as we have seen, his liminal subject position made of him a rare witness, better positioned, perhaps, to offer an open critique of America's military efforts and the machinery of war itself than someone with less conflicted loyalties.

Apess became peculiarly politicized by the war, forced as he was to confront the double bind of Native identity in colonial service. Years later, looking back on the events in which he participated at the Battle of Plattsburgh, Apess would write, "This was indeed a proud day for *our* country."[2] The use of the inclusive pronoun "our" was atypical of Apess's wartime recollections, particularly when speaking of the United States as a discrete political entity. Like many a soldier and warrior, Apess expressed pride in his combat experience, the role he played at Plattsburgh, and the courage he demonstrated under fire. And within this context, he may indeed have felt a sense of camaraderie, of shared experience with other men, both white and Native, who fought bravely alongside him.

In the pointed syntax that follows, however, we can perceive the divisions that continued to split Apess in regard to his claiming a sense of group identity. He writes, "On land we had compelled the enemy to seek safety in flight. *Our* army did not lose many men, but on the lake [Lake Champlain] many a brave man fell—fell in the defense of *his* country's rights."[3] As Apess's narrative suddenly runs up against the presumed causes of the war—the things for which men profess to fight and die—he once more finds himself on unstable ground, poised between the honor he would claim for participating in acts of valor and, conversely, the impossibility of recognizing any "rights" that the United States might extend to Native peoples as a result of those acts. These tensions would force Apess in unpredictable new directions in the years to come, pushing him even further from his home at the close of the war, and dropping him astride an imposed U.S.-Canadian borderline that cut directly through what was once the undivided Longhouse of the Iroquois, or Haudenosaunee.

Gloria Anzaldúa's 1987 book, *Borderlands/La Frontera,* invokes the often-traumatic nature of border regions. "A borderland," she writes, "is a vague and undetermined place created by the emotional residue of an unnatural boundary." It is a place where trespassers may be "raped, maimed, strangled, gassed, shot."[4] Rules, customs, long-established moral codes often break down on the borders as the protections offered by a collectively understood national identity become blurred and indistinct.

Native reservations (and First Nation reserves in Canada) always constitute the imposition of a border, whether they sit astride well-defined international boundary lines like the homelands of the Akwesasne–Saint Regis Indians of upstate New York and Canada or lay embedded within fully developed sites of colonial containment like Apess's Pequot homeland. Reservations are terrains wrested into being by the aggressive incursions of settler colonialism, islands of indigeneity in a sea of white, and, as the political scientist Kevin Bruyneel points out, their legal status is always highly ambiguous, assuming political sovereignty on the one hand but remaining under the jurisdiction of colonial powers on the other. This ambivalence, or "third space," enables a great deal of exploitation while simultaneously becoming a locus of indigenous *survivance.* Or, put another way, reservations were created as sites of violent containment meant to drain the lifeblood out of indigenous culture and tradition, but the very colonial imperatives that forged them into being have paradoxically provided the legal and cultural framework for maintaining Native space, identity, and sovereignty in the twenty-first century.[5]

As a Pequot in the early nineteenth century, Apess had already lived the harrowing after effects of the loss of cultural cohesion through settler colonialism. The attempted destruction of the Pequots hovers at the epicenter of New England colonial history, itself a gaping wound that festers beyond sound and representation. Apess was, in a sense, the product of the centuries-long repercussions made manifest through loss of land, language, and culture, resulting in mass depression, alcoholism, poverty, forced prostitution, and the layers of neglect and abuse endemic to such conditions. In a very real sense, the borders that had been imposed on Apess's life to this point had engendered precisely the kinds of violent social conditions described by Anzaldúa. And, as Anzaldúa observes, such forces were the equivalent of an

> open wound
> dividing a pueblo, a culture,
> running down the length of my body,
> staking fence rods in my flesh,
> . splits me   splits me.[6]

Although borders are obviously meant to delineate secure, stable lines designed to mark off and divide separate realms, border studies scholars draw attention to the chaotic instability of borders, their intrinsic artificiality, and their inability to determine difference save through externalized acts of violence and coercion. Rachel St. John observes, "Rather than a clear line that defines the limits of national territory and state power," borders are more often spaces "where categories blurred and power was compromised."[7] A case in point is that many U.S. citizens before the War of 1812 still considered themselves to be Loyalists in support of the crown, and many Canadians were transplanted Americans who had come seeking open land but still felt strongly allied to the cause of American independence and would have been sympathetic to the notion of the United States expanding its boundaries northward.[8] As the historian Laurence Hauptman notes, however, for Native peoples these newly imagined lines "intruded on nearly every aspect of Indian existence" and were sorely contested by many indigenous communities.[9] The border was a place of ambiguous, shifting, and divided loyalties.

With the cessation of hostilities in 1814, the Iroquois in particular saw their best opportunity at retaining a contiguous land base in the buffer zone between colonial powers crumble. They were to remain an artificially divided people, with two council fires in place of the one that had been maintained for over five hundred years at Onondaga.[10] Already, in the era preceding the war, the Haudenosaunee had seen 95 percent of their land base wrested from them. Once encompassing the entire region of upstate New York, with influence fanning northward into Canada, westward into the Ohio Valley, and southward into Cherokee country, the holdings of the Six Nations now represented only a fraction of their former size, consisting of ten greatly reduced reservations in the Empire State and six in Canada.[11] Construction of the Erie Canal would begin as soon as 1817, and the already highly desirous fertile valleys of Iroquoia achieved even greater commercial value to white speculators, who began pushing in at an ever more alarming rate.[12] These incursions, replete with highways, railroads, tolls, and the construction of new towns, worked to further fracture the psychic and geographical links connecting the Haudenosaunee as a people.

Nowhere at this time was the imposition of a colonial border more evident than in the Akwesasne–Saint Regis community. Akwesasne, meaning "Where the Partridge Drums," sits along the Saint Lawrence River due west of Plattsburgh and was a place of rich natural resources, proving a desirable refuge for Mohawks and other families in the 1740s and 1750s as forces of colonial disruption rippled throughout the Northeast and set indigenous communities in search of secure new areas for settlement.[13] As Akwesasne grew in size, however, European missions followed, and the French Jesuits soon established a presence, naming their mission Saint Francis Regis, after a beloved Jesuit priest, or more simply, Saint Regis.

Following the Revolutionary War, the 1783 Treaty of Paris and the subsequent border commission drew its international boundary line along the banks of the Saint Lawrence River and, consequently, directly through Akwesasne, so that its residents were now one people under the authority of two competing nationalities. Eileen Luna-Firebaugh writes that, prior to the establishment of the U.S.-Canadian border, "indigenous peoples had territories with boundaries that were recognized and honored by their neighbors. Villages and other types of settlements existed where water, agricultural possibilities, and trade made the location reasonable. When, however, the international borders were drawn up, little if any regard was given to the separation of Native villages, and Native nations were not consulted. The lines imposed by the colonizers ignored traditional hunting lands, areas of resource procurement and religious sites."[14] Although the Jay Treaty of 1794 promised the Natives of Akwesasne free and unlimited crossing of the international border within the confines of their reservation, this was contested by the Canadian side, which did not feel obligated to recognize the authority of the Jay Treaty over Natives who were considered British "subjects" prior to the line being drawn.

This artificial boundary remains a scarred wound stitched across Mohawk land and identity to this day. But it also situates Akwesasne–Saint Regis on legally unstable ground, a third space of sovereignty that is at once under colonial control and yet in defiance of the markers by which colonialism polices its perimeters. As Luna-Firebaugh observes, since 1815 the Mohawk Nation has "asserted that the border is largely irrelevant." Although this assertion continues to be contested to this day, the ambiguous third space it creates would, in a sense, prove fortuitous for William Apess when he found himself, following the war, in need of crossing over into Canada.[15]

When Apess left the army sometime around the late summer of 1815, rather than turning homeward, he spent the next two years tracking the U.S.-Canadian borderlands, drawn there most likely by the presence of his Mohawk "brethren." He seems to have sought something out in these postwar hinterlands that either had not been available to him in the country of his birth or that he had been too young, displaced, or emotionally traumatized to formerly recognize among his own people. Apess devotes only a few pages of text to chronicling this chapter of his odyssey, and yet clearly, within the two years he spent drifting across these border regions between 1815 and 1817, Apess was forced to confront the perilous ambiguities of his own liminal status. What he ultimately discovered, however, were pockets of indigenous culture that, although shaken by centuries of colonialism and the fury of unrelenting war, were still politically coherent and intent on self-preservation. Even if this was not the traditional culture of his Pequot ancestors, Apess became witness to the possibility of indigenous lifeways and beliefs sustaining themselves in a hostile environment. I maintain that this discovery was of utmost importance to his development and survival—that it would plant seeds to help Apess spiritually heal and grow after his own traumatic upbringing, find purpose in a heretofore aimless condition, and eventually lead him to carry such possibilities homeward with him to his own country.

"I Could Never Think That the Government Acted Right toward the '*Natives*'"

Apess wrote in *A Son of the Forest* that following the "proud" victories on Lake Champlain, "we remained in Plattsburgh until the peace. As soon as it was known that the war had terminated, and the army disbanded, the soldiers were clamorous for their discharge, but it was concluded to retain our company in the service—I, however, obtained my release."[16] His enlistment records tell a slightly different story, however, showing Apess as having deserted on September 14, 1815.[17] Given that his conscription at the age of fifteen was illegal to begin with, it seems unfair to quibble over Apess's early departure from the army. But, as is so often the case with the documentation of Native lives by the U.S. government, there is also always the chance that the archive here serves an institutional bias. As a "deserter," Apess would not be eligible for the forty-dollar enrollment "bounty" owed him, the sixteen months back pay, or the one hundred and sixty acres of land the federal government had promised to veterans of the war (lands that, ironically, would be wrested from both the Six Nations and the Native peoples of the Ohio Valley) in an effort to encourage what had been lackluster enlistment for an unpopular war.[18] Whether he actually deserted or not, Apess gained insight into the systemic mechanisms by which Native people were disenfranchised in the United States, regardless of their affiliations or service.

Apess's comments pertaining to his departure from the ranks of servicemen speak to the larger, more complex borderland consciousness beginning to arise from the ashes of his war-ravaged youth. He notes that there are many

who are willing to roll in their coaches upon the tears and blood of the poor and unoffending Natives—those who are ready at all times to speculate on the Indians and defraud them out of their rightful possessions. Let the poor Indian attempt to resist the encroachments of his white neighbors, what a hue and cry is instantly raised against him. It has been considered as a trifling thing for the whites to make war on the Indians for the purpose of driving them from their country and taking possession thereof. This was in their estimation, all right, as it helped to extend the territory and enriched some individuals. But let the thing be changed. Suppose an overwhelming army should march into the United States for the purpose of subduing it and enslaving the citizens; how quick would they fly to arms, gather in multitude around the tree of liberty, and contend for their rights with the last drop of their blood.[19]

Apess is not speaking here of distant historic events in need of redressing, but of the very real consequences of the war in which he had so recently been engaged. Detailing the promises that had been made to all U.S. soldiers fighting in the war, he tells us, "I have not seen anything of bounty money, land, or arrearages, from that day to this. I am not, however, alone in this—hundreds were served in the same manner. But I could never think the government acted right toward the '*Natives*,' [original emphasis] not merely in refusing to pay us but in claiming our services in cases of perilous emergency, and still deny us the right of citizenship; and as long as *our nation* is debarred the privilege of voting for civil officers, I shall believe that the government has no claim on *our* services."[20] Apess speaks not just as an individual here, but collectively for those Natives ("our nation") who, like himself, served in the regular army, as well as for the combined members of the Akwesasne, Oneida, and Buffalo Creek reservations that had reluctantly thrown their weight in with the U.S. endeavor as "Indian" companies under their own leadership. His declaration of nationhood and the inclusive pronoun "our" reflect his emerging notions of Native sovereignty, which stand quite apart from his allegiance to the United States.

Other Native leaders were making similar claims. As early as 1813, the Seneca orator Red Jacket had lamented to General James Wilkinson, "We have not received pay according to promise . . . we do not fight for conquest, but we fight for our rights—for our lands—for our country. We hope our request will be granted."[21] Hauptman reports that many Natives had trouble securing their pensions. In the case of Seneca enlistee Thomas John, who had fought with the United States at the Battles of Fort Erie, Chippewa, and Lundy's Lane (and had been wounded in the last), no amount of arbitration was able to secure him the pension of eight dollars a month he'd been promised. After he died, his widow, known as Aunt Dinah John, who herself had served as a cook in the army, spent the next seventy years trying unsuccessfully to secure her promised widow's pension.[22]

Apess clearly invokes this larger community of shared nationhood and grievance in his pronouncement of rights withheld. Thousands of indigenous warriors had put their lives on the line despite conflicted loyalties and were ultimately abandoned by the federal governments to whom they had pledged their allegiance. Within this grievance, then, is forged a discrete Native identity that recognizes the politics of third-space sovereignty. Because Native people ("our nation") were not accorded their rights, they were under no further obligation to the federal government, and the federal government had no further claim on their services. It is the ambiguous state accorded Native peoples that ultimately creates a space for sovereignty to emerge in this case. And it allows for Apess to, if nothing else, justify departure from the armed services on his own terms. If the price of his desertion was to be withheld pay, enlistment bonuses, and promises of land, this seems, in the final analysis, no different from the price all Natives who enlisted in the American cause ended up paying.

Assuming that Apess sought out the company of other Natives during his extended travels and sounded them out about their lives, their customs, and their experiences, it would make sense that he not only knew something of their grievances, but that he might court their companionship and community in more intimate ways following the war. This becomes apparent in his claim, "When I left the army, I had not a shilling in my pocket. I depended upon the precarious bounty of the inhabitants, until I reached the place where some of my brethren dwelt."[23] By "my brethren" Apess of course meant other Native people. Rather than wait to be mustered out with the rest of his unit or track a path back to the splintered remains of his family in Connecticut, Apess determined to travel to Native lands on or near the border in search of a space to heal and recover before charting his *nostos,* or journey home.

A reasonable assumption is that, on leaving Plattsburgh, Apess initially made his way west to Akwesasne. The farmsteads Apess encountered along the way were themselves in the midst of hard times following three years of war, and this would explain their "precarious bounty." But he had marched the path west to Akwesasne a number of times in his military campaigns and knew the way well enough to get himself there alone or in company. Certainly, deserters were still tracked down and punished at this point, but even during the thick of the war the border here had been alarmingly porous, allowing individuals the opportunity to escape capture. The American general George Izard wrote to the secretary of war just prior to the Battle of Plattsburgh, "From the St. Lawrence to the ocean, an open disregard prevails for the laws prohibiting intercourse with the enemy. The road to St. Regis is covered with droves of cattle, and the river with rafts, destined for the enemy."[24] This unchecked flow of people and goods continued apace after the war as well, and it was often Native peoples who operated the boats and rafts that slipped unchecked across the international waterway. From the Akwesasne reservation, Apess would have been able to cross into the Saint Regis reserve on the Canadian side of the river with little concern of being detected by American forces. It would have been a comparatively easy river ride down the Saint Lawrence to Montreal from there.

Once in Montreal, Apess immediately sought work. He apprenticed himself out to a baker and speaks kindly of this "master." But he also had trouble shaking the bad habits he had cultivated while in the army. As he expresses it, he frequently "fell in company" and turned to the liquor bottle. He recounts running into one of the "king's soldiers" during a drinking binge and, "after abusing him with my tongue, I gave him a sound flogging."[25] This seems an impetuous act for a young Native deserter trying to make a go of it in a country not his own, and it goes against the grain of everything that might otherwise be said of Apess. Rarely if ever does Apess come across as a hothead or a bully, and his later ethos will be one of studied nonviolence.

If at this moment he appears to be embracing the ethos of the soldier who bears continued antagonism toward his former enemy, the scene is complicated by Apess's ever-present liminality. Any colonial soldier is an occupying soldier in Native space. Had Apess been in "company" with other former U.S. soldiers (unlikely under the circumstances), such an outburst of braggadocio might have been encouraged. Had he been in "company" with Canadian Mohawks, he might have shared their grievance toward the Canadian Army for failing to pay soldier's salaries and for the sorry terms brokered on their behalf in the Treaty of Ghent. Whatever company he kept, Apess might reasonably have felt antagonism toward any man in uniform at this point in his career. Either way, Apess's loyalties must have felt more confused than ever, and he seems to lash out at the world in dangerous and ill-advised ways, in this instance, costing him his job.

After his stint as a baker in Montreal, Apess worked as a field hand for a short time. This did not suit him, however, and neither did his return to the life of a domestic servant. As a cook, he earned twelve dollars a month aboard a sloop traveling the Saint Lawrence River. He worked odd jobs for the farmers with whom he stayed, and served under a merchant for a season, but each of these occupations seems to have rapidly dissolved into some kind of falling-out with his employers or a restless lapse back into drink, forcing him to sever his ties.

Like many a soldier grappling to reintegrate himself into a peacetime economy after combat, Apess had a great deal of difficulty adjusting and found himself subject to violent mood swings and the need to self-medicate with alcohol. He floundered from one opportunity to the next in search of a safe piece of ground on which to stand. He even claims to have had a brief flirtation with the Methodist Church at this time, but as he reflects, "it soon wore off."[26] Apess speaks of wandering to the Kingston area and working through that winter with a Dutch farmer, a situation with which he professes to have been "much pleased." But for the most part, his account is fragmentary, and he appears in his own narrative as a frail vessel at sea, buffeted by winds and storms over which he has little or no control.[27]

It is quite probable that Apess blurred at least some of the events of two years into one at this point, as there does not seem to have been enough time for him to have accomplished all he claims to in the given timeframe. In *The Experiences of Five Christian Indians of the Pequot Tribe,* however, Apess offers a slightly different chronology. Whether a result of faulty memory or, perhaps, merely different narrative objectives, in this latter memoir Apess writes of traveling from "Montreal to Upper Canada, Fort Niagara; from thence to Kingston, and through the wilderness," where he "saw many of my brethren."[28] The difference between the two accounts is significant. Fort Niagara was on the contested strip of land between Lake Ontario and Lake Erie where the British, at least initially, refused to withdraw their troops following the war in defiance of the 1814 treaty. If Apess was at Fort Niagara in the months leading up to the winter of 1815, as this timeline suggests, he would have been in direct proximity to Fort George, on the Canadian side of the Niagara River, at the time that a meeting occurred between the two divided councils of the Six Nations who had agreed to come together to exchange wampum and make peace.

In fact, there is reason again to believe that Apess's travels during this time are much more interwoven with the movements of his "brethren" than he ever lets on. A large contingency of Natives were gathering for the council and could expect, among other things, to be provided with food and trade goods from the British authorities who presided over the meeting. Given the rampant hunger of that season and the prospect of a poor harvest, Apess would have had compelling reasons to make this trip. The fact that he omits his travels to Fort Niagara in *A Son of the Forest* may simply suggest one of those strategic silences to which I earlier alluded. Apess was piecing together a new sense of identity through his association with his Haudenosaunee brethren, but it was not an identity that conformed to the concerns of his later Christian mission. If he did, in fact, arrive at the area of Fort Niagara with a company of Mohawks that September, he would have had an opportunity to observe the highly ritualized structures of the condolence ceremony, and would have been a participant in the processes of healing that took place there on the very border where four nations now converged: the United States, Canada, and the two divided nations of the Iroquois.

Embracing a Narrative: Creating the Codes of "Forest" Diplomacy

The ritual of wampum exchange has its origins in what Arthur Parker referred to as "the [Peacemaker] Legend."[29] The "legend" is actually the cultural history of the formation of the Five Nations of the Haudenosaunee (People of the Longhouse), or Iroquois, and it is important to know something of this narrative—its origin, maintenance, and the traditions it establishes—in order to understand crucial undercurrents of Apess's autobiographical journey. One recorded version of the narrative begins as such: "North of the beautiful lake (Ontario) in the land of the Crooked Tongues, was a long winding bay and at a certain spot was the Huron town, Ka-ha-nah-yenh. Near by was the great hill, Ti-ro-nat-ha-ra-da-donh. In the village lived a good woman who had a virgin daughter. Now strangely this virgin conceived and her mother knew that she was about to bear a child. The daughter about this time went into a long sleep and dreamed that her child should be a son whom she should name [Peacemaker]."[30]

The story, dating back perhaps as far as the eleventh century, tells of the creation of the Haudenosaunee Confederacy and has been passed down through generations as part of the Great Binding Law or Constitution of the Five (later Six) Nations. Although the constitution serves as a set of laws and protocols for Haudenosaunee leadership and succession, Parker, who helped compile the narrative from multiple sources in 1923, emphasizes in his introduction to this document that "the version of the constitution now held authentic by the Iroquois of New York and Ontario, embraces a narrative."[31] In other words, the Great Law, or Kaianerekown, that binds the people together is inseparable from the story of its creation and cannot be properly appreciated or understood apart from the narrative structure that consecrates its cultural relevance.

According to the narrative, the Peacemaker was born at a place called Kah-ha-nah-yenh in the area of the Bay of Quinte near Kingston, Ontario. The child of virgin birth was not well received, we are told, and in one version of the story, at the grandmother's behest, three attempts were made to drown the child in the bay. After each attempt, however, he materialized once more unharmed at his mother's bosom, forcing the grandmother to concede that they best care for him, for "he may become an important man."[32] As the child came of age, however, he was despised by his own people, resented for his "handsome face and his good mind." He was compelled to leave the land of the Crooked Tongues because "their hearts were bitter against a man who loved not war better than all things."[33] And so, as the story goes, the Peacemaker "began to build his canoe out of a white rock," and informed his mother and grandmother of his plan to embark on a journey of many years carrying the Ka-rih-wi-yoh (sometimes Gawaiio), or "the message of the Good Tidings of Peace and Power." Launching his stone canoe on the waters of Lake Ontario, he bid his family farewell and paddled into history, announcing himself to all he encountered on his journey as one "who came from the west and am going eastward and am called [Peacemaker] in the world."[34]

The story goes on to relate how, through the agency of the culture heroes Peacemaker and Hayonwhatha (variant of Hiawatha), a message of peace, power, and unity was carried through the warring regions of their world, disrupting the cycles of vengeance and trauma that, once set in motion, perpetuate strife, and producing circumstances under which a cohesive new nation could bind together. At the heart of the narrative lies the creation of wampum, an indigenous medium for healing traumatic grief and creating a space for reconciliation between warring parties. The wampum, as envisioned by Hayonwhatha, would console those who were burdened with grief, as was Hayonwhatha himself following the deaths of his daughters.

In the wake of his loss, Hayonwantha described his condition as one of dividedness—not only of self but of national identity. In a larger sense, his dividedness split the very firmaments. He lamented, "My sorrow and my rage have been bitter. I can only rove about since now I have cast myself away from my people. I am only a wanderer. I split the heavens when I went away from my house and my nation."[35] Those whose minds are similarly blighted by devastating events, particularly in wartime, become, in Hayonwhatha's language, "covered with night and wrapped in darkness. This would I lift with words of condolence and these strands of beads would become words with which I would address them."[36] Through the agency of wampum, parties could reconcile their differences and assuage one another's grief by wiping away the tears in the eyes, removing the dirt from the ears, and unplugging the obstructions from the throat, thus freeing up all the processes necessary to see, hear, and speak beyond the distorting emotional constraints of traumatic rage and grief.

The wampum represents not only a highly ritualized spiritual conduit through which to counteract the effects of cultural trauma, but, as Parker notes, the wampum belts that have passed down from generation to generation comprise the "ancient archives [of] the Six Nations of New York Indians."[37] The use of wampum belts, therefore, in diplomacy and healing alike, must be understood as both a culturally creative solution to end cycles of violence and a highly generative textualized process. Lisa Brooks tells us that "when an agreement, an alliance, or an event was put in wampum, a transformation in Native space was solidified."[38] The transformation wrought by the Peacemaker and Hayonwhatha in the pre-Columbian era resulted in the creation of a powerful group identity for the Haudenosaunee. By the second decade of the nineteenth century, however, that group identity had already been under aggravated assault for some two hundred years.

A main factor in preserving indigenous land and culture amidst the onslaught of colonialism was the preservation of stories. When the Haudenosaunee determined to collect and publish their constitution in the late nineteenth and early twentieth century, it was with a conscious determination to preserve their narrative traditions "as others have done," and to protect them from further corruptions and inaccuracies that had crept in via cultural ero-sion, language loss, and the interpretations of white ethnographers and his-torians.[39] By embracing the narrative, the Haudenosaunee maintained their law, and, as Parker relates, "Through the law as a guiding force and through the heroes as ideals the Iroquois have preserved their national identity and much of their native culture and lore. . . . This is a remarkable fact when it is considered that they are surrounded by a dominant culture whose encroach-ments are persistent and unrelenting in the very nature of things."[40]

Many contemporary trauma scholars observe that psychic well-being actu-ally relies on the maintenance of strong, enduring, cultural frameworks, or the ability to fully *embrace a narrative*.[41] We secure ourselves in the world through the connection we feel to our sustaining narratives and the sense of community we derive from them. Such stories, which are nothing less than the materials of which culture is forged, are essential in structuring the illu-sion of integrated linearity through which our lives are ordered. An event becomes traumatic when it exerts an unanticipated force capable of shattering our sustaining narratives, posing a violation of the moral and temporal terms on which we previously understood the world to operate. After such violent experiences, it becomes difficult to reintegrate oneself into a former life or find a community of listeners to properly honor one's rudely awakened sense of the world. It is due to this very fact that veterans, as well as other survivors of trauma, typically have such difficulty communicating their stories to others who do not share the same frame of experience.

The trauma specialist Jonathan Shay uses the Greek word *themis* to suggest an understanding of "what's right," or the narrative contours of cognition that encompass notions of "moral order, convention, normative expecta-tions, ethics, and commonly understood social values." Trauma, Shay tells us, is the "betrayal of *themis*," the violent and unanticipated fragmentation of what once seemed a safe and integrated worldview.[42] Soldiers at war are particularly vulnerable to this phenomenon, as their service, and often their sacrifice, is highly bound up in moral terms revolving around concepts of patriotism, honor, manhood, and performing "what's right" for one's country. But too often the conditions of warfare, once engaged, cannot sustain these moral trappings. Trauma sufferers find themselves violently shaken from the narrative structures that had previously sustained them, leading not only to a profound sense of isolation and betrayal, but to an inability to reestablish the sequential order of their cognitive processes. The traumatic moment is so unexpectedly catastrophic that it shatters the social-narrative framework upon which the sufferer based his or her perceptions. There is no place in the story for such egregious occurrences, and therefore the narrative framework by which one has ordered one's life shatters. Shay tells us that "although the *themis* of narrative temporality is one of the deepest structures of our culture, severe trauma destroys the capacity to think a future or a past."[43] The moment of trauma itself becomes a gaping wound or fissure that sufferers cannot bridge, spiritually paralyzing them within the rupture of that psychic moment.

When entire cultures endure prolonged violent assault on their lifeways and traditions, as Native peoples have done under the sustained operations of colonialism, they too experience trauma, their cohesive order becoming strained beyond its capacity to maintain shape and structure. The societal ills that arise from such an assault fester and boil under the imposition of foreign values and imposed narratives specifically designed to disparage social order as it was once understood. Maria Yellow Horse Brave Heart and Lymera DeBruyn refer to this phenomenon as "historical unresolved grief" and speak of the intergenerational transfer of trauma resulting from the loss of lives, land, and vital aspects of Native culture "promulgated by the European conquest of the Americas."[44] Surely in Apess's time these conditions were experienced all across the indigenous borderlands of the Northeast.

The path to overcoming trauma, according to Shay, "depends upon communalization of the trauma—being able safely to tell the story to someone who is listening and who can be trusted to retell it truthfully to others in the community."[45] It would seem, then, that the path to healing personal and historical wounds we witness in our own time is in significant ways similar to the methods that served the Haudenosaunee in the time of the Peacemaker. In both cases, a community of listeners must be established so that the trauma narrative can be heard and acknowledged, and grievances addressed. On the borderlands between Canada and the United States, Apess, too, would seek out an opportunity to begin to pull together the materials of a new narrative framework that would prove crucial to his own healing and form the philosophical core of his literary accomplishment from that point on. It is a narrative that begins to recognize historical grievances and places them in a newly revitalized textualized space. As Hayonwhatha stated, "This would I do if I found anyone burdened with grief even as I am. I would console them for they would be covered with night and wrapped in darkness. This would I lift with words of condolence and these strands of beads would become words with which I would address them."[46]

The council at Fort Niagara in 1815 included not just Iroquois but other groups as well, such as the Hurons, Delawares, and Tutelos who had placed themselves "beneath the tree" of the Six Nations for protection. Speaking for the Canadian branch of the Iroquois was the Mohawk Henry Tekarihoga, an elder statesmen who over the preceding quarter century had found himself allied to both British and colonial causes at various times. The most recent conflict found him sided with the British, with whom he had led a Native detachment at Beaver Dams in 1813. His long experience as a warrior and diplomat on either side of the "medicine line" made him the perfect representative of the Mohawk council. Because the British government officially hosted the event, however, it was incumbent on the British officer present, Colonel Robertson, to offer the opening words of condolence and "uncover" the "King's council fire." This would have involved invoking the ritualized language of wiping tears from the eyes, and removing obstructions from the ears and throat. As related by Parker, "When a person is brought to grief by death, he seems to lose sight of the sky (blinded with grief) and he is crushed by sorrow."[47] The wampum would be used to wipe the sorrow clean and create conditions of clear seeing, hearing, and speaking.

After the first string of wampum was received, Tekarihoga addressed the council, acknowledging the correct performance of the opening ceremonies by Colonel Robertson and explaining of this ritual that it was "customary with our ancestors," and one that "we endeavor to continue." It is unavoidable that Tekarihoga's speech would be political in nature, as were the speeches by the other Native orators assembled, and was meant as much for the British officers in attendance as it was for his compatriots. As such, words had to be chosen with great care, and skilled orators were needed to perform the ritual.

Tekarihoga remarked that the assembled nations from Canada "salute you from the other side—we are the same people with you, we are relations, and of the same colour notwithstanding our having been opposed to each other in the Field during the late Contest between our Father the King of England and the Americans." Tekarihoga stressed the significance of shared bonds of kinship and culture that must withstand the losses sustained due to the squabbling of two foreign nations. He emphasized how those bonds must be able to transcend the divisions, both emotional and geographical, placed there by colonial politics. The uncovering of the council fire had "removed all obstructions," and the minds of all were "set at ease." He continued by asserting, "The River which separates us is opened that we may have a free passage at all times—The Roads are cleared of all briars," and friendly intercourse could once again be renewed. Although Tekarihoga is presumed to be speaking metaphorically to a certain degree, he also seems to allude to the conditions of the border itself and to the right of Native people to cross from one side to the other and engage in trade and fishing without being held to the restrictions of settler customs or international boundary lines. The conclusion of his address was sealed, of course, by the extension of a string of white wampum.[48]

Tekarihoga was followed by Choi, an Onondaga chief from the U.S. side, who also elaborated on the ancient ritual components of the ceremony, intoning "All ill blood has been removed from our hearts. We put the tomahawk to the depth of a pine tree underground; and that it may not be removed, we place over it a tree that the roots may so cover it that it cannot be found again." He appealed to those assembled to forget the occurrences of the past, and, speaking specifically to his Native brethren, Choi said, "We condole with you from the bottom of our Hearts for the loss of your friends and wipe the tears from your eyes. We open the throats that no obstruction shall remain, that you may speak freely and with the same friendship which formerly existed between us." Choi's words invoked the white roots of peace which first emanated from the pine tree planted by the Peacemaker at the forming of the Haudenosaunee Nation, as well as the function of wampum to condole individuals suffering from grief. Within the structure of the ceremony always lay the words and symbols of the original alliance and constitution. The words of the speech were sealed with strings of black and white wampum, ensuring the cultural and spiritual validity of their offering.

Lastly, the old Seneca orator Red Jacket stood and addressed the assembled nations. Red Jacket, too, had lived through his share of colonial conflicts over the years, and was well versed in the expectations of the ceremony from both an indigenous and a colonial perspective. Like the other speakers, he too regretted the loss of blood between what were essentially one people. Red Jacket acknowledged the constrained condition of his people, and their economic hardship and inability to operate outside colonial authority. What had previously occurred in wartime, he assured his audience, "was not from any animosity towards an ancient father and friends." As he maintained, "We are a poor people—we cannot do as we would—we are as Prisoners." Nevertheless, he recommended that all who were there labor to "be united and become one Body."

Red Jacket's speech seems to offer a reminder that despite drastic transformations to Haudenosaunee culture—despite, in fact, being held hostage to settler colonial expectations and agendas—traditional values still needed to be minded. He asked of all who were present to return to their "occupations of hunting and agriculture," and that they "pay due attention to your women, who by our ancient customs have a voice in bringing up our young People to the practice of truth and industry." The clan mothers had always played a vital role in the maintenance of Haudenosaunee community, not just in a domestic sense but also as advisers in matters of governance, diplomacy, and even war. Red Jacket, who in the past had provided a voice for the clan mothers in diplomatic ceremonies, remained aware of the importance of this role to the sustenance of community, and apparently sought to add a counterweight to the threat of hierarchical gender transformations he already anticipated from the colonizing culture.

Finally, Red Jacket extended an offer to the Grand River Mohawk to go live with the Delaware at White River in the Ohio country, where there were still "fine lands and Game of every kind in great abundance." These last words were met with confusion and were ultimately rejected by Tekarihoga (the suggestion more than likely was not Red Jacket's own, but came from U.S. authorities who were invested in pushing all Native groups westward to clear ground for white settlement), but the rest of Red Jacket's speech was sealed with wampum strings. Finally, Tekarihoga, mindful of the road home, returned for his closing statement, directing his speech to the British officials as well as to his own brethren. "We hope," he said, "we will be able to travel along the road peaceably without being insulted by the inhabitants." He knew full well that although Native alliances had been sought and valued during wartime, the cessation of battle meant the renewal of hostilities between vulnerable Native communities and those of European descent who looked to recoup their war losses at the expense of Native communities. The response could not have been encouraging, as he was tersely reminded by the Indian superintendent that only if the "Indian children" behaved well would they see such kind treatment reciprocated.

All the differences that had fallen between the two divisions of the Iroquois could not be set right in this single gathering, but the ceremony allowed a process of healing to be set in motion. What was begun here would eventually lead to the collaborative effort between the divided groups to forge a new articulation of the Great Law and constitution decades later, with the various ancient nations of the longhouse contributing a voice. The meeting at Fort George allowed the Natives to condole with one another over their wartime losses and metaphorically "bury the Tomahawk." Gifts were exchanged, and supply goods were provided by the English government for the return journey. Like other Natives present, Apess (assuming he was there) would have found his way to Fort George as much for the "gifts" as the diplomatic proceedings, but the event would also have afforded him an opportunity to witness what is often referred to as "forest diplomacy"—indigenous structures for resisting power and maintaining cultural autonomy. The combined speeches of Tekarihoga, Choi, and Red Jacket offered powerful expressions of Native sovereignty and tradition, and there were avenues for resistance in these rituals that may have impressed themselves on the mind of a young man.

Ceremony

Once the rekindling ceremony was concluded, Apess would have followed the Tyendinaga Mohawk from Fort Niagara back to the Kingston area where his autobiography places him in the winter of 1815–16. Though he writes of laboring under pleasant conditions for a Dutch farmer at this location, he also recounts spending a great deal of time with his Native brethren, and he "often went around with them on hunting excursions." In fact, he tells us, "they were all around me, and it therefore seemed like home."[49]

We might well pause here to consider what such a statement implied. Apess's home life, what we know of it at least, had been something of a nullity. He had been more or less abandoned by his parents; had endured hunger, deprivation, and beatings that nearly cost him his life; and from then on, home had been a series of positions as an indentured servant in which he was poorly treated and sold from one master to another, not unlike a slave. It was to escape this situation that Apess had run off and became a soldier in the first place. But clearly here was a place that Apess felt nurtured and at ease, and experienced some semblance of what he understood home should feel like. It meant for the first time being part of a stable community of indigenous people and learning how this community still maintained its traditional values, still spoke its own language, adhered to ancient ceremonies, and acknowledged a law and a spirituality that had deep roots in the soil. Although it is difficult to extrapolate a great deal from the brief glimpses he affords, we can still posit that Apess felt a certain level of inclusion in the seasonal activities of the Tyendinaga, and was exposed to their practices and customs. As Parker asserts, the Canadian branch of the Iroquois in 1815, having united "all their tribes in a general council, continued to govern themselves in the ancient way and under the laws of [Peacemaker], and Hiawatha [Heyonwatha]."[50]

These were not topics that Apess was at liberty to write openly about in his Christian conversion narratives, or explicate in positive terms, although it is clear that he desires his readers to gather something of his experience and the Native pride he felt in this community to which he attached himself. As such, he resorts to a kind of slant narrative to unburden himself of the deep emotions raised by this moment in his life. In *A Son of the Forest,* Apess recounts a number of opaque experiences suggesting an undercurrent of spiritual power flowing in hidden opposition to the surface waters of expressed Christian faith. He recalls,

> I was now in the Bay of Quinte; the scenery was diversified. There were also some natural curiosities. On the very top of a high mountain in the neighborhood was a large pond of water, to which there was no visible outlet— this pond was unfathomable. It was very surprising to me that so great a body of water should be found so far above the common level of the earth. There was also in the neighborhood a rock that had the appearance of being hollowed out by the hand of a skillful artificer; through this rock wound a narrow stream of water: It had the most beautiful and romantic appearance, and I could not but admire the wisdom of God in the order, regularity, and beauty of creation.[51]

Lisa Brooks, sensing a profound, if subversive, spiritual realignment taking place in this passage, has referred to it as "the scene of his [Apess's] rebirth."[52] Brooks's reading of this is affirmed when one learns that the features Apess describes can still be located today on the Bay of Quinte in Prince Edward County, Ontario.

The Lake on the Mountain is a peculiar geological phenomenon that has long held spiritual significance for local Natives inhabiting the region. Sitting atop a prominent hill overlooking Lake Ontario, the lake is fed by an underground spring and only prevented from draining into the greater body of water below by its soft limestone bed encased in a much harder shell of solid granite. Thought for many ages to be bottomless, the lake has since been determined to be thirty-seven meters deep, and, though other theories exist, was probably dredged into place by a passing glacier at the retreat of the last ice age. It is a singular curiosity to stand on a level with its serene waters on one side and then to turn and look out over the greater expanse of Lake Ontario, some one hundred feet below, on the opposite side.

The Lake on the Mountain is said to be the place where the Peacemaker began his journey in his stone canoe. Apess's narrative seems to suggest that he simply happened upon this natural curiosity, as though a mere tourist in the region, but there can be little doubt that his association with his "brethren" at the Bay of Quinte guided him to this site for very specific purposes. Not only would he have been introduced to the stories invested in the mysterious natural landmark, but his purpose for being there was no doubt ceremonial. The Tyendinaga Mohawk come to this place in the spring to gather waters flowing from the lake that are used ceremonially to regenerate the land. Apess would likely have been impressed as much by the natural beauty of the location as by the deep historical and cultural roots that had been nourished here.

As such, there is reason to surmise that Apess's own spiritual regeneration springs from this place and moment. He had now become a participant in certain practices and mysteries that had been in continuance for centuries and suggested depths of indigenous tradition that previously seemed nonexistent or unfathomable to him. Here stories came together, revealed their hidden currents, merged practice with theory, and incorporated the landscape itself into their narrative cohesion. Traditional indigenous culture still manifested itself here on the border, in this place of mystery sandwiched between colonial powers, this narrow strip between bodies of water, this third space between earth and sky, in ways that simply could not be spoken of in the Christian tracts for which Apess would become well known in his later adulthood.

To follow the thread of the mystery, however, was in a sense to follow the Peacemaker's journey in an impossible vessel from a landlocked lake on the mountain to the broader sparkling sea below. To accomplish this required a leap of faith, perhaps, or the ability to trace the channels of power to where they ran hidden beneath the ground only to come gushing out through a natural cavity in the very granite, "a rock that had the appearance of being hollowed out by the hand of a skillful artificer" or some greater force yet. Here, Apess observed, "a narrow stream of water" wound its way through and plummeted to the bay one hundred feet below. At the base of this formation, which must be attained by precarious descent down steep walls of granite, one finds a number of rocks that thrust up violently from the earth like giant shafts or like the stern, perhaps, of a great white stone canoe having spilled from the cavity in the rock wall above and completed its watery trajectory.

Apess's deference to the "wisdom of God" in his description of these features might readily be viewed as Christian revelation, particularly given the evangelical concerns of *A Son of the Forest.* Such an interpretation is tempered, however, by his ensuing observation that, from the vantage of this place of power and tradition, he then "turned my eyes to the forest, and it seemed alive with its sons and daughters. There seemed to be the utmost order and regularity in their encampment."[53]

If Apess stands at this very moment geographically situated between the borders of two colonial powers, he firmly locates himself in Native space, a space defined against the persistent denigrations of the dominant culture. This is no desolate chaos full of wild beasts and wild men, as the Puritan William Bradford once described it, but rather a space of order and beauty. For Brooks, such a space includes the "spirit of creation" and "the forest and its network of relations, which contained all the Native inhabitants of the region, including Apess himself."[54]

Once one has situated the account within its proper spiritual geography, the passage can only be seen as equating the order of God's creation with the order and harmony of Native ceremony.[55] Apess relates how the woods of this newly regenerated space became "vocal with the songs of birds; all nature seemed to smile and rejoice in the freshness and beauty of spring. My brethren appeared very cheerful on account of its return and enjoyed themselves in hunting, fishing, basket making, etc."[56] Although Apess does not reflect long upon the insights inspired by these events, he is nevertheless acknowledging a personal awakening that seems to arise from a sense—a space—of community the likes of which he had not previously communicated.

The Mohegan medicine woman Gladys Tantaquidgeon once described a similar natural phenomenon sacred to the peoples along the Thames River (formerly the Pequot River) in Connecticut, where "icy cold pure water surfaced from beneath a capped flat-topped rock" atop Mohegan Hill and was believed to have magical properties. According to Tantaquidgeon, the water "makes one strong and healthy."[57] Brooks, too, has observed that Apess's

"There was also in the neighborhood a rock that had the appearance of being hollowed out by the hand of a skillful artificer, through this rock wound a narrow stream of water" (Apess *SOF,* 32–33). *Photo by the author, 2014.*

View from below of the rock at the Bay of Quinte. *Photo by the author, 2014.*

reference to a "skillful artificer" in this passage invokes Algonquian stories of the culture hero Maushop, whose actions were responsible for shaping the natural landscape.[58] If Apess, in his childhood, learned anything of traditions indigenous to the region, he never lets on. But we will see in following chapters how the Christian practices he engages with on his home ground take on syncretic shapes, merging his Bible learning with deep-rooted local indigenous traditions. Perhaps he had experienced some intercourse with these traditions all along and was open to such spiritual fortification as these stories provided following his war experiences. Certainly Apess's mentioning of it here, in an autobiography largely designed to gain him entrance to the evangelical Christian community, alerts us to the continuous hidden tensions and moments of Native resistance that inform all of Apess's works. But it also suggests the sort of syncretic awareness in which Christian and Native organizational rhetoric are often bound together.

In the 1829 edition of *A Son of the Forest,* when Apess referred to the "regularity" and "order" of the Native encampments he glimpsed at the Lake on the Mountain, he included the observation: "And they held all things in common."[59] From a Christian context, the phrase alludes to Acts 2:44–47, which tells of the apostle Peter baptizing the citizens of Jerusalem, after which "all that believed were together, and had all things in common; And sold their possessions and goods, and parted them to all men, as every man had need. And they continuing daily with one accord in the temple, and breaking bread from house to house, did eat their meat with gladness and singleness of heart." But in Apess's hands the phrase equally alludes to the traditional Native practice of holding land in common and eschewing the accumulation of material wealth upon which colonial economies insisted.

For Apess, the ethos of shared land and shared resources stood at the foundation of both Christian and Native community. And the baptism by which the biblical community was forged held striking similarities to the indigenous baptism Apess himself had just undergone, his immersion in the restorative waters that proved a source of regeneration for Haudenosaunee culture and tradition. This would be the first of many passages in which Apess the preacher found cause to hold up the traditional practices of Native peoples as more intrinsically Christian than anything practiced by whites. Although the provocative phrase "they held all things in common" was excised from the later 1831 edition of *Son of the Forest,* it speaks directly to a particular indigenous aesthetic that must certainly have been striking to Apess at the time. And perhaps it was his hope that such a community, in which order, peace, and an aesthetic of shared resources were the apparent norm, might be rekindled among his own people in New England should the proper bearer of the message happen along.

"Placing the Wood Together"

For trauma specialist Shay, the important considerations when dealing with trauma are social and political. Shay asks how we might attempt to heal trauma by restoring the integrity of cultural narratives. For even though an instance of unanticipated violence may disrupt an illusion of narrative continuity for one individual (a disruption that leads to feelings of rage, helplessness, severe depression, and, at times, amnesia), that illusion is nevertheless always studiously policed by the culture at large. When the trauma sufferer attempts to make his or her own story known, it is roundly dismissed by those who apprehend the maintenance of *themis* to be threatened by that particular narrative. In other words, the narrative of the trauma survivor threatens the sense of "what's right" for the rest of society, as it intimates what is, in fact, so terribly wrong.

The master narrative of the colonizers is one that strategically represses the awful outrages that were committed against indigenous peoples of this country. In a sense, culture itself is a construction that attempts to contain traumatic knowledge through coercive hegemonic power. If, as Shay asserts, the trauma narrative "is a challenge to the rightness of the social order, to the trustworthiness of *themis*," then the ideal response would be that we all "strive to be a trustworthy audience for victims of abuse of power." To do this, Shay says, "we must overcome all the good reasons why normal adults do not want to hear trauma narratives. If forced to hear them, normal people deny their truth. If forced to accept them as true, they often forget them."[60] The true restoration of *themis* must involve an accommodation of the trauma sufferer's narrative. As long as such narratives are tamped down and kept silent, the symptomatic social ills of rage, denial, depression, and so on will continue on both ends. Therefore, as Judith Herman has suggested, "an understanding of psychological trauma begins with rediscovering history."[61]

Here, then, is a final bit of history that is rarely found in the books that get written and read today. When the United States emerged victorious from the Revolutionary War, the Iroquois siding with the British under the leadership of the Mohawk Joseph Brant were forced to relocate to Canada, forming the Six Nations Reserve and, shortly thereafter, the Tyendinaga Mohawk Territory. Perhaps, given the forced fragmentation and dislocation of the Iroquois in this period, we should consider it ironic that Tyendinaga, translated from the Mohawk, means "placing the wood together."[62] Then again, what could no longer be geographically reconstituted could, perhaps, retain cohesion through narrative strategies, the framework of shared stories and beliefs.

The Tyendinaga Mohawk were promised land in return for their service to the British during the Revolution. When Captain John Deserontyon broke new ground with twenty other families on a tract along the Bay of Quinte in 1784, he understood that, despite violent relocation, he was placing his people back into geographical continuity with an ancient story. The 92,700 square acres of the Tyendinaga Mohawk Territory were officially granted in 1793 with the Simcoe Deed. This meant that the Mohawk had reestablished themselves in the place of their cultural origins. Only a few miles distant from the "curious" lake Apess described is Eagle Mountain, where the Peacemaker was said to have been born. Placing the wood together was accomplished by embracing the narrative and locating oneself within it, by the creative insistence of holding on to traditional frameworks and a sense of shared identity even in times of great sorrow and rupture.

When Apess, in a seemingly off-hand passage in his autobiography, speaks of climbing that high hill near Kingston, Ontario, and seeing wonders that defied the agency of human hands, he too was placing himself within an indigenous narrative construct, although one that was indecipherable to non-Native audiences. As Brooks notes, this moment served as Apess's "Native conversion experience," an epiphany that offered him a newly formed consciousness of Native community and advocacy generated from within Native space.[63] Although Apess is circumspect about his motives for visiting this site, he clearly comprehended its spiritual significance to the community with which he was encamped and became a participant in the ceremonial practices that have arisen from this space. He would continue to make veiled reference to Native customs and spiritual structures throughout his written works.

At the Lake on the Mountain, Apess was standing on firm Native ground, and when he wrote of it in his 1829 autobiography, he was textually locating himself within the story by which the Haudenosaunee had organized and preserved their culture for hundreds of years. In a sense, from this point on he would follow a path that partially emulated that of the Peacemaker, cultivating the law of peace as he traveled, a retrograde wanderer, from the west to the east, against the grain of "civilization" typically charted by colonial powers. His own life story strangely mirrored the story of the Peacemaker in some respects. The legendary lawgiver was, like Apess, said to have been abused by his maternal grandmother, who tried to kill him. It was only through supernatural agency that he avoided death, and from then on the Peacemaker would go to live among other people (the Iroquois), away from his own relations. He came of age in a time of war and violence and would spend the rest of his days attempting to negotiate peace between conflicted parties by issuing words sealed by textual processes that would heal and help institute one law that all might follow. Such words and metaphors will continue to play a part in Apess's rhetoric as his vision matures in the coming years.

As he comes down from this spiritual high ground, however, Apess laments to his Christian audience, "Oh, what a pity that this state of things should change. How much better would it be if the whites would act like civilized people and, instead of giving my brethren of the woods 'rum!' in exchange for their furs, give them food and clothing for themselves and children."[64] It is a strange and sudden rhetorical turn. On the one hand, Apess wishes to preserve the vision of order and shared resources that he sees among the "children of the forest," and yet he laments the incursion of those settler vices that are ever forwarded in Christian literature as the downfall of the Native race.

Apess, in coming down to earth, also returns to the enumeration of vices and missteps that chart the path of the Christian conversion narrative. He returns to the dominant tropes, and leaves the visions of order and harmony in the margins of his text, an incomplete presence on the borderlines of representation. He returns to the strategies of syncretism whereby Native people curry social favor and civil rights by playing the part of "children of the forest." And yet in Apess's hands these "children" are a people of beauty and integrity, and it is the whites who seem to lack the qualities of a "civilized people." If this could only change, he intones, "God would bless both the whites and natives threefold." As things stand, however, Apess can only look at how the white missionaries devise schemes and speculations "to the advantage of themselves, regardless of the rights, feelings, and interests of the untutored sons of the forest." In this way, he laments, "many a good man's path is hedged up, and he is prevented from doing good among the natives, in consequence of the bad conduct of those who are, properly speaking, only 'wolves in sheep's clothing.'" What is needed, he suggests, are good missionaries to go among them. And this is what Apess himself proposes to become—a good missionary.[65]

One of the challenges for Apess, moving forward, will be to forge a rhetoric that can bridge the gap between the life experiences of Native peoples and the limited ability of the dominant culture to play the role of audience to such histories. But as he descended the Lake on the Mountain in the spring of 1816, such thoughts were still quite distant from his mind. Apess had not yet adopted Christian rhetoric as a means of delivering his message of peace. His heart was still full with the indigenous customs and narratives made tangible to him along the border regions of the United States and Canada. He would soon trace a year-long trajectory homeward, following the Mohawk River, traversing the lands through which the Peacemaker himself had traveled, sometimes staying with his brethren, sometimes laboring among the whites, falling into "company" more often than not, wrestling with his recurrent dalliances with alcohol. Apess had not found the answers that would sustain him as of yet, but a seed was planted, the roots were growing, the bloody hatchet of war would eventually recede from view, and a path was opening up before him.

CHAPTER FIVE
Becoming a Son of the Forest

I had become now a wanderer alone, as it were, in my native woods.

—Aunt Sally George

Lazarus

William Apess spent the spring of 1816 among his "brethren" of the Tyendinaga Mohawk in the forests of Upper Canada, harvesting maple sugar for the Dutch farmer who had hired him out through the winter. This was relatively light work, and a great deal of leisure time remained for other activities, such as fishing, hunting, and basket making among his "brethren." But Apess, now in his nineteenth year and recollecting his "kindred friends who had long before buried me beneath the sods of the forest," was suddenly ready to return home.[1]

With the emergence of spring, he bade farewell to the farmer and his Mohawk acquaintances and charted a path back to Kingston, Ontario. Here Apess records that he was once again but "a poor, destitute, helpless child of the forest, all alone in the world as it were," and, as a result, the journey hit upon a number of snags.[2] He found himself living for a spell in a household of a husband and wife who were both terrible drunks. Apess is vague about this experience, but writes that he found "much trouble in the wigwam," and the domestic situation soon fell apart. Soon after, as he had become something of an experienced hand on a boat, he landed a job as a guide for four American sportsmen interested in hunting and fishing along Lake Ontario. On this excursion, there was very little rum to drink, and by degrees, he recalls, he recovered his appetite, suggesting the extent to which his debouched lifestyle over the previous months had played havoc with his system and left him in a physically depleted state. The backwoods excursion helped restore his health, and with the assistance of his new employers, Apess seems to have, at some point, stepped off the boat and back onto American soil somewhere in the area of Oswego, New York.[3]

Using his earnings to purchase a new pair of shoes, Apess rededicated himself to the road home, some three hundred miles yet to travel and "a long journey to perform alone, and on foot," as he thought. But there were "friends" to be found along the way, many of whom proved willing to supply him with food, shelter, and assistance. The implication seems to be, once again, that he met with Native people on his journey who took him in and cared for him. He may have stopped at Oneida en route to Utica and visited with Pequot relations in Brothertown, where it seems likely his father and mother had once sojourned. It is interesting to think that, as fragmented by colonial violence as his family relations were, that still, even here, he probably had kin who would know his name and be happy to receive news of his adventures and whatever else he might impart of things back home.

Refusing to linger at any one place too long, however, Apess continued, following the course of the Mohawk River eastward along the old wampum trade routes. He found labor as a boatman on the Mohawk, allowing him to work off part of his passage. At times he "fell into company" again, as he called it, lapsing all too easily into bad habits he had acquired, and other times he was forced to beg from door to door. If there were friends to be found on certain legs of the journey, he also encountered prejudice and antipathy regarding his Indian identity and skin color, was treated cruelly at times, and felt compelled to remark on the dark underbelly of the so-called civilized world, which, even in peacetime, appeared to be driven by corruption, greed, violence, and other distinct markers of "the brute creation." He found cause to examine his own vengeful urges, his capacity for violence honed in the theater of war, but was able to check these passions. He summoned in their stead feelings of pity toward a people whose lives were closed shut to channels of human kindness and knew not the Native customs of hospitality and charity that had sustained him at other points in his travels. "A son of the forest would never stoop so low," he believed, as these wretches of the earth now encountered along the road.[4]

In Albany Apess stood witness while the body of a man who had been struck by lightning the day before was lowered into the ground. Drawn to the churchyard no doubt by the promise of shelter and perhaps a bite to eat, he was struck by the randomness of God's judgment, the frailty and happenstance of existence, and other mournful considerations that seemed to peal through him as he inwardly marked the tolling of the church bell. He was himself a wayward pilgrim with but the most precarious perch on life, facing yet another uncertain winter season and no assurance of welcome anywhere in the world. Perhaps he too easily identified with the stranger being laid beneath the turf. He had seen his share of death at that point, had witnessed the incalculable circumstances that swept off multitudes and yet left others standing unharmed fast beside without deference to rank, race, creed, or moral imperative. Continuing on from Albany, he wandered through the "pleasant" streets of Troy, New York, a town that was destined to open its arms to him in future years.[5]

Hesitant to return home with empty pockets, dressed in rags, and having made no account of himself in life, Apess halted his journey and took on work as a farmhand in time to help bring in that year's harvest. When the seasonal work ended, he crossed into Connecticut, following the course the great river cut through the landscape, winter fast on his heels. He turned nineteen among a group of unsavory companions he had fallen in with who spent their time in drink and in dance halls with promiscuous ladies. These companions persuaded Apess that he should take his chances on a whaling boat at sea as so many young Native men of New England before him had done.

An earlier "writing Indian," Joseph Johnson of Mohegan, had shipped out for a number of years on a whaling boat in the 1760s, and wrote in his journal of having been where "dangers were and great dangers too. . . . I have been Preserved on the mighty Waters, and have been kept safe from the rage of the great whales who obey his Voice."[6] Apess's own brothers and sons would lead whaling lives, whaling being one of the few steady jobs always available to Native men. And yet Apess was unable to secure a shipboard position in either Hartford or New Haven and so missed out on the opportunity to partake of the rigors, dangers, and, no doubt, overly romanticized glories of a life at sea.

Apess describes a difficult winter and generally hard times, but he seems to have remained determined not to return home in a state of desperation, drunkenness, or dependency. Perhaps he recalled the circumstances under which he had left his father, their last parting having been one tainted by an act of deception. What, if anything, did his family know of his fate following his running away from home, and in what condition could Apess hope to find his family now? Were they still in the same place he had left them, regardless of their tendency to travel "from river to river and from mountain to mountain"? Had they weathered the war years and the economic uncertainties that followed—uncertainties bound to afflict Native communities more than others? His previous homecomings had all been tentative affairs, fleeting moments of refuge before being tossed back out into the world. He could not count on simply playing the role of returning war hero. Apess's father had made it clear on a number of occasions that his eldest son could expect little in the way of assistance or nurture and would have to make his own way in life, regardless of what accomplishments he might have scored in the fields of martial glory. There would be few laurels upon which to rest.

Nevertheless, in the spring of 1817, Apess finally directed himself to the place of his early upbringing in southern Connecticut, apparently bypassing Colchester and making his way to Groton, the heart of Pequot country. He appeared before his small community like Lazarus called up from the tomb. On his arrival, he wrote, "My people looked at me as one risen from the dead. Not having heard from me since I left home, being more than four years, they thought I must certainly have died, and the days of mourning had almost passed. They were rejoiced to see me once more in the land of the living, and I was as equally rejoiced to find all my folks alive."[7] And so Apess was once again among his people.

Nothing in Apess's autobiographical works up to this point truly prepares one for the homecoming he claims to have received and the community of devout Natives with whom he now engages. Apess tells us that when he first took leave of his father and ran away to New York in 1813, it would be eight years before they would set eyes on each other again. This suggests that, at this point in his narrative, Apess's reunion with his father is still four years in the future. Apess also wrote that when his parents parted ways when he was but a child of four, it would be another twenty years before he ever saw his mother's face again. That meeting was therefore also some years off. The question then becomes, who exactly was it that rejoiced to see the young Apess risen from the dead? Who were these "folks" that, thinking him dead, had previously mourned for him? Perhaps his maternal grandparents could be counted among those who rejoiced to see him, despite their woeful treatment of him in years past. Or maybe his siblings remained in the region, still laboring under the oversight of wealthy white families. But this is the first time Apess allows us to apprehend something of the otherwise invisible extended kinship network within which he had evidently dwelt all along, even as an indentured servant living among the white families of his childhood.

As earlier noted, it is very difficult to identify with any certainty Apess's extended kinship networks, but we can make some inferences. A Eunice Apes still lived in Colchester in 1814, as evidenced by a letter held for her at the post office listed in the local *Gazette* for that year. In fact, it was in all probability Apess himself who sent her the letter from his barracks in Plattsburgh, whether or not she ever received it.[8] This same Eunice was living in Groton in the 1820s and was probably there when Apes returned. Given that she married in 1825, she was roughly Apess's age, give or take a year, and may have been the frail younger sister of whom he writes of being so sorely neglected as a child living in the shack of his grandparents. This sister passed the years in his absence as a bond servant in white households, where, as he would later write in *Indian Nullification of the Unconstitutional Laws of Massachusetts Relative to the Marshpee Tribe; Or, The Pretended Riot Explained,* she was treated more like a dog than a human being, "slavishly used and half-starved."[9] There was also the uncle, a Lemuel Ashbo, who had rescued him from the abuse of his grandparents, and a few other Apes women, such as Tyra and Polly, who in 1798 married Peter Gorge in the Separatist church in nearby Preston. This marriage links the Apes family to the George family that would prove to be such a powerful force on the reservation in the years to come.

The Pequot identity of the Georges had been contested some years earlier by the white overseer Samuel Mott, who reported in letters to both William Hillhouse and the Connecticut General Assembly that the Pequot "match and propagate with Negroes which makes us some trouble." To the white community, any claim to Native identity was compromised by intermixing with blacks, as this was perceived to detract from notions of racial purity. Mott claimed of his charges, "There is but few of the Tribe now Left. Except some who are aged and some Lame and Lost their Limbs, Some are Blind, so that there is now several who are an constant Expense for Boarding and for Doctoring from the rents of some lots that are let out yearly." Mott singles out two Indians, "Benjamin George and Peter George who all the tribe says does not belong." Overseers such as Mott (and Apess's former "master" William Williams), whatever their character, had extraordinary power to influence Pequot affairs to their advantage and to make life difficult for Pequot individuals who fell out of favor. Lurking behind Mott's indictments was undoubtedly a great deal of tribal unrest over the ongoing theft of land and timber and an overall sense that the overseers were turning a blind eye to these abuses—if not actively contributing to them. The Georges seemed to be agitating for new oversight even as Mott assured Connecticut officials, "The Tribe in General . . . are much against altering the overseers."[10]

In April of 1819, two years after Apess's homecoming, many of the Georges would sign their name to a petition stating that "the tribe of Mashuntoc Indian in Groton . . . are Disattfied with there overseer" and asking that someone else of their own choosing (specifically, a Captain Enos Morgan) be given the office. This petition not only speaks to the continuing tensions between the Georges and the Pequot overseer (which was William Williams at this time) but also reveals to a great extent the political and familial ties to which Apess became attached. Among the Georges who signed the petition were Peter and Polly (formerly Apes) George, as well as Anna Wampe (Anne Wampy) and her sister Betty. (Anne Wampy, as you may recall, was the old basket-seller who made such an impression on the town historian of Ledyard as, decades later, he reminisced of his childhood memories there. Wampy was a colorful local character who left a strong impression on those who came within her compass, including Apess himself.) Also attaching his name to the petition was one Jonathan Wood, who may have been a relation to Mary Wood, a woman with whom Apess soon became romantically involved and would marry in two year's time.

The Pequot petition concludes with a rhetorical flourish deserving of our attention: "This Indians [sic] prays that they may hold their possessions as long as wood grows and water runs." The phrase "as long as wood grows and water runs," or some variant thereof, has a long genealogy in the treaty-making history between the United States and sovereign Indian nations. In fact, it traces its roots all the way back to one of the first recorded treaties between the Dutch and the Haudenosaunee in Albany in 1613, and sealed the understanding that the two parties would be as "brothers" and share the resources of the land. As chronicled by Onondaga Chief Irving Powless Jr., the Native delegation in Albany "informed the Dutch people that we would put our record of this event in a wampum belt," as the Haudenosaunee were skeptical of the permanence of paper documents and wanted to ensure that the record of the treaty would last forever. "Forever," as Powless states, was

> described by our ancestors . . . in the following words: "As long as the grass is green, as long as the water flows downhill, and as long as the sun rises in the east and sets in the west." This is the first place that these words were spoken. Subsequently you hear them in movies, you hear them in various places. The United States used these actual words in some of the treaties that were made in the 1800s. But they were first spoken here by the Haudenos-aunee to show that we would make this treaty last forever. We did not think that your paper would survive the times.[11]

The Teiohâte Kaswenta, or two-row wampum, is, in fact, the only remaining record of the 1613 treaty, its parallel rows of purple wampum shells on a field of white meant to represent the two paths on which the Natives and the Europeans found themselves, one group in their canoe and the other in their boat of sails, separate but equal in their cultural journeys through the shared landscape.[12]

The word "forever" appears often in the old land transactions documented between New England Natives and colonists. In the original Algonquian (the language in which many of these written transactions are recorded and preserved), the word signifying this is *michime,* which, ironically given the historical outcome, appears more often than almost any other word in this troubled archive.[13] But the extended phrase "grass growing and water flow-ing" is often associated with later eighteenth-century removal policies among the Cherokee and Creek, this having been a phrase Andrew Jackson included in some of his infamous land grabs. I am not aware of it appearing anywhere, however, in the documented transactions between Natives and colonists of

New England.[14] Its presence here seems to be an improvised rhetorical twist, and suggests that Apess may have been the scribe of this particular petition.

Although basic literacy skills were more widespread among Native communities than is commonly believed, it still required a special level of competency to write for the tribe in an official capacity. Samson Occom, a few decades earlier, had often supplied this office among the Mohegans and other New England Natives, penning petitions, letters, and "what writings they wanted" as part of his overall advocacy for the tribes. Many of these documents in Occom's hand are still extant.[15] William Apess was one of only a handful of Natives in Groton at the time whose literacy skills, although still raw, approached this level and, as we will see, it is a role he would continue to fulfill for Native communities, looking to forward their appeals to resistant overseers. He might have had the opportunity to overhear this phrase "as long as wood grows and water runs" in his time among the Mohawks and other tribes of Canada. The curious use of pronouns in the short statement seems to suggest that the scribe, "this Indian," although Native himself, is not a member of the tribe, even though he wishes "they" might hold "their" land in perpetuity. Even more suggestive, however, is the ironic wordplay replacing "grass" with "wood," for, as Apess well knew, the illegal harvesting of wood was one of the major factors prompting the petition. This kind of verbal alteration will become a hallmark of Apess's literary style.

Apess would have been well positioned to pen this petition for his Pequot relations and would have felt an investment in the outcome. If he did not place his own signature on the petition, it may be because his tribal designation was uncertain, as was his legal designation as runaway or deserter. In fact, there is great irony in the notion that Apess may have penned the petition that pressured his former master, William Williams, into resigning his post, and this may suggest one more reason Apess left his name off the document. Either way, the written petition, coming out of the George faction of the Pequot community, may owe its very being to the fact that a literate Native was on hand to write it. If the wording does not show the mastery of the form that Apess would demonstrate in his later writings, he had ten years ahead of him yet to hone his skills and ply his art.

The communities that the Natives of the Northeast had managed to hold together after two hundred years of colonial turmoil were places greatly in need of such skills. As Apess would write some fourteen years later in his stinging indictment of white racism, "An Indian's Looking-Glass for the White Man," any casual visitor to an Indian reservation would be stunned by the appalling neglect, the scenes of "prodigality and prostitution" on display. "Let a gentleman and lady of integrity and respectability visit these places," he prodded. "As they wandered from one hut to the other they would view, with the females who are left alone, children half-starved and some almost naked as they came into the world . . . the females are left without protection, and are seduced by white men, and are finally left to be common prostitutes for them and to be destroyed by that burning, fiery curse, that has swept millions, both of red and white men, into the grave with sorrow and disgrace—rum."

As Apess went on to explain, the main reason for this vulnerable status was the lack of economic opportunity, blatant exploitation by the overseers, and a negation of basic civil rights among Native communities. The women were left unprotected because the most "sensible and active" men were at sea, making their perilous livings as whalers, which kept them from home for years at a time with no way, in the interim, of helping to supplement the incomes of those left behind. With no legal protection and no steady support, those who remained on the reservation were highly vulnerable and driven to eke out a living however they could, often manufacturing "a few little items such as baskets and brooms."[16] Many of the agents assigned to oversee and improve conditions on Indian lands (as a result of the politically dependent legal status of Natives) were themselves corrupt, unfaithful, and could care less "whether the Indians live or die." As such, Native communities were "much imposed upon by their neighbors, who have no principle. They would think it no crime to go upon Indian lands and cut and carry off their most valuable timber, or anything else they choose; and I doubt not but they think it clear gain."[17]

The nascent reform movement generated within these Native spaces of subjection and injustice achieved legitimacy through its connections to Christianity, and, with the men mostly absent, it was the women who formed the core of this community resistance. Sarah George, better known as Sally, became the spiritual leader of this small band, and she worked on young Apess, drawing him into her sphere of influence and ultimately into the Separatist flock. Sally George, like most other Natives of her community, had herself been a servant, working in the household of Hezekiah Park of Preston, Connecticut, in the 1790s. She was almost certainly exposed as a young girl to the teachings of Samson Occom, who made regular visits to the Park family a generation earlier. She acquired land through marriage to the Georges and eventually became comfortable enough to live off the rents she collected from white tenants.[18] Apess, although feeling it more pragmatic to throw in with the Methodists, was clearly drawn to Sally George's more informal Native-centered spiritual stylings. As he put it, she "meted out to my soul the sincere milk of the word, which gave me strength in the Lord to persevere."[19] George served as a surrogate mother for Apess and he came to emulate her political and spiritual stances, singled out, it seems, as the bearer of her legacy after she died. Although Apess downplays his local political entanglements in his earliest autobiographical writings, his mentorship at the hands of powerful Pequot women such as his Aunt Sally George, Anne Wampy, and others firmly locates Apess within a network of social and spiritual reform movements taking place on the reservations.

As much as being home brought the comfort of familial relations, spiritual community, and new political purpose to Apess's life, he continued to bear physical and emotional signs of the trauma with which he would do battle throughout his life. He sought out and found more or less steady seasonal employment, but he notes how he could scarcely eat and declares, "The anguish of my soul afflicted my body to such a degree that I was almost too weak to perform my labor. Sleep seldom visited my eyelids."[20] If he struggled to maintain steady habits and kept altogether from drinking, he still carried around with him his wartime scars, as well as what he felt to be an oppressive weight of shame as a result of behaviors he had picked up while in the military. As with many a veteran, the war continued to rage inside him long after the peace papers had been signed. To make matters worse, the farmhands with whom he labored were given to taunting him for his pious stances, taking the Lord's name in vain in his presence and committing other casual apostasies that apparently tried Apess's soul in this time of torment. He felt he had brought these oppressions upon himself, having become wretched with sin, and found himself filled to over brimming with despair. It suddenly seemed to him, in fact, that his situation was worse than it had ever been and "nothing but thick darkness gathered around me."[21]

It was while away from home, in the midst of all this torment and self-doubt, working such odd jobs as he could find, that Apess once again began attending Methodist meetings in earnest. The historian Karim Tiro observes that the ranks of Methodists in the first quarter of the nineteenth century "were still drawn primarily from the lower echelons of society, and they developed an enthusiastic, fervent religious style that contrasted most sharply with the rationalism of the orthodox Congregationalists and Presbyterians."[22] The Methodists privileged extemporaneous prayer over prepared performances, and were famous for their physically demonstrative style of address, an effluence of speech that poured directly from the heart, presumably infused with the grace of God, that worked powerfully on economically disadvantaged audiences, which were often illiterate and less staid in their devotions than the buttoned-up congregations of the more "respectable" classes. Methodism rejected the old Congregationalist notion of predestination and its chosen class of "Elect." It preached instead the more egalitarian notion that every individual contained the spark of "original grace," and that life was a gradual journey away from sin and toward salvation. Because of this vestige of original grace, every human had innate reason enough to see through the veil of man's fallen condition and to pursue a righteous path based on moral choices, using that small spark of Godly presence within as a guiding light to negotiate a world of sin. Methodism encouraged salvation as a process. The first step, as always, was to admit one's need for salvation and put one's self on the path to mercy.

Because it was anticipated that the individual would experience emotional fluctuations regarding such a commitment, a six-month trial period was advised, which Apess began that fall.[23] As part of that commitment, he attended a Methodist camp meeting, "astonished by their proceedings" and "charmed by their songs of praise."[24] The camp meeting was a staple of Methodism and usually consisted of anywhere from three to six days spent in the forest groves, with large gatherings from near and far sleeping in tents, sharing food, chanting hymns, and worshipping while the preachers stood raised above the crowd on their wooden platforms leading the throngs in sermon, prayer, and song. The Methodists typically had no meetinghouses of their own at this point. Their preachers were itinerants, known as "circuit riders," assigned to a particular district or region and preaching wherever they could find a pulpit—whether it be a private household, school, tavern, courthouse, barn—or as guest ministers in some other church. But the forests and groves where the camp meetings were held presented a more intimate sense of shared space that they could call their own for the duration of the meeting.

Services were typically announced by the blast of a bugle, with the congregation singing "Come hungry, come thirsty, come ragged, come bare, / Come filthy, come lousy, come just as you are."[25] Worship continued from the break of day until far into the night, when the multitudes became encircled by the light of a bonfire and raised their voices to the star-strewn heavens. As the editors of the *Christian Advocate* wrote in 1826, though many sincere Christians who had never tried it might criticize the efficacy of the camp meeting, "we have good reason to believe, that, to spend a few days in the year, in this way, is well pleasing in the sight of the Lord. . . . Leaving our worldly concerns behind us for a season, and retiring into the shades of the wilderness, we have a better opportunity to call to remembrance our sins and our transgressions."[26] Anticipating a note of early Emersonian philosophy, the passage continues, "In the stillness of the forest and in the retirement of Nature, it is well known from experience, that religious discourses often make the most lasting impressions on the human heart."

Apess recalled how at his first such meeting he was singled out and called on to pray. While endeavoring to do this, he feared "my words would choke me—the cold chills run over my body—my feelings were indescribably awful."[27] But as he overcame his great anxiety and cultivated his desire to please God rather than man, he found more and more that he had the strength of calling and could in fact summon up a fluid language of devotion. These

"Methodist Camp Meeting," 1836. *Harry T. Peters "America on Stone" Collection, National Museum of American History, Smithsonian Institution.*

experiences seemed to bring great comfort to Apess, as they had in his early childhood, enfolding him in a spirit of communal warmth and belonging that promised relief for his anguished condition.

American Methodism was officially founded in 1783 and became a vital force in America's early national period, its growth as an organization following directly on the heels of American expansionism. It held a particular appeal for fledgling communities on the so-called frontier but also appealed strongly to communities of eastern blacks and Natives who were either marginalized or shunned by the more traditional churches. The preachers themselves were characterized as rough types, often unschooled and not required to attend seminary on the path to ordination. As one early twentieth-century historian observed, the preachers were typically "ignorant men" and "graduates of 'Brush College' as they facetiously called the itinerant method of study. Their saddlebags contained their library, and whenever they could they studied."[28] Although it lacked brick-and-mortar infrastructure, the church spread through the marshaling of these mobile lay preachers, or circuit riders, who were sent out to cover the nooks and crannies of America's back settlements, spreading God's word to whites, blacks, and Indians alike. Their unstudied, enthusiastic style, favoring extemporaneous speech over prepared sermons, spoke powerfully to these audiences, who were all too often unschooled and illiterate themselves. Effective preaching was likely to have been accompanied by "weeping, shouting, loud praying, clapping of hands, and bodily motions," all of which pointed to the power of God working through the preacher.[29]

Although the church, by the 1830s, would begin to pivot away from such demonstrative displays, they were in all likelihood a part of Apess's repertoire when he worked the Watervliet, New York, circuit in 1828–29 and when he was later assigned to minister to the Pequot.

Circuit riders might travel fifty miles in one day by horse, mule, or on foot over rough roads and among rough people with little or no compensation beyond that which they could wring from the crowd. The early Methodist circuit rider Billy Hibbard claimed to have made only eight cents in the first quarter of his circuit but was happy with the outcome, crying "Blessed ar the poor!"[30] The preachers were not universally welcomed and were quite often reviled for their ostensibly inclusive racial doctrines, making them prone to persecution and harassment. The circuit rider Freeborn Garrettson, who would eventually introduce Methodism to the city of Providence in 1816, wrote of being "imprisoned, beaten twice, left on the highway speechless and senseless . . . once shot at, guns and pistols presented at my breast . . . surrounded frequently by mobs; stoned frequently."[31] Apess, in his later travels, would experience many like dangers, anxieties, threats, and wonders.

With their gesticulating and speaking in tongues, the upstart Methodists were often accused of merely riling up crowds and whipping them into a chaotic, rather than a religious, frenzy. One Episcopal minister, Edward Sharman, claiming to hold up a "looking-glass" in which the Methodists might view themselves, sneered that the "extreme yelling and screaming, those indecent gestures and tumbling topsey-turvy manifested at camp meetings, appear more like Indian powwowing, or the ravings of insanity, than imitating the meek and holy Jesus."[32] Nevertheless, Frederick Norwood, writing on the history of American Methodism, observes that, to the Methodist circuit rider, "the whole country was a vast field ripe for the harvest of souls," and the effort to reap this harvest could be likened to a "battle of souls on the frontier."[33]

Methodism prided itself, to a certain extent, on being nondoctrinaire. It outlined a process toward salvation while avoiding direct involvement in battles of orthodoxy, informing its preachers that they "had nothing to do but to save souls."[34] Methodism therefore had great appeal to someone in Apess's condition and initially presented rare opportunities for participation and advancement. When Apess returned to the Pequot reservation, however, after a season's labor, he found his small kinship network uninterested in officially classing themselves among this group. A portion of his family seemed indifferent to his spiritual calling. Others were simply content with Sally George, whose practice, if similar to Methodism on the face of it, always retained a level of autonomy that allowed for the insertion of Native spiritual leanings. Like the Methodists, George labored "to save souls," held meetings outdoors, spoke extemporaneously, and was probably every bit as physically demonstrative as the early Methodist circuit riders. Apess remarks that although she had not the skill to read or write, she could "almost preach," and she was "the handmaid of the Lord."[35] Apess's autobiography was, of course, written under the auspices of the Methodist Church, and I imagine the caveat that George could "almost preach" was added to appease Methodist orthodoxy, which, if more progressive than some other denominations, would still never have allowed a woman to become a licensed preacher.[36]

Despite Apess's apparent denominational woes, he reserves for Sally George more lavish praise than he confers on anyone else in his writings, singling her out as his one true mentor. Aunt Sally George, as he recalls, endeavored to "give me much instruction," and was a woman much admired, apparently, by both whites and Natives in the community.[37] She possessed what Apess referred to as an "organic power of communication," which, when tuned toward spiritual discourse, was "delightful, charming and eloquent," bringing her audiences to tears. Aside from being the spiritual leader of her community, Sally George also fulfilled the role of medicine woman in attending to the sick and was much in demand wherever she traveled. Like Anne Wampy, she was known to make her seasonal rounds—long journeys that took her on her own self-ordained circuit as both healer and exhorter. Apess, serving as her apprentice, recalls that he would have trouble keeping up with her on these occasions, as "her limbs would play as lively over the ground as a deer." But her home, of which as a widow she had sole ownership, was also known as a place of refuge where, in accordance with Native custom, all who came seeking shelter would be accommodated.[38]

Apess writes that he lived with his aunt through the winter of 1817–18 and had what he described as "very good times." Although this remains a silence in his narrative, he was undoubtedly courting Mary Wood at this time and she may already have been pregnant with their first child, William Elisha, even though their official church marriage was still a couple of years off. Wood seems to have been active in the Methodist Church prior to meeting Apess, and writes of being a camp-meeting enthusiast. I am inclined to believe that the two initially consummated their relationship at the Methodist camp meeting Apess first attended, and that his early interest in Methodism was fueled, at least in part, by his romantic prospects.

Whatever the case, this happy interlude continued, and he warmly recalls how Sally George held meetings every four weeks, "where God's children" gathered and people would attend from as far away as Rhode Island. In an intriguingly opaque passage that could be read as sympathetic to Methodist ideology or, conversely, as hinting at a syncretic style of worship enfolding various remnants of traditional Native spirituality, he notes that "the seasons were glorious. We observed particular forms, although we knew nothing

about the dead languages, except that the knowledge thereof was not necessary for us to serve God. We had no house of divine worship, and believing
'that the groves were God's first temples,' thither we would repair when the
weather permitted." The fact that Apess intersperses his recollection of Sally
George's meetings with lines from the popular nineteenth-century poet William Cullen Bryant suggests that he was becoming more comfortable in the
world of print literacy at the time of his writing this and again points toward
a certain sympathy with nascent tremors of transcendentalism. But more
importantly the passage highlights hidden currents of Native spirituality that
course like underground rivers through Apess's text, bubbling up in vibrant
prose from which his more attuned readers might drink.[39]

Apess concludes the above passage by observing how the Lord often met
with them in these groves, "and we were happy in spite of the devil." As in
the earlier passage in which the devil appears at Hell Gate in a stone canoe,
this strange invocation points to the veiled vocabulary Apess often employs
when skirting around the necessarily silenced topic of Native tradition. The
colonial mindset, of course, viewed Native spirituality as "devil's work," but
Apess seems to suggest it was a force that remained present at these meetings,
in spite of its fierce denigration by mainstream culture and the evil they projected on it. Barry O'Connell goes so far as to suppose that these meetings
were conducted largely in the Pequot language (not a "dead language," as was
often supposed), and that the "particular forms" in question contained "elements of Pequot spiritual traditions."[40] To speak openly of Native spirituality
was not permissible as an aspiring Methodist missionary and carried with it
unpopular political undertones. But Apess learned to wield his indigenous
"negative voice" in his writings to convey his desired meanings.

Apess would ultimately model his own mission on the one that his Aunt
Sally George set for him, attempting to emulate her emotionally compelling,
free, and organic style of address as well as her sense of Native advocacy. Even
so, he retained his footing among the Methodists. In the fall of 1818, he spoke
out for the first time in meeting, in a trembling voice, finding himself powerfully inspired to shepherd poor sinners into the flock. Whether it was the
example of Sally George or his usage among the Methodists that compelled
him to this action, he felt his voice lifted up and drawn from him, harnessed,
as it were, to the work of God. He may have found added inspiration in the
fact that, according to the town records of Preston, Connecticut, his second
child, Solomon Apes, was born earlier in the year. He attended his second
Methodist camp meeting that season, and shortly thereafter, in December of
1818, on what must have been a frigid day for dunking, he, along with three
others, was administered the ordinance of baptism by immersion at the hands
of a Reverend Mr. Barnes in the Yantic River at Bozrah, Connecticut.[41]

This moment represents Apess's rebirth within the Christian community. It was the completion, of sorts, of his spiritual rebirth in the wake of war that had begun with the Tyendinaga regeneration ceremony at the Lake on the Mountain in Ontario, proceeded through his returning home to his Pequot community, a Lazarus reborn, progressing onto his season of healing with Aunt Sally George, and now finding culmination within the Christian faith in this latest rebirth, of which he noted, "I was brought again from the dead to praise God."[42]

From this moment on, though still "weak and ignorant as to the letter" and regarded by the world at large "as a hissing stock and a byword" simply because he was born "a child of the forest," Apess determined his course, to carry the word of peace and love to whoever would hear it. Like the Peacemaker who had to confront the Tadodaho, a powerful wizard of the Onondaga whose mind was so crooked it sprouted snakes, Apess saw that he would soon enough find "men like adders, with poison under their tongues, hissing around me; and to this day, I find now and then one hissing at me [still]." But Apess's mission became focused on a rhetoric of peaceful rather than violent resistance. The light of truth appeared to shine on his path, offering its awakening power and launching him on yet another new journey. Before he could begin with a clean slate, however, he had one last quest to make, "a difficult place for me to reach, being a dark and winding way, through mire." The time had come for Apess to return to the place of his birth and at last reunite with his father.[43]

Return to Colrain

It is no small trek from Groton to Colrain, some one hundred and twenty miles straight up the Connecticut River valley through village, forest, field, and swamp. If Apess had friends, acquaintances, or Native brethren he might have lodged with along the way, he does not mention it, but he carried with him his certificate of standing with the Methodist church, and this may have afforded him room and board at certain stops. Although he had already started a small family of his own, he seems to have left them behind for the time being as he made his way north on foot. But in some measure, his new role as husband and father must have provided at least part of the impetus for his trip. He would return to his father a father himself.

Colrain was still just a minor dot on the map at this time, but it was less of a frontier town in 1819 than it had been in 1798, its hills now denuded of a great deal of forest and the town center below grown into a small industrial nucleus to the cluster of hill settlements that lay scattered about. Apess had not been back since the year of his birth, but his father had returned often, seeming to divide his time between Colrain and Colchester. As such, Apess would have had to ask directions of the locals when he finally arrived in "the neighborhood of my father's residence." Eager to make home, he determined to press on through the night, expecting to arrive unannounced in the pre-dawn hours like the prodigal returned.[44]

But having mistakenly turned off the road, he found himself suddenly engulfed in what was known to the locals as "the old dismal swamp of St. Peter's" with its "dense growth of pines and hidden marshy bogs."[45] He penetrated into this "labyrinth of darkness with hope of gaining the main road," believing he had heard a team of horses passing on the far side and persuading himself he had not strayed far off the beaten track. But as he pressed forward, "at every step I became more and more entangled—the thickness of the branches above me shut out the little light afforded by the stars, and to my horror I found that the further I went, the deeper the mire." Before long he apprehended himself in a desperate place, "shut out from the light of heaven—surrounded by appalling darkness—standing on uncertain ground—and having proceeded so far that to return, if possible, were as 'dangerous as to go over.' This was the hour of peril—I could not call for assistance on my fellow creatures; there was no mortal ear to listen to my cry. I was shut out from the world and did not know but that I should perish there, and my fate forever remain a mystery to my friends." Such a dire scene was likely familiar to many a Methodist circuit rider, and in this moment of doubt and horror, Apess turned his eyes upward to heaven, calling upon his faith to deliver him from the crisis.[46]

Critics have read this scene in Apess's autobiography as symbolic of his spiritual redemption, a kind of experiential as well as self-consciously literary (he goes so far as to paraphrase from Shakespeare's *Macbeth*) reaffirmation of his faith, coming as it does so closely on the heels of his baptism.[47] But it opens itself up to other layers of interpretation as well. Barry O'Connell reads Apess's "getting lost" as a moment of subtle irony, standing in contrast to literary productions of the day, such as James Fenimore Cooper's *The Last of the Mohicans,* which painted Indians as inveterate scouts and trackers perfectly at home in the dismal abodes of the deep forest. As such, the swamp passage serves not only "as a metaphor for his spiritual struggle for his Christian vocation but also as a commentary on all that had happened to actual Native Americans in the East who were lost from the sight of the dominant culture, lost from cultural consciousness, and also lost in terms of ancestral heritage."[48]

Still others, such as Jace Weaver and Ron Welburn, have wondered whether this passage doesn't actually relocate Apess, to some extent, within the framework of his Pequot heritage. Swamps were often viewed by Native communities of the Northeast as generative places abundant in important herbs, roots, and other materials sustaining to life. They were places of refuge during

"Western View of Coleraine," 1830s, with the Methodist church on the right.
Courtesy Henry N. Flynt Library of Historic Deerfield, Special Collections, folder no. 6, Miscellaneous.

wartime but also places of tragedy within the colonial tableau in which entire communities were hunted down and slaughtered without regard to mercy, Christian or otherwise. Swamps were also known, in Algonquian tradition, as home to mysterious forces, including the Little People, whose tendency to play tricks on the unsuspecting might have accounted for the sounds Apess first heard summoning him into the dark interior of the bog. As Welburn notes, the Little People "are acknowledged for using phosphorescence to lure unwary travelers from their paths . . . variously referred to as will-o'-the wisp, jack-o'-lantern lights, or foxfire."[49] Welburn sees Apess's journey into the swamp as contingent on these forces. He characterizes it as a "vision quest," an essential rite of passage for the young man. This crucial section in Apess's autobiography is not simply indicative of "his passage into a new and white religion, but into a state of mind preparing his commitment first to 'saving' the souls of his 'brethren' and, more importantly, to his learning to negotiate the images of Christianity in order to attack white hypocrisy."[50]

It is difficult not to regard the passage within its array of possible symbolic meanings, positioning Apess somewhere in-between worlds, or, as he suggests, "shut out from the world" entirely, in a space of liminality, with no solid ground upon which to stand. As in certain indigenous stories detailing how the world was made, he must seek outside assistance to restore order and place the world back on its proper footing. In one indigenous tale told by many in the Northeast, a woman fallen from the sky comes to rest upon the back of a turtle, which prevents her from sinking into the watery waste below. Requiring solid earth upon which to live and sow the seeds brought with her from the above world, she enlists the assistance of the sea creatures—the duck, otter, beaver, and muskrat among them, to scour earth from the water's bottom and bring it back to the surface. When the lowly muskrat succeeds in this effort, the woman is able to take this dollop of mud, spread it on the turtle's back, and, from so small an offering, constitute the world as we know it.

Apess, putting his trust in higher powers, makes his way from the swamp beginning with one "small piece of solid earth" upon which he can test his strength, and spreading out from there until the very world mended beneath him and he was released from peril. Homecomings were difficult for Apess. Before he could reunite with his family, he needed to reconstruct the universe to his new spiritual coordinates and be confident of his ability to stand on his own ground. The encircling watery waste having regained its solidity, he fell to his knees, thanking the master of the universe for this delivery, and reached "home" shortly after sunrise, finding his father well, and all his family rejoiced to see him.

According to the 1820 census for Franklin County, there were at least five people living in the Apes household at this time. Although most critics assume that Apess's parents were reunited, I suspect that his father had taken up with another woman with whom he had at least three other children, Mary Ann, Gilbert, and Griswold. Griswold, the youngest at five or six years of age, had been an infant when, years before, Apess had left his father's house in Colchester to become a soldier, but the others might very well have remembered him and "rejoiced" at his homecoming. It is also possible that Apess came into contact with his grandmother on his father's side for the first time while back in Colrain, learning from her stories of his Pequot lineage, including the notion, whether true or not, that he was descended from the seventeenth-century Wampanoag leader King Philip. Critics typically assume that Apess had little or no connection with his Pequot heritage, but his grandmother may have been the repository of a great deal of narrative and practical tradition.

While typically the census at this time was very particular about distinguishing Native Americans and blacks from whites (the 1820 census for Franklin County had a special column for "Slaves and Free Colored"), Apes's father is not listed under any special category. He was apparently able to pass for white, which further suggests he may have lived in the largely white community on Catamount Hill, managing to meld in to some extent. His trade is listed as "manufacture," which is to say, he was a shoemaker. Apess tells us, "I now agreed with my father to tarry with him all winter, and he agreed to learn me how to make shoes. In this new business I made some progress."[51]

We can trace a fairly good image of life in the backwoods of Colrain at this time from the first-hand reminiscences of certain residents, preserved by their late nineteenth-century descendants, and perhaps from this we may gather a sense of the lives of the Apes family. Dr. Davenport, a young "barefoot boy" in the 1820s, remembers living on Catamount Hill, among some fifty other families populating the hilltop, in a one-story wooden house separated into two rooms by a large chimney "eight foot square at the base with a brick oven on one side" and nothing but the earth itself for a floor. This was likely typical of other lodgings in Colrain as well. Most houses had some kind of earthen cellar in which fruits, vegetables, and pork were stored. Each household was its own place of manufacture for sundry goods such as brooms, butter, cheese, wax, wool, and clothing. Children on the hill would practice their letters and multiplication tables by firelight, learning to write on tablets made of birch bark and quills cut from hen feathers. They manufactured their own thick black ink by boiling together the resins of different kinds of bark.

Of course, some of the dwellers on the hill were not as well off as others, and Davenport recalls how at one time a neighbor's boy came to the house and peeked his head through the door, saying, "Us wants some butter." Davenport also recalls how a shoemaker was "hired, who came to the house with his lasts, bench and kit, and took measures of the feet, and shod up the family for the winter's campaign." We might read the experiences of Apess's family into such reminiscences and the shoemaker referenced may very well have been Apess's own father.[52]

Although Apess's father had joined with the Baptist Church, Catamount Hill became the center of a small Methodist community "firmly united to each other" and referring to itself as the Methodist Reformed Church of Colrain. They were recalled as "a strange denomination that preached in the open air." According to one town historian, they "did not believe that buildings were necessary for their purpose. Meetings were held in groves, caves and barns. The Hill meetings were held at the Oven Den and in the newly erected school house." At the time Apess was living in Colrain, Pardon Haynes, a country doctor from nearby Rowe, was the circuit rider appointed by the Methodist Conference in Troy, New York. James Covel may have been another rider appointed to the district. The so-called Oven (or sometimes "Devil's Oven") is a sort of small natural amphitheater, centrally located on the hill, and must have provided a romantic backdrop for outdoor meetings, with its natural pulpit, nearby spring, and a cave hollowed out in the rock in which the large felines for which the hill was named apparently once dwelt. The Oven was located about a mile down the road from where the Apes family most likely lived, and Apess, who reports that he was actively attending meetings at this point, would have had many an opportunity to exhort on this spot. As he recalls, "I cast in my lot with this small band and had many precious seasons."[53]

Apess writes, "While in Colrain the Lord moved upon my heart in a peculiarly powerful manner, and by it I was led to believe that I was called upon to preach the Gospel of our Lord and Savior Jesus Christ."[54] This determination was not reached without great soul-searching, periods of prolonged self-doubt, and a recognition by Apess himself that "I was nothing but a poor ignorant Indian" who was likely to be despised and ignored by white congregants. But clearly Apess received some sort of encouragement from the local Methodist organization, either because they recognized his rhetorical abilities or because they saw some merit in cultivating the powers of an Indian exhorter who might prove a novelty and crowd pleaser.[55]

From this point on, realizing that he was "weak and ignorant as to the letter," Apess began his study of scripture in full measure. If in his private moments he suffered through torrents of pained self-doubt, in the evening meetings he would suddenly find his voice infused with Godly power and he would speak unabashedly, "exhorting sinners to repentance and striving to comfort the saints." He spoke with a kind of other-worldly fervor, in a trance or spell, the words rushing forth from the floodgates of his heart. In his dreams, however, Apess returned to the dreaded swamp, finding himself lost once more in the mire, paralyzed with fear and uncertainty. But if these dreams spoke of hidden terrors and doubts, they also offered him assurances that he must continue on his perilous path. In one dream, as he struggled through the darkness, attaining at last the refuge of a sun-drenched plain, an angel appeared before him and, blocking his progress, held discourse with him, offering at last words of direct scripture from the Gospel of John concerning the word of life. By publishing this dream visitation to the world, Apess was, in fact, claiming a direct connection to the fountains of truth and authorizing his own ability to preach the gospel. He was also responding to traditional Native practice that placed a great deal of reliance on the power of dreams. He writes that he was encouraged by this angel to persevere.[56]

Seeking an opportunity to exercise his calling, Apess was able to secure an appointment for a meeting to take place at the home of a "friend" whose advice he had sought on the subject. As Apess relates it, there arose some confusion regarding his authority to appear in such a manner, although, as he well knew, Aunt Sally George had never waited on any such authority. Apess's unnamed friend apparently advertised Apess's appearance as a "sermon" rather than the more appropriate "exhortation." This distinction speaks to the various stages of accreditation within the Methodist organization. Following proper procedure, anyone who wished to preach would first have to act for a period of time as a class leader, then be promoted to exhorter with the ability to hold meetings in the absence of a preacher; from there one might be appointed preacher—or, more significantly from the Methodist's standpoint, circuit rider.

Given that circuit riders often had a great deal of ground to cover, in places such as Colrain, far off the beaten path and lacking institutionalized structure and memory, their visits were probably infrequent, and the governing rules of the larger organization were no doubt loosely followed. Apess, in fact, met none of the criteria to stand before a crowd and lecture in the name of the church. His own reading of scripture, however, assured him that, in biblical times, holy men and prophets "spoke as they were moved by the holy ghost." Apess believed this was all the validity one required to preach the word of God, and felt he had been given sufficient light to proceed.[57]

On the appointed day he found the congregation so large that it became necessary to move the meeting down the road to the schoolhouse. As a result of this, we can make a fairly good guess as to the location of Apess's first delivered "sermon." The schoolhouse on Catamount Hill has remained a Colrain landmark due to local tradition which remembers it as the first school building to raise the American flag over its roof at the start of the War of 1812. While the original structure commemorated as such burned down sometime around 1815, another schoolhouse was quickly erected on the same spot, and it was in this building that Apess most likely preached, with its long wooden benches ranged around the room and a fire crackling in the large fireplace at the far end.

It was not uncommon in the nineteenth century, especially in just such a hilltop settlement, for people to come out to hear a sermon regardless of denomination. The local historians tell of the many old personages who "preached with power" at the schoolhouse, "not to empty seats, but a crowded house; eager listeners who came from the hillsides and valleys below to listen to the Word."[58] Although an honor roll of names is offered of such speakers— Stearns, Myers, Strong, Wolcott—all noted for their powerful oratory and Godly administrations in this place, Apess, their most famous preacher, is never counted among them. Nevertheless, he seems to have packed the house that evening. When Apess entered the small structure, he found every eye fixed on him. Managing to choke down his nerves to some extent, he powered through his sermon, lips quivering, knees shaking. Apparently the locals approved, but they also quickly spread the word abroad of the curiosity in their midst, and when Apess was asked to preach again in the same spot a short time later, he returned to find "a great concourse of people who had come out to hear the Indian preach."[59]

It had been a primary concern of the original New England colonists to "come over and help" the poor heathen, who, in the language of the Puritans, had "long sat in hellish darkness," by converting them to Christianity, whether they desired it or not. Their failure to achieve this goal through peaceable means remains a compelling mark against their endeavor and calls into question the sincerity of their claims. Here, however, was the spectacle of the Indian standing before the white congregation and presuming to exhort them on the status of their souls. It was a rare spectacle, and one that was as likely to provoke ridicule and hostility as pious attention.

As Apess launched into his second sermon, the crowd began to unleash a torrent of abuse, hurling sticks and other objects at him. Perhaps he had anticipated such a response. It was not entirely unusual for Methodists to be reviled and persecuted, as they had been in Colchester in Apess's youth. But the added affront of his being an "Indian Preacher" almost assuredly provoked the crowd to greater abuse. Still, Apess persevered, defying the audience with his controlled yet energetic manner, and with his text of avoiding the temptations that fall in one's path. Who knew better of this than the preacher himself? Still, as he observed afterward, no Native audience would ever have treated a speaker in such a manner, and he bemoaned the thousands of immortal souls who knew no better and were now "sitting in darkness" themselves. One wonders if the readers of his autobiography picked up on the sly reversal, in which it was the Native son of the forest now "come over to help" the white settlers lift themselves out of their benighted state. Whatever his audience might have initially expected from the Indian Preacher, he could well note afterward that "the sons of night were confused" by his performance.[60]

If crowds were riled up by Apess's preaching, it seems that he also continued to be a draw. He began preaching throughout the community of northwestern Massachusetts, visiting parishes in Greenfield and elsewhere. He would sometimes preach twice a day, preparing nothing formal for these events but trusting in the spirit and his own charismatic presence to carry the day. He often wrung tears from the repentant sinners in the crowd and vocal praise from the faithful. But his preaching, however successful, soon got him in trouble with the Methodist organization, and following the appointment of a new "elder" to his district, Apess was censured by the church. He also had a falling-out with his father, who was apparently getting pushback from the community regarding his son overstepping his bounds. But Apess could not be induced to "sheath his sword." This notion that no person of God must preach His word unless ordained by man carried little weight with Apess.[61]

Eulogy on Aunt Sally George

Apess left the Methodists at Colrain for the time being and returned again to his "first love," the Pequots of Connecticut. He continued to preach where he could find a congregation, mostly among "colored people," and no doubt he furthered his apprenticeship with Aunt Sally George, who continued to wield God's word without authorization from man or church. He made ends meet by plying the cobbler's trade, learned from his father, and he went on, a mender of souls, traveling throughout southern Connecticut, honing his skills as an unlicensed itinerant preacher. Although, as mentioned earlier, he allows no reference to any kind of romance or courtship, we learn that on December 16, 1821, precisely three years after his baptism, Apess was married to Mary Wood of Salem, Connecticut—a "woman of nearly the same color as myself"—and for a short time Apess could claim that he got along "prosperously."[62]

Mary Wood was born in Lyme, Connecticut, on January 3, 1788. She records in her own autobiographical sketch, found in Apess's *The Experiences of Five Christian Indians of the Pequot Tribe,* that her mother was English and her father "a descendant of the Spanish islands or a Native of Spain." Her family may have been in some manner associated with the Pequot tribe, as she informs us that the Wood family name was taken from her mother's side, "the Woods family of Lyme," and not her father's.[63] The birth records of Apess's children suggest that he met Mary Wood a few years before marrying her. From her short account and other glancing references, there is reason to believe she was involved with the tight circle of people who worshipped with Aunt Sally George and may have been among those welcoming Apess when he returned from war in 1817.

Wood's father died when she was young, and, like Apess and "all other fatherless children," she was placed out as an indentured servant in the home of a white family characterized as proud, haughty, and impious.[64] Her memories are clouded by the abuse and neglect she suffered under these circumstances, and she laments, "How much little children have to undergo, who are fatherless and motherless in the world. . . . How much I wanted a tender, and affectionate, and pious mother to take me by the hand and instruct me, or some pious friend. How much good it would have done to me; but I had none but a wicked and unholy tyrant to discourage me."[65] Like Apess, she found her way to Methodism through a number of fits and starts, but ultimately sought solace and support within the arms of the church, which she came to view as a surrogate family to replace the systematically fractured kinship networks of her youth. Her connection to the church grew strong, and she probably had a role to play in drawing Apess toward Methodism.

Now a husband and father himself, Apess confronted many of the uncertainties and anxieties his own father had faced. To support his family he frequently had to seek labor elsewhere, traveling from town to town, holding down seasonal work and other positions that always seemed to terminate after a month or two. He set up shop as a cobbler for a short while in Middletown,

Connecticut, but could not make ends meet. It is likely that within the Methodist organization there were attempts to help establish congregants in their trades and to patronize one another, but the Methodists in general had little economic clout, and Apess often found his best endeavors foiled by ill treatment, false claims, and other countless minor abuses that worked in silent concert to prevent Natives from trafficking within the networks of white commerce. Forced from self-employment, he took to being a tavern keeper, a farm hand, and an odd jobber, traveling as far off as Gloucester, Massachusetts, that year in search of work and forwarding his wages along to his wife.

In the very same paragraph in which he tells of his marriage, he relates, "I prayed that my family might not suffer, as I knew that they were innocent, and my little ones too small to help themselves." This partially suggests what the town records confirm—that Apess already had at least two children at this point, William and Solomon. A third, Leonard, was born on December 30, 1820, but, despite Apess's efforts and prayers, the child died before his first birthday. This would have been, in fact, one month before Apess and Wood were actually married, and so their little family was already touched by grief before the couple ever even took their official vows. It is also quite possible that Wood, who was ten years Apess's senior, had at least one child from a previous marriage, and so there were multiple mouths to feed. On March 4, 1822, Abby Ann Apes was born in Colrain, most likely in Apess's absence. Just as Apess, as a child, had been forced to live with his grandparents, so it seems that Mary, in a time of travail, took up with Apess's family in Colrain. Perhaps Apess's paternal Pequot grandmother was on hand to serve as midwife.

To save money for his growing family, Apess remarks that he negotiated extra wages by abstaining from the traditional half pint of spirits many employers doled out to their workers during harvest. His motto at this point was "Touch not, taste not, handle not," and although he was ridiculed by the other hands, it afforded him "a sum sufficient to buy my poor dear children some clothes."[66] Through steady labor, pious observance, and temperate habits, Apess began to feel rising reservoirs of strength, and, for the first time, perhaps, in memory, he could finally report, "My mind was calm."[67] On December 4, 1823, Sally George Apes was born in Colrain—named, of course, after Aunt Sally George—and in 1824 a fifth child, taking the name of his departed infant brother, Leonard, was born, his birth recorded in the town records of neighboring Leyden, Massachusetts. Apess had noted that he spent "many precious seasons" in the area of Colrain, and it was, in turn, the place that formed the earliest memories of his own children.[68]

On May 6, 1824, Aunt Sally George died. She was only forty-five years old, and her death must have had a profound effect on Apess, whether or not he was on hand to witness it. Apess seems to have already, at this point, entertained some thoughts of compiling for publication a series of written testimonies involving Indian conversion to Christianity. Perhaps he saw the market potential of such a tract, in keeping as it was with a long and complicated tradition of colonial publications involving Indian converts. And perhaps, as a Native himself, he could do justice to the cultural and economic complexity of these conversions in ways that colonial writers of the past could not. With this in mind, he had apparently taken the time to gather Sally George's personal testimony prior to her death. Although it is only a few pages in length, it offers revealing details of her life and her complex relationship with Christianity.

George was born in Groton, Connecticut, in 1779, and although she labored as a young woman with the family of the reformist minister Paul Park, she apparently was not afforded the improvements of education that were supposed to come with indenture. Lacking proper instruction, George as a young girl was often led astray by her acquaintances, but she speaks of receiving "good advice from those who were mothers of Israel," by whom she meant other Pequot women who were her "own kin." This passage in her testimony subtly speaks to the network of women within the tribe who sought to maintain the spiritual balance of the community, often performing this function with "streaming eyes and melted hearts." Sally George was not an anomaly as a female spiritual leader to the tribe, but one who carried on existing traditions at a time when men were frequently absent in search of work or rendered incapable of furthering such goals by decades of colonial degradation and emasculation.

George's conversion to Christianity occurred amid the kind of overwhelming doubt and torment one comes to expect from the spiritual discourse of the day, but it retains as well certain elements peculiar to Native conversion narratives, with their many inverted references and veiled critiques of colonialism. She observes how, as she "wandered up and down in the forest," the "enemy" of her soul would take advantage of her youthful mind, suggesting there could be no happiness for her in life. This enemy "followed hard after me and withal tempted me to destroy myself." She became a "wanderer alone, as it were, in my native woods," and it was here, by a deep brook in the forest, that rather than take her own life she gave herself up to a higher power, and by the "washing of regeneration and renewing of the Holy Ghost" her soul was ultimately bathed in the love of God and she was "translated" into the kingdom of heaven.[69]

George's curious evocation of a condition of transience—wandering "to and fro, up and down the forest"—was in some ways common in describing Native peoples of New England, although, in fact, they were not nomadic, nor did they live in the forests.[70] The phrase seems to have been designed to suggest the restless state of indigenous souls in their heathen condition, and echoed passages from Job in which God's messenger, Satan, speaks of "going to and fro in the earth and from walking up and down in it" (Job 1:7, 2:2). But when Native people such as Sally George use it to invoke their own state, it takes on a crucial difference, in some ways embracing the intended critique and subverting it to new purposes. The Mohegan preacher Samson Occom, who often visited Groton in George's childhood, also drew from this scriptural reference in his autobiographical sketch, remarking of his people that "they led a wandering Life up and down in the Wilderness, for my Father was a great Hunter, thus I liv'd with them, till I was Sixteen years old."[71] If George's rebirth occurs within the framework of Christian salvation rhetoric, she is also careful to allow that it occurs within her Native woods, at a traditional site of spiritual power and renewal, where she seems to preside over her own baptism. Her wanderings up and down and to and fro move her along these lines of power, and she returns home to her friends to exhort her young mates to repentance.[72]

As Apess testified, Sally George could never speak before a congregation without the entire gathering being "watered by an overwhelming flood of tears." Her language was "free and lively and animating." She styled herself a member of the Free-Will Baptist Church, but Apess assured his readers that, like himself, "she was no sectarian" but "would go among all orders of Christians and worship God with them, *and was entirely free to do so.*"[73] She was well beloved and mourned by both Natives and whites, who in the end afforded her the dubious honor of allowing her to be interred in the white cemetery. In Apess's recollection she had never known "a barren season to her soul" and "was always diligent to seek Jesus in the way. The fences, the groves, the forest." All might witness to the fact, he proclaimed, although if not for his testimony we might never have known it. He closed his eulogy with some lines from Isaac Watts's "Funeral Hymn" and beseeched his readers to "strive to meet her there" in her place of heavenly rest. "Her name was Sally George, and she was deservedly esteemed for her piety."[74]

William Apess: Circuit Rider

Sometime in the summer of 1824 Apess moved to Providence, Rhode Island, where he had a sister who was "very kind" to him. It may be this was Mary Ann Apes, born in 1805 when Apess was bound out to the Furmans, or perhaps it was Eunice, who I presume to be his closest younger sister. He had earlier mentioned that people came from as far off as Providence to attend Aunt Sally George's camp meetings, and this sister was most likely associated with that tight circle of friends and brethren moving within the margins of the Methodist church but still equally attached to the social and cultural ritual of George's gatherings. Providence, Rhode Island, and New London, Connecticut, were both joined to the same circuit at this time, so Apess had most likely forged connections in the church linking him to both cities. The Methodists had been able to make successful inroads in Providence so that by 1820 a second meetinghouse was erected on the corner of Chestnut and Clifford Streets.

As usual, whether by accident or design, Apess seems to have placed himself in the center of controversy as, by the autumn of 1824, Providence was in the throes of racial unrest resulting in what is known as the Hardscrabble Riot. The riot apparently broke out when a number of black men failed to show deference to a group of whites on the sidewalk by refusing to step aside and offer the right-of-way. This would have been in violation of unwritten, but strictly observed, nineteenth-century codes regarding the racial hierarchy of New England's public spaces, and suggests the precarious rituals people of color were forced to observe as they strove for middle-class respectability in urban spheres that refused to recognize them as equals. The next evening local whites pounced on this opportunity of perceived social overreach to converge on the Hardscrabble District, where many in the black community lived. They proceeded to burn, loot, and destroy property throughout the neighborhood, terrorizing the residents while upward of a thousand white onlookers gathered to cheer on the proceedings.

According to the historian John Wood Sweet, far from being an isolated incident, the 1824 riot was the "brutal harbinger of a trend toward widespread antiblack violence in the antebellum North, a crucial turning point in race relations as the regions last slaves were becoming free."[75] Although a number of the whites involved in this act of terror were subsequently tried, not one was convicted. A Nathaniel Metcalf was, in fact, found guilty of "riot" (a charge for which Apess himself would later do jail time) but was deemed mentally unfit to face charges.[76] Apess would have to negotiate these volatile racial tensions as he spent the next six months working, exhorting, and adding souls to the Methodist Church's rolls.

After five months in Providence, Apess summoned his family to come live with him. Because a city statute required a registry be kept of all "strangers" boarding in Providence, we find that Apess lived in the Hardscrabble District, listed as a "Colloured man" from Connecticut, along with his wife and two children, supporting himself by following "trucking for a living."[77] Whatever he may or may not have "trucked" (most likely he sold books for the Methodist concern), he would spend two full years performing the role of class leader connected to the Chestnut Street church.

The "class meeting" structure had been implemented by the Methodists to

ensure an informed and disciplined congregation in the absence of permanent preachers. New converts to the church were to undergo a six-month trial
period, and class meetings, held weekly under the guidance of an appointed
leader, helped to keep new recruits connected to the larger community of
congregants.[78] Class leaders were appointed by the presiding minister, which
in Providence at this time was Daniel Webb. Webb most likely saw the efficacy of appointing a person of color to preside over his growing black and
Indian congregation, and Apess seems to owe his footing in the church to
Webb's sponsorship. Apess was responsible for thirty or more class members
and would lead them in Bible study, prayer, testimony, and the tenets of
church discipline.

As one nineteenth-century account of a Methodist class meeting records,
"The [class] leader . . . opened the speaking exercises by relating a portion
of his own experience, in which he spoke feelingly of the goodness of God
to his soul." Such rehearsed performances over time would have afforded
Apess the opportunity to hone the finer points of his own Christian conversion narrative and provided him with the materials for a first draft of his
autobiographical writings. The account of the meeting continues, "After this
he [the class leader] spoke to the rest in order, inquiring into their spiritual
prosperity; addressing to them such language of instruction, encouragement,
or reproof, as their spiritual states seemed to require. It was a time of profound and powerful feeling; every soul seemed to be engaged in the work
of salvation. I was astonished beyond all expression. Instead of the ranting,
incoherent declarations which I had been told they made on such occasions,
I never heard more plain, simple, Scriptural, common-sense, yet eloquent
views of Christian experience expressed in my life."[79]

In 1826, Brother Webb was replaced as circuit rider by Asa Kent. Kent was
known as an "uncompromising disciplinarian" who performed his duty without regard to friend or foe, and many apparently found his methods to be
"exceedingly severe."[80] He had, however, been appointed to New London on
and off throughout his career, so it is possible that he and Apess had a long-
standing acquaintanceship.[81] Nevertheless, when at the end of his second
year as teacher Apess finally applied for an exhorter's license, he was opposed
by certain members of the congregation, Brother Kent most likely among
them. As Apess tells it, the discord arising over his candidacy nearly split the
congregation.

At this time there were some thirty-seven "colored" members in the church
at Providence, making up about a sixth of the total congregation. Apess
seems to have been responsible for all thirty-seven of them (he describes his
class as consisting of "about thirty in number"), and this provided him some
clout in his bid for a license. Surely racial tensions were still running high

in Providence, and as Apess noted, "a division had like to have been the consequence of withholding it from me."[82] Echoing the language of Aunt Sally George, he wryly commented on how "many a severe combat have I had with the *enemy* respecting my competency."[83] Here and elsewhere it is extremely unclear whether the "enemy" is the devil or the white power structure that obstructed his advancement and confounded the aspirations of people of color everywhere, often rendering their lives a misery. In the end he was awarded the title of exhorter, the penultimate step on the road to becoming a circuit-riding preacher, and he began traveling "from place to place, improving my gift."[84]

To defray the costs of travel associated with being an itinerant exhorter, Apess now added bookseller to his list of professions. It wasn't uncommon for itinerant ministers to sell books, and it often afforded them the opportunity to circulate their own pamphlets and tracts as well. Mason Weems, the man responsible for immortalizing the story of George Washington and the cherry tree among other noteworthy national fables, was both traveling minister and bookseller, and he used his firsthand knowledge of popular tastes based on book sales to inform his topics for writing. Aside from his 1800 publication of *The Life and Memorable Actions of George Washington,* Weems published little tracts of popular interest such as his 1812 *The Drunkard's Looking Glass* and his 1823 *The Bad Wife's Looking Glass.* As he wrote to his publisher, Matthew Cary, "Experience has taught me that small, i.e. quarter of dollar books, on subjects calculated to *strike* the Popular Curiosity, printed in very large numbers and properly *distributed,* wd prove an immense revenue to the prudent and industrious Undertakers."[85]

One of the reasons the Methodists were so successful in this period was because they capitalized on new paper-production and printing technologies that allowed for the proliferation of such inexpensive tracts, propaganda, and—most important for their purposes—hymnals. Ironically, given their abhorrence of the written sermon, the Methodists, according to Karim Tiro, "simply managed to out-publish their more orthodox opponents."[86] Apess writes that he had "some success in selling my books and made enough to support my little family and defray my necessary traveling expenses. So I concluded to travel, and the Lord went with me."[87]

The enumeration of cities and towns that follows, all of which Apess visited in the space of two or three seasons of travel, is staggering to consider. He traveled from Providence to New London to Montauk on Long Island, treading in the footsteps of Samson Occom and following traditional seasonal subsistence routes that the Pequot and Mohegan had long traversed. Next he returned to New York City, where he had been conscripted into the army so many years earlier, and probably visited the Methodist printing house on

Cherry Street (where he once lived) to pick up books and perhaps solicit interest in his own narrative which would be published from this office in 1829. From there Apess traveled up the Hudson to Albany, "where the lord poured out his spirit in a powerful manner," then to Boston, New Bedford, Martha's Vineyard, Salem, Newburyport, and Portland, Maine.[88] He preached "wherever a door was opened" and found that "being a native, the people were willing to receive me." In other words, when he could advertise himself as the "Indian Preacher" he was sure to draw a crowd. Interspersed with his travels were quick visits "home"—whether that was in Providence, Colrain, or elsewhere at this point. He notes the difficulty of travel and the heartache accompanying such long absences from his family. But he also remarks that it "was good to be afflicted," believing as he did that his work was for the greater benefit of all.[89]

When the quarter conference came around in 1828, Apess went up for his preaching license but was denied. He had run into conflict with a Brother Foster in Newburyport, Massachusetts, who was apparently unwilling to be schooled on points of doctrine from an Indian. This misunderstanding resulted in the church fathers hearing "evil reports" of Apess, and rather than receiving his license, Apess was asked to improve upon the Watervliet circuit west of Albany, New York. The regional circuit rider at this time was James Covel Jr., son of James Covel, who now presided over the New York Methodist conference. Traveling as far west as Bath, through Utica, Troy, and back to Albany, Apess revisited old haunts from his postwar wanderings. This portion of the world had been immeasurably transformed with the completion of the Erie Canal, bringing in a flood of white settlement and commerce, resulting in the transplanting of more indigenous communities. Still, it is likely that Apess visited old Native "friends" at Brothertown, Oneida, and elsewhere. He spoke of holding lively meetings with congregations of both white and "colored people" and finding souls eager for conversion. As he noted, "Crowds flocked out, some to *hear* the truth and others to *see* the 'Indian.' "[90] But either way he met with great success, and his evangelical efforts were greeted with tears and other appropriately pious outpourings.

It cannot be said with certainty what type of sermons—or more precisely, exhortations—Apess delivered at this time. Perhaps he drew inspiration from the moment and, as the traditional Methodist circuit riders were wont to do, simply located a suitable scriptural passage to spark a topic and, like ice in a skillet, skated extemporaneously along its own melting. He found the reading of prewritten sermons, to quote from Corinthians, to be "like an empty sound and a tinkling cymbal."[91] Nevertheless, he would have had recurring themes, passages, and rehearsed bits that he could tap into at will, and the few existing accounts of his performative style suggest that he was a forceful and charismatic speaker. Apess published only one traditional sermon in his lifetime, *The Increase of the Kingdom of Christ,* appearing in 1831, and it offers some indication of his preaching style. *Kingdom of Christ* is Apess's most conventional and, as Barry O'Connell observes, his most "regressive" tract.[92] The timing of its publication suggests that he prepared this sermon for his ordination and therefore hewed closely to the expectations of the church hierarchy, some of whom would have been in attendance for the performance. But the sermon probably echoed many themes that he took with him on the circuit, and despite its conformity to certain dominant white frameworks, it contains interesting allusions to Native spirituality and agency.

Apess had always drawn inspiration from the Gospel of John, and the title of his sermon was taken from John 3:30: "He must increase." John tells of John the Baptist, the "mighty prophet of the wilderness," who seems to have rendered his own messianic urges subordinate to those of the Christ whom he baptizes. The regressive aspects of the sermon built on the theme that John the Baptist's *race* "should wane away before a [one] greater than himself." Such language closely paralleled language often trotted out concerning nineteenth-century Indians, who were viewed as an inferior and perishable race "melting away like dewdrops in the morning sun."[93] This goes against every rhetorical stance Apess would make in his publishing career and begs the question of whether or not the text was editorially enhanced at some point in the production. Liberties may have been taken in bringing the sermon to press and items inserted without Apess's approval. Still, this was language that would have met with tacit acceptance by almost any nineteenth-century audience and even today would raise few eyebrows.

But the sermon, taken as a whole, contains a number of powerful passages, and when one peels away the cursory layer of dominant platitudes there emerges a surprising superstructure of indigenous advocacy and belief. This "prophet of the wilderness" of whom Apess speaks bears more than passing resemblance to that other prophet of the wilderness, the Haudenosaunee Peacemaker who came among the Five Nations aboard his stone canoe and, along with Hiawatha, put in place a ceremonial structure that brought an end to the continuous cycles of war that had ravaged the people. By creating wampum, initiating the condolence ceremony, and burying the weapons of war underground ("burying the hatchet" in contemporary parlance) and in that spot planting the great world tree from which spring the white roots of peace, these indigenous prophets ended generations of senseless feuding and laid the foundation for an enduring civic structure. If to a certain extent all religious narratives are likely to have compelling similarities and moments of narrative intersection, Apess's language appears calculated to exploit these moments of intersection rather than simply stumble over them. Of the new age he predicts is coming, he writes, "The axe is laid at the root of the tree of human corruption, and the tall branches of pride and avarice, and lust and cruelty, wither, and in their place spring up the trees of Paradise, loaded with the fruits of the spirit. . . . Large communities, long disturbed by quarrels and wars, strangely forget to fight and live in gentleness and peace."[94]

Just months earlier, Apess had traveled through the lands of Mohawk, Oneida, and Onondaga as circuit rider in training, spreading his own syncretic brand of Christian rhetoric. It would not be surprising if the generative powers of these indigenous belief systems were freshly planted in his thoughts when he committed this particular sermon to writing. But it was nothing new to him. There is a strong chance that he had, long before in Fort Niagara, witnessed the way that the narrative structure of Haudenosuanee belief systems insinuated themselves into their diplomatic procedures on the world and national stage. He had been to the birthplace of the Peacemaker, partaken in the ritual structure of the spring renewal ceremonies at the Lake on the Mountain, and stood at the very spot where the Peacemaker is said to have begun his mission of peace, drinking deeply of those waters. In Apess's sermon he writes (and we must imagine that he spoke these words before the Methodist conference committee members and their congregation as well), "It is a blessed thing to stand on some of the great landmarks of time and be able to look back on a long line of prophecy fulfilled." We can forgive his audience if they assumed he was speaking of Christian prophecy, but, as we will see, there are indeed other prophets in Apess's rhetorical bag of tricks, and while he sings the praises of such Christian worthies as Wesley, Whitefield, and Edwards, he also declares that "the stone cut out of the mountain without hands shall fill the whole earth."[95]

Schism

While Apess made his way along the circuit path for months at a time in 1829, his family faced hardships in Albany, where they were lodging. His wife fell ill in his absence and was refused treatment or assistance. Despite the fact that all were "brethren" connected to the Methodist organization, she had been treated in a manner "not fit for a dog." Experience had taught Apess to expect such treatment from the white community, and yet the Methodists had always stood apart for him in that respect. When the weather turned and his wife had recovered, he moved his family to Troy, New York. It seems as though Troy harbored a small Methodist community that had always been welcoming of Apess, even in his Colrain days, and he expresses his regard for the "good Christian friends" he communed with at this place.

Apess would continue to encounter prejudice throughout his career, having to confront ingrained attitudes of intolerance and the thousands of obstacles, seen and unseen, that were thrown in his path. These obstructions were indicative of larger forces moving through the Methodist organization at this time, for although the church had begun amid an overall rhetoric of uplift and inclusion, as it continued to spread and become more respectable, it sought to distance itself from many of its earlier stances. Gains in the South and in the West had in many ways split the early abolitionist mandate of Methodism, and, even among the more progressive elements of the society, ingrained racism persisted.

Other splits in the church were occurring over the issue of itinerancy and the lesser status of parish preachers who tended fixed congregations. When the Protestant Methodist Church, which officially organized itself in 1830, began publishing its own propaganda materials, it cited the "burdensome role of presiding elders" and the antirepublican governing structure of the Methodist Episcopals, particularly in regard to nonitinerant ministers, as their main reasons for leaving the official church. If Apess thought the Protestant Methodist Church would prove more sensitive to racial issues, it is unfortunate that racial tolerance was not discussed in their inaugural Baltimore convention. When their constitution was drafted and printed, it contained specific clauses asserting that among the laity only white male members could be franchised to vote, and that each annual conference would have exclusive power to make its own rules concerning the admission of "coloured members."[96] Although Apess would soon switch over to this newly formed Protestant Methodist Church, there was little apparent reason to hope that it would prove more open to placing people of color in leading roles.

Troy, where Apess now lived, was home to the 1829 Methodist Episcopal regional conference which was held in May of that year. Apess was on hand, expecting to be ordained at this point. When the meeting gathered and his case came up, the presiding elder asked Apess a series of questions, including whether or not he thought the Lord had called him to preach and if he was prepared to conform to the doctrine and discipline of the church. Having answered all questions in the affirmative, he was then asked to leave the room while his fate was determined. After a half hour of deliberation, a Brother Strong approached Apess and rendered the judgment that, for the second year in a row, the conference did not see fit to grant his request, and they wished to know if he would receive an exhorter's license for another season. Without offering specifics, they claimed that there were questions regarding Apess's character, and that more time would be needed for ordination. When Apess later approached Brother Covel personally to decline the invitation and tell him he would join with the newly formed Methodist Association instead, Covel expressed surprise. But as Apess coolly informed him, there was "too much oppression in the old church." Covel and the council tried to persuade him otherwise, and implied that he was in the wrong to disobey church discipline and judgment, having publicly consented to its doctrines at the conference. Apess responded merely that he could not view it "through the same glass."[97]

Only after the persuasion of the elders had failed and Apess had tendered his withdrawal from the organization did Covel allow that a vague accusation against Apess had prevented his advancement. According to Covel, in Apess's absence, his wife Mary had threatened to "expose" him, although in what manner remains unclear. On further investigation, Apess determined that it was, in fact, the Albany landlady responsible for cruelly neglecting his wife in her illness who had begun spreading unsavory rumors about him. He chastised Covel and the elders for not directly confronting him with this information earlier and affording him the chance to defend himself against false accusations rooted, as he believed, in racial prejudice. But it was too late, and Apess claims that from here on in, wherever he saw "the image of Christ" there would he claim fellowship and perform as the "mouth for God," warning sinners of the wrath to come. He prays to God to banish prejudice everywhere, "that it may die forever should be the prayer of every person." "But," he added, "I suspect that this will not be the case with many of my brethren in the Methodist Episcopal Church."[98]

The rejection of Apess's ordination at the Troy Conference occurred sometime around May 11, 1829.[99] Just a little over two months later, on July 25, he deposited the manuscript of his autobiography, *A Son of the Forest*, with Fred J. Betts, clerk of the Southern District of New York patent office for copyright. Refused ordination in the church, he located another bold avenue to begin to offer his message to the world. "Look brethren," he concludes his autobiography, "at the natives of the forest—they come, notwithstanding you call them '*savage*,' from the 'east and from the west, the north and the south,' and will occupy seats in the kingdom of heaven before you." Events were surging forward, and Apess felt himself at the forefront of this great tide of progress for his Native people, leading the call, standing before his audiences "as a monument" of God's unfailing goodness.[100]

CHAPTER SIX
Indian Preacher

I have preached for all that would open their doors; and sects have bid me welcome; and this is as it should be.
> —WILLIAM APESS, *The Experiences of Five Christian Indians*

The pale-faces are masters of the earth, and the time of the red-men has not yet come again.
> —JAMES FENIMORE COOPER, *The Last of the Mohicans*

Literary Landscapes

Although William Apess was not actually ordained in 1829, as critics have uniformly assumed, he joined up with the seceding Protestant Methodists in May of that year and sealed his union with this new organization by writing and publishing his autobiography, *A Son of the Forest*. His official ordination would come later, but in a sense Apess announced his ministry to the world in his 1829 memoir and therein defined the shape and scope it would take. The young nation had turned its eye westward, its vision of Manifest Destiny demanding of Native peoples that they either assimilate to Western norms, thereby renouncing what was left of their cultural identities in exchange for the role of third-class citizenship, or be ruthlessly swept from the scene. But Apess made his identity as a Pequot and a Native central to his creation of self, insisting on the sustainability of Native community even within a Christian framework, thereby forcing the tensions of American racial intolerance to center stage. In this newly acquired public voice, Apess called for sovereignty for Native people and asked that past violations against that sovereignty be, if not forgotten, then forgiven. "All nations are equally free," he proclaimed. "One nation has no right to infringe upon the freedom of another. Let us do to these people [the Christian nations], as we would have them have done to us."[1]

This chapter follows Apess's labors as Indian Preacher, as they progressed through his eventual ordination, his ministry to the Pequots, and ultimately his mission at Mashpee. Apess would rely on peaceful means in his attempts to transform the conditions of Native space under a settler regime, becoming a student not only of the causes of historical prejudice against Indians, but of tools and strategies for peaceful resistance. This makes him one of the earliest voices of civil disobedience in American literature as his writings put into play bold methodologies for Native people to assert sovereign rights in a historically hostile environment.

Apess's *A Son of the Forest* continues to stand as the earliest known book-length autobiographical narrative written and published by a Native American. Noteworthy for this alone, it is also remarkable for the crucial snapshot it affords of Native lives in the American Northeast at this time, exposing the social conditions in which Native people were forced to live and shattering the clownish façade of noble savagery that had been so clumsily painted over the figure of the Indian in American arts and letters up to this point. Although contemporaneous Native writers such as David Cusick and Elias Boudinot had published works prior to this and John Norton and Eleazar Williams had written their extensively detailed journals, there was simply nothing with which to compare Apess's narrative in the publication history of the continent to this date. Even Samson Occom's published writings (including his posthumously published short autobiographical account) from fifty years earlier, although prompted by similar cultural exigencies, lacked the scope and verve of Apess's extended personal narrative.

Many books about Indian peoples had, of course, flooded the market by 1829 and proven remarkably successful. James Fenimore Cooper's *The Pioneers* had recently appeared before the reading public in 1823, followed by its equally successful and admired sequels, *The Last of the Mohicans* (1826) and *The Prairie* (1827). Cooper's books helped to fashion a vision of American nationhood that was ostensibly sympathetic to the plight of the "Indian" but also worked to usher this figure off the American stage.

Lydia Maria Child's *Hobomok* appeared in 1823, the tale of a Puritan woman who, unlucky in love, resigns herself to marrying the quasi-historical Wampanoag warrior Hobomok. The novel boldly imagines what previous Puritan captivity narratives had figured the "fate worse than death" for a white woman—to marry an Indian and bear his offspring.[2] Child's book was roundly criticized for this transgression, and yet her story, like Cooper's, played with powerful colonial desires and taboos that others would continue to probe in more acceptable forms.

Catharine Maria Sedgwick published her nascent feminist revisionist novel *Hope Leslie* in 1827, offering a sympathetic, if still colonially clouded, retelling of the Pequot War. In Sedgwick's story, the tragic Pequot heroine Magawisca offers her account of the 1637 massacre of the Pequot village at Mystic from what passes as a "Native perspective," allowing for an element of moral uncertainty to infiltrate the historical record. And yet, despite this revisionist appeal, the novel ultimately manages to reinscribe white settler superiority through every last narrative thread, leaving no place for Magawisca and the Pequots in the end save to vanish into the vast forest wilderness never to be seen or heard from again. Although Hope's sister, Faith Leslie, winds up being captured and marrying into the Pequot tribe, her experience among the Indians renders her an empty cipher, incapable of anything beyond childlike impulses that induce a wave of horror in the otherwise resourceful and unflappable Hope (the character of Faith was clearly modeled on the real-life captive Eunice Williams, who married into the Mohawk tribe, much to the distress of her Puritan preacher father, John Williams, and became great-grandmother to Eleazar Williams, the Mohawk who fought alongside Apess in the Battle of Plattsburgh).

John Augustus Stone's immensely popular theatrical production *Metamora: Or, The Last of the Wampanoags,* also about King Philip's (or Metacom's) War, packed theaters from 1829 through the 1850s, thrilling audiences with the self-pronounced eulogy of the king of the forest. And Cooper, too, published on the subject of King Philip's War with his 1829 *The Wept of Wish-ton-Wish,* a novel that again flirts with interracial liaisons but is careful to keep the lines of racial inheritance emphatically policed.

These works (along with many others), taken together, performed the task of sharpening and refining into an extraordinarily precise edge a deterministic vision of Native peoples as vaporizing from the continent like soft dew lifted from the grass by the morning sun while white settlers imbibed their essence, their skills, their lands. Suddenly every Indian to appear on the national stage, be it in novels, plays, histories, or newspaper articles, was the "last of his race"—a kind of tragic holdover from a bygone Heroic Age, soliloquizing in Shakespearian cadences and shaking an angry hatchet at the fickle Gods for condemning his people to play out their final days in such a misbegotten season. These works collaborated in perpetuating the notion that Indian peoples, although perhaps admirable in certain retrograde ways, were inherently unfit for this new age of presumed forward progress and highly organized civic structure. The children of the forest could not compete with the demands of Western civilization and so became prophets of their own doom, heralds of an inescapable racial destiny. Such books were remarkably effective at rousing sympathetic feelings for Native people while simultaneously disposing of them in the dustbin of history, asking readers to wipe away a tear alongside any sense of guilt or cultural culpability for the violent acts of colonial aggression that conspired to bring about this outcome. As the historian Maureen Konkle has observed, "Such elaborate sympathy for Indians served only to justify political oppression."[3]

Apess was certainly aware of these literary manifestations of Indianness, and despite their reductive nature even played into them to a certain extent when he titled his book *A Son of the Forest* and advertised himself as such in sermons and lectures. One wonders to what extent, given his upbringing as a servant in the homes of urban white landowners, he appreciated the self-inflicted irony of being figured a kind of noble forest dweller. Furthermore, given his family history, it would be difficult to stress just how absurd the notion must have appeared to Apess that the different "races of man" were somehow to be kept separate at all costs. This false imperative of racial purity was not simply the fancy of literary romancers but formed a cornerstone of America's national identity that was hammered into law in most states. And yet Apess's own experience made it readily apparent to him that nothing could be more erroneous in practice.

In every one of his major publications, Apess draws attention to the hypocrisy of this fantastical colonial notion of uncorrupted bloodlines, noting that the white colonizer has "committed violence of the most revolting kind upon the persons of the female portion of the tribe."[4] The dominant white culture propagated the myth of strictly policed bloodlines because, in theory at least, whiteness was the very quality that shored up their dominance. For Apess, however, to be a "son of the forest" did not indicate racial purity so much as it acknowledged the complicated and often painful legacies of bodies of peoples coming together amid highly unequal power differentials. Within the scheme of Apess's poetics, "a son of the forest" is not a puerile and romantic appellation but one that implies specific inherited and inalienable rights that have been unlawfully negated through willful violations of body and statute.

For an Indian to address white audiences in Apess's time required not only rare determination, but a very particular kind of performance. One could not simply ignore the meticulously manufactured presence of the literary Indian or pretend it did not exist. But as one literary scholar, John Kucich, points out, if the construct of the noble savage had long been "a carefully cultivated persona for elite European Americans," it had also become "by the nineteenth century a mask through which a Native American could speak."[5] It seems Apess must at least partially don this mask before he could expect to capture the attention of colonial audiences reared on such pabulum and begin to realign their perceptions. As one newspaper advertisement announced, "A son of the forest says 'Great is the novelty of man—but how small his intentions to do good.'" In a sense, Apess learns to leverage the fluctuating public perception of savage nobility and legitimate Indian grievance into a position of moral candor from which to exhort the colonial conscience—not on the subject of some immutable past to which the colonial gaze had drifted, but on the current condition of living Native communities.[6]

A Son of the Forest relates Apess's entire life story right up until roughly two months before the manuscript was published, which is suggestive of the immediacy with which he sat down to record these events. Quite likely, he had already scripted portions of the text or rehearsed elements of his personal narrative in his many public appearances. But the refusal of the Methodist Episcopal Church to elevate him to the role of preacher at the 1829 Troy Conference may have driven Apess to rethink his strategy and redouble his efforts. In *A Son of the Forest* Apess constantly grapples with the problem of self-representation of a Native identity so firmly entrenched within a sphere of colonial containment. The solution that presents itself to him, as I have already suggested, is to perform a kind of "negative work" in which the assumptions of the dominant culture are systematically dismantled and inverted, reflected back on a predominantly white audience in harshly critical terms.

The long-established imposition of racial hierarchies in North America rendered moot the usual rhetorical strategies of debate. Racial bias is founded not in reason but in the systemic abuse of power that involves the negation of reason. Therefore, persuasion had to be achieved through other means, by wedging open narrative possibilities within seemingly closed discourses and carefully cultivating an audience for the voice of historical trauma by subverting rhetorical expectations—all while speaking from a platform of approved spirituality. Apess, who had honed his delivery one northeastern backwoods pulpit at a time, learned that the only way to make his words stick was to maintain the distortion that white viewers had already internalized while reflecting that image back at them, situating them within their own abusive scheme. Rather than shy away from troubling social ills such as child abuse, alcoholism, prostitution, and the dissolution of family structures, Apess addresses them head-on, inviting critique while simultaneously redirecting the source of culpability from the "inherent limitations of the red man" to an ongoing history of colonial greed, violence, intolerance, and exploitation, using Christian doctrine as both shield and wedge to drive home his points.

The medium of the written text afforded Apess new rhetorical avenues by which to pursue this strategy. As the book historian Phillip Round notes, simply the act of copyrighting the book itself was, for a Native individual, a "remarkable and unlikely step into proprietary authorship." It announced Apess's bold and almost unprecedented bid to be recognized not just in the sense of full personhood but as an elite shaper of ideas and opinions with ownership and title to his own words.[7] For Native peoples in New England, the idea of private property had never truly figured into their traditions and was met with ambivalence in colonial times until lands and subsequent titles to lands were systematically swept away. But Apess was laying a new kind of foundation by claiming ownership of words and ideas that might, within the colonial milieu, ultimately translate into greater extensions of rights. The results are necessarily imperfect and yet constantly provocative, enabling him to carve out a fully realized indigenous subject position that had yet to appear anywhere in American letters.

"In the Character of a White Man": Critical Receptions

As might be expected, Apess's bold claims were not greeted with universal applause. Apess sold his books in conjunction with sermons he delivered as an itinerant minister, and there is reason to assume that, given his growing reputation as a powerful and provocative speaker, he dispensed with a great many copies of his autobiography in this manner. Boston booksellers advertised *A Son of the Forest* at fifty cents apiece, touting it as "the Experiences of William Apes, a native of the forest—written by himself."[8] One newspaper editor opined that Apess's method "was to preach then to offer his book for sale; and he succeeded, we are told, in disposing of a large number at very extravagant prices."[9] But the few critical mentions appearing in the press, while acknowledging that Apess had "of late become considerably known in the New England states," were more concerned with Apess's assertions of identity than his accomplishments as writer and speaker.

One critic in the *American Monthly Review* ignores the entire content of the book except to take issue with Apess's claim to be descended from "the royal family of Philip, king of the Pequot tribe of Indians."[10] The skeptical reviewer hastens to note that no authority is provided for this heritage claim "other than the tradition of the natives themselves" and takes Apess to task for misidentifying Philip as a "Pequot." [11] Another reviewer, William Snelling, takes the debate one step further, however, by denying Apess's claim to Native identity altogether. In his 1835 review of *The Life of Black Hawk*, Snelling observes, "It is the only autobiography of an Indian extant, for we do not consider Mr. Apes and a few other persons of unmixed Indian blood, who have written books, to be Indians." Regardless of their heritage, Snelling asserts, "their tastes, feelings and train of ideas, were derived from the whites."

Rather than view Apess's alleged "whiteness" as a potential positive, Snelling, in the complicated double bind by which colonization worked to contain Indian identity, perceives such *improvements* as having hopelessly compromised Apess's ability to speak for his own people. "Take an Indian child from his parents," Snelling asserts, "in the hope of making him useful as a missionary or instructor, give him an insight into the truths of religion, and a competent knowledge of the benefits of art, science, and literature, and his expected usefulness is destroyed by the very means used to increase it." The Indian child, thus educated, will return to his people a stranger, whitewashed of the very qualities that "savages" admire and heed. Snelling concludes that if such an Indian writes at all, "it is in the character of a white man."[12]

The implication that Apess and other literate Natives could only write "white" has had enormous staying power in the almost two hundred years since. Well-meaning critics have echoed Snelling's assertion that, by entering through the rabbit hole of colonization and assimilation into the sphere of Western discourse, indigenous peoples inevitably shed their epistemological moorings and could speak only within the structural framework of their colonizers. These are by no means simple claims to shrug off, but they are typically attended by a host of problematic assumptions concerning the nature of authenticity: that indigenous tradition must somehow remain pure and unsullied to remain indigenous; that colonial culture itself is somehow immune to the infiltration of indigenous knowledge and perspectives; and that cultures are, in fact, actually capable of subsuming other cultures in their entirety, leaving no trace of the thought processes or identity structures peculiar to their geographical and cultural orientations.

Apess was undoubtedly forced to operate within the tightly controlled discourse of colonial agendas and expectations, but it remains evident that nothing about his own written output is entirely derivative of, or could ever be replicated by, his white contemporaries. His sensibility remains rooted in the politics and concerns of indigeneity—even if to claim that identity he must assume highly problematic identity markers like "poor Indian" or "son of the forest." One indicator, however, of his intellectual and rhetorical sovereignty over dominant paradigms is precisely the fact that the semantics of colonial discourse can never properly register with him but rather send discordant shock waves through his cognitive perception. Words such as "savage," "barbaric," "wild," and other perfectly common markers of Indian identity remain unstable referents for Apess, becoming the loci of his negative work, the rhetorical lynchpins by which he begins to expose and dismantle the bankrupt genealogies of colonial history and forge his resistance to colonial dictates and norms. Largely hidden from view, however, are the ways common readers responded to Apess's work, such as William O'Bryan, an Englishman who stumbled upon a copy of Apess's *A Son of the Forest* while journeying from Ohio to New York City in April of 1833. O'Bryan remarked approvingly of Apess in his journal, cautioning his audience to "Remember, he was a converted Indian and could read the Bible. I could extract a great deal more, but let this suffice for the present."[13]

The Road to Ordination

The 1830 census locates Apess as living on King Street in Manhattan, a small lane just south of Houston Street on what was, at that time, the northernmost limit of the city proper. Suggestive of the ever-shifting racial categories under which he labored, Apess is listed in the census as a white male with three white children all under fifteen years of age. Apess and his wife Mary had at least five living children at this point, although the older children were either indentured out to white families in Connecticut or simply not on hand when the census taker made his rounds. The children counted were probably Leonard, who was about five years old at the time; Abby Ann, who was seven; and Sarah, or Sally, who was listed as being under five years of age but would have been about six years old. There is good reason to believe that the Apesses had another younger child by the name of Bethel at this point as well. Given that at least some of his children were living with him, it stands to reason that the "free colored female" of the household was his wife, Mary. The census also lists one "female slave" as being attached to the household, presenting a minor mystery. Might she have been a sister to either Apess or his wife whom the census taker erroneously catalogued?[14] It remains an improbable coincidence that, of only seventeen individuals identified as slaves in the 1830 census for New York City, one of them would just happen to be living with William Apess.[15]

Patrick Rael observes that, while slavery had been terminated in New York State by 1830, it died "not suddenly and decisively but gradually and with ambivalence."[16] The Gradual Emancipation Act of 1799, similar to Connecticut's abolition laws, allowed that all slaves born after the year 1827 would be freed when they reached twenty-one years of age, but all born before that arbitrary cutoff point would remain in slavery until they died, with their children placed under an additional twenty-five-year indenture period. The law was revised, however, in 1817, ensuring that slavery would come to an end as a legal institution in New York by 1827. Still, by 1830, it was possible for southern slaves to be brought to New York and remain property, and children under the age of twenty-one might still be held under the indenture laws enacted in 1799 and 1817. The 1840 census would mark the end of this two-hundred-year-old institution in New York, although the city's black population would continue to struggle for basic civil rights and equal employment opportunities. In the meantime, the one slave situated in the Apess household on King Street might also speak to Apess's hidden connections with the abolitionist movement in the city, and quite possibly he was providing refuge.[17]

Critics have speculated about the ethnicity or racial designation of Mary

Apes, who described herself in *The Experiences of Five Christian Indians of the Pequot Tribe* as the descendant of an English mother and a father from the Spanish Islands or "a native of Spain."[18] This ambiguous self-classification leaves itself open to multiple interpretations, as does Apess's declaration at the close of his "An Indian's Looking-Glass for the White Man" that he has "a wife of the finest cast."[19] His point, of course, was that skin color did not enter into his calculations about what determined an individual's character or worth. The census taker, however, perceived Mary as a "colored female," which placed her one precarious step above the position of slave. This darker "cast" may explain the shameful treatment she received from the landlady in Albany who refused her medical treatment and circulated malicious rumors about Apess just prior to the Troy conference the previous winter.

Despite these complex racial dynamics, New York City proved fertile ground for Apess throughout his career, as it was a center of intellectual and cultural transformations occurring in the nation. That summer Apess held regular services across town for the Associate Methodist Church (with which he was now aligned) on the corner of Frankfort and Williams Streets, with the design of raising money for a "house of worship" he intended to build for the Pequots in Groton.[20] He preached at this location on the Fourth of July, 1830, when he had occasion to pronounce upon the incomplete promise this celebrated day in American history held out for people of color. It was a theme, a kind of negative work, that would find its way into a number of his later published tracts and one that would be famously echoed in later years by Frederick Douglass.[21] But economic exigencies kept Apess on the move as always, and by August he was apparently back in Connecticut, with five of his children listed as enrolled in the Ledyard School District.[22] Advertisements appearing in Connecticut papers in September promoted Apess as both a "Pequod" and a "descendant of the celebrated King Philip." He lectured at least two nights at the state House in Hartford, capitalizing on his connection to that romanticized figure of colonial lore and promoting, among other things, the idea that America's indigenous peoples were descended from the ten lost tribes of Israel.[23]

The lost tribes theory had been in circulation going all the way back to Puritan times, having been proposed by such colonial luminaries as Roger Williams, John Eliot, Cotton Mather, and others.[24] More recently, the New Jersey statesmen Elias Boudinot (from whom the Cherokee editor of the *Phoenix* received his Anglicized name) had championed this view in his 1816 *A Star in the West,* which Apess liberally cribbed from in the long appendix to *A Son of the Forest.* Mohegan writers Samson Occom and Joseph Johnson had also found the lost tribes theory to be a serviceable rhetoric. As the literary historian Rochelle Raineri Zuck sees it, "The Brothertown founders invoked the model of the Hebrew tribes of the old Testament to show that a nation could be multi-tribal and mobile, able to be remade in new locations" and constitute themselves as one "Body Politck."[25]

Whether Apess truly subscribed to this belief or not, he, too, found it to be a provocative weapon in his rhetorical arsenal with which to argue for Native legitimacy within an acceptable Christian framework. In a previously undiscovered article by Apess published in the *Monthly Repository and Library of Entertaining Knowledge* in August of 1830, he writes, "I have been asked time and again, whether I did not sincerely believe that God had more respect to the white man, than to the untutored son of the forest? I answer, and always answer such, in the language of scripture, 'No: God is no respecter of persons.'" Nevertheless it remained helpful for Apess to enlist the intellectual support of "white men" such as Boudinot, known for their "profound reasoning and deep and studious research," who maintained that the Indian tribes were the remnant of that nation "peculiarly and emphatically blessed of God—his own highly favored and chosen people."[26] Later in life Apess apparently came to reject the lost tribes scenario as he staged a number of open debates with the newspaper editor and New York political operator Mordecai Noah, "combatting" Noah's prominent public stances on lost tribes mythology.[27] Whatever problems the lost tribes theory might have presented, however, it nevertheless offered a notion of universal personhood that worked to obstruct prevalent racial classifications and helped to rhetorically elevate Native people above the role of denominated savage. Apess would later attach his *Ten Lost Tribes* essay as an appendix to his 1831 tract, *The Increase of the Kingdom of Christ,* and the theory seems to have been a staple of his preaching at this time.[28]

The Protestant Methodist organization had its first official conference in Baltimore in early November of 1830. It is unclear whether Apess attended or not, although his presence would have afforded him the opportunity to promote himself within the greater organization, advertise his book as a possible vehicle for Native conversion, and lobby for his own ordination within the church. It seems more likely, however, that he circulated that season between New York City and Connecticut, preaching and preparing the second edition of his autobiography. Nevertheless Apess's sustained success on the lecture circuit could not be denied, and the newly configured Protestant Methodist coalition must have determined that a second edition of *A Son of the Forest* was merited.

The church's rival, the Methodist Episcopal Church, had been reporting ongoing victories in converting the "heathen Indians" of the western nations, jubilantly inviting readers through their press releases to "witness with what delight many of them now hear the words of eternal life."[29] Peter Jones of the Missassaugua of Canada had been making the rounds in Boston in 1829, garnering positive publicity for the Methodist Episcopal Church.[30] Realizing they had their own "Indian Preacher" on hand, the Protestant Methodist Church divined an opportunity to broadcast that asset more aggressively to the world at large. Therefore, the second edition of Apess's book, published simultaneously with his sermon *The Increase of the Kingdom of Christ,* was a more "elegant" affair than the previous edition, with improved type and better-quality paper.[31] Apess made minor improvements in the overall structure of the work, deleting the perhaps contentious episodes detailing his switching of church affiliations. The new edition also boasted a handsome portrait of Apess on the frontispiece, to which we are indebted for a singular frozen glimpse into the aspect of the enigmatic Indian author, our only visual impression of the figure the bold young missionary cut on the streets of Manhattan and elsewhere.

The portrait was painted by John Paradise, a resident of New York City, and was engraved by the firm Illman and Pilbrow located on Hudson Street. The surviving engraving that adorns the inside cover of the 1831 edition of *A Son of the Forest* portrays a confident, almost suave, young Apess, of boyish but handsome features, gazing intimately at the viewer, with slicked-back black hair and the slightest intimation of a smile on his lips. The collar of his shirt is turned up beneath his thick, gray, buttoned-up overcoat and he appears, in the portrait, to have just rushed in off the blustery Manhattan street, a true itinerant, making the briefest of stops in-between missionary sojourns. The artist seems to have captured something of the ironic, even world-weary, expression in Apess's eyes. Apess had seen and experienced more in his now thirty-two years than many people would in a lifetime, and as he gazes back at his audience, his aspect almost dares the reader to question the integrity and authority of the unusual tale he prepares to relate. But it is also true that the image reflects a kind of middle-class propriety on Apess's part, accompanied by an almost radiant calm denoting the figure's Christian fortitude. There is nothing here to signal Apess's indigenous roots save, perhaps, the darkness of his skin and hair. The artist seems almost unconcerned with the identity politics that surround virtually every aspect of Indian representation in the nineteenth century, or, perhaps more accurately, the artist reflects an agenda of the Methodist Church which claims that the untamed savages can be brought around to the Christian faith and made useful domesticated citizens of the new republic.

John Paradise was not only a painter but an enthusiastic supporter of the Methodist cause, and many of the engravings appearing in the *Methodist Magazine* in the 1830s were taken from his portraits. Although little is known about Paradise, an 1833 eulogy fondly recalls his role as a cherished class leader in the Methodist Episcopal Church of New York, and as such he might very well have been a member of Apess's circle of acquaintances in 1830 when the portrait was done. It was said of Paradise that "few, if any, ever sat for their likeness, but that while he was sketching the outlines of their form he entertained them with religious conversation, and thus endeavored to impress on their minds the likeness of Jesus Christ."[32] As it turns out, Apess was not the only Indian Preacher within the Methodist Organization that Paradise painted. Two other engravings exist, to be found in the *Methodist Magazine,* of Paradise Indians: Monocue and Between the Logs, both of the Wyandot, or Huron, Nation. These two Native leaders from the area of modern-day Detroit were hastily ordained by the Methodist organization under the supervision of the itinerant minister James Finley in the 1820s. In 1826 they went as part of an Indian delegation to Washington, DC, and then New York City, where they addressed the New York Missionary Society and apparently sat with Paradise to have their portraits done pro bono while receiving an earful of kindly Methodist evangelizing.

In 1826, Paradise, along with Hudson River school artist Asher Durand, was one of twenty-six founding members of the National Academy of Arts and Design, which, by fall of 1830, had just relocated to the newly erected Clinton Hall on the corner of Beekman and Nassau Streets. Clinton Hall was established with the stated aim of servicing "literature and the diffusion of useful knowledge," and it soon became the intellectual epicenter of New York City, housing not only the academy, but also the Mercantile Library Association, which boasted a collection of some nine thousand books, a sizable lecture hall, and the earliest classrooms for New York University. Also claiming offices at Clinton Hall was the *Protestant Magazine,* official organ of the newly formed Protestant Methodist Church. Apess himself would offer a series of lectures at Clinton Hall a few years later, suggesting his deep hidden connections with the leaders of New York's intellectual, religious, and artistic circles.[33]

Given what can be known about Apess's whereabouts at this time, it stands to reason that he sat for his portrait in New York City sometime in late October or early November (just after the earlier mentioned engagements in Hartford), possibly in the academy's new studios at Clinton Hall. The portrait, which remained in his possession throughout his life, was brought directly to the engravers and was ready for printing by early January of 1831. We know the book must have come out in January because the Methodist Book Concern in Baltimore, newly established by the conference, would immediately begin advertising sales of Apess's second edition of *A Son of the Forest* in the same month, January of 1831, suggesting that, directly following the publication of the book in New York, Apess quickly made his way to Baltimore, by land or by boat, to drop off copies of the new edition.

As manic as this timetable may sound, it is at least partially corroborated by the fact that the newspapers definitively place Apess in Washington and Georgetown just a few weeks later, in early March of that year. He had multiple engagements at the Protestant Methodist Church in Georgetown, often preaching two or three times a day. The newspaper advertisements were careful to note that Apess was an "Indian of the Pequod" tribe, and it seems the thrust of his preaching at this time was to promote his mission to the Pequots and to continue to raise money for a house of worship. The same newspapers that advertised Apess's sermons also ran ads for the sale and purchase of slaves, often on the very same page, with one advertisement boasting, "We are determined to give higher prices for slaves than any purchasers [sic] who is now or may be hereafter in this market."[34]

Solomon Northrup, a free black man from Saratoga, New York, would be illegally kidnapped in this same town some ten years later and sold into slavery in Louisiana. One can imagine that Apess, who met with his fair share of racial prejudice in the North, encountered even more explicit tensions and resistance in his southern travels and continued there under grave personal risk. Apess traveled back north by land, preaching at every pulpit he could find along the way. An entry in the records for the Dutch Church in New Brunswick, New Jersey, informs us that "an Indian named William Apess, of the Pequod Tribe" built a sermon around the biblical tale of Noah and the flood on April 6, 1831.[35]

By mid-spring Apess had made his way back to New England with a mandate from the Protestant Methodists to administer to the Pequots.[36] Little is known of Apess's actual ministry in Groton, but he is likely to have learned many hard, if valuable, lessons at this time regarding the difficult politics of preaching on reservation lands—experience that would stand him well in years to come. Although he notes that he took pleasure in the assignment of working with his own people, he found them in a "poor, miserable" condition, the result, as he would later add, of being the "small remnant left from the massacre of the whites."[37] Apess had been a presence in the Pequot community for many years, of course, closely allying himself with Sally George and the Pequot/Christian faction she represented. If this had previously provided a safe haven of sorts, the Georges had their detractors, too, and undoubtedly encountered considerable resistance. George was regarded as a powerful insider with strong support in the surrounding community, but also she was a woman, and as such did not pose a credible threat to the established ministries assigned to that region. Apess, however, was moving now under the authority of a newly formed, if somewhat vilified, church and was prepared to make ripples in the waterways that George could not. In his newly elevated role it became easy for others to target him as an outsider and an agitator.

Apess's *Experiences of Five Christian Indians* (published two years after *A Son of the Forest*, in 1833) provides the clearest lens through which to view his mission to the Pequot. The work is organized in a series of firsthand accounts, the first belonging to Apess himself, in which he offers a slightly truncated version of his autobiography as already related in *A Son of the Forest*. This version, although similar in regard to the details of his life, seems to have been intended for younger audiences, and often Apess's narration will pause to directly address young (white) readers, reminding them how fortunate they were not to have been raised under the same conditions or circumstances as the poor Indian child. Possibly he intended to serialize the tract in one of the many children's journals becoming popular at the time. His short personal account is followed by the narrative of his "consort," or wife, Mary, and concludes with the transcribed narratives of three exemplary Christian women of the Pequot community, consisting of Sally George, Hannah Caleb, and that aged "veteran of the woods," Anne Wampy, who was known throughout the region as a kind of picturesque Indian medicine woman and basket seller.

Curiously, of these three women, only one was apparently still alive in 1831 when Apess began his official mission to the tribe. He was of course well acquainted with Sally George, and must have either gathered her narrative before she passed on in 1824 or known it so well that he felt capable of paraphrasing her experiences. He must also have known Anne Wampy from his time in Groton. He was not intimately acquainted with Hannah Caleb, however, and seems to have received her narrative second hand from a lady of "respectability and piety," perhaps his wife, sometime before Caleb's death. I imagine all of these women were linked together by ties of tradition and kinship, and that Mary Apes, before marrying into the family, had been part of their circle as well. Together they must have formed a kind of unofficial tribal center, the "kitchen table" of which the Abenaki historian Lisa Brooks speaks, where stories are created and told, history passed on, and tradition preserved.[38] It was into this bustling feminine sphere that Apess had first insinuated, and later apprenticed, himself as a young man returning home from the war, anxious to experience a sense of community and cultural identity. And it is thus that the Pequot conversion stories he relates, other than his own, all belong to women.

The written "experiences" of these women contained interesting parallels. Each woman admitted to feelings of despair that had brought her to the verge of wishing to end her life, and each, in turn, discovered her faith in an epiphany of renewal and regeneration, alone in the woods, in what Mary Apes describes as a "shelter from the rain . . . among the rocks."[39] Sally George spoke of being a "wanderer alone, as it were, in my native woods" when revelation came by the side of a bubbling brook. And Hannah Caleb, too, speaks of striking out "into the wilderness" to seek solace and spiritual comfort in her darkest moment of doubt. Caleb spends the entire night in this solitary space, returning the next morning, as she relates, "with the lightness of an angel."[40] Their stories all speak of the forest (often regarded in Western rhetoric as a place of spiritual darkness and temptation) as the very fountain of Godly light, much as Apess seems to have discovered some assurance of his spiritual moorings lost in the miry swamp on the way to Colrain. This particular strain of discourse, shared by all three women, seems to have been well in keeping with the spiritual teachings of Sally George, who, of course, held her camp meetings in the groves that were "God's first temples."[41]

If Anne Wampy was, in fact, in league with these God-empowered women, she nevertheless presented a singular challenge to the Christian missionary, formerly despising "all that was said to her upon the subject of salvation" and using "very bad language in her way, being not able to speak plain English." Apess, from his time as class leader in Providence up until this time, found personal narrative to be a powerful vehicle to exercise the mind toward redemption. Most likely, in keeping with Methodist practice, he established a classlike setting for potential converts and encouraged everyone present to recount his or her life stories. Wampy would relate that "when Christians come to talk with me, me no like 'em; me no want to see 'em; me love nobody; I want no religion. But Sister Amy no let me alone; she talk a great deal to me about Jesus. Sister Apess, too, come talk pray for me. I be afraid I should see 'em, and me no want to hear 'em; by me, by me come trouble very much, me very much troubled. Me no like Christians, me hate 'em, hate everybody."[42]

There are phrases here that provoke hard questions, particularly in regard to Wampy's spitefulness, her expressed hatred of Christians, the repetition of the word "hate." "Do you hate me?" Apess's grandmother had asked after coming in from selling her baskets on a long ago night. Apess seemed unable to comprehend those words as a child, perhaps because, like Anne Wampy, his grandmother's English was poor. Wampy confesses here, "By me come trouble very much, me very much troubled." It is possible, after all, that Anne Wampy was Apess's grandmother. All of the women in *Five Christian Indians* seem to belong within a tight circle of Pequot relations, including his wife and aunt, and this would explain Apess's motives for harvesting the story of this one important convert, even if he doesn't explicitly identify her as his grandmother. He simply relates, "Our sister was born in Groton, Conn., A.D. 1760; lived in sin rising 70 years, brought up in ignorance and prodigality till old age, and then snatched as a brand from the burning . . . and made an heir to all things."[43]

Apess apparently transcribed Wampy's story in 1831 when he was appointed missionary to the Pequots, and published the narrative in 1833 with his

Experiences of Five Christian Indians, but the story of Anne Wampy was reconfigured many years later by the Protestant Methodist missionary Joseph Snelling (no apparent relation to the William Snelling who slammed Apess's Indian credentials in his review of *The Life of Black Hawk*). Snelling was president of the Protestant Methodist chapter of Boston, and in his memoir, published in 1847, he tells of his own visit to the "Pequods" in Groton, many of whom he reports "are descendants of the celebrated King Philip," and where he finds "several of them converted but in a lukewarm state."[44] Cribbing liberally from Apess's life story, but failing to directly credit him at any point, Snelling relates a camp meeting where "I preached in a grove to a large and attentive congregation." A "glorious time" was had, and "five persons [five Christian Indians] professed to find the pearl of great price." One of the presumed five was a boy of fourteen who sounds a great deal like a younger Apess, his contributions to the Pequot mission cast aside and his boyhood experiences conflated with the contemporaneous telling of the tale (see chapter 2).[45]

This case of literary theft by the president of the Boston wing of the church was probably deemed safe given how quickly, stunningly, Apess's star had faded by 1847, his memory in the church archives virtually erased. As such, Snelling could go on to record how, on the following morning, "a considerable number came to my lodgings. We sang and prayed together and had a blessed season." The narrative reaches a crescendo, however, when "a female Indian, who was between seventy and eighty years of age was brought into the liberty of the Children of God, and related her experience in a public meeting which I held on Tuesday evening following, before a large congregation. As it appeared very interesting to me, I will relate some of it in her own simple though impressive language." Snelling goes on to offer nearly verbatim the entire speech given by Wampy in Apess's *Five Christian Indians*. He even goes so far as to have Wampy relate how "Sister Amy" and "Sister Apes" kept visiting her in an effort to "wear me out." In his attempt to write the Indian Preacher out of the scene, he inadvertently leaves the Indian Preacher's wife in the script.[46] Snelling concludes the narrative by recalling how, as he was descending from the pulpit, "I stepped towards her to bid farewell, when looking on me with tears flowing down her furrowed cheeks, and heaven beaming in her countenance, she said 'I am sorry you going away, I want you to pray for me; I want to meet you in heaven.'" Snelling reports that he tarried a few more days, praying, conversing, and establishing a class meeting. Apparently he never returned—if he ever actually went there at all.[47]

Apess, however, continued to pursue his own mission among the Pequot and paid a heavy price for his efforts. On May 9, 1831, New London court papers show that Apess's place of residence in Groton, Connecticut, was broken into and Apess was attacked and severely beaten by a white man, Henry Halleck. Although the circumstances of the case are ambiguously detailed, the Hallecks were small landowners whose property bordered the Pequot reservation at Mashantucket in 1831, and who were possibly involved in attempts to intimidate and harass Pequot landowners into surrendering their claims. This would be consistent in every way with the mounting racial tensions that had recently come to a boil at Hardscrabble in Providence as a result of people of color publicly overstepping their bounds. Apess, as preacher to the community, may have suddenly emerged on the scene as an upstart and an obstacle to white encroachments. As such, his home was entered in the night and, in the language of the court docket, "Henry did then and there seize, beat, bruise, wound, and ill treat and other wrongs to the said William," using a long stick in the service of his assault. The attack, according to court documents, left Apess "in great pain of body—his head badly swelled and bruised so that said Apes life was greatly endangered." Aside from the swelling of his head, Apess suffered a two-inch gash or wound over his eye and bruises all over his body, and was in "great danger of loosing his life."[48]

This case was not an isolated incident, but appears to intersect with at least one other case before the New London County Court that season. A few months earlier a "colored person" by the name of James Pierce had been accused of threatening a Charles Braiton, one of Halleck's neighbors and accomplices, with force of arms. Braiton, himself a "colored man," had been repeatedly accused of harvesting wood from Pequot lands without author-ity.[49] Apess, probably in keeping with his missionary aims, appears to have extended himself in some role of advocacy, showing himself willing to speak up in Pierce's defense, which, in turn, seems to have led to the assault on Apess.

Although it may be difficult to parse the social dynamic behind these vaguely documented incidents, the judicial imbalances plaguing the Pequots might be perfectly gleaned from the sentencing that followed. For allegedly threatening to beat Charles Braiton, James Pierce was fined five hundred dol-lars, a sum that he undoubtedly would not be able to pay, possibly leading to forfeiture of property, loss of liberty, or both. Two women were allowed to testify in Braiton's defense. Apess, the only witness for Pierce, was apparently called into court but never actually brought to the stand. Halleck, on the other hand, the man who actually did break into Apess's place of residence and beat him within an inch of his life, was fined a mere seventy dollars for his crime. These systemic imbalances, repeating endlessly over a thousand invisible lines of power, made up the daily existence of Native people under colonial rule, a social and economic structure similar in every way to the Jim Crow regime of the late nineteenth and twentieth centuries. The operations of pressure meant to keep the Pequot down and ultimately disenfranchise them of their land and legitimacy as a people were intricately layered into the fabric of society and held together by myriad interlocking pieces working seamlessly in support of the regime of power.[50]

One ironic indicator of the interconnectivity of this system of power and abuse was the fact that the presiding justice in the James Pierce case was Apess's old master, Judge William Williams. One can only imagine the scene as Apess faced the former owner of his indenture in court. Their last positively known dealing with one another, sixteen years earlier, had been when Williams had placed an advertisement in the *Norwich Courier* for the return of his runaway servant for a one-cent reward. Now here Apess had surprisingly turned up again, bad-penny-like, except instead of fulfilling his scripted fate as a destitute "poor Indian" remorseful for his actions, he stood before Williams a preacher of the Protestant Methodist Church, advocating for the rights of his people. It is interesting, under such circumstances, that he was not allowed to testify, but then again, as Williams and Apess both knew, the testimony of a person of color would have had little or no weight in the court system at that time.

To better understand how a leading authority such as Williams, with the power to make or break lives on the Pequot reservation, thought, we need only look at his own words offered in 1832, one year after the trial, when Williams wrote a short sketch of the Pequot Nation for the perusal of Connecticut Governor Jonathan Trumbull and other state officials. Although Williams maintains an officious level of sympathy for the Indians, his tone is decidedly unflattering. He observes that a "remnant" of the Pequots still persisted in the town of Groton of about "forty souls" living on roughly eleven acres of "poor land reserved to them." He writes, "They are more mixed than the Mohegans with negro and white blood, yet are a distinct tribe and still retain a hatred of the Mohegans. . . . They are more vicious, and not so decent or so good looking a people as the Mohegans. This however may be owing to their being more mixed with other blood."[51] Williams fully understood that to characterize the Pequot as a vicious and indolent people was to keep them tied to the patriarchal codes of government oversight used to order their fates and strip them of resources. By emphasizing that the tribe had "mixed" with "negroes," he was also discrediting the validity of a "pure" Pequot identity, further disenfranchising them as a people. All of these dynamics would come into greater relief as Apess, in the coming year, involved himself in the dispute between the Mashpee Wampanoag and their overseers.

Mindful of these dominant perceptions and strategies, Apess was beginning to decipher the workings of the settler colonial system from a new angle, both inside and out, and if he left Groton without a victory in this particular round of struggle, he was neither crippled nor cowed by the experience. If anyone had a right or sufficient cause to back out at this point, it was Apess. The world had done everything within its power to beat him back and bow him down since the day he was born. He had been abused, outcast, mistreated, and trampled upon. "It is a fact," Apess wrote, "that I had a difficult road to travel before I really got to preaching."[52] But he would not allow himself to be intimidated by the physical threats to his livelihood or by the more subtle but equally sinister threat of the legal apparatus of white power over Indians. Instead he would pick himself up once more and continue to operate not just as "a mouth for God," as he states in the first edition of *A Son of the Forest*, but as a mouth, a voice, for Native people.[53]

To that end, a few months later, in August, having barely had time to heal from his grievous wounds, Apess found himself in Malden, Massachusetts, a small town north of Boston, for the Protestant Methodist's quarterly conference. On the eighth day of that month William Apess, aged thirty-three, was ordained a licensed minister of the church. As one of the ministers at the meeting recalled,

> On the Sabbath, the "holy Supper" was administered; and ordination conferred on Rev. Mr. Apes. This gentleman is a son of the forest, and is engaged as a Missionary from the P. M. Church to his brethren, the Pequod tribe of Indians, in the state of Connecticut. For this service he appears to be well qualified, both by native talent and learning, and the peculiar bent and warm piety of his soul. We feel an interest in his prosperity; a brief acquaintance has endeared him to our hearts; and we pray the equal Father of all His creatures to make him an instrument of salvation to his neglected and injured brethren.[54]

Apess's impossibly long road to ordination was finally complete.

The Cherokee Delegation

In 1830 Congress had passed the Indian Removal Act, designed to "provide for the exchange of lands with the Indians residing in any of the states or territories, and for their removal west of the river Mississippi."[55] The language of the act might almost sound benign and, perhaps, beneficial to Native people if you could forget for a moment that most, if not all, Natives had no desire to exchange their lands, communities, social identities, or national sovereignties for some vague promise of land in a far-off place. In the warped paternalistic vision of the newly elected Jackson administration, however, this was indeed a charitable offer.

Jackson, in his 1830 State of the Union address, lamented, "Humanity has often wept over the fate of the aborigines of this country." Natives were regarded as objects of pity because of their seeming inability to adapt to the demands of Western progress. According to Jackson and his ilk, the only benevolent course of action left was to remove Native peoples from their expansive landholdings in the East and place them beyond the corrupting influence of white progress, which had proved so destructive to their continued well-being. In a sense, Jacksonian policy was the real-life equivalent of the figurative role carved out for Natives in the fiction of the day. Jackson rationalized that it would be best for all concerned if Natives could simply be sent to a land "where their existence may be prolonged and perhaps made perpetual. Doubtless it will be painful to leave the graves of their fathers; but . . . is it supposed that the wandering savage has a stronger attachment to his home than the settled, civilized Christian?"[56] Jackson's argument readily conceded that white settlers had already begun to illegally seize Indian land, but posited that, given that both parties now made claims to the land, it was more just to remove the "wandering savage" than to uproot a "civilized" people who would naturally have stronger attachments despite their brief tenure. Note the power of words—repeated qualifiers such as "wandering" and "savage"—to hammer out historical identities and impose irrepressible realities from the ether of perception.

Even so, such opportunistic logic should not have carried far in a nation of laws, save for the fact that, as Charles Mills has observed, the egalitarian principles of the revolution were never meant to extend to people of color. Lewis Cass, governor of Michigan Territory and mouthpiece for the Jackson administration, observed without irony, "The Creator intended the earth should be reclaimed from a state of nature and cultivated." Wild bands of roving Indians leaping through the vast forest primeval, hunting deer and chasing buffalo, simply did not agree with the plan the creator had so clearly mapped out for earthly occupation. Never mind that the Native nations subject to removal were all traditionally agricultural peoples and by this point in time had largely converted to Christianity. Never mind that many lived in wood-framed houses—and in the case of the Cherokee had also framed a constitutional form of government deliberately following that of the United States, had their own newspaper and syllabary, and in some cases had cultivated successful plantations, perversely becoming slave owners themselves. Cass could still somehow insist that "a barbarous people, depending for their subsistence upon the scanty and precarious supplies furnished by the chase, cannot live in contact with a civilized community."[57]

The Jackson administration was not invested in drawing an accurate picture of Native land tenancy (perhaps any more than was William Williams in his 1832 sketch of the Pequot). Jackson had made his name and wealth through a particular brand of land speculation that entailed mobilizing frontier militias in the wake of the War of 1812 to violently force the Seminoles, Creeks, and Choctaws off their lands in flagrant disregard of treaties. This decades-long process of clearing and policing conquered territories in northern Alabama and Mississippi made Jackson a popular figure among southern land speculators and ultimately carved a path for cotton kings to expand their empires. This had the added benefit of opening new markets for slave labor and helped to exponentially expand the domestic slave trade. In the state of Georgia, where the pressure to remove Natives off their land was, perhaps, the strongest, a lottery system was initiated in the 1830s so that, if Native people could be "persuaded" to remove, their land was parceled out at below-market prices to whichever white citizens were lucky enough to draw the lot. This, as one historian notes, "gave every white family in Georgia a personal stake in Indian removal."[58]

By 1832 the Cherokee were in the thick of a defensive media campaign of their own to bring attention to the gross mischaracterizations being used as propaganda against them. Despite disagreements and internal strife about how best to pursue their own national interests, the Cherokee sent two representatives to lobby for their cause, Elias Boudinot and John Ridge. Boudinot had achieved national fame as the editor of the *Cherokee Phoenix,* which served not only as a mouthpiece for the embattled Cherokee nation but as a symbol of Cherokee learning and progress, giving the lie to claims by those who, like Jackson and Cass, insisted that Native peoples were simply "wandering hordes of barbarians, seeking a precarious subsistence."[59] Ridge was Boudinot's cousin, and, like Boudinot, had been educated at the American Board for Commissioners of Foreign Missions school in Cornwall, Connecticut. Both were extremely well versed in forms of white literacy, politics, and culture, and both had devoted most of their adult lives to fighting removal policies.

Ralph Waldo Emerson, having seen the two speak in early March of 1832, had admired Ridge in particular for his "plain, right on, & fine Indian eloquence."[60] When the Cherokee came to speak in Federal Hall in Boston in late April, however, Ridge was apparently unavailable to offer his usual address. The historian Maureen Konkle has posited that it was William Apess who showed up in Ridge's place that evening, making an equally powerful impression on the listeners in the audience. Apess, a known figure in the metropolitan Northeast by this time, had made the acquaintance of church leaders, newspapermen, reformers, and abolitionists. It is certainly possible that, as the most well-established local Native speaker, he was able to insinuate himself into this public debate and temporarily fill in for the crowd-pleasing Ridge. As Konkle notes, Apess was in Boston at the time and was advertised to be giving his own speech, "The Principles of Civilization," the following week at Boylston Hall, a theater that seated up to a thousand people.[61]

An account of the Cherokee lecture was preserved by Louisa Park, a young socialite who was in attendance and recorded the event in a letter written to her mother in late April of 1832. As she describes the event, the meetinghouse, which was presided over by the famed Unitarian minister William Ellery Channing, was packed. Park, who arrived a bit late, had never seen a church so filled, and she and her companions were forced to find a seat next to the door at the very back. Park shows herself to be a studied critic of the oratorical genre, all too familiar with the local speakers and their particular styles.

When the famous statesman Edward Everett takes the podium, Park is intimately aware of his tics and flaws, finding the "great man" to be something of an awkward parody of himself. She writes, "He set my teeth on edge for he hisses like a serpent; every S told . . . and he annoyed me by the ungracefulness and sameness of his gesticulation; he perpetually waved his arm on high and brought it down with a rat tat tat upon the paper he held in his left hand. He must have been brought up to the trade of a single handed drummer." She overcomes her distaste, however, enough to praise the forthrightness of his address and the history of abuses it tracked. Boudinot followed, and Park, describing him as a "swarthy, independent looking gentleman," found his talk to be dry and overly long.

Park was apparently unaware of the identity of the second Native speaker, referring to him simply as the "other of our 'red brethren.'" Nevertheless, as she notes, his "palaver" seemed to hit the taste of the audience more decidedly. This unknown speaker presented

> a few tropes and metaphors which never failed of applause, some of them manifestly clap traps; but on the whole I was both surprised and pleased; this man was evidently not quite as well educated, had not the same familiarity with choice language, and was not so civilized as his companion, but there was more native eloquence in his address, his earnestness was evidently sincere, and I felt the difference between hearing an actor on the stage, or even a lawyer defending a client—and listening to a patriot engaged bonafide, with all his heart and soul in stating the wrongs and pleading the cause of his oppressed country. He was sometimes vehement and Gen. Jackson had one or two side knocks, to my great satisfaction.[62]

If Apess (assuming he was the speaker) came off as less educated than Boudinot, or for that matter, Ridge, it was because unlike the two Cherokee orators, Apess had no formal education. He was self-taught in every sense of the word and so had not the "choice language" of his colleagues. If this made him seem somehow less "civilized" than Boudinot, Park was also quick to note how her more dull-witted companions were at odds to explain the seeming discrepancy of "wild Indians" dressed in civilized attire. But Apess had long been on this public stage by this point and had mastered many of the intricacies of performing Native identity to white audiences. He was fully capable of insert-ing himself into the discussion of Cherokee resistance to removal policies and outperforming some of the leading speakers of his day.[63]

Apess's star seems to rise shortly after the Federal Hall lecture, lending more credence to the notion that he was the speaker in question. When he was engaged to speak at Jefferson Hall in Boston later that spring, William Lloyd Garrison commented in the *Liberator,* "We intend to be among his hearers. A short interview with him has given us a very favorable opinion of his talents and piety."[64] Apess soon acquired a series of Boston speaking engagements, including a steady gig every Sabbath throughout that summer at Franklin Hall, where he lectured on slavery, the purity of the gospel, and the Pequot tribe of Indians.

Franklin Hall was a habitual meeting place for the abolitionist society in Boston at this time, and running concurrently with Apess's Sunday sermons were weekly meetings, held Monday evenings, of the Anti-Colonization Soci-ety, sponsored by Garrison and meant to garner consensus against the other "removal" policy of this era, which sought to recolonize free blacks in Africa.[65] It is difficult to imagine that Apess was not a participant in these discussions, which the historian Andy Doolen has characterized as a groundbreaking new "guide for a radical abolitionism" in America.[66] Also appearing at Franklin Hall was the black abolitionist Maria Stewart, who delivered her most famous address, "Why Sit Ye Here and Die?" in this space in September of that same year. All of this suggests that Apess was very much in step with the front lines of abolitionist discourse. In July of that year, two prominent Mormon mis-sionaries, Orson Hyde and Samuel Smith, also paid a visit to Apess, passing two to three hours in what was described as "quite an interesting time" as they sat down "with an intelligent son of Abraham" and found their interview with him to be "something agreeable." Their talk concluded with an invitation from Apess "to Preach in *his* hall (Franklin Hall)."[67]

Apess tailored his speeches to the abolitionist crowd but, apparently with the manuscript for *Five Christian Indians* in mind, he also seasoned his talks with an account of Anne Wampy, or the relation of "a miraculous conver-sion of an aged Indian woman of his tribe," which seems to have become the new centerpiece of his performance.[68] But then, as always, just as Apess was achieving the kind of steady notice and income that might help stabilize his life, calamity struck. Sometime in August of 1832 a Methodist preacher, John Reynolds, publicly accused Apess of being a "deceiver and an imposter" guilty of misrepresenting himself and the Methodist organization by partaking in the scandalous practice of "buying lottery tickets" and misappropriating monies collected by him for the church.[69] These charges would trail Apess for the rest of his career, although there appears to have been no foundation for them. Interestingly, it was Reynolds, in the previous year, who had posted the announcement of Apess's ordination in the *Christian Watchman* and noted the "interest" he and the church held in Apess's prosperity. Now, suddenly, Apess was an "imposter," his credibility as a minister called into question. It may be that when Apess was awarded his license to preach among the Pequot, it was not anticipated that he would become a feature among the white churches of Boston and achieve so much success on his seemingly self-prescribed circuits. Apess immediately sued Reynolds for libel, but Reynolds, appearing in court sometime in October, stood by his claims, causing the Boston establishment to shrink back from Apess's ministry.[70]

Apess's speaking engagements suddenly dropped off, and in January of 1833 the *Norwich Courier* of Connecticut continued to pursue the story, demonstrating just how tenacious such claims could be, particularly if you were an Indian. The *Courier* reported that all those of a benevolent stripe within the community were "probably acquainted with a young man of the Pequot tribe of Indians by the name of William Apes, who claims to be a licensed preacher of either the Methodist or Baptist Denomination. . . . For sometime past he has been travelling about the country preaching and soliciting charity for the ostensible purpose of building a church upon the Pequot Reservation." The editor of the paper presumes that such funds must surely have been procured by this point and wonders how they have been allocated. Nowhere is it mentioned that Apess's mission to the Pequots came to an abrupt end when he was beaten within an inch of his life. But the editor does recall meeting with a "very respectable" woman of the tribe who cautioned against giving Apess additional funds. A "white man from the same neighborhood" also came forward to support this opinion. One wonders if the white man wasn't Henry Halleck, the same man who severely beat Apess a year earlier.

As always, there were forces in and around the reservation more than willing to take Apess down, forces that had become adept at making impassioned pleas for the conversion of the poor Indians but did everything within their power to inhibit Native prospects. The newspaper article advised against anyone offering Apess funds toward his otherwise noble endeavor.[71] Other papers also retracted their support of Apess and refused to print any more notices of his lectures. The *Boston Recorder* went so far as to openly criticize Apess's "methods" and wondered at the value of a book such as *A Son of the Forest,* which seemed to celebrate the debauched vices of a runaway and flagrant drunk.[72]

Through an Indian's Looking-Glass

Apess probably spent that winter pursuing his mission, not just with the Pequots but among the other New England tribes. But he spent the deepest part of winter preparing his manuscript, *The Experiences of Five Christian Indians of the Pequot Tribe,* for publication. After the slander he had endured, it may be no wonder that he decided to attach to the end of this document his most powerful essay "An Indian's Looking-Glass for the White Man," which tackles the racism of the dominant culture head-on, and offers a sample of the fiery brand of rhetoric with which Apess engaged his audiences at this time.

The mirror, or looking-glass, was a common rhetorical trope at the turn of the nineteenth century, and countless tracts employed this literary device, suggesting that the text itself, the words on the page, presented a kind of mirror that reflected back a true representation of the world—one that might have been previously hidden or shielded from the eyes of the reader. This was often deployed as a rhetorical device, in which a text proposed to make apparent certain faults that had remained obscure to the object of its critique. Benjamin Franklin performed this task for the British government with his "Rules for Reducing a Great Empire to a Small One" by noting, "I have held up a Looking-Glass in which some ministers may see their ugly Faces and the Nation its Injustice."[73]

But Apess demonstrates his usual innovation and audacity by suggesting that the entire white race must look at itself, and not in just any mirror, but through an Indian's looking-glass. For it was readily apparent to Apess that if texts operated like mirrors, then the textual productions of colonial culture to date had collaborated in forming a powerful looking-glass that only magnified the qualities white people wanted to see. The American historical and literary canon up until this point was a kind of immense reflecting pool of white desires, justifications, and rationalizations that obscured a repository of crimes and abuses that had failed to substantially imprint themselves in the captured light of history but instead slipped, phantom-like, unwitnessed, from the surface of the glass. An Indian's looking-glass promised to reflect back something quite different, and Apess was one of only a handful of Native people of his generation who had the learning, will, and rhetorical skill to raise such a glass and place it before the whitened aspect of the dominant culture.

Suppose all the crimes of humanity were put together, Apess proposes, and "each skin had its natural crimes written upon it—which skin do you think would have the greatest?" In posing such a question, Apess exonerated people of color from the savagery historically projected upon them, reassigning that history of mindless violence to the white settler race that had robbed one "nation almost of their whole continent . . . murdering their women and children, and then depriving the remainder of their lawful rights, that nature and God require them to have." Furthermore, it enslaved "another nation to till their grounds and welter out their days under the lash with hunger and fatigue under the scorching rays of the burning sun."[74]

The Declaration of Independence had declared all men created equal. Yet it had also decried "the merciless Indian savages whose known Rule of Warfare is an undistinguished Destruction of all Ages, Sexes, and Conditions." In his essay, Apess called out the lie. It had been the Puritans of the Massachusetts Bay Colony, in fact, who had burned his people alive in their fortress without regard to age, sex, or condition. The Pequots, and thousands of other Natives, still labored under the "awful injustice" that kept them a subjugated people nearly two hundred years later, as though their darker pigmentation were a curse God himself had indelibly imprinted on their skin, a visible reminder of their lesser humanity, a justification for mistreatment and exploitation, the mark of Cain. But Apess upends this notion, raising the specter that even Jesus Christ himself, the Son of God, was almost assuredly not white. This provocative claim could not have sat comfortably with mainstream nineteenth-century audiences. Still, Apess observed that "when I cast my eye upon that white skin and if I saw those crimes written upon it, I should enter my protest against it immediately and cleave to that which is more honorable. And I can tell you that I am fully satisfied with the manner of my creation, fully—whether others are or not."[75]

Apess's point was not to shift the terms of race-based prejudice in a new direction and vilify whiteness itself. Rather, he wished to reveal to white audiences the unreflective quality of their most cherished cultural certainties, reveal the "skin deep" nature of their prejudices. He calls for an end to laws prohibiting miscegenation. Apess's complex lineage offered standing proof that anti-miscegenation laws were no protection against racial mixing, whatever horrors it presumably held for white people. Exposing the absurd contradiction of these fears, he coolly observes how whites had already "taken the liberty to choose my brethren, the Indians, hundreds and thousands of them, as partners." Apess alludes here to the sexual predation to which Native women were (and in many cases continue to be) subjected, and the historical inequities that had forced them into poverty, servitude, and prostitution, a painful legacy that informed the shadowed contours of his own life. And, finally, Apess confronts the white ministry itself, asking, "Is it not the case that everybody that is not white is treated with contempt and counted as barbarians? . . . My white brother, what better are you than God? And if no better, why do you, who profess his Gospel and to have his spirit, act so contrary to it? Let me ask why the men of a different skin are so despised."[76] He continues to exhort, "I should not wonder if some of the most selfish and ignorant would spout a charge of their principles now and then at me. But I would ask: How are you to love your neighbors as yourself? Is it to cheat them? Is it to wrong them in anything?"[77]

While Apess was building a case of systemic mistreatment against Native people in general, his own sense of grievance at the hands of the white ministry shines through in this tract. Nowhere else, perhaps, is Apess so openly disdainful of the raw prejudice of white people against Natives. Apess had no use for human distinctions based on the color of one's skin, and he begins here to forge a discourse relevant not only to Natives or whites but to all people of color on the American landscape. He concludes, "Do not get tired, ye noblehearted . . . the Lord will reward you, and pray you stop not till this tree of distinction shall be levelled to the earth, and the mantle of prejudice torn from every American heart—then shall peace pervade the Union."[78]

"This Riotous and Mischief-Making Indian": The Mashpee Revolt

The pockets of media silence that occur from time to time in Apess's career, when no known newspaper advertisement or other type of notice registers his name, may represent periods spent traveling among the Indian tribes of New England, beneath the radar of the mainstream press. He notes that, "it being my desire, as well as my duty as a preacher of the Gospel, to do as much good as lay in me to my red brethren, I occasionally paid them a visit."[79] And so it was in May of 1833 when Apess directed his path to the Mashpee Wampanoag Indians of Cape Cod. According to the family memories of some Mashpees, Apess was accompanied on his journey by the Pequot George Ockree (later known by the more anglicized George Oakley), who would go on to marry into the influential Attaquin family at Mashpee. In keeping with this tradition, Apess's presence had been formally requested by the leading men of Mashpee, including Solomon Attaquin and Daniel Amos, to assist in their long-standing struggles with the town overseers. Loaded down with copies of *The Experiences of Five Christian Indians* hot off the presses, Apess made his way along the old Post Road, presiding over encouraging gatherings in places such as Scituate, Kingston, and Plymouth. Along the way he conversed with other reform-minded religious leaders and was further forewarned of the situation in Mashpee.[80]

The habitual disregard of Native rights on reservations was, of course, nothing new to Apess. As he observes, "I knew that no people on earth were more neglected; yet, whenever I attempted to supply their spiritual wants, I was opposed and obstructed by the whites around them, as was the practice of those who dwelt about my native tribe (the Pequots)."[81] Nevertheless, having managed to obtain proper letters of introduction from the ministers he had encountered en route, Apess now presented himself at the home of one Phineas Fish, the white pastor assigned to Mashpee. Apess, with the help of Ockree, had taken the precaution of broadcasting throughout the town his intention to preach at the Mashpee church the very next day, and Fish, having perhaps felt his hand forced, graciously ceded Apess his pulpit.

Thus it was that the next morning Apess was brought by carriage to the old Mashpee meetinghouse. He looked upon the simple structure with reverence, appreciating the complex history of the one-hundred-year-old "sacred edifice" planted in the midst of a "noble forest." The church had been erected in 1757 specifically for the use of the Indians at Mashpee, a relic of the age-old colonial endeavor to bring light to "those poore Indians, who have ever sate in hellish darknesse."[82] No one understood better than Apess the double-edged nature of that mission and the manner in which policies of presumed Christian benevolence were undergirded with schemes of colonial control and containment. And yet, as in Mashantucket and elsewhere, the church still presented itself as a center of tradition, a place where the indigenous community might anchor itself against the relentless tsunami of colonial assault.

The Mashpee church stood before Apess as a kind of "x-mark," a site of consent and coercion representing struggle and transformation for the Mashpee Indians, but also the possibility of hope for the future. The history of that struggle was further suggested by the Indian burial ground that stood "hard by," as Apess noted, overgrown with pines and a "delightful brook, fed by some of the sweetest streams in Massachusetts." The literature of the day, as recorded by major poets such as Philip Freneau, William Cullen Bryant, and Lydia Sigourney, viewed the "Indian Burial Ground" as a resonant space marking the closure of Indian tenure on the land—an unstable referent so effaced by time and weather that meaning could no longer adhere to it, save for its signifying the tragic demise of the Indian race. This same trope had been powerfully summoned by Colrain historians who, when speaking of Pequot maidens married to white settlers, consigned their burials to lonesome plots under unmarked stones. But Apess determined to view this site as a space of continuance, the gravestones suggestive of the deep history embedded in the land and the commitment to spiritual and cultural perseverance by the people still living there.

On entering the church, however, Apess was struck by the "hue of death" that sat upon the countenances of the congregation. Expecting to encounter the "cheerful" aspect of his red brethren, he found instead a strange "paleness was upon all their faces." In this moment, Apess has positioned his reader once more before his Indian's looking-glass, wherein the pall of death, dislocation, and impermanence typically reserved for descriptions of Natives is strategically reversed. For in place of the Mashpee Wampanoag he came to address, Apess finds the meetinghouse usurped by whites, and it is this gathering that bears the twisted hue of impending mortality captured in his glass. As in the earlier "berry picking" episode in *A Son of the Forest,* Apess shifts the scene one hundred and eighty degrees, suggesting a kind of inverted congregation, so that the racial preconceptions of the reader become crossed in the process and the meetinghouse is rendered a house of mirrors. "I must do these Indians the justice to say that they performed their parts very well," he quips. But when, in his sermon, Apess projects the inconsistency of an Indian meetinghouse devoid of Indians back at his congregation, he quickly discovers that "plain dealing was disagreeable to my white auditory."[83]

Following the sermon, Apess inquired of Fish where all the actual Indians were to whom Fish had been assigned as minister. He was told that they met separately in a different location under the pastoral guidance of one Blind Joe Amos. Armed with this information, Apess quickly set Fish further on his heels by determining on the spot to arrange for a second sermon at the meetinghouse, this time with the local Natives in attendance. Fish could do little but go along, although he cautioned Apess against bringing up the issue of "oppression," that being the very thing that made the local Natives discontented. Not surprisingly, Apess disregarded this advice, and was soon publicly confronting Fish on his apparent failure to uplift the Mashpee from their miserable condition, which Apess intimated had more to do with lack of education, civil rights, and spiritual guidance than the "disposition to be idle . . . and to lie drunken under their fences," as Fish contended.[84]

Although his meeting with the Natives was well received, Apess continued on his way afterward, pursuing speaking engagements "on the soul-harrowing theme of Indian degradation" in Hyannis, Great Marshes, and Barnstable (where he found no resting place for the "sole of my foot").[85] *The Barnstable Patriot,* taking upon itself the responsibility of tracking Apess's movements, gloated that this "itinerant Indian Apsotle" came to their village "burdened with tracts purporting to be 'Indian Experience' to distribute in his tour" but met with a "cool reception. . . . The next we heard of him was that he succeeded in finding a vineyard wherein to labour and was proselyting the poor, ignorant dwellers upon the Marshpee Plantation." Apess did, in fact, come back through Mashpee on his return route, ostensibly to meet with the Natives of the township one last time, but as the *Patriot* colored it, it was here Apess had "concluded to lay aside his staff and scrip and locate."[86]

Apess likely harbored deeper commitments than openly admitted to in *Indian Nullification of the Unconstitutional Laws of Massachusetts Relative to the Marshpee Tribe; Or, The Pretended Riot Explained,* his written tract on the subject. Nevertheless, at this "one last" gathering, rather than simply preach, Apess opened up the floor for the Mashpee to voice concerns and grievances. He then read to them from his own work, perhaps relating choice sections from his *Experiences of Five Christian Indians,* and, in particular, his "Indian's Looking-Glass," to help illustrate similar circumstances experienced in places like Mashantucket. His reading was met with cries of "Truth! truth!," and Apess suddenly felt himself compelled to remain in Mashpee indefinitely to further educate himself on the dynamic there and strategize with the prevailing leadership as to what might be done. As events will show, Apess had been giving a great deal of thought to the subject of Indian rights from a civil and legal perspective. It was one thing to preach that all men were descended from one root and one tree—or, for that matter, that all men were created equal—but these rhetorical strategies seemed not to operate or promote change on a systemic level. Something more was needed.

Scholars have marveled at the organizational skills Apess exhibited at Mashpee, as though they had sprung organically from thin soil. But it is by now readily apparent that Apess, as an Indian exhorter and preacher, had been pushing the limits of rhetorical discourse and resistance on Native communities for many years by this point. There is reason to believe he had witnessed the Haudenosaunee in Canada using tradition, ritual, and formal address to set themselves on even footing with the whites; he had lobbied for reform in Mashantucket and petitioned to gain control of the oversight process on the reservation there; he had closely followed the Cherokee resistance, which was ongoing, and had quite possibly lectured alongside Boudinot, encountering new strategies for asserting nationhood and sovereignty; he had attended abolitionist meetings and preached in their hall in Boston; he had faced oppression in the church and in the courts, had been threatened, attacked, and discouraged by countless other means; he had learned from community-level organizers such as Sally George and Hannah Caleb, but he had also made a study of the grand spiritual narratives of the Haudenosaunee Peacemaker and Christ—until he finally appears to have landed in Mashpee with a fully formed set of strategies that had been honed to perfection over a decade or more of struggle. Although the Mashpee, too, had long maintained legal and personal battles for political autonomy, Apess brought with him a body of knowledge and experience that broke new ground and created new opportunities for political advancement.

Apess remarks in *Indian Nullification* that "the causes of prevalent prejudice against his race [Apess speaks of himself in the third person here] have been his study from his childhood upwards."[87] In other words, Apess's commitment to understanding and combating racism had been his lifelong passion, a broken and tormented riddle he had puzzled over since his grandmother first confronted him as a child of four with the question, "Do you hate me?" Small wonder, then, that a full decade before Thoreau and the transcendentalists would fully hit upon this ideology, Apess apprehended how the resiliency and effectiveness of a marginalized resistance to power would have to be conducted through the acquired moral authority of directed nonviolent action or civil disobedience. As he continued to lecture the local circuit on the topic of "Indian affairs," he noted, "Many of the advocates of oppression became clamorous, on hearing the truth from a simple Indian's lips, and a strong excitement took place in that quarter. Some feared that an insurrection might break out among the colored people, in which blood might be shed. Some called me an imposter, and others approved of my proceedings." Having already assessed the general temper of the region, Apess was fully aware that those who prophesized "savage" bloodshed were typically the ones most determined to provoke it.[88]

The so-called Mashpee Revolt of 1833 arose in response to the conditions of protectorship under which the Mashpee, like other Natives of New England, were reduced to serfdom on their own land. As seen elsewhere, the white overseers appointed to look after Mashpee interests had used their positions of authority and power to rent land, sell lumber, and parcel out other resources for personal gain. The indigenous residents found themselves economically marginalized and in dire straits, stripped of all civil liberties and fully dependent on the overseers for nearly every necessity. Nevertheless, they had organized their own church in defiance of their appointed minister, Reverend Fish, and had begun to agitate for political autonomy. When Apess arrived, he immediately seems to have read the situation and allied himself with indigenous leaders of Mashpee such as Blind Jo Amos, Ezra Attaquin, and Isaac Coombs. These local leaders had been spearheading political and cultural resistance to the white power structure for years, but in combining with them, Apess was able to immediately set in motion a detailed plan to bring the situation at Mashpee to a highly publicized crisis.

He began by assisting the Mashpee in the production of a number of formal resolutions, the first of which was to adopt Apess and his family into the tribe. This may seem like an unusual request, and it raises questions about Apess's ongoing affiliation as a Pequot. But whatever events may have strained Apess's status at Mashantucket, the move to be adopted by the Mashpee proved essential in warding off charges, already anticipated by Apess, that he was an "imposter" and outside agitator. He had encountered similar accusations on the Pequot reservation and sought to preempt them here with an official declaration by the tribe—something it was within their limited legal rights to do—of his adoption. As he explained, "If they wished me to assist them, it would be necessary for them to give me a right to act in their behalf. . . . They must be aware that all the evil reports calumny could invent would be put in circulation against me by the whites interested, and that no means to set them against me would be neglected."[89]

A second document, sent to the Massachusetts governor, the state legislature, and the Corporation of Harvard College (which held the Mashpee lands in trust), declared the right of the tribe to rule itself, given that all men were "born free and equal." It further announced the resolution that no white man would be permitted to cut or carry off wood or hay or any other resource from Mashpee. Anyone caught doing so would be removed from the "plantation" (the archaic term for colonial patents). The third document was sent to the Harvard overseers to declare Mashpee dissatisfaction with Fish as their appointed minister. Fish had received hundreds of dollars in compensation annually to preach to the Indians, and yet had failed, according to the tribe, to administer this trust or convert even one Native. They wrote, "We think it our duty to let you know . . . that we as a tribe, for a long time, have had no desire to hear Mr. Fish preach (which is about ten years), and do say sincerely that we, as a body, wish to have him discharged." Their dissatisfaction with Fish was not only in regard to his preaching, but a result of the fact that he had "possession of five or six hundred acres of the tribe's best woodland, without their consent or approbation, and converted them to his own exclusive use, pretending that his claim and right to the same was better than that of the owners themselves."[90]

Although the petition was signed by the tribal president and secretary, Ebenezer Attaquin and Israel Amos, respectively, one can hear Apess's distinct voice in the language, the ironic application of negative work, such as when the petition states, "We wonder how the good citizens of Boston, or any town, would like to have the Indians send them a preacher and force him into the pulpit and then send other Indians to crowd the whites out of their own meeting house, and not pay one cent for it." As always, the reversal was key to Apess's rhetorical strategy, prompting dominant audiences to reflect on the absurdity of their own systemic injustices. Rather than invite focus on Native peoples as incapable of being converted or of modernizing, Apess asked white audiences to reverse the lens and consider how such schemes would play out in accordance to their own sense of justice or inalienable rights. The document concluded by comparing the plight of the Mashpee to that of the Cherokee, noting that the latter had been the beneficiaries of a great deal of sympathy among northern white communities, and yet these same audiences seemed to not consider the injustices to Indian peoples taking place right at their doorsteps. As such, the Mashpees claimed the right to choose their own preacher, and the choice they made was the Reverend William Apess.[91]

Part of Apess's scheme was to make these resolutions public, openly proclaiming the tribe's intentions to the power structure that lorded it over them and also to the press, which Apess had learned to manage so cannily in promoting his own speaking campaigns. Therefore, sometime in mid-June, Apess and Joe Amos traveled to Boston together to personally deliver their petition to the Massachusetts governor, Levi Lincoln. Although the governor would not meet with them, they were given an audience with the lieutenant governor, Samuel Armstrong, who advised them that their resolutions were invalid unless passed through normal legislative channels. As such, Amos and Apess promptly delivered their petition and resolutions to the secretary of state to be submitted to council. This done, Apess then notified William Lloyd Garrison, who, in the June 22 edition of the *Liberator,* announced to the world that "Rev. Wm. Apes has requested us to publish the following resolutions, which he said were passed at a recent meeting of the tribe of Indians at Mashpee."[92]

With the press now engaged in the process, the Boston legislature would be forced to act rather than simply table the Mashpee resolutions. All in all, Apess had set in motion a sure-footed and surprisingly modern media campaign that forced all the issues at Mashpee to a head. Perhaps the most savvy component of Apess's plan, however, was that it set a firm deadline of July 1 for its resolutions to be put into effect, whether sanctioned by the state legislature or not. By imposing this timeframe, Apess ensured the complete transparency of the tribe's intentions. No one could claim to be blindsided by ensuing events. The Mashpee provided themselves moral, if not legal, cover for their actions.

Apess returned to Mashpee by ship in late June, and the *Barnstable Patriot* was once again on hand to observe him "freighted with his implements of housekeeping . . . wending his way, with his bag and baggage, Squaw and pappooses to his new abiding place." The newspaper was clearly already wary of Apess's presence and hoped aloud that "the spirit shown by the authorities of Georgia in a somewhat similar instance will be exercised towards him."[93]

Nevertheless, with his family now situated alongside him in Mashpee, Apess and his allies immediately began to draft a constitution, elect representatives, and make other arrangements in preparation for the storm they knew to be coming. Apess was taking a page from the handbook of the Cherokee by making a demonstration of Mashpee progress and sovereignty. Daniel Amos, the well-educated and successful owner of an oyster concern, was recruited for the role of president. For the first time, Apess writes, a form of government "suited to the spirit and capacity of freeborn sons of the forest" had been put in writing and, if it was modeled in some ways after "the pattern set us by our white brethren," there was one exception in that the Mashpee "were to be held free and equal, *in truth,* as well as in letter." They also made public their resolution to keep all those who would deprive the Mashpee of their own resources, those who daily "degraded and robbed" them, off the reservation, noting that the Mashpee wanted "nothing but their rights betwixt man and man."[94]

What followed in the next few days set the local media on its feet for months to come and sent corresponding ripples throughout the national press. As Apess relates it, he was innocently walking through the woods on July 1, 1833, when he encountered two men preparing to haul off a wagonload of wood from the reservation. Of course, Apess did not just happen to be there. July 1 was the date the Mashpees had set for their resolutions to go into effect. A "Nullifying Ordinance" composed in "good handwriting" had been posted at the meetinghouse, on trees, and at various other places throughout the community, and undoubtedly the Mashpees had organized patrols along the paths leading in and out of the reservation, understanding that their assertion to self-governance would be immediately challenged.[95]

Apess writes that he "mildly" informed the trespassers of the intentions and views of the tribe, noting it was not their design "to wrong or harm any man in the least" but that, until the matter was resolved with the overseers, all former practices of wood harvesting must cease. He remarks, "I begged them to desist, for the sake of peace; but it was to no purpose." What followed was undoubtedly a tense confrontation. Apess had been beaten back by blunt force in the past, but this time the Mashpees stood by him. He is careful to note that he had "previously cautioned the Indians to do no bodily injury to any man, unless in their own defense, but to stand for their rights." Without so much as a "threat or an unkind word," the Mashpees proceeded to unload the wagon. Despite all this, the trespassers, two brothers by the name of Sampson, "used very bitter language at being thus, for the first time, hindered from taking away what had always been as a lawful spoil to them."[96]

This action, having violated an essential privilege of white hegemony, erupted in precisely the way Apess anticipated it would, and in a matter of days the governor suddenly desired to appoint a time and place for the Mashpees to meet with an agent of the state. The Mashpees, however, quickly fired back a message of their own, insisting that any meeting be held on their own ground at the contested Mashpee meetinghouse. The literary scholar Theresa Strouth Gaul has written, "To the Mashpee, reclaiming the space of the meetinghouse from the whites became an important symbolic maneuver in their effort to gain the right of self-governance."[97] In effect, it shifted the very ground on which matters stood, converting the meetinghouse from a site of colonial control to a space of Native resistance.

And so, on July 4, 1833, the two parties assembled, even though the Mashpees had to break into their own church to gain access to it. This time it was not an inverted congregation seated before Apess but the true people for whom the meetinghouse had originally been built. The governor's agent, J. J. Fiske, along with the "high sheriff" of Barnstable County, John Reed, a local judge by the name of Marston, members of the press, and other curious onlookers all piled into a room that was already packed with a hundred or so of the Mashpees themselves. At the insistence of the Natives, time was allowed to fetch the reservation's overseers to ensure that they, too, would hear the grievances to be aired out, and then, in the words of Apess, "they now heard preaching in our meetinghouse as they had never heard before."[98]

The reconstructed Mashpee meetinghouse, where Apess was arrested on July 4, 1833. *Photo by the author, 2015.*

Apess observes that the locals were expecting to encounter wild Indians armed with "tomahawk and scalping knife; that death and destruction, and all the horrors of a savage war, were impending," and many were too easily persuaded that white people had already been butchered. Apparently, prior to the meeting, the governor had considered calling out the militia due to hysterical reports by the Indian agent, Gideon Hawley, who insisted that "the Indians were in open rebellion and that blood was likely to be shed."[99] The county had readied itself for some kind of full-on revolt, but calmer heads prevailed, and the government agent gave audience to the charges of the Mashpee over the course of the day, although a few in the surrounding community still conspired to ratchet up prevailing tensions by portending "bloodshed and murder."

These claims of a barely averted riot would echo through the ensuing press reports for months to come, despite Apess's attempts to ridicule the notion of calling out some "fifty or sixty thousand militia; especially when the great strength and power of the Marshpee tribe was considered."[100] Apparently three of the Mashpee Natives, coming in from hunting deer, had brought their old broken-down rifles with them into the meetinghouse, and this was

interpreted by some as armed insurrection. Such false claims and provoca-
tions to violence fully demonstrate the efficacy of Apess's careful approach, his
insistence on full transparency and peaceful means. The slightest gesture of
aggression would have justified for the colonial powers every disproportionate
countermeasure and was likely to have brought terrible reprisals down upon
the Natives at Mashpee. As it was, a militarized crackdown was just barely
averted.

One wonders if Apess not only precisely orchestrated the Mashpee resistance, but actually planned for it all to come to a dramatic head on the day
that America celebrated the birth of its democratic institutions. Having been
told that their claims were illegal, Apess stood up to address the agents of
state power, speaking "with an energy that alarmed some of the whites present
considerably."[101] He reminded them that their laws were unconstitutional and
stripped Native people of their rights as citizens. He reminded Massachusetts of its own revolutionary legacy—how, when faced with the crushing
weight of an oppressive regime that refused to address their grievances, they at
length "determined to try some other method." He recollected for the white
members of his audience how their forefathers had thrown British tea into
the harbor (dressed as Indians, no less, though Apess leaves this detail aside),
and ultimately fought a terrible war "that your fathers sealed with their blood
a covenant made with liberty." He also reminded those assembled that the
Mashpee themselves had fought alongside the colonists in that long ago war,
furnishing them "with some of her bravest men to fight your battles. Yes, by
the side of your fathers they fought and bled, and now their blood cries to
you from the ground to restore that liberty so unjustly taken from us by their
sons."[102]

But the result of such loyalty and patriotism, Apess exhorted his listeners,
had been imposed bondage, a people kept in darkness, ignorance, and vice.
Rising to a rhetorical pitch, he exclaimed that, rather than set up schools,
as was promised, the Mashpee children were "put out to service. . . . Many
of those who held them in servitude used them more like dogs than human
beings, feeding them scantily, lodging them hard, and clothing them with
rags." Clearly Apess's own childhood memories and traumas were rising to
the fore. Recollections of abuse and betrayal intermingled with the threat
of violence, the horrors of war. Bringing it all home, he continued, "Such,
I believe, has always been the case about Indian reservations. I had a sister
who was slavishly used and half starved; and I have not forgotten, nor can I
ever forget, the abuse I received myself." Apess concluded by declaring to his
audience that the Fourth of July was no day of celebration to the Indian, but a
day of mourning and lamentation, and a sore annual reminder of the ills they
continued to suffer.[103]

No doubt, it was a fiery and disconcerting history lesson for the white people in attendance. For his troubles, Apess was promptly arrested, and apparently some sort of examination was held that evening at the nearby Cotuit courthouse in which a hostile township gathered to ensure "justice" was done. Apess recalls that, "excitement ran very high," and he intimated that, had the white mob gotten its way, "I doubt not that I should have been ruined forever." In fact, had he not taken such meticulous preparations and precautions prior to his arrest, such would have been his fate. Still, he went along peaceably, insisting, "I was glad they had taken me into custody, as it would lead to an investigation of the whole ground in dispute."[104] Apess perceived that he maintained the moral high ground and, as such, understood that a jail sentence would only further publicize the case, bringing into focus the irresponsible use of force at the hands of the state in ways that powerfully negated treasured principles of democracy.

In a sense, Apess foresaw that jail time under these circumstances performed a valuable kind of negative work. It was one thing for such abuses of power to happen in isolation (as they so often did), safely out of view of the public eye, but for someone to be arrested on the Fourth of July before a large audience, with the press in attendance, for the crime of trespassing on one's own property, seemed to strain the very limits of nineteenth-century democratic discourse, even if the "trespasser" in question was an Indian. Apess wryly observed, "Now if I had taken any neighbor's wood without his leave, and he had thrown it out of my cart, and told me to go away, and had given me no further molestation, I should think I had gotten off very easily," adding that, "if a poor Indian wishes to get into jail, this is just the course I would advise him to pursue . . . many and many a red man has been butchered for a less wrong than the Mashpee complain of." Under such circumstances, Apess reckoned that the Fourth of July held little joy "for the man of color." From his established position of moral high ground, Apess used his night in jail as a means of holding up American democracy itself before his Indian's looking-glass, and the reflection proved unsettling to a number of people in relatively high places.[105]

Apess would have been obliged to spend many months in jail awaiting trial had his bail, which had been set at two hundred dollars, not been paid by Lemuel Ewer, a former white treasurer of the tribe. Even this expediency seems to have been mapped out in advance by Apess, but the townspeople, still wanting blood, were blindsided by the event. Apess didn't think it an exaggeration to claim they "bellowed like mad bulls and spouted like whales gored mortally by harpoons" when they heard of his release. Sprung from prison, Apess was now, in the words of certain townspeople, "the leader of the Nullifiers at Mashpee [and] going about the plantation in full command of all its disposable force and treasure, ordering every white man he meets to quit, and not to touch a stick of wood, under penalty of being dealt with according to his Proclamation." Such a hyperbolic and unintentionally ironic account pictured out Apess as a kind of little Napoleon leading a sizable force of combatants rather than an ordained Methodist minister lobbying for Indian use of Indian land through peaceful acts of resistance.[106] The local press, which stood in forceful opposition to this assault on Barnstable's long-standing usages, was forced into untenable stances, complaining that somehow Native people were not entitled to the use of their own property, their own resources or "treasure." The inherent stinginess of such claims proved additional fodder for Apess, who happily published many of these tirades in *Indian Nullification* and gently alluded to the lack of both Christian and democratic principles in such rantings.

Other newspapers ran alarming headlines declaring "Hostilities Commenced in Mashpee," "Indian War in Massachusetts," and "Trouble in the Wigwam," etc.[107] It would be easy to understand how people removed from the actual situation might think a minor Indian revolt had flared up and the eagerly hyperbolic nature of such headlines speaks volumes to the type of reporting that would be generated by the struggles of western indigenous nations in years to come. A New Jersey paper, getting wind of the story, suggested that Apess, "a half-breed . . . who sometime since went about the country in the character of a preacher . . . wishes to be made Governor of his nation. He has stirred his people up to commit various depredations in that vicinity."[108] Another exclaimed, "The Indians, inflamed by the appeals of Apes, are now ready for a nullification of all the state laws."[109]

A few newspaper editors came out in support of the Mashpees, however, including of course, the *Liberator,* but also the *Boston Daily Advocate* and the *Hampden Whig* of Springfield, Massachusetts. The *Whig* emphasized the peaceful restraint of the Natives at Mashpee, noting, "they offered no violence to the whites." The paper further reported,

> It appears by statute that the Indians in this State are placed under guardianship, and we are informed that it is no uncommon occurrence for the Overseers to bind the young Indians to serve on board the whalemen, and to send them to the Pacific, away for years at a time. It appears that the overseers claim the wood growing on the Indian lands, and that the forcibly taking it away is the cause of the present trouble. We think it would be well for our friends "down east" to treat *our own Indians* like human beings before they make any more complaints against the government of Georgia. Altho' it is out of the power of the Marshpee Indians to nullify by physical force the laws of the state, their present movements will induce public inquiry into their grievances and procure for them a redress of wrongs. . . . Will they [the State] endeavor to build up the Massapees, whose title to their lands is

undisputable and according to the ancient treaty cannot be ever conveyed away, into *an independent nation.*[110]

Apess was roundly vilified for forcing these questions to the fore, and took most of the heat from the local community. As one newspaper reported, the Mashpee were "lead on by one Apes, a well known half breed preacher of the itinerant order." He was described as having "considerable shrewdness and talent as a preacher . . . and, as is supposed, has had a material influence in organizing the disaffected Indians." The *Barnstable Patriot,* always Apess's strongest critic, proclaimed, "This Mr. Apes is an Indian Preacher, whom some of our readers may remember, as having preached a very odd sort of sermon in this town, full of premises and conclusions, but destitute of argument, injudicious, and somewhat offensive. He is now charged with stirring up the Marshpee (Massachusetts) Indians, to make difficulty with the whites, and thus to bring trouble upon themselves." The *Patriot* concluded by noting of the Mashpee, "at the time of Apes' coming among them, they were quiet and peaceable, and their condition mentally, morally, and pecuniarily improving. At this time . . . comes this intruder, this disturber, this riotous and mischief-making Indian, from the Pequot tribe, in Connecticut. He goes among the inhabitants of Marshpee, and by all the arts of a talented, educated, wily, unprincipled Indian, professing with all, to be an apostle of Christianity; he stirs them up in sedition, riot, *treason!* Instigates them to declare their independence of the laws of Massachusetts, and to *arm themselves* to defend it."[111]

In these statements and many others the colonial ambivalence that attaches itself to the project of Native assimilation is laid bare. The Mashpees were of little concern to the presiding colonial power as long as they remained in abject poverty and lacked the tools to compete or exercise even a shred of agency in the economic straightjacket designed for their "improvement." But as soon as Natives were allowed to become educated or to develop their own talents through the profession of Christianity, or by any other means, they became a threat to the community at large. The dominant culture had long maintained that Indians were inherently incapable of cultivating such "arts," but Apess's intervention at Mashpee quickly teased out the falsehood of such claims, making available instead the explicit intention to deprive Native peoples of such "mischief-making" abilities. The very talents that were supposed to "civilize" the Indian on the contrary rendered him "shrewd," "wily," and "unprincipled," making of him a treasonous "imposter" merely for exercising those talents to the advantage of himself and his community. No wonder, at the start of *Indian Nullification,* Apess could wryly announce himself still "the same unbelieving Indian that he ever was."[112]

Indian Nullification, which recounts the events of the 1833 "revolt," is Apess's longest and, not coincidentally, his most politically engaged book.

It presents Apess in what is, perhaps, his finest moment, when the brutal struggle, astounding persistence, and astonishing intellect that informed so many pursuits of his adult career finally come to successful fruition. Many have viewed the organized resistance at Mashpee as a bid for full inclusion in the constitutional set of rights guaranteed to every American citizen. The historian Jean O'Brien argues that Apess lobbied for a kind of "dual citizen-ship," which, practically speaking, was probably always the end goal.[113] As the above editorials suggest, however, Apess and the Mashpee were lobbying for sovereign control of their own lands and livelihood as supported by their long-standing relationship with the colonial and then U.S. government. They hoped to assert themselves as "*an independent nation.*" In an "appeal" written in the formal voice of the tribe, we are told that the Mashpee should be "an independent people, having the privileges of the white man . . . we are not free. We wish to be so, as much as the red men of Georgia."[114]

Indian Nullification laid out the case for this plea for sovereignty to the American people, constituting a cleared space where many voices could come together, a space where different sides and different grievances could be aired out and a clear path forward might be delineated. By including the editorials of his opponents, the formal appeals of the tribe, the decisions of the state government alongside his own "powerful negative voice," Apess constructed a unique spatially conceived text—one which, as Strouth Gaul notes, "empha-sizes the existence of multiple and contradictory viewpoints" in a single tex-tualized space.[115] It is a decidedly indigenous approach to conflict resolution, indicative in some ways of the condolence ceremony of the Haudenosaunee that asks all parties to join in a cleared space to ritually wipe away the tears and obstructions of grief, rage, and self-interest that endlessly divert us from good decision-making. As Apess noted, many would like to see the Mash-pee perish, but these forces were destined to be bitterly disappointed, and the Mashpee stood ready to "exhort them to dry their tears, or suffer a poor Indian to wipe them away."[116]

In brief, *Indian Nullification* works to nullify or negate, through public exposure in a provocatively heightened environment, the series of harmful practices and undemocratic abuses that had been codified into law over time to the detriment of Native peoples. Apess maintains that the plight of the Natives at Mashpee and elsewhere had nothing to do with racial destiny, but was a result of unjust laws "calculated to drive the tribes from their posses-sions and annihilate them as a people; and I presume they would work the same effect upon any other people; for human nature is the same under skins of all colors. Degradation is degradation, all the world over."[117] The Mashpee Natives were declaring themselves "an independent community," but one that enjoyed the same inalienable rights enjoyed by U.S. citizens. An integral component to the design of Apess's textual output was to insist on a continued Native presence in New England that was—somewhat paradoxically given the presumed association with the abolitionist movement—*separate but equal.* In other words, the Mashpee were not seeking inclusion in the American government but rather, as Apess told the *Liberator,* "We as a tribe will rule ourselves, and have a right so to do, for all men are born free and equal."[118] For freely voicing such sentiments, in mid-September of that year, Apess was sentenced to thirty days in prison.

CHAPTER SEVEN
The Bizarre Theater of Empire

In the bizarre theater of empire, the stage is a kind of mirror in which the audience, moved to delightful tears, watches a blurred reflection of its own passivity.

— MICHELLE BURNHAM, *Captivity and Sentiment*

Let us drop a compassionate tear also for these benighted children of the forest . . . It was not for them, dark and uninstructed even in the wisdom of man—to comprehend the great design of Providence, of which their wilderness was the appointed theater.

— EDWARD EVERETT, "Oration at the Celebration of the 160th Anniversary of Lathrop's Battle with the Indians"

Combing the Snakes from the Hair

The early twentieth-century Seneca historian Arthur Parker tells us that when the Haudenosaunee Peacemaker first appeared in the lands of the Flint Nation, he declared to all who would listen that the "Creator from whom we all are descended sent me to establish the Great Peace among you. No longer shall you kill one another and nations shall cease warring upon each other." To prove his worthiness and resolve, he was then made to perch himself in a tall pine by the side of the great falls and suffer the tree to be chopped down. "A multitude of people saw him fall into the chasm and plunge into the water. So they were satisfied that he was surely drowned." But the next day the Peacemaker was found once again at the village edge cooking his breakfast as though nothing of great notice had occurred.[1] Having previously survived attempted drowning at the hands of his grandmother and arrived at the Flint Nation on a stone canoe, this final occurrence persuaded the people that the Peacemaker was a worker of miracles and a prophet of peace.

The Haudenosaunee epic details the many obstacles that the Peacemaker and his compatriot, Hayonwhatha, must overcome to bring peace to a warring people. They meet with obstructions wherever they go, confront the blindness of those whose lives are ruled by grief and rage. Hayonwhatha must be consoled of his own grief at the loss of his daughters, a trauma that splits the very heavens in two. The wampum was created to perform this function and open up a ceremonial space for grieving peoples to come together in mutual understanding. In the end, however, the final obstacle to overcome was the defiance of the tyrannical Tatodaho, whose great power kept the surrounding people in a state of terror. Tatodaho is a darkness lurking at the fringes of the narrative, an emblem of human depravity, his mind turned so crooked from corruption and greed that he gnawed on his own fingertips and sprouted snakes from his hair. For Western readers who encounter this tale, Tatodaho promises to provide the springs for narrative action and ultimate resolution. A confrontation is brewing, and if peace is to prevail, it must ultimately require a show of force to overcome this evil resistance. It is the story we are reared upon, the paradox that governs Western thought and principle in its most lucid hours.

The epic of the Northeast woodlands defies expectations, however, when the Peacemaker confronts his nemesis and, rather than vanquish him in mortal battle, endeavors to set his mind right. Although various versions of the tale offer different details, the outcome is always the same. There is no violent confrontation, no struggle, no show of dominance. If the defiant sachem has been twisted and made crooked by past events, Hayonwhatha is finally able to comb the snakes from his hair, thus removing the final obstruction to forming the Confederation of the Longhouse. It is, perhaps, a strange anticlimax for those reared on more oppositional stuff. But it is consistent with the dictates of the white roots of peace and the protocols of condolence. War and violence warp the mind, enrage us, and lead us into cycles of unremitting conflict and trauma. Force can only offer the most fleeting of resolutions. To achieve lasting peace, one must address the root causes, must seek to smooth out the wrinkled and distorted patterns of thought that twist us into tortured versions of our better selves. The community must band behind this notion and a place must be made at the table for the narrative of the former outcast, whose mind has been made crooked by war, to be honored. For all too often, that crooked mind is our own.

William Apess, of course, was unable to perform miracles, other than the everyday down-to-earth variety of withstanding persecution, violence, and incarceration with a good mind—and the equally minor miracle of being able to face the crooked image of his oppressors and endeavor to make it smooth so that formerly warring people might live in peace. I maintain that all of Apess's writings are informed by this intention and that his philosophical commitment to peaceful resistance is a remarkable achievement in and of itself. I have referred to his methodology throughout this book as "negative work," and so it is, as it moves against a nearly inviolable fortress of white history making, of unwitnessing, of the twisted aspect of irresponsible power sprouting writhing snakes from the tortured brow of this country's narrative consciousness.

History itself is the result of cultural trauma, a narrative of elisions and shifting improvisations sprung from conflict, designed to halt the flow of troubling knowledge, of truth too hideous to bear, and which runs the risk of turning any who dare to lift aside its veil into cold unfeeling stone. Power aggressively pushes back all who attempt to unmask its hidden aspect, or, failing that, finds creative ways to ameliorate the unmasking, enfolding its horror into a somehow more acceptable narrative framework. Dominant history will always forcefully resist the types of decolonizing methodologies that someone like William Apess brings to bear. Whatever horrors or injustices are witnessed, the processes of power will unwitness. Attempts will be made to silence, discredit, or beat down the testimony of the wronged and replace it with simulations of dominance.

Apess sees this happening in his own time in a variety of ways, not least of all in the emergence of the noble vanishing savage motif, a narrative so insidiously integrated into the pageant of American history keeping that it enabled reams of violent colonial encounters to read like small sentimental accidents of fate, the forced pogroms of entire populations to seem but a sad "trail of tears," the usurpation of land and resources to appear the inevitable result of savagery hitting up against civilization. As Apess is quoted as saying in one of his many public lectures on the troubles at Mashpee, "The Indians have no way in which to tell their story to the world; but the whites would blazon forth the matter in their papers, and represent their opponents [the Natives] as aggressors, when in truth they were abused and insulted sufferers."[2] We must allow, however, that the "negative voice" needed to confront and reshape such constructs was, nevertheless, a *positive* force, waged against great odds. It operated on the belief that violence would not reap the same results as would peaceful engagement through the courage of personal testimony. Apess used his writings as a means of combing the snakes from the hair of colonial history. In some ways, he *was* a worker of miracles, a prophet of peace. In other ways, it was Apess himself who was in need of condoling.

Letter from Barnstable Jail

The charge against Apess and six of his Mashpee cohorts was that "with force and arms" they did "unlawfully" and "riotously . . . assemble and gather themselves together to disturb the peace," resulting in "a great noise, riot, tumult, and disturbance . . . to the great terror of the people of the said Commonwealth." For this charge Apess was sentenced to thirty days imprisonment, while his cohorts Jacob Pocknet and Charles de Grasse seem to have received a lesser punishment of ten days each.[3] Apess quietly served out his sentence through September and into October of 1833. He used his time in prison to, among other things, draft a detailed petition that the tribe would later submit to be read in the Boston legislature.[4] As he would explain after the fact to the Barton commission in charge of investigating the affairs at Mashpee (as preserved in the clipped transcription of the stenographer), he had written the letter "as voice of people."[5]

The letter, or "memorial," was immediately circulated throughout Mashpee, where, in keeping with traditional processes, it was read to the gathered tribe and discussed and amended where necessary until all were in agreement with its language. The memorial was signed or approved by well over half the residents of Mashpee and laid out the case for the Mashpees' complaint, citing a list of long-standing grievances, and enumerating the unjust and opportunistic means by which the tribe had been oppressed over time.[6] As Apess observes, the laws governing the tribe were so difficult to access and of such complexity, that the Natives themselves had no clear sense of the very rules by which they were governed, making it all the easier to manipulate and exploit their weaknesses.[7] He scolds the august rulers of the state, "While ye are filled with the fat of our father's land and enjoy your liberties without molestation will not this Honorable Body be as benevolent to us, poor Marshpee Indians, who are sighing and weeping under bondage, as ye are to the poor Cherokees?" The memorial concluded with a general cry for release from bondage, exclaiming, "*Oh, White man! white man!* the blood of our fathers, spilt in the Revolutionary War, cries from the ground of our native soil, to break the chains of oppression, and let our children go *free*."[8]

Apess's "Memorial," although first published in the *Liberator* in 1834, has not been reprinted anywhere since. I include it as an appendix to this work as a seminal contribution to Native literature. Although indigenous prison protest literature as a genre can be said to have already had a complex history in the colonies—including documents from Katherine Garret, Moses Paul, and arguably even Black Hawk—Apess's petition stands as a centerpiece in the textualized struggle for Native rights emerging from the heart of colonial containment.

But for Apess, the hall-of-mirrors abuses persisted. White reporters remarked of Apess's trial, "In our opinion, never was there a more just conviction, or a milder sentence." This, in spite of the fact that potential jurors voicing sympathy for the Natives were released without explanation, and a judge in the case, Judge Charles Marston, openly "swore in court that he thought Indians were an inferior race of men, and, of course, were incapable of handling their own affairs."[9] The newspapers concurred, proclaiming that the Natives at Mashpee were "as helpless and incapable of taking care of themselves as little children or slaves."[10] Apess had little recourse but to reflect these pale inconsistencies, formed of the logics of oppression, back at his audience in the hope that, somehow, they might give pause. He maintained that "since this affair took place, I have been kindly informed by a gentleman of Barnstable that my punishment was not half severe enough. I replied that, in my mind, it was no punishment at all; and I am yet to learn what punishment can dismay a man conscious of his own innocence."[11]

Such calm and enlightened responses from an allegedly cunning and riot-mongering Indian must have rankled Apess's opponents. They unexpectedly found themselves cast in the role of frothing tyrants accusing noble Socrates of corrupting the youth of Athens. But perhaps most galling of all for Apess's detractors was the fact that, upon his release, he continued to travel freely about the country, preaching, lecturing, and "endeavoring to enlist public sympathy in his favor . . . stigmatizing and calumniating the Court and Jury who tried and convicted him, and flinging his sarcasms and sneers upon the Attorney and Jury who indicted him. And for all this, he is receiving the applause of an audience who must be ignorant of his character; and blinded by the pretenses of this imposter."[12]

As the above commentary implies, Apess, as soon as he was released from prison, began publicizing the abuses at Mashpee in yet another of his tireless campaigns, stretching from Rhode Island to Connecticut and then back up through Worcester, Springfield, as far north as Concord, New Hampshire, and then back down through Salem, Massachusetts, all in roughly two months' time. It is difficult to imagine anyone, no less a member of the oppressed class, with the energy, will, and organizational skills to manage such a campaign with virtually no support, financial or otherwise. But the response was largely positive. The *Rhode Island Republican* reported that "the son of the forest told many historical truths which could not be very palatable to those who term themselves civilized. He spoke charitably, fearlessly, but unfavorably of the conduct of the white Missionaries among them."[13] And the *New Hampshire Observer* observed, "The object of the address was to awaken public sentiment to the expediency of a measure which will be proposed to the Legislature at its coming session" to extend the rights of the Indians.[14] Apess ended his whirlwind publicity tour in Boston, where, along with his "Marshpee Deputation," consisting of Daniel Amos and Deacon Coombs, he once again packed Boylston Hall and apparently brought the crowd to its feet with what the *Barnstable Patriot* sourly described as his "ribaldry, misrepresentation and nonsense."[15] One might imagine that Apess almost exhausted his rivals as he persisted in pressing the matter coming up before the Massachusetts legislature.

In mid-January of 1834 the Mashpee delegation presented their "memorial" to the House of Representatives in Boston. All three of the Mashpee leaders spoke, beginning with Deacon Coombs. The *Liberator,* which had taken a special interest in the case by this point, provided commentary, noting that Coombs was brief but "somewhat indefinite" in his remarks. Coombs was followed by the newly elected Mashpee president, Daniel Amos, who gave a short account of himself, his years spent traveling the globe on whaling boats, and his pride in never having been imprisoned for either crime or debt, apparently a rare achievement under the Mashpee regime as it existed. The *Liberator* wrote that Amos's words were few and his "language broken." These were not men who, whatever their strengths, were practiced at performing in the halls of power before all-white audiences.

When Apess rose to speak, however, we are told that he was "fearless, comprehensive and eloquent." He "illustrated the manner in which extortions were made from the poor Indians, and plainly declared that they wanted their rights as men and as freemen," and "endeavored to prove that, under such laws and such overseers, no people could rise from their degradation." Apess demanded to know by what right the Mashpee were held under such obligations and made what the *Liberator* referred to as some "dexterous and pointed thrusts at the whites for their treatment of the sons of the forest since the time of the pilgrims." Whether or not everyone was as inspired by Apess's speech as the correspondent for the *Liberator,* Apess probably prompted more than one legislator to shake off his ambivalence concerning the racially motivated laws by which Native people were governed. The *Liberator* concluded, "The cries of the Indians have reached their ears, and we trust affected their hearts."[16]

It must be noted that some hearts also remained unaffected. The Boston lawmakers were divided over the issue, and many argued that the presented memorial did not even merit so much as a reading on the house floor, although, as Mr. Allen, the representative from Worcester, objected, such a course of action had never before been adopted, in his memory, toward a respectful petition. The issue was hotly debated, with many still maintaining, against all available evidence, that Apess was an outside agitator who had instigated a "riot." This misinformation was at least partially due to the fact that Phineas Fish, the reviled Mashpee preacher, had presented his own memorial to the floor, complete with signatures from tribal members, which, of course, contradicted everything stated in the Mashpee memorial. It would later be revealed that Fish's signatories were largely belonging to the family of Nathan Pocknet, who was likely bought off by Fish, and a few other disreputable or uneducated stragglers who, not surprisingly, did not understand what they were signing and later recanted. Although the reading of the Mashpee memorial ultimately prevailed in the legislature, it still remained for it to be debated and passed as a bill.

William Lloyd Garrison continued to champion the cause of Apess and the Mashpee. On February 7, 1834, he orchestrated a fundraiser for the benefit of the Mashpee delegation, featuring a singing performance by his very own Garrison Juvenile Choir. No doubt Apess attended and took part in the proceedings, which consisted of hymnody, national anthems, and spoken dialogues on subjects both religious and moral. The cause was further championed by Benjamin Hallett, a young attorney and editor of the *Boston Advocate,* one of the few public supporters of the Mashpee cause. Hallett chose to represent the case of the Mashpee as counsel before a joint committee of state leaders in March of that year. His court argument, which was published at the request of the Mashpee delegates in April of 1834, is a brilliant defense of Native rights put forward by a white lawyer, in a voice that seems to have had very little precedent in nineteenth-century print discourse. Recognizing the divisive redirection employed when people spoke of Native issues, Hallett argued in his suit, "White men of the present day console themselves by attributing all the wrongs of the Indians to our ancestors. It is as unjust as it is false. Modern men have done the worst wrongs to the remnant of the Indian tribes all over the country . . . as the whites have become more free in Massachusetts, they have increased the slavery and disabilities of the Mashpee Indians."[17]

As has already been suggested, the abuses the Mashpees faced went well beyond the white privilege of taking wood off the reservation (Apess estimated some fourteen hundred cords of wood a year) or the struggle to control the meetinghouse. These were significant matters in and of themselves, but the average reader would likely be mortified to fully comprehend the system of peonage under which Natives of New England lived and labored. Hallett, in his argument, observed that the overseers

> were vested with full power to regulate the police of the plantation; to establish rules for managing the affairs, interests, and concerns of the Indians and inhabitants. They may improve and lease the lands . . . regulate their streams, ponds, and fisheries; mete out lots for their improvement; control and regulate absolutely their bargains, contracts, wages, and other dealings; take due care of their poor, and bind out their children to suitable persons, the parents having no voice in the disposition of their children, and there being no appeal, in any exercise of the above unlimited powers, from the overseers to any other tribunal.[18]

In other words, the overseers held power over the Indians equivalent to that of "overlords." If an Indian was deemed to be an "idler," the overseers had the authority to forcibly bind him into service strictly based on their own arbitrary judgment, a power Hallett rightly characterized as "despotic." No small wonder that the minister, Fish, could indiscriminately label the whole tribe a nation of idlers, as it gave him and the overseers even greater authority in managing and suppressing Mashpee lives and ambitions.[19]

Hallett took issue with the suggestion that any group of landowners (which the Mashpee were) who regularly paid their taxes (which the Mashpee ostensibly did, through the relinquishing of their resources at a highly exorbitant rate) could be called paupers or "indolent." In fact, Hallett observed, the Mashpee had served as an open source of revenue for the surrounding community, strengthening the coffers of the Commonwealth at a rate four times higher than any other township in Massachusetts.[20] And yet they received no services in return, no schools, no roads, not even the use of their own meetinghouse (unless one somehow considered the appointment of the unwanted Phineas Fish as their minister a "service"). If the Mashpee were neither paupers nor slaves nor enemies of the state, the question raised then was, by what right, legal or otherwise, did the state rule over the Mashpee people?

Hallett's defense is lengthy and thorough, reviewing the entire history of the Mashpee as a legal entity under the colonial regime and firmly rebutting every claim made by the Mashpee opponents. While Hallett reports that he had no desire to enter into the religious concerns of the tribe, he dismantles the arguments in Fish's memorial to the legislature piece by piece, wryly observing that he regrets its "spirit" and that "in comparison with that of the Indians [written by Apess], I must say it loses in style, in dignity, and in Christian temper." Hallett also observes that it is not his business to defend the character of Mr. Apess, who, as he notes, "is charged with being the ring leader of the 'sedition.'" But given the despicable laws in place at Mashpee, Hallett wonders how we can blame them if

> when they found an educated Indian, with Indian sympathies and feelings, they employed him to present their complaints. . . . Look at this circumstance fairly, and I think you will find in it the origin of all the prejudice against William Apess, which may be traced to those of the whites who are opposed to any change in the present government of Marshpee. If aught can be shown against him, I hope it will be produced here in proof, that the Indians may not be deceived. If no other proof is produced, except his zeal in securing freedom for the Indians, are you not to conclude that it cannot be done? But his individual character has nothing to do with the merits of the question, though I here pronounce it is unimpeached.[21]

Hallett proved the perfect advocate at the perfect moment and the Marshpee Act passed both branches of the legislature unanimously on March 29, 1834. The bill gave to the Mashpee the right to self-government as a township with its own town officers, and power to oversee schools, highways, management of the poor, and management over all the proprietary lands held in common. It was a substantial victory, although in the end, the legislature did not feel it had the power to evict Fish as minister at Mashpee. Use of the Meetinghouse was to be divided between the competing denominations and Marston, the racist judge, retained his position as commissioner over the district. Still, Apess's collaboration with the existing leadership at Mashpee had lasting effects so that even now, he is recalled by some in the tribe as "Marshpee's first Indian/political/social activist."[22]

Indian Nullification

Apess made the events at Mashpee the topic of his lectures in the days and months ahead, again traveling from Rhode Island to New Hampshire and as far as Portland, Maine, speaking in prideful terms of the advances at Mashpee now that the Natives were self-governing. He boasted (as Samson Occom had done at Brothertown some fifty years earlier) that Mashpee had now formed a "body politic and appoint the usual town officers. They have about 60 houses. . . . One hundred of them can read the bible, forty-four can write, and a few can cypher. They have a church of about fifty members and a temperance society of about 60 members. They have eight teams, thirty cows, and a few sheep. Since they were relieved by the last legislature, they built a house 36 feet by 18, designed in part for a school house and in part for a dwelling house for a teacher."[23]

In his time at Mashpee, Apess also began to acquire a more sophisticated understanding of regional indigenous history and, in particular, the history of King Philip's, or Metacom's, War of 1675–76, to which he had long claimed a connection while commanding very few specifics. Rather than merely gleaning this history from the colonial records, however, Apess was able to center his knowledge in Mashpee oral tradition and began, more and more, to structure his lectures and sermons on a framework informed by indigenous history keeping.

When Apess began to place that framework before a colonial audience in his 1836 *Eulogy on King Philip,* he would specifically demand if it were not truth, for as he was quick to remind, "Indians think it is."[24] For the Mashpee, King Philip's War was still a vivid memory and open wound that could not so easily be dissolved into sentimental absolution by the distance of time. It had resulted in the death of nearly 40 percent of their population, the breaking up of the Wampanoag people as a self-governing nation, and the fragmentation of family and social structures, with many of the survivors being sold into slavery in the West Indies following the war. Apess was now a bearer of this history. He spoke before crowds of the peace treaty between the Wampanoag sachem Massasoit and the Pilgrims, kept inviolate for forty years, and reminded his listeners of Native involvement in the Revolutionary War, in which the Mashpee posted more volunteers than any other district in Barnstable County, all but a handful of whom gave up their lives for the cause of American democracy and freedom.[25]

Apess must have once again used the winter to begin compiling the manuscript that would be titled *Indian Nullification of the Unconstitutional Laws of Massachusetts Relative to the Marshpee Tribe; Or, The Pretended Riot Explained.*[26] This tract fulfilled two purposes for Apess. It provided a durable print accounting of the events that had occurred in 1833–34 at Mashpee, ensuring that the indigenous witness to these events could not be shrouded over by reams of newspaper print still insisting on calling it a "riot" and a "revolt." But it served the dual purpose of publicly exonerating Apess of the many charges that had dogged him even prior to the peaceful resistance at Mashpee. The old slanders had refused to go away and, in many instances, the events at Mashpee had only exacerbated them.

On May 29, 1835, the *Boston Recorder* asserted in an open letter to the public said to be written by ranking Native officials at Mashpee that "where-as a colored man by the name of William Apess, calling himself a preacher of the Gospel, has repeatedly made collections of various amounts of money in different parts of the country, pleading for this purpose (as we are informed) the necessity of the people of this place [Mashpee]: This is to allow, that said Apes is wholly unauthorized by us. We never have realized any benefit from anything bestowed upon him, nor if we might be profited do we wish for anything by *his* means."[27] The letter, signed by William Mings and Ebenezer Attaquin, both now enjoying the office of selectmen to the district of Mashpee, was designed to discredit every aspect of Apess's identity, first by declaring him a "colored man" rather than either a Pequot or an adopted member of the Mashpee tribe, then by calling into dispute his ordination, and, finally, by bringing up the old charge that he had collected church monies for his own private gain.

In direct response, *Indian Nullification,* which came out in late May or early June of 1835, opens with a testimony from the primary leaders at Mashpee, styled in traditional Native address from "the red children of the soil of America" to the "descendants of the pale men who come across the big waters." Signed by three other Mashpee selectmen, Israel Amos, Isaac Coombs, and Ezra Attaquin, it immediately and thoroughly discredits the former report, stating of Apess that "many of our white brethren hate him, and revile him, and say all manner of evil of him, falsely calling him an imposter. Know, all men, that our brother Apes is not such a man as they say . . . we say that we love our brother, the Rev. William Apes, who preaches to us, and have all the confidence in him that we can put in any man." Benjamin Hallett also weighs in, averring that "William Apes, an Indian preacher, of the Pequot Tribe, regularly ordained as a minister, came among these Indians to preach. They invited him to assist them in getting their liberty. He had the talent they most stood in need of."[28]

Apess also comes to his own defense, observing, "It appears that I, William Apess, have been much persecuted and abused, merely for desiring the welfare of myself and my brethren."[29] He enumerates the crimes laid against his name and one by one dismantles the claims, providing written testimony from the church leadership in Boston and full retractions from those who had originally slandered him. One such letter of support, from Thomas Norris, president of the Protestant Methodist organization in Boston, is dated May 7, 1835, demonstrating that less than one month before *Indian Nullification* was published, Apess was still actively seeking redress for his wrongs, careful to leave no stone unturned.[30]

Of John Reynolds, who had initially published the libels against Apess in 1832, it is revealed that he had spent time in prison and been denounced by other members of the church. It seems Apess had initially won the enmity of Reynolds because at the regional Methodist conference in 1832 Apess had voted against his advancement to the status of church elder. This rejection at the hands of an Indian was apparently a slight that Reynolds could not forgive, and it inspired the backlash against Apess's own name and reputation as a preacher. Apess sued his accusers for libel (there being two others), and each of them was held at fifteen hundred dollars bail.

Although Apess might have left them to suffer the consequences of their actions, he notes that he promptly dropped the charges against the men in return for their written retractions and "in order to show them that I wanted nothing but right, and not revenge, and that they might know that an Indian's character was as dearly valued by him as theirs by them." He concluded by wondering, "Would they ever have thus yielded to an Indian, if they had not been compelled?"[31] Apess concludes *Indian Nullification* by noting, "I have been assaulted by the vilest calumnies, represented as an exciter of sedition, a hypocrite, a gambler. These slanders, though disproved, still continue to circulate. Though an Indian, I am at least a man, with all the feelings proper to humanity, and my reputation is dear to me; and I conceive it to be my duty to the children I shall leave behind me, as well as to myself, not to leave them the inheritance of a blasted name."[32]

To help keep that good name, on June 5, 1835, a mere week after the *Boston Recorder* had published its letter slandering Apess's credentials and intentions, Apess personally dropped by the paper's offices. He had in hand his own statement of support from Coombs and Attaquin signed by the Mashpee justice of the peace, as well as a receipt indicating that he had put down money for the building of a meetinghouse at Mashpee and a certificate of his position there as a preacher in good standing with the church. Apess left nothing to chance. He also apparently dropped off a copy of his new book, *Indian Nullification,* for the editors to peruse.[33] The book, published by the Boston printer Jonathan Howe, promised to set the record straight about the "pretended riot" in Mashpee and sported a woodcut frontispiece depicting a cynical vision of exchange in which an Indian trades his harvest of wood for a bottle of rum that unfortunately detracted from, rather than explicated, the political realities at Mashpee.

The publication of *Indian Nullification* in late spring marked the beginning of a new tour in which Apess made his usual rounds, promoting the book throughout the states of Massachusetts, New Hampshire, Maine, and probably Rhode Island and Connecticut as well. The *Portsmouth Journal* announced on July 18 that "Wm. Apes an Indian Preacher, yesterday handed us a book . . . [that] explains the circumstances of the pretended riot at Cape Cod in 1833—and also gives a concise history of that tribe for many years." The article added that he would remain in town a day or two with copies to sell.[34] Another New Hampshire paper, the *Gazette,* praised the "memorable spirit of 76" invoked by the Mashpee in the book, noting that the Natives simply wished to be "mantled to those truths which our fathers once proclaimed to the despots of the world."[35] *New England Magazine's* review of the book observed, "It is written far better than could have been expected from an Indian, and is well worth reading. The only fault we find is, that the author has allowed himself to be exasperated by the persecution he endured."[36] And the *New England Galaxy* said of the book that "it exhibits considerable powers of argument and a vein of sarcasm. . . . The work is also rather witty, and in our opinion worth reading. There will be some, however, who will no doubt think the affairs of a few Indians on Cape Cod unworthy of their attention."[37] Only the *Massachusetts Spy* was not so generous, noting of the book that "its tone and language are violent and denunciatory."[38]

Of Monuments and Men: The Bloody Brook Monument Commission

Still making the rounds to promote his new book, Apess stopped at the Universalist meetinghouse in Portsmouth, New Hampshire, on July 21, 1835, and gave what appears to have been the very first performance of what is arguably his most powerful piece of writing, the *Eulogy on King Philip.*[39] In all likelihood he had yet to fit together all the myriad historical pieces of what would become the finished document. Perhaps the title had been an on-the-spot improvisation—just another provocative way to promote himself to a local audience. But ultimately the *Eulogy on King Philip* was to become the sweeping repurposing of dominant historical narrative hegemony that Apess had been working toward his entire career. He finally hit upon the theme, the historical locus, around which all his other concerns and rhetorical strategies could calibrate themselves, creating a kind of critical mass, an improbable imploding and unfolding of narrative possibilities, all of them swirling and gathering around the unstable vortex of the figure of King Philip.

Apess had long claimed a kinship to Philip, invoked his name, and hovered around the vague and distorted brushstrokes of colonial image making that had so crudely smeared the Wampanoag leader's life and name across the canvas of white history. Apess's experiences and connections at Mashpee, however, had allowed him to newly locate Philip within indigenous perspectives, opening up a newfound center of gravity with which he could begin to recount the bloody cost of the colonial encounter; a center that, rather than disintegrating into misty fables of Native vanishing with each revolution, accrued mass and power in its insistence on a livable indigenous present and future. "Where shall we place the hero of the wilderness?" Apess would ask in his finished address, although the answer was always clear. Philip was right there at the center.[40]

The early nineteenth-century fascination with the figure of King Philip was in full swing in 1835, with America's favorite thespian, Edwin Forrest, still the toast of the nation in his starring role in *Metamora: Or, The Last of the Wampanoags.* The 1829 play, written by John Augustus Stone, served as the ultimate wish-fulfillment fiction whereby colonial audiences were permitted to valorize that which they actively sought to destroy, displacing their own agency in this destruction by wiping out the historical record of war, murder, and slavery in one fell rhetorical gesture. The play was wildly successful, remaining in production for the next two decades, with Forrest coming to inhabit the title role.[41] As the historian Jill Lepore observes, the play ultimately spotlighted Philip's death, "a tragic death, yes, but a necessary one." Lepore writes that if "*Metamora* mourned the passing of Philip and the disappearance of New England's Indians . . . it mourned these losses as inevitable and right."[42]

Interestingly, Washington Irving's 1819 sketch "Philip of Pokanoket" was also enjoying a brief revival in August of 1835, in a digested format as "The Death of King Philip," appearing in a flurry of major newspapers across the East Coast. In addition, *King Philip* was the name of a well-traveled steamer in the 1830s doing brisk business throughout the eastern seaports. There was even a thoroughbred racing horse named King Philip gaining notice on the tracks. But the events of Philip's life made their most significant intersection with other mandates of colonial history keeping that late summer at the

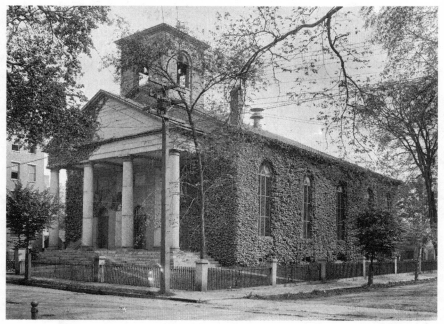

The Stone Church in Portsmouth, NH, where Apess performed the earliest-known version of his *Eulogy on King Philip*. Photo 190515, Detroit Publishing Company, Library of Congress Prints and Photographs Division, LC-DIG-det-4a23742.

commemoration of what is known as "Lathrop's battle," or, more infamously, the "Bloody Brook massacre."

Bloody Brook proved one of the more decisive losses suffered by the colonists in King Philip's War. Captain Thomas Lathrop, returning from a mission to evacuate vulnerable trading posts in the Connecticut River valley in September of 1675, was taken off guard by a Native war party claimed to number about seven hundred. All but a handful of Lathrop's men were killed in the attack, the Puritan historian William Hubbard referring to this day as "the Saddest that ever befel *New-England*."[43] Now, one hundred and sixty years later, it behooved the local inhabitants of South Deerfield to erect a monument on the spot of this hallowed ground. So, on September 30, 1835, a number of luminaries were called in to assist in marking the day, most notably, the poet Lydia Sigourney and the statesmen and orator Edward Everett. Although no one thought to invite William Apess, the self-styled descendent of King Philip, to the event, some of the main motifs of his own *Eulogy* would be on display.

The ceremony took place in a large open field in South Deerfield, known to be the site of the actual battle. Papers reported that the day was hot but carried a stiff breeze that swallowed up the words of the less powerful orators. Some six thousand people appeared for the event, spread out in a semicircle across the field, eager to pay homage to the fallen ancestors who, with their life's blood, had secured for themselves this land. A stage was erected and chairs set up for the ladies in attendance. Directly across from the stage, rising up from the level plane of the field and presiding over all, was a prominent ridge culminating in the summit known as Sugarloaf, richly decked in its "September robes."[44] A band played, politicians pontificated, and Sigourney read her commemorative poem, penned especially for the occasion. But it was Mr. Everett's speech that "attracted the ears and eyes of the audience."[45]

If Louisa Park had found Everett to be tendentious and outdated in his speaking style when he addressed the cause of the Cherokee three years earlier, he still seems to have been pleasing to the tastes of most audiences of the time and, if nothing else, had a voice capable of carrying across a large open field crowded with people. But Everett was also known for the informed historical breadth that he brought to his speeches and his ability to bring all of the various elements of his address to a pitched crescendo calculated to inspire in the crowd a redemptive pathos, steeped as it was in deep stentorian considerations of fateful happenstance and nationalistic import. His speech at Bloody Brook lasted for an hour and a half and was delivered, as was his style, without notes. Everett opened by setting the scene, asking his audience to go back in time and imagine themselves still surrounded by "gloomy forest" and "tangled swamp." He invited them to cast their glances back to the few huddled cabins thrown up in "the bosom of the primeval forest" and a cornfield or two raised up against "the all surrounding wilderness," lair of "the wolf, of the rattlesnake, of the savage." The landscape Everett mapped out for his listeners was a savage and unredeemed space, and if it was sorrowfully "in the possession of the Native tribes, it was obviously the purpose of Providence that it should become the abode of civilization, the arts, and Christianity."[46]

Given such oppositional language, it is difficult to imagine Everett a so-called friend of the Indian, even though considered a thorough reformist who had been called in to support the cause of the Cherokee just a few years earlier. "What good man would prefer a country covered with forests and ranged by a few thousand savages to our extensive Republic, studded with cities, towns, and prosperous farms?" Andrew Jackson had queried five years earlier.[47] Everett's rhetoric frames the precise same question, revealing a man deeply embedded in the linguistic operations of colonialism still locating Native peoples in a space of unabated intellectual and spiritual darkness, their removal from the land an act of divine Providence. In the very same year that a Cherokee party consisting of Elias Boudinot and John Ridge felt coerced into signing the Treaty of New Echota (that fateful x-mark providing cover for the federal government to forcefully drive the Cherokee off their land), Everett stood before this immense gathering in Massachusetts and declared that the conquest of Natives by European culture was, in fact, a "moral necessity," for how else could "the forests have been cleared, and its place taken by the cornfield?" The Indian, Everett surmised, "seen as he really is," stands "low on the scale of humanity . . . he leads an indolent, a squalid, and a cheerless existence," with scarcely anything "that one can call agriculture," addicted to war and the "scalping knife." One can almost imagine Everett slicing the air up and down with his hand here, as Louisa Park described him in his earlier address, hissing his *s*'s along the way.

For all this, however, Everett seems to have found a racial exception in the figure of Philip, as one who was somehow "greatly the superior both of his elder brother and his father, in reach of policy, capacity, vigor, and resource." Philip, it seemed, due to some happy accident of genetic disposition, was practically a white guy. Interestingly, in earlier colonial times, Philip had served the precise opposite role, emerging in the literature of his day as the most reviled and debased of the savages.[48] The subsequent elevation of Philip in the nineteenth century was in keeping with popular notions of racial hierarchies existing even within a particular racial category. Pocahontas was often regarded in such a light, as one who stood apart from her otherwise degraded kin, as was the Shawnee warrior Tecumseh. This trope served the complex rhetoric of early nationalism by allowing sympathy and remorse to devolve on a single individual rather than an entire race of people, whose demise, if properly considered, might rightly reek of genocide. As such, Philip himself, as in the play *Metamora* and Irving's sketch, becomes the locus of our mourning, one tragic deficit in an otherwise balanced accounting sheet.

Everett's speech goes on to rehearse the popular details of the war, leading inexorably to Philip's death. There is no tangible acknowledgment in his address that Native people still walked the earth, that they might have a stake in the history keeping invoked, or that the lowly rank in human affairs he assigns them in his speech could be accepted as anything other than racial destiny. In the course of his oration, the figure of the Indian managed to run the full gauntlet from reviled savage worthy of extermination to noble king of the forest, stripped of power and resources, felled by his own savage proclivities, and yet worthy of a tear and even forgiveness now that the foreseen termination had come to pass. Everett even manages, at last, to offer a few words in reproach of the white man, who perhaps wrongfully, stripped the Indian of his lands—although too late, for sure, to do anything about it.

But Everett's showstopper, saved for the near end of his speech, is when he asks his audience to consider "the fate of Philip's wife and his son?" Few probably knew, as Everett seems to have uncovered, that "they were sold into slavery; West Indian slavery! . . . to gasp under the lash, beneath the blazing sun of the tropics. . . . Is there anything—I do not say in the range of human-ity;—is there anything animated, that would not struggle against this?" This was classic Everett—an appeal to what was best in humanity, sprung from a completely unexpected corner of his discourse. No matter that untold num-bers of New England Natives had been sold into slavery since the time of the Pequot War. By bringing the innocent "squaw" and "papoose" of Philip to the fore of his lament, Everett managed to shift the ground of his speech from the ambivalent regrets of past colonial aggressions to the ongoing immorality of southern slavery. He offers all this with a kind of sentimental preening liberally dotted with exclamation points of remorse.

Lest anyone lose the thread of his talk, however, Everett concludes by reca-librating his colonial gaze once more to the present, fixing it on "the hills cultivated or covered with flocks. . . . I see roads, bridges, the canals, the rail-ways which spread their busy network over the face of the country." In other words, there was none standing who could question the great improvements wrought by the sacrifice of those "who on this sacred spot . . . poured out their life blood in defense of the heritage which has descended to us." Where he began by locating his audience in a wild space devoid of art, agriculture, law, or religion, Everett concludes by restoring his listeners to the cultivated improvements of civilization, his speech at the last redeeming the very ground upon which they all stood, consecrating the sacrifice of their forefathers within a cartography of unimpeachable improvements. And for all this, Ever-ett was rewarded with the immense delight and thundering applause of his audience. Newspapers would continue to print excerpts from his speech for the next three months. The *Liberator* even gushed that, in the wake of such a speech, "hereafter we claim Mr. Everett an anti-slavery man."[49]

In her book *The Common Pot,* the Abenaki historian Lisa Brooks begins her discussion of Apess by coincidentally revisiting the very same location where Everett delivered his Bloody Brook address. Brooks, however, traces the contours of this landscape along a quite different set of narrative delineations than the one Everett plotted out, understanding that the Connecticut River valley was not simply howling forest and tangled swamp in the time of King Philip but rather what she calls a "deeply situated social and ecological envi-ronment." It was a space not only of indigenous village life, but of other, non-human habitats sustained by rich alluvial fields where corn, beans, squash, and other produce were cultivated through Native arts, and by a variety of other shared resources that constitute what Brooks refers to as the "common pot." In Brooks's rendering, the tall peak marking the termination of the ridge that loomed over South Deerfield that day is not Sugarloaf but Ktsi Amiskw, the Great Beaver. Abenaki lore tells how it was Ktsi Amiskw who built a giant dam over the Connecticut River, hoarding the water for himself and causing the fields and wetlands below to dry up—an act that brought suffering and devastation to the land. As punishment the Creator turned Ktsi Amiskw to stone. He stands over the valley today as a reminder of the interconnectivity of all those who dwell in the land, regardless of skin color or creed, and of their responsibility not to take more than needed from the village dish to survive.

The evils of colonialism encountered by Apess in his day were, in a sense, no different from those described in the story of the Great Beaver. A few selfish and shortsighted individuals attempted to horde the best of the resources for themselves, heedless of the pain and deprivation it caused others. This is the story of colonialism, simply told, and its practices and values continue to wreak havoc to this day, keeping the world in a state of precarious imbalance. When Apess composed his *Eulogy*, however, Brooks notes that he drew on indigenous tradition by "establishing New England as Native space into which Europeans entered, by invoking the centrality of Native rights, and by seducing his audience into the conceptual space of the common pot."[50]

"O What Cursed Doctrine Is This?": Apess's *Eulogy on King Philip*

For a certainty, when Apess spoke before a crowd, he could never afford the luxury of imagining the absence of *white* auditors. Every public word he uttered was specifically crafted to take into account the intractable prejudices of white culture and the granite foundations of their history making. This was still very much the case on January 1, 1836, when Boston newspapers first began to advertise the performance of "an Eulogy" on the subject of "The Indian King Philip," at the Odeon Theater, to be "pronounced" by an Indian Preacher. Critics and historians long believed there were only two performances of Apess's *Eulogy*, but it is now clear, thanks largely to improved electronic databases of historical newspapers and materials, that the *Eulogy* had multiple readings across the stages, lecture halls, and pulpits of the East Coast. As with his other set lectures and publications, Apess took this show on the road, hammering out its particulars from one audience to the next, devising ways to bring his performance to an Everett-like peak of pathos and portent, but in a manner that took into account the needs of multiple audiences and ethnicities rather than simply planting itself as a monolithic ornament of truth.

There seem to have been two performances at the Odeon in early January, on the first and eighth of the month.[51] Tickets were sold at local bookstores or at the door of the theater, where twenty-five cents might purchase admission for both a gentleman and a lady. One Boston paper, in anticipation of the talk, offered a dubious endorsement, announcing, "Here is something worth while. Be it known, that on the eighth of January, 1836, a native American Indian is to pronounce . . . an eulogy on this great sachem. . . . Well, strange things have happened. Our fathers stuck the warrior's head upon a pole, and his limbs adorned the spires of Boston by way of weather-cocks; now let us make amends by hearing from one of his fallen race."[52] On January 26, Apess was invited to perform his *Eulogy* yet again at Boylston Hall, in a slightly abridged version, the papers hinting at "some dissatisfaction at the previous performance at the Odeon."[53] The implication seems to be that people were upset with the tone or content of the Odeon performance, and there was, in truth, plenty in Apess's speech to upset them. The *Eulogy* was next performed at the Lyceum Hall in Salem, Massachusetts, on the 29th, where, it was promised, attendees would have their "only chance to hear the *true* character of the mighty Philip."[54] As the advertisement intimates, Apess was intent on breaking down the image American audiences had constructed of Philip over the previous century, offering a version that would stand in contrast to that of Everett, Irving, Cooper, and Forrest.

On February 22, the country was celebrating the birthday of its first president, George Washington, and Apess likely used this commemoration as a rhetorical springboard when he launched into his *Eulogy* that evening in Worcester, Massachusetts. The reporter for the *Massachusetts Spy* wrote that the Indian orator "feelingly told the story of the Red man's wrongs," and although it was found that he was "too severe upon our fathers," it was nevertheless concluded that "the history was interesting, and the orator was, in some passages, really eloquent."[55] By March, Apess was in Hartford, once again to pronounce upon the "great personage of the Woods." The *Eulogy* was delivered at least twice at Union Hall, with the *Hartford Times* graciously wishing "the Indian success and a full house."[56] Most likely Apess performed the *Eulogy* at additional stops along the way and at this point had the printed version in hand to sell at his performances. His *Eulogy on King Philip* was to be the last, and perhaps most accomplished, of Apess's works.

The *Eulogy* stands apart from Apess's other works as the least autobiographical and the most cohesive literary offering of his career. The fact that it reads more self-consciously as a performance than his other works lends it an added element of immediacy, vigor, and stagecraft. Eulogies were a popular genre at the time, and not a month went by when someone wasn't appearing in a hall somewhere to eulogize the likes of Washington, Jefferson, Lafayette, or some other cherished luminary of the Revolution. By determining that his life and career deserved equal treatment, Apess was removing the figure of Philip from a rarified atmosphere of colonial handwringing, what Michelle Burnham refers to as the "bizarre theater of empire," and placing him in a grounded perspective that acknowledged Philip as a man of accomplishment and merit in appreciative historical terms.

Had he merely wanted to counter the words of Everett at Bloody Brook, Apess might have offered a more pointed speech. It had been impressed upon Apess, however, that he would need to widen his scope, that history itself was the fault line upon which every misperception concerning Native peoples was built. As he had observed as early as 1829 in *A Son of the Forest,* the Indian character had been greatly misrepresented and "justice has not and, I may add, justice cannot be fully done to them by the historian. My people have had no press to record their sufferings or to make known their grievances; on this account many a tale of blood and woe has never been known to the public."[57]

A Native view of history had been so thoroughly obscured and distorted that there was, Apess seems to concede, no way to tease it fully back into being. But through a kind of negative work one could begin to unmake the history of the colonist. If the past could not be fully resuscitated in any serviceable form, there was still the opportunity to reshape the narrative of colonialism that served in its stead—to repurpose the litany of slaughters, thefts, and misdeeds that retained shape and force in the memories of eastern Native peoples and seek a new verdict. "It will be well for us to lay those deeds and depredations committed by whites upon Indians before the civilized world," he proclaimed.[58] But the *Eulogy* is also, from start to finish, a document that unwaveringly privileges peaceful resolution as the only course toward universal equality. It is an act of literary condolence designed to heal the wounds of a historical past.

David Reynolds has observed that early nineteenth-century theatrical performances could quickly devolve into moblike affairs, with audiences tending to be rowdy and easily provoked.[59] It must have been with a fair amount of trepidation then that Apess, the Indian, took the stage and first stared down that large unwieldy crowd at the Odeon, drawing a deep breath and reserves of courage before pronouncing his greatest orchestration of negative work: "I do not arise to spread before you the fame of a noted warrior, whose natural abilities shone like those of the great and mighty Philip of Greece, or of Alexander the Great, or like those of George Washington," he cried, and "neither do I approve of war as being the best method of bowing to the haughty tyrant. No, far from me be such a thought."[60]

If Everett had privileged the spilled blood of colonial patriots in his Bloody Brook address, Apess made clear to his audience from the start that the "son of the forest" was a man of peace, a being made "by the God of Nature," within whom had been planted "sympathies that shall live forever in the memory of the world." Forbearance, sympathy, permanence—these were the heretofore unacknowledged Native virtues Apess sang, while knowing all along that

there were those of the so-called civilized world who would "think it no crime
to wreak their vengeance upon whole nations and communities [of Indians],
until the fields are covered with blood and the rivers turned into purple
fountains, while groans, like distant thunder, are heard from the wounded
and the tens of thousands of the dying." Apess's audience had no inkling of
such atrocities committed *against,* rather than *by,* Native peoples, or, more
accurately, they had successfully unwitnessed such events, failing to allow the
horror of sustained violence against Natives to gain purchase in their cognitive worlds. But as Apess tallies up one example after another of depredations
committed in the name of "civilization," it behooves him to enquire of his
audience, "Who, my dear sirs, were wanting of the name of savages—whites
or Indians? Let justice answer."[61] It becomes readily apparent how some in the
audience might have taken offense or called for an "abridgment."

The *Eulogy* is not just a critique of colonialism, but a scathing indictment
of Christianity itself, or at least the version of it practiced by a settler nation.
The hospitality and forbearance first practiced by the Wampanoag sachem
Massasoit in helping to provide for the Pilgrims at Plymouth suggested to
Apess a greater sense of Christian virtue than those merely "pretended pious,"
as he often refers to the Puritans.[62] He observes how "Christianity" was thrust
upon the Native nations through the weapons of "rum and powder and ball,"
and he asserts that diseases such as smallpox were intentionally introduced to
Native populations "on purpose to destroy them." Apess reprises his theme
from *Indian Nullification* in which he called for the 4th of July and the 22nd
of December (the day he gives for the Pilgrims having landed at Plymouth
Rock) to be "forgotten in your celebration, in your speeches, and by the burying of the rock that your fathers first put their foot upon . . . let every man
of color wrap himself in mourning," for these were "days of mourning and
not of joy." When Christians continued to celebrate these days, he reminded
his audience, they tacitly demonstrated their ongoing allegiance to works of
colonial violence and intolerance. "Although in words they deny it, yet in
the works they approve."[63] It is a complex claim, forcing his contemporary
audience to consider the contradictory forces binding their own sense of progressive enlightenment to acts of conquest and human depravity.

Apess's critique of Christianity springs, of course, from his own precarious
subject position as Indian Preacher, and yet, more so in the *Eulogy* than in
his previous texts, that subject position becomes confused and radicalized by
the performative aspects of the historical journey upon which he guides us.
Through the imposition of stubborn binaries, Apess cannot but locate himself
in opposition to the Puritan targets of his critique, thus positioning himself
firmly in the camp of his "heathen" indigenous ancestors. At times he seems
even to channel the voice of Philip himself, as he intones, "O Christians, can

you answer for those beings you have destroyed by your hostilities, and beings too that lie endeared to God as yourselves?" He calls for the "children of the Pilgrims" to blush while "the son of the forest drops a tear and groans over the fate of his murdered and departed fathers." He goes so far as to suggest that all people of color would be better served to "pray to the great Spirit, the Indian's God, who deals out mercy to his red children, and not destruction."[64]

Who is this "Indian God" Apess invokes, and in what relation does the Indian Preacher on the stage place himself to this incantation of indigenous tradition and belief? Apess once again summons filaments of Native tradition with which he has come in contact throughout his life, transports himself to that long-ago summit on the Bay of Quinte, before the soundless lake of mystery, whose waters, sprung from underground currents, continued to feed the fluid materials of a spiritual narrative that cascade downward from that pure source through hollowed rock and into the earth's moving waters. Of this place, where the people of the forest "held all things in common," Apess cannot speak. Nevertheless, by calling for the cessation of celebration and the burying of Plymouth Rock—these ceremonial markers pertaining to the dominant order—he invokes the treaty language of Native tradition and seeks a restoration of balance in the cognitive structure of the world. The weapons of war must be buried, obstructions removed so words can flow freely, and if there are tears, they must be wiped away.

Having rhetorically cleared this ground, Apess's *Eulogy* begins to reconstruct a history of King Philip's War—a history that argues for the rights and cultural legitimacy of the Native peoples of New England, building his case with the same assiduous attention to detail with which he had studied and argued the case for Mashpee sovereignty a few years earlier. Although he has drawn authority for his witness from internal sources of Wampanoag tradition and practice, he compiles further evidence from the colonial archive, poring over ancient histories, hard-to-find documents, and rare land deeds, teasing out a vision of Native civility from the jaundiced inscriptions of a "corrupt" people "calling themselves Christians."[65] In this reframing of colonial history, Apess is able to identify Native society as one governed by laws and well-established rights concerning land, boundaries, social order, and even war itself. King Philip's War, as he observes "was no savage war of surprise, as some suppose, but one sorely provoked by the Pilgrims themselves." Nevertheless, he cautions, "it must be recollected that this war was legally declared by Philip, so that the colonies had fair warning."[66]

Like Everett's speech, the *Eulogy* ultimately builds to the moment of Philip's death, after his having been pursued through forest and swamp by the colonial officer Captain Benjamin Church. Apess recalls Church's indelicate observation upon the occasion, preserved in Church's own account (and strategically omitted by Everett), where he remarks what a "doleful, great, naked, dirty beast, he [Philip] look'd like."[67] Church ordered the lifeless body mutilated, its quartered parts hung from the trees, "for as much as he has caused many a Pilgrim to lie above ground unburied, to rot, not one of his bones shall be buried." Philip's head and hand were separated from the whole to be paraded around the area of Plymouth, and, as Apess notes, Philip's head was finally "exposed upon a gibbet" at the gates of Plymouth for the next twenty years.

Everett, even in sympathy for Philip, was able to locate a brand of universal justice in his death. Apess, however, decries the moral negligence and brutal ugliness of it all, descrying in this one moment a systemic pattern of denigration and destruction by which the entire colonial endeavor was underwritten. He laments the refusal to do honor to a great leader, the lack of a proper burial, the twisted Puritan mindset that praised God not only for the death of Philip but for the destruction of Native peoples throughout the region, exhorting his audience that such "prayers" and "preaching" of the "pretended pious has been the foundation of all the slavery and degradation in the American colonies towards colored people."[68]

But Apess, too, saves his greatest measure of outrage for the sale of Philip's wife and child into slavery. Undoubtedly, as he paced the stage, his voice rose to its highest timbre at this moment. Seeming to lurch from the very pages of his own manuscript even, he exclaims, "While I am writing, I can hardly restrain my feelings, to think a people calling themselves Christians should conduct so scandalous, so outrageous, making themselves appear so despicable in the eyes of the Indians; and even now in this audience, I doubt but there is men honorable enough to despise the conduct of those pretended Christians." Apess warns, "He that will advocate slavery is worse than a beast, is a being devoid of shame, and has gathered around him the most corrupt and debasing principles in the world—and he that will not set his face against its corrupt principles is a coward not worthy of being numbered among men and Christians." And finally, Apess assures those assembled that he has "no manner of doubt but that all my countrymen would have been enslaved if they had tamely submitted."[69]

Apess's soaring rhetoric and invocations of injustice must have pierced his audience in some way, however unwelcome the emotions it wrangled to the fore. By so closely associating the Puritan endeavor with slavery, massacre, and other decidedly un-Christian qualities, Apess's *Eulogy* directly challenged the powerful narrative of American exceptionalism, lambasting and dismembering its rituals of false mourning. Unlike Everett, Apess did not seek to locate the Native world in forest darkness. When he speaks of his home continent, Apess maps out a land "where nature shone in beauty," delineating a space of abundant light, agricultural plenty, and extraordinary generosity.[70] But when Puritans entered that space, landing at Plymouth, Apess writes, "Without asking liberty from anyone they possessed themselves of a portion of the country, and built themselves houses, and then made a treaty, and commanded them (the Natives) to accede to it. This, if now done, it would be called an insult, and every white man would be called to go out and act the part of patriot, to defend their country's rights; and if every intruder were butchered, it would be sung upon every hilltop in the Union that victory and Patriotism were the order of the day."[71] Apess sought to indict colonial practices by tracing a continuous line of abusive policies from past to present. His construction of a history that recognized and catalogued the abuses committed against Native Americans over the course of two hundred years was a first step toward ensuring not only basic civil rights for "people of color," but the recognition of legitimate treaties that had been trampled by the U.S. government.

Be that as it may, Apess finally calls on his audience to look forward and put aside bad feelings, to lay aside the desire for vengeance, as he himself has done, and abide by one general law. Rather than ask "What do they, the Indians, want?" he advises for all to think what it is they wish for themselves and to treat others just so. He acknowledges that the deep and tortured history between Native peoples and colonists has laid the ground for profound distrust and antipathy. Two hundred years of colonial rule had spread "like a fire, a canker, created by the pilgrims from across the Atlantic, to burn and destroy my poor unfortunate brethren and it cannot be denied." But when he calls for both parties to "bury the hatchet and those unjust laws and Plymouth Rock" together, he is not simply seeking to exile colonial history under "a mantle of darkness."[72] Rather he is acknowledging the symbol of Plymouth Rock itself as a weapon of war, as an obstruction that must be removed in order for truth to be heard and words to flow freely.

When the Peacemaker ended the wars between the various tribes in pre-Columbian times and brought together the original Five Nations of the Iroquois, one of his final gestures was to "uproot the tallest pine tree and into the cavity thereby made . . . cast all the weapons of war. Into the depths of the earth, down into the deep underneath currents of water flowing to unknown regions we cast all the weapons of strife. We bury them from sight and we plant again the tree. Thus shall the Great Peace be established and hostilities shall no longer be known."[73] Apess draws from this wellspring of tradition in order to affect a certain outcome. When he calls for "the burying of the rock that your fathers first put their foot upon," asking his audience to "let it be forgotten," he is suggesting that a new offshoot of democracy and peace might rise in its place. For peace and equality to be achieved between nations it was necessary for the controlling narratives of occupation and domination to be identified and laid to rest, to "bury the hatchet and those unjust laws and Plymouth Rock together and become friends."[74]

Apess had come to realize that he was in conflict with history itself. The myths, symbols, and narrative projections of colonial print discourse had worked to violently displace Native peoples from their traditional homes. It had cast them in the role of savage beast and configured knowledge itself in a manner that disenfranchised Natives from any claim to their legitimate birthrights. The process was deep, complex, insidious. Apess took the stage in his attempt to seek its source, stem its tide, apply contrary pressure to all the leaks and springs through which power exerted itself. It was a truly surprising and singular performance. He concluded by noting, "We have not to answer for our fathers' crimes. Neither shall we do right to charge them to one another. We can only regret it and flee from it; and from henceforth, let peace and righteousness be written upon our hearts and hands forever. Such is the wish of a poor Indian."[75]

Apess's last known performance of the *Eulogy* was in Hartford around the second week of March. From there he must have visited relations in Hartford, Groton, and elsewhere. Apess's mother, Candace, lived in Hartford and died

Ticket to Admit One to Apess's performance of *A Eulogy on King Philip* fastened to the inside cover of an 1831 edition of *A Son of the Forest. Courtesy American Antiquarian Society.*

there two years later, in 1838. Might she have seen him perform, and if so, what could she have made of such a performance, springing so powerfully from the lips of her wayward son?

By the 28th of that month Apess was in Montville, Connecticut, where he stopped, at the request of some Mohegans to draw up a petition for the tribe. Just as in Mashpee, Mashantucket, and probably other places we have yet to discover, Apess's skill with a pen was in demand at Mohegan. The petition addressed to the state senate, House of Representatives, and the General Court appears in Apess's hand, even if his name (given that he is not a member of the tribe) is not among the signers. The petition calls out abuses similar to those experienced in Native space throughout New England, and demands abrogation of "the Laws which bind us to be State paupers—which open a door for white men to rob us of our temporal rights and, the more respected, our natural rights." As with his *Eulogy on King Philip,* Apess works to position the Mohegan complaint within a historical framework that recognizes past wrongs and obligations. It reads, "Your Fathers were willing enough to put them Selves under the protection of Uncas our Chief until they were able to protect them Selves. And our Chief never deprived the white man of his rights."[76] The 1836 Mohegan petition adds just one more intriguing piece to the emerging pattern of Apess's consistent advocacy for Native causes throughout Native space in New England.

Completing the Ceremony

As the winter of 1836 gave way to spring, Apess returned home to Mashpee to tend to his neglected family and flock. Given that the *Eulogy* was Apess's last published work, there has been a tendency to view his career as having peaked at this moment and to assume that from this point on his physical and spiritual trajectory was downward, his star faded, his health in ruins, his reputation at Mashpee strained, and his lofty dreams and ambitions for Native peoples, which he dared to speak aloud at the public lecterns, come finally to naught. But it should be emphasized that if his wick was burning too fast and bright in this, his thirty-eighth year, he was not yet conscious of it himself and remained as active as ever. Aside from drafting the petition at Mohegan, Apess represented the people of Mashpee at the annual Temperance Convention of People of Color in New England that spring at his old stomping grounds in Providence, Rhode Island. Temperance remained a significant component of Apess's mission, and he could boast that Mashpee now counted some sixty members in the temperance society he had instituted.[77] Writing to William Lloyd Garrison of the *Liberator* later that summer, Apess proudly exclaimed, "Permit me to say to you that our situation is improving, though we have had some difficulties to encounter, which grew out of the persecution of our malignant foes, who have always waged war against our liberties. But our new government works well, and our people are becoming more industrious, and all begin to feel that they are men, instead of being deers and wild partridges, as many have said about us."[78]

In his role as pastor of what he branded the Free and United Church in Mashpee, Apess advertised for a three-day camp meeting to be held that August. Even here, his playfully circular rhetoric was on display as he welcomed "all people of every sect who are on the Lord's side, without distinction of color, to come and help us, and all God's ministers to aid us in every good word and work. For if we are good, it will do no harm to do us more good, (and we shall not harm you,) and if we are not good, it will be the very work good people are called to do; that is, strive to make us as good as yourselves." The meeting hoped to bring people in from places as far off as New Bedford, Nantucket, and elsewhere.[79]

The camp meeting had always stood at the spiritual center of Apess's identity and practice as a Christian. It was during meetings such as this, in the groves that "were God's first temples," that he first realized his faith and connected it with the maintenance of community and tradition among his own Pequot tribe. The camp meeting had provided a place for the young Apess to speak the anguish of his heart; it offered shelter for his wayward soul when he traveled alone among oppressors, helped soothe the torment of his postwar homecoming, and his relationship with Mary Wood also flourished amid the warm loving embrace of the Methodist camp meeting. But if in the previous three years he had organized these meetings at Mashpee with Blind Joe Amos, Apess seemed to be operating on his own now. It is possible that his ministry in Mashpee was declining, not because of any falling-out with the Mashpee leadership, as some have assumed, but simply because he was hardly present. As a result of his endless campaigns—whether promoting the rights of the Mashpee or attending to his own reputation as author, preacher, and public speaker—Apess was infrequently at home, and the residents at Mashpee, including his own family members, would have needed to look elsewhere than Apess's Free and United Church for the daily spiritual sustenance they sought.

Which raises an issue that yet groans from the gaps and silences surrounding Apess's life even as it inescapably forms the connective tissue by which we might still trace his restless path. As has been noted, it was difficult for any Native man in nineteenth-century New England to sit still. The economics of the age forced people of color to range far and wide for income, serving as itinerant labor wherever work presented itself, or taking to the seas for years at a time on whaling boats. Paul Cuffe Jr., a Wampanoag of New Bedford who penned his own short memoir in 1839, writes of spending but one or two weeks at home for every two years at sea, this pattern beginning at the age of fourteen and continuing throughout his life. Although Apess's father never took to sea, as far as we know, he too was rarely able to maintain a stable residency or directly care for his children, despite having been a landowner and craftsman in his trade as cobbler. To maintain steady employment conducive to domestic stability was, for most Native men of the era, an option that was simply out of reach.

Apess labored under the same circumstances as his brethren, despite his particular genius at speaking and self-promotion. He was compelled to hustle and scrape to make his living, forever lighting out on new campaigns to raise awareness, build audiences, and collect funding for his missions. Advancement within the Methodist organization was as unlikely as it was unprofitable and, at this point, it isn't clear that Apess retained any affiliation with the church. But it seems as though he might possibly have carved out a niche as preacher at Mashpee. The community had thrown its grateful support around him and, if the newspaper stories were correct, it appears as though he finally followed through on his promise to erect a schoolhouse for Indian education, affording him his own pulpit from which to preach and build a permanent home.

In fact, sometime in the late summer of 1836 Apess was able to take out a mortgage on a piece of property on prime land located on the northeastern shore of Dean's Pond in Mashpee, borrowing some fourteen hundred dollars from a Richard Johnson of New Bedford to supply this need for his wife and children.[80] The many possessions he itemized as security against his mortgage—including, among other things silver spoons, tea plates, wine glasses, a featherbed with Chinese bed curtains, and one large looking-glass—speak in an offhand way to middle-class aspirations all but attained.[81] Nevertheless, the early August camp meeting at Mashpee in 1836 may have proved the last moment in which Apess was to experience that potential for sustained community within a group that included his family and the extended circle of neighbors and brethren who flocked to attend such meetings. They prayed, held hands, sang hymns in one unified voice under the open heavens, and there was faith that good people might do good work to help keep hope alive.

And yet Apess could not be still. He had been constantly on the move since the day he first took breath in Colrain in 1798. The longest he had ever stayed in one place was the six years he worked as a bond servant for David Furman as a child, and even this had been marked by episodes of flight. It is likely that his wounds and war memories pursued him yet, the lid of his unease pried open again and again by an unrelenting series of insults, oppressions, and abuses. The role Apess had carved out for himself in the economic infrastructure of his times was one of instigator, agitator, peacemaker, constantly placing himself in the path of power only to be scoured clean in the process, divested of defenses, slammed to the earth time and again.

Apess was unable find personal peace in the domestic sphere. His family was neglected and, no doubt, Mary, his wife, had a difficult life, uprooted again and again by the forces that drove her husband, finding herself, as the "consort" of an itinerant minister, transplanted among strangers in cities, towns, and backwoods settlements and reservations. Her children, too, were to be scattered about New England. If Leonard, Abby Ann, and Sally (twelve, fourteen, and fifteen, respectively) still lived in Mashpee with their mother, the official records do not show it. The Mashpee town clerk's office mentions only William, Mary, and twelve-year-old Bethel, all of whom were registered as "strangers come here in 1833" (Apess is listed as "Indian and white," whereas Mary and Bethel are listed as "mulatto"). Who was twelve-year-old Bethel Apes? She must have been born shortly after Leonard, perhaps in the hills of Colrain, Massachusetts or neighboring Leyden. Abby's name appears, along with Bethel's, on the Mashpee memorial petition, suggesting she was in Mashpee in 1833 when, with her father in jail, the petition was first drawn up. Sally and Leonard, at least, would find their way back to Connecticut some years later, where court records suggest that they became servants in the Williams household back in New London. The older children, Elisha and Solomon, would soon take up whaling.

Perhaps Mary Apes hoped her wayward husband would finally slow down and sink roots. However, neither the domestic security offered by Mashpee, nor the ceremony, communion, human warmth, and brotherhood that welled up from the camp meeting of 1836 proved enough in the end to quiet Apess's restless soul. Come November, we find Apess on the streets of New Bedford, canvassing for one Mr. Crocker, who was running as a Democrat for senator.[82] And three months later, in February of 1837 Apess was back in New York City, on the lecture circuit once again, inhabiting yet a new role on the American stage.

The newspaper advertisements for this phase of Apess's career leave a great deal to the imagination, for there is no printed book to fortify this latest and, perhaps, strangest of his performative incarnations. In various engagements from February through April, it was announced that "an educated Indian of the Pequot tribe" was to appear before audiences under the exotic mantle of Gos-kuk-wa-na-kon-ni-di-yu to expound on the topic of "the Indian origin and character." Subsequent talks promised to broach the subject of "wars and treaties made by the red men with this country," with the proceeds earmarked for the establishment of an Indian academy.[83] Apess had in hand newly published editions of his *Eulogy on King Philip* and *The Experiences of Five*

Christian Indians of the Pequot Tribe to sell at these engagements, and the press seemed as interested as ever in the curious figure he struck, with notice of his Clinton Hall lectures appearing in newspapers as far away as New Orleans.[84]

Although Apess, for some reason, did not advertise himself by name for these lectures, he was still remembered by New York newspaper editors and Clinton Hall illuminati, who saw through his assumed persona, with one paper suggesting that he was Mohawk but others insisting he was Pequot. The confusion stemmed from the fact that Apess was presenting himself as a figure from Haudenosaunee tradition, and there is reason to believe that he even began to wear something that resembled traditional Mohawk regalia for these performances. An ad in the *New York Colored American* boasted in April of that year that the lecturer would "appear in the full dress of an Indian Chief. Ladies will do well to come in season, as the house may be crowded."[85]

Apess came across the name Gos-kuk-wa-na-kon-ni-di-yu in Samuel Drake's *Book of the Indians,* where it is written that he was known as "the Prophet" and brother to "Cornplant," a reference to the Seneca prophet Handsome Lake, who was responsible for reviving the Longhouse religion at the latter end of the eighteenth century. Handsome Lake reportedly had been a man of little consequence among his people until, at a very advanced age, while wasting away on his deathbed, he was suddenly roused by the force of a revelatory dream that lifted him from his torpor and compelled him to spearhead a religious revitalization movement among the Seneca. Apess might have known something of Handsome Lake's history given that he himself had lived among the Haudenosaunee at the time immediately following the prophet's death in 1815, when the movement was at its peak. Then again, it is quite possible that Apess did not make these connections but simply adopted the lengthy pseudonym for his own purposes.

The name Gos-kuk-wa-na-kon-ni-di-yu, at least in typographical appearance (as it appears in all the newspaper announcements), bore some resemblance to Black Hawk's name, given in his memoir as Ma-ka-tai-me-she-kia-kiak. Apess might have felt there was an "authentic" Indian appeal for audiences in such an exotic title. Drake, in his book, had been dismissive of Handsome Lake's influence, but Apess probably sensed there was more there than Drake was capable of allowing, some vital link that might be of central importance to his own personal narrative and sense of identity. Although the figure of the "Prophet" surely served theatrical purposes, the name Gos-kuk-wa-na-kon-ni-di-yu (in English, "Large Beautiful Lake") resonated with Apess in other ways.[86]

I suspect that Apess, in keeping with his practice, was working on a new literary or historical tract to accompany this performance. Newspaper announcements suggested that the scope of his historical interests was widening. His talk not only would cover the old ground of Indian origins and history, but was focused on treaty law as well and promised to "descant on the character of Osceola," who was generating a great deal of news in relation to the ongoing Seminole War in Florida. Apess apparently also planned to dispute recent statements made by Rabbi Mordecai Noah, known across the Eastern Seaboard as Major Noah, a newspaper editor, playwright, and proto-Zionist who was busy pursuing his own series of "Indian lectures" at Clinton Hall on the topic of the old lost tribes theory. Noah had been involved in a bizarre scheme to create a new Jewish homeland on Indian Territory in Grand River. The *New York Herald* had proclaimed Noah's intention of endeavoring to "organize all the Indian tribes west of the Mississippi, and to become their Meshiah or Moses and to lead them into a new Canaan."[87] Apess, who had either abandoned his old defense of Native peoples as descendants of the lost tribes of Israel or objected to some other aspect of Noah's performance, seems to have constructed his lectures, at least in part, in response to Noah's public appearances.

As for Apess's own performance, the *Herald* suggested (under the headline "Rabbi Noah at Discount") that it "could not fail to be of a highly interesting and novel character. The bare fact of an aboriginal addressing and instructing an audience of whites on a subject so involving the fate of his own unfortunate race, is an epoch in the progress of civilization."[88] Yet another advertisement proclaimed, almost tongue in cheek, "Metacomet, a Mohawk Indian, and what is more, a very gentlemanly savage, gives a lecture in Clinton Hall tomorrow. We shall go and hear him."[89]

Apparently the ability of Apess's *Eulogy on King Philip* to fill theaters had persuaded him that the performative possibilities of playing "Indian prophet" were more persuasive and potentially more lucrative than traveling from pulpit to pulpit, offering sermons for mere room and board. The United States was experiencing a major depression in 1837 in the wake of Andrew Jackson's dissolution of the Bank of America, and Apess, for the first time in his life, was accruing debts that he could not seem to get out from under. New York City itself had experienced the leanest of winters, with mobs parading through the streets demanding relief from the high costs of fuel, rent, food, and flour. Within a week of the launch of Apess's Clinton Hall lecture series, some twenty thousand people "of all ranks of society" turned up at city hall to protest living conditions. The *Herald* railed against "the politicians and speculators" who had been the cause of so much misery, and boldly called for nothing less than "an entire reconstruction of things."[90]

But all economic considerations aside, there was a certain logic and continuity in Apess's adopting the role of "Indian prophet." Throughout his public career, one could feel Apess, the "unbelieving Indian," straining at the margins of acceptable discourse, playing the role of pious preacher, but always as a means to critique dominant paradigms, to challenge discourse from within and upend its violent assumptions. If noble savagery was a mask that a Native might wear to address his white audiences, Christianity, too, was a kind of mask. Maybe both were sincere to some extent, and yet neither mask truly fit, and what might we rightly call the fluid turmoil of competing identities that lay just underneath, the confluence of passions, grievances, traumas, and desires? Under which category might someone of Apess's experience and condition place his x-mark?

Hayonwhatha had seen his world destroyed by malevolent forces. He cried, "My sorrow and rage have been bitter. I can only rove about since now I have cast myself away from my people. I am only a wanderer. I split the heavens when I went away from my house and nation."[91] Trauma, as clinically understood, is the disruption of cultural narratives, the forceful fragmentation of the cohesive cognitive functions by which one comprehends the thread of order holding the world together. It is a force that, if not treated, works to split the heavens, disintegrate the self, situates the individual in a paralysis of fractured moments that cannot be restored to linearity despite the psyche's repeated attempts to force the individual beyond the incident of rupture. As the psychiatrist Judith Herman writes, "Reliving a trauma may offer an opportunity for mastery, but most survivors do not seek or welcome the opportunity," for it forces them to experience anew the horror that provoked the trauma in the first place. However, any "attempt to avoid reliving the trauma" has equally negative effects, too often resulting "in a narrowing of consciousness, a withdrawal from engagement with others, and an impoverished life."[92] Even today, some one in four homeless persons are veterans of war.

Apess had stayed ahead of these neuroses most of his adult life by recreating himself, recentering himself within indigenous traditions of spiritual regeneration, shielding himself from colonial violence in the embrace of what had seemed, initially, at least, a Methodist movement committed to advancing the rights of people of color, and placing himself at the forefront of Native advocacy movements in the small regional sphere in which he operated. He committed his adult life, with amazing resolve and decision, to seeking out new narrative threads by which to bind the wounds of history and create a welcoming space for sustaining narratives of indigeneity.

One wonders, however, if Apess's own wounds had yet to heal. In the old stories it was Hiawatha who, in his time of greatest grief, said "Men boast what they will do in extremity but they do not do what they say. If I should see anyone in deep grief I would remove these shell strings from the pole and console them. The strings would become words and lift away the darkness with which they are covered. Moreover what I say I would surely do."[93]

Apess had grappled with the lack of traditional structure, fractured kinship networks, the piecemeal historical knowledge that shivered into tantalizing patterns in the crackling spaces between the pronouncements of his impassioned spontaneous oratory. He sensed the whispered connections from his own Pequot origins, where the wampum had originally been gathered and carried along water routes to find its way to the Haudenosaunee Longhouse, thus binding the Northeast in networks of ritual and reciprocity, on pathways that Apess had tracked throughout his life. I might suggest, however, that there was no one who came forward to bind Apess's wounds. There was no one who could. "Do not get tired, ye noble-hearted," he encouraged in his "Indian's Looking-Glass for the White Man," but "only think how many poor Indians want their wounds done up daily."[94]

William Apess drove himself relentlessly onward, divining yet one more way of locating himself within a generative narrative framework by appropriating an identity that carried him back to the Lake on the Mountain, the large beautiful lake that stood at the source of spiritual regeneration and good-mindedness. The legend of the Peacemaker lay aback of his mind. But how to reconnect with such distant and seemingly irretrievable stories? The notion behind the condolence ceremony was always that, in the space cleared by wampum, two parties in conflict might forward their narratives in a way that divested the interaction of all the rage, greed, and ill feelings called up by the pain and violence of war. But the discourse that rose from the storm of colonialism invested itself in devouring all resistance, opposing any narrative that respected Native identity, memory, and tradition, and casting it within a mantle of darkness. Apess took to the bizarre stage of empire again and again, in role after role, seeking to tease an indigenous worldview back to the fore, to clear the dark clouds surrounding his people and rekindle their traditions, to comb the snakes from the hair of the writhing whirling beast that is dominant white history. And we leave him there on that stage, exhorting, praying, dancing, seeking out the ceremony that will heal the wound.

Apess's full signature. Barnstable Court House Index of Defendants, A–K, 1827–1886, case no. 1069, *Ezra Toby vs. William Apess*, 1837. *Photo by the author, 2015.*

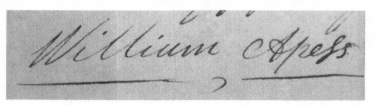

CONCLUSION

"He Possessed the Real Traits of the Indian Character"

I was born from the mountain
I leave a path of wildflowers
A raindrop falls from me
I'm walking home
I'm walking back to belonging
I'm walking home to happiness
I'm walking back to long life

—LESLIE MARMON SILKO, *Ceremony*

On a spring day in 2014, I found my way to 31 Washington Street in New York City, in the Wall Street district near the waterfront—the place where, according to the official coroner's report, William Apess was residing when he died on April 10, 1839.[1] What had once been a boardinghouse some two hundred years earlier is now an expansive multistoried upscale apartment complex encompassing half a city block. But I positioned myself nonetheless in the place where I imagined Apess's final residence to be and made an offering of tobacco, which the wind driving off the river lifted up and scattered a little ways over the incongruent asphalt and concrete. The gesture felt compromised by the absence of any true structure to which I could attach my complicated thoughts and sentiments concerning the man whose life I had spent the last five years researching. Nothing in the hulking monolith of a building before me presented itself as a touchstone by which my own journey could achieve some kind of closure. But this had been the nature of the endeavor from start to finish. I came closer to tracking the arc of William Apess's extraordinary life and experiences than I had ever expected to come, and yet could it ever amount to more than the fleeting projections of stray bits of light, ink, paper, and thought glimpsed but through a glass darkly? We hope, on such occasions, to stand in the presence of history, just as we hope, on some level, to channel the essence, the spirit, the soul of the individuals who inspire us to spend years tracking down their stories. But oftentimes, particularly when investigating the lives of Native people, we find their history dramatically dispossessed by a daunting edifice of colonization that has all but obliterated the landscape alongside our hopes of coming into contact with some trace particulate of the past.

But William Apess had indeed been here, and many times he would have strolled the Manhattan streets to this particular address where I now stood, not distant from the centers of nineteenth-century New York commerce, the bowling green, the docks, the tavern where George Washington bid farewell to his troops after the Revolutionary War, and the halls where he later served out his terms as president of the United States. Old Clinton Hall, where Apess lectured as Gos-kuk-wa-na-kon-ni-di-yu, was within easy walking distance, a few blocks uptown. Just a little way up the road is the John Street Church, where the black Methodist community formed their own congregation in the 1790s, and also Trinity Church, where you may peruse old grave markers of the likes of Alexander Hamilton and Stanley Fulton, inventor of the steamboat engine. There is even a tombstone in the yard bearing the name of Charlotte Temple, the fictional heroine of the popular late eighteenth-century novel of the same name, written by Susanna Rowson.

But just as you will find no record or marker of William Apess's birth in Colrain, Massachusetts, there is nothing to indicate his final resting place here in New York City. It is not the sort of history of which city fathers or later historians took notice. In a sense, it still isn't. As a "colored person," Apess was most likely buried in a pauper's grave in the old Negro burial grounds now entombed beneath the concrete of lower Manhattan. Not so much as an *x* marks the spot.

The cause of death was said to be apoplexy, which was a sort of ambiguous catchall medical term in the nineteenth century indicating internal damage resulting in aggravated infection and a rush of fluids to one organ or another. One surprising aspect of the report, which Barry O'Connell's research helped to uncover in 1997, is that it offers us the only shred of evidence that Apess had taken up with another woman at this point in his life, calling herself "Elizabeth Apes" in the report and claiming to have been married to Apess for two years. The *New York Transcript,* reporting on Apess's death, described Elizabeth as "a good-looking white woman with whom he lived happily," although there is no indication as to how Elizabeth's ethnicity or appearance was determined.[2] Still, it is well within the realm of possibility that Apess had left his family in Mashpee and, as his father seems to have done before him, forged new relationships to accommodate a difficult and transient life.

Although a marriage certificate has yet to emerge, it is clear from the reports of witnesses at the boardinghouse where the Apesses stayed that the two had been together for some time and, as all of the testimonies verify, had lived on good terms. Catherine Garlick, housekeeper and daughter of the boarding house manager, observed that the couple were "affectionate and kind to each other." And Elizabeth herself reported that "we have always lived on good terms" and that she "never had any words" with her husband.[3] This abrupt emergence of Apess's second wife may appear, perhaps, through some jaundiced moral lens, as a kind of blot on his character and further evidence that his life was on a downward trajectory at this stage. But these are difficult claims to support in any time, and particularly given the stress Native families were under and the consideration that monogamy was yet another Western value (loosely observed) that had been forced upon Native communities. Apess was probably not aware of many successful marriages in the circles among which he traveled, and few intimate acquaintances had been able to model this ideal in his life.

Apess began to feel sick on a Friday in April. Still feeling ill the next day, he visited with a doctor and was given some medicine. After another twenty-four hours of vomiting and purging, a "botanic physician" was called and found Apess with a high fever and complaining of pain in his right side. Some roots and herbs were given for Elizabeth to make into a tea, including thirty grams of lobelia, or Indian tobacco, a common nineteenth-century remedy used to induce vomiting. By Monday a doctor was called for again and administered some other medicines. These apparently only increased Apess's discomfort. But come Tuesday morning, Elizabeth claimed that Apess felt better. He rose from his bed "and walked to the glass and took a tooth brush and cleaned his teeth." Then he made some toast and ate a few bites, claiming to feel revived. Within two hours, William Apess was dead.[4]

Elizabeth offered this information in her testimony to the medical examiner. She added, for the record, that Apess had been born in Massachusetts, had formerly been a preacher with the Methodist society, and that he had "wrote some books which he sold and lectured on the history of the Indians." It seems like such a vague and incomplete summation of his life, and quite probably, the medical examiner offered the most truncated account of Elizabeth's testimony. Nevertheless, one wonders if Apess was still actively lecturing, as she seems to suggest, and if, somewhere in that boarding house apartment, there were bundles of Apess's books, yet unsold. Was he working on a new manuscript, a yet more complex and engaging examination of indigenous history, wars, and treaties? Was his enigmatic fascination with

Gos-kuk-wa-na-kon-ni-di-yu something that would have been drawn into greater relief in a future text?

The incidents of his life up until this point, clarified by new findings and deep archival research, suggest that Apess was on a continued path to connect the fragmented markers of his Native identity—a piecemeal identity that he had been able, thus far, to harvest from the scattered indigenous communities with which he had sheltered and worshipped. Thrust into the world with few solid handholds by which he might assemble a sense of national pride or tradition, blasted into a state of persistent liminality by the violent forces of colonial power that diligently labored to dismantle all bastions of indigenous strength and self-worth, Apess had nevertheless managed throughout his journey to cobble together something serviceable, a construction of Native being, history, identity, spirituality that might serve to lift his people up from the haunts of economic and cultural disempowerment and knit the frayed ends of their collective memories together again.

And perhaps he might have been remembered and even eulogized in this generous light, if not for the fact that his new wife seems to have been prodded by the examiner into uttering something about Apess's recent behavior—his alleged drinking. "He has lately been somewhat intemperate," she is quoted as saying. The unfortunate phrase was then echoed by the two other witnesses at the boarding house, as though, in their brief testimonies, there was nothing else of merit they might say, and the accusation was thus reprinted in every newspaper across the Eastern Seaboard, leaving the indelible impression that Apess's lofty and energetic commitments to Native uplift and advocacy had inevitably given way to the presumed defects of his race.

He has "indulged much too freely in drink," the *Albany Evening Journal* exclaimed, "and would take frolics that would continue for a week or two."[5] "It appears that Apes has been of late much in the habit of intoxication," reported a Philadelphia paper, the *North American.*[6] The *Christian Watchman* sniffed that "for some time he had ceased to enjoy the confidence of the best portion of the community."[7] And the *Olive Branch,* a New England Methodist Protestant newspaper, went a step further in suggesting that Apess had "fallen into bad company and took to drinking too freely."[8] By 1844 the *Boston Recorder* could recall that "this man whose name was Apes, died in the almshouse of the City of New York, a miserable, degraded wretch."[9] All this extrapolated from the merest suggestion by Elizabeth that he had "lately been somewhat intemperate."

From the moment he first launched his career, forces had conspired to tear down Apess's pretensions as an indigenous man appropriating the rhetorical and spiritual authority typically reserved for whites. As far as the press was concerned, the narrative had finally come full circle, and the racial destiny reserved for a son of the forest had played itself out perfectly according to script. History was doing its work. The mold was so well worn and malleable to the touch that it could be cast into any situation and made to justify any kind of encounter involving Native peoples.

Robert Warrior, in his "Eulogy for William Apess," imagines that, as an Indian intellectual up against such daunting and unrelenting odds, Apess was ultimately broken down into a state of despondency that was neither uncommon in the face of unremitting racial oppression nor unwarranted. Warrior wonders what it must "have been like to be a writer and feel like a writer" and yet to have no outlet for such impulses, no cultural mechanism acknowledging your ability, or even right, to partake in such discourse? He concludes from this that "Apess's drinking career caught up with him in New York, a conclusion consistent with [a] combination of factors," not the least of which were the all-too-familiar results of battling the explicit and implicit aggressions of racism and the predictable effects of what Warrior refers to as "intellectual despair."[10]

It is not difficult to see Apess on the edge of that precipice, shouldering such a heavy load of personal and political expectations, his life hanging precariously in the balance. I have maintained throughout this book that Apess was pursued not only by the forces of oppression and a legacy of cultural destruction, but by smaller, more personal, traumas that were all nevertheless implicated in the same web of circumstances and consequences that insinuated themselves into the lives of countless Native individuals. And yet, I prefer, in the light of more recent findings, to see Apess still very much in the game, like all of us, perhaps, slipping at times, given to human shortcomings and complications, and overburdened with the weight of enormous cultural and personal scars. But for all that, still in the struggle, still capable of generating controversy, of bringing crowds into the room and stirring up their emotions, challenging their assumptions, messing with their history.

In fact, his career didn't come to a screeching halt playing the role of Indian prophet in the New York lecture halls. Apess was in the Washington, DC, area again by the winter of 1837, apparently in conjunction with a tour of Pawnee and Ottawa Natives who were visiting the city to receive medals of peace from the Van Buren administration. As one DC reporter noted, "Among the arrivals yesterday was a delegation of Indians who have been on a visit or tour to the North; but the curiosity which the first arrivals had excited with regard to these savages, has now died off, and will not be revived until a '*wardance*' or some *refined* exhibition of the sort is advertised." The reporter continues disapprovingly, "I last night listened to Mr. Apess, an Indian missionary who resented in strong language, the treatment of the Indians, taking them out on the commons for the gratification of the people;

indeed, those who have charge of the Indians would better consult, not only their own propriety, but also that of the citizens of this city, by stopping such exhibitions." Do I read this correctly? Did Apess escort a group of visiting Native dignitaries, described in the local press as "more savage than any near our border," out on the Mall in Washington, DC, inviting the crowd to join them as they pronounced their political grievances to the streets of the nation's capital? Perhaps Apess not only was still energized in his mission, but actively seeking out greater ties within ever-larger spheres of indigenous presence.[11]

I have passed Apess's coroner's report along to a number of physicians, who have declared it a textbook case of appendicitis. The pain identified on the right side more or less rules out liver failure, and it is not uncommon for there to be a sensation of relief after an appendix ruptures, accounting for Apess's claim that he felt better on the Tuesday morning of April 10, just hours before his death. I maintain that Apess's life came to an end not as the result of some prolonged fall from grace but due to a random medical condition to which anyone would be susceptible and for which there was no cure in the nineteenth century. "Thus ignobly ended the life of this rather famous 'son of the forest,'" the *Olive Branch* fairly gloated. "O thou destroyer Rum, what hast thou done, especially to the poor Indian!"[12]

It is tragic, in a sense, that Elizabeth Apes felt compelled to refer to her husband's intemperance. The legacy of exaggeration and abuse it opened up was incommensurate with the evidence offered by her brief statement. If a white man had been known to take a few drinks just prior to his unrelated demise, no one would have thought to mention it. Barring any mitigating circumstances, no one would have even thought to ask. But I would wager that the medical examiner, understanding Apess to be an Indian, reflexively inquired about his drinking in an attempt to write off a case that might otherwise prove more ambiguous and require more paperwork. The fact that two other witnesses supported the story does not verify its accuracy so much as it suggests the examiner pointedly presented them with Elizabeth's testimony and asked them to approve it. The narrative had already been written. All the other minor players had to do was go along with the shopworn script.

Many of the newspaper reports of Apess's death identified him as the "Indian preacher." They recalled him as the author of a number of sermons and the "life of Philip." But it was the Methodist Protestant *Olive Branch* again that offered, paradoxically, the most demeaning characterization and the most brilliant praise. They had intended to have "said something about this singular and gifted Indian preacher," the newsletter confessed. "He was a man of superior powers of mind" in possession of "a Native eloquence that was truly powerful and had it not been for the demon rum, he would have made a most useful preacher." The reporter goes on to note that Apess "possessed the real traits of the Indian character, *cunning* and the disposition never to *forgive an enemy.*"[13]

I think of Apess on that final morning, shuffling out of bed, as his wife Elizabeth testified, and standing before the glass one last time to brush his teeth before sitting down to eat his toast. It is a surprisingly domestic conclusion to a life defined by such unrelenting activity and controversy. I cannot help but wonder if, when he met his reflection in the looking-glass, he could catch even a glimpse of the regard with which future scholars would view him—as a man who made an indelible mark in the literature of his people, offering an articulation of Native identity and resistance that would continue to register down through the centuries—or, conversely, if he had difficulty making out such an image in the dim urban light of his Manhattan flat. Did he see himself as a repository of fortitude and genius, ready to pick himself up and reengage the struggle, or was he confronted with an aspect of wreck and decay, a man at the end of his trajectory? Did he behold a Native prophet or a Methodist minister? A Pequot or a "poor Indian"? Which history had been written on *his* skin? Which narrative reflected back from the glass—that of the agitator for Native rights, education, and sovereignty, or was it that old chimera of dominant discourse that saw every indigenous face as a predictable composite quantity, an "Indian," known to be cunning, unforgiving of a slight, prone to excessive drink?

Could Apess see himself at all in such light?

Some of William Apess's kin and descendants would go on to have remarkable lives. Others would struggle in almost complete obscurity. In July of 1839, a letter addressed to a Louisa Apes awaited pick up at the Hartford post office. More than likely it carried news of her relative's sudden demise. Louisa was Apess's sister-in-law, married to his brother Elisha, who was possibly away at sea on a whaling ship at the time. The invisible strands of Apess's extended family reveal themselves only at certain moments and in the most intricate patterns, suggesting that his kinship networks are always more involved than the archive allows. If Elizabeth did send this note to Hartford, and knew to whom she should address it, then we might also conclude that Apess's second marriage was not something performed in secret or kept in the dark but was known among his relations. They were all still within the circle of family.

As for his first marriage, some have speculated that perhaps Mary Apes had passed away at this point, thus prompting Apess to take a new wife. But records show at least three members of the Apes family were wards of the state of Connecticut in the summer of 1839, Mary Apes among them. She was accompanied by both Sally and William Apes, who are all listed as having spent multiple weeks boarding at the expense of the Norwich county prison system. Although it is the Norwich town "jailor" who records their expenses, I would imagine they were actually placed in a boarding house for the poor rather than in an actual prison. It makes a certain amount of sense that Mary Apes would have returned home to Connecticut in the wake of her husband's prolonged absence. She remained unable to make ends meet and quickly found herself destitute of means. If it was shameful for Apess's wife and children to find themselves in such a situation, it was not an unusual place for women in the Native community to find themselves, and she shared her fate with Tantaquidgeons and Fieldings, some of the leading families of the Mohegan tribe, who were also registered as temporary wards of the Norwich poor house at this time.[14]

My best guess is that the "William Apes" mentioned in this record is William Elisha, Apess's oldest son. He would have been roughly twenty-three years old at this time, and, like so many other young Pequot men before him, had little choice but to take to the whaling industry to help support his indigent family. The socioeconomic conditions that fostered such circumstances were the very things his father had fought against so passionately at Mashpee. Nevertheless, William Elisha Apes would go on to have a storied career at sea, becoming involved in a mutiny on the *Ann Maria* that was instigated when Apes protested the mistreatment of the ship's apprentice boy. The six-foot-one-inch tall Apes apparently managed to subdue the first mate and, with the help of the ship's carpenter, take control of the firearms in the captain's cabin. The two then boarded a whaleboat loaded with supplies and rowed themselves to land. Once in New Zealand, Apes married into a Maori family in Dunedin, where the Apeses continue to live to this day and still recall their Pequot ancestry. He would name his first child, born in 1842, Mary, after his mother, whom he had been forced to leave behind a world away. He was married in the Methodist church in 1844 and named his first son William.[15]

Apess's second-eldest son, Solomon, also worked as a whaler, and an index of New London whaling crews shows him shipping out to the coast of Patagonia on the schooner *Francis* in April of 1837. The record offers no details concerning Solomon's features save for his complexion, which is given as "Indian." Leonard, Apess's third-eldest son, would also have a life at sea and held the position of first mate on a number of ships, including the *Erie* and the *Oriole,* both out of Norwich. He was described by other seaman as having "a bold, daring appearance, his eye was piercing, he had high cheek bones; in short, his was a grim and resolute mien." Another noted that Leonard had "sailed many seas, visited many strange lands, and in his home had a collection of rare and curious souvenirs of his adventurous life." For a family of "poor Indians," the Apesses had seen their share of the world, more than many white families of New England could ever possibly imagine.[16]

Apess's younger brother, Griswold, would marry Sophia Quash in 1835, joined together in matrimony by Lyman Strong, one of the Methodist ministers who had so diligently worked to block William Apess's ordination into the Methodist Episcopal Church back in 1829. Their sons, Elias and Gad, would both serve with the Northern army in the Civil War, although it appears that Elias fought with the regular troops, and Gad was placed in a colored regiment. These seemingly arbitrary designations serve as a reminder of how fluid racial identity could be in the nineteenth century and how difficult it must have been at times to negotiate the shifting perceptions and projections of identity in a world in which skin color to a large degree determined one's fate. Throughout their lives, Apess's descendants would variously be listed as white, black, or Indian in the census rolls right up into the twentieth century.

William Apess received recognition in his day as a Native "son of the forest" who preached the Christian gospel, enough of a curiosity to draw attention and, typically, fill a room. The figure he struck, as a charismatic minister offering fiery rhetoric from the pulpit and the stage, caused a brief stir in the Northeast, as it challenged the racial constructions and hierarchies of nineteenth-century American life and history that continue to haunt us today. Then as now, the cultural response to such rhetoric has been a kind of ambivalent silencing through neglect. Apess's impassioned pleas for Native self-determination and sovereignty are greeted with studied inattention not only by the dominant culture that fails to posit a remembrance of his birth, life, and death, but even to a certain extent among the Pequot themselves, with whom Apess identified in his personal narratives but who have some-where along the way dropped the Apes name from their tribal rolls.

This book has been an attempt to interrogate the cultural silences surrounding Apess's life while simultaneously seeking to secure Apess's place on the literary, cultural, and historical map. Apess himself was adept at addressing historical silences, at locating the moments in colonial history and praxis in which Native agency was displaced by the hegemonic discourse of the settler state. His writings brilliantly exposed these ruptures, teasing out alternative realities to rhetorically lift Native identity out from the dark enclosures of the settler state. The particulars of his life have never before been patched together with the level of intricacy that this book offers.

My hope, of course, is that the new understandings that emerge from this study will break ground for further findings, some of which will support what I've noted here, and some of which will undoubtedly contradict it. But whereas previously the chronology of Apess's life was vague, jumbled, and filled with murky gaps and silences that prevented us from seeing how the pieces all came together, it is now possible to examine Apess's literary accomplishment in the light of his personal activities and whereabouts, to trace his path over a large geographical, experiential, and even spiritual expanse, which will hopefully shed light on a worthy topic that as of yet has been seen but through a glass darkly. Such is the hope of a poor scholar.

APPENDIX

Memorial of the Marshpee Indians, January 1834

To the Honorable the Senate House of Representatives, in General Court assembled:-

Where it is expected, by the inhabitants of this Commonwealth, that justice and equity will reign in the hearts of all—that national prejudices and peculiar feelings, attending religionists, will not be permitted to rule the hearts of any—but, that every enlightened and judicious Representative, as we trust they all are that compose this Body, will be willing to do as they would wish to be done by; and we wish this Honorable Body to consider our oppression. While ye are filled with the fat of our fathers' land, and enjoy your liberties without molestation, will not this Honorable Body be as benevolent to us, poor Marshpee Indians, who are sighing and weeping under bondage, as ye are to the poor Cherokees? And have we not groaned under the weight of degradation long enough? Are ye willing that we should go down to the grave with sorrow and disgrace, as our fathers have before us, when we are willing to try to take care of ourselves? And we fear that our petitions have been laid aside without much notice heretofore; and our complaints that come before common Courts, as well as this Honorable Body, have been looked at as being mere cyphers. But we hope that this indifferent spirit is dying away, and that the true spirit of the Christian philanthropist is beginning to reign in the hearts of the people, and those who compose their Legislative Bodies. If so, may we not expect to share a part, although we are looked upon to be but poor and insignificant creatures? And why are we so?—Because we have not had the opportunity; no particular pains have been taken to instruct us; we are wanting the same privilege that your Honors have, in order to make us what we ought to be, good and wholesome citizens; and we do say that we can never rise to a state of cultivation, under existing circumstances. We can assure your Honors that there is not one enlightened and respectable Indian upon the plantation, that wants Overseers or the present minister, Mr. Phineas Fish. We say that all of our rulers, and he who is said to be our preacher, were placed here amongst us without our consent; and it has been the policy of these interested men to work upon the feelings of some of our most ignorant and dissipated men and women, to keep us divided. We are sure that none but those who are in the habit of drinking, and such as do not attend meeting any where, would, or have signed his paper, to hear him preach; and many of them have said they did not know what it contained. Why we mention this, is, because we have discharged him, and passed Resolutions that we will not hear him preach; and we are of the same mind still. We do not believe he cares any thing for our souls, but the fleece we believe he loves well. If he did care for us, we believe that twenty years would have been long enough to have secured our confidence, and reared to himself a respectable church and society; but he has not a male member belonging to his church that has one drop of the royal, or real native blood in him. We therefore wish to have him removed peaceable from our borders, by this Honorable Body, who we believe will try to do us justice, especially when your Honors hear the Bill of Complaints, laid before you by us, your humble petitioners, the Marshpee Indians.

Bill of Complaints.

Honored Gentlemen:

It is not possible for us to give you a full statement of wrongs that we have to suffer, in consequence of having Overseers to manage for us, who, we believe, felt more interested for themselves than for us; and we purpose only to give you a few statements of facts, such as generally can be sustained by us, whose fathers were the original proprietors of the soil where this stately edifice now stands, and whose laws have ground us to the dust.

First: We are certain that the Marshpee Government is unconstitutional, and far transcends the Constitution of the country, and of course is extremely defective and injurious to us as a people.

This law was imposed upon us by the consent of a few of our forefathers, aided by the designing white man, whose artful voice inspired in their breasts cheering hopes that their property should be secured to them, and they one day should be equalized and respected with the white man; for we have no idea that our fathers would have bound us, so as to take away all of our rights from us, for Indians have too much affection for each other, to use that kind of treachery towards their children. We believe they would as soon given up their own lives, but for the promise of bettering their condition, and that of their children. But since our fathers fell asleep, we have heard but little about law or liberty, or any thing else, but imposition upon the back of imposition, and in the following manner:

We have been obliged to submit to a hereditary government, as we believe, son succeeding father, and brothers brothers, to the Overseership: for this lineage of government has been kept up for nearly forty years, and we think it is time for a change. Neither do we think it right for us to abide by an unconstitutional law, made by our fathers forty years ago, and others, meaning the whites, who had their interest in view, we believe, altogether—for our sufferings by that law have been immense.

For we as a people have not been permitted to worship God according to our own views and feelings, and as conscience dictated us; for the preacher that was placed among us was altogether by the power of the Overseers, without asking one of us whether we would like to have him or no, and of course ordained without the particular knowledge of us—to be supported out of our property for life, without being any service to us, or our consent to have it so. Is the like known any where amongst other towns in this State peopled by white men? This preacher has moved principally amongst white people, and taught them, whilst we have been compelled to support him, and sigh in bondage; and the presumption is, that the whites have had three times the benefit of the preacher and our funds, that we have ourselves.

This government also admits two ministerial farms upon our plantation, occupied by Phineas Fish and Gideon Holly. Mr. Holly succeeded his father, who was Preacher and Overseer—the latter now being Overseer—and these two gentlemen occupy about fifteen hundred acres of our best land, and do us no essential service whatever, but contrariwise, a bill of expense, and as destructive to us as a famine would be, in gradually wasting away the people before it.

We have been kept out of our own meeting house and school houses till very recently;—have had no privileges to hold any kind of meetings in them, although we should have been glad to have done something to improve our minds, in the way of meetings, either for debating societies or the worship of God; and our meeting house has been vacated for nearly ten years by most all of our people. We have no idea it would average ten of a Sabbath, and our meeting house is almost worn out by white people. It is not actually fit for respectable people to meet in. When we wanted a meeting for the benefit of the town, the Overseers have appointed them in other towns, and incurred a large bill of expense in this way, while they have insulted and pushed us out of doors: our women and our widows neglected, and our orphan children crying for bread. The expense has been very great in this way of doing business, for they (the Overseers) generally had a fine dinner, and we believe the expense came altogether out of our funds. The General Court provides but three for us to pay, but they (the Overseers) provide three of four more for us to pay, and they all find such good picking, they are loth to leave us; but we should rather not maintain them any longer, for we do not see that they are any service to us in raising us in the world; but we find the same deep stain of degradation hanging upon our persons and property, all apparently devoted to the will of unholy and unpriciplod [sic] men, that prowl around our borders.

This present government admits that the scum of the white population amöngst us that cannot remain in those towns where your Honors dwell, and our young people are not slow to learn their vices; and it is impossible, under existing laws, to have it otherwise. It also admits those characters to more privileges under our lands than ourselves, and if we say a word, we are then made out highway robbers, condemned, and hauled to the prison, and calumniated to the foulest extent by those very persons, who, we believe, have reaped the benefit of our property.

It furthermore withholds from us the necessaries of life that many of our people might enjoy; for it is a fact, that it gives power to the Overseers to take from us our grain if they choose, which they in fact have done. Whilst their husbands were absent at sea, our wives, and mothers, and sisters, would go to the Overseers for assistance. Sometimes they would hear, and at other times they would not; and when they did, they would give them a writing or order for the value of twenty-five cents, and then send them nine or ten miles to procure the value of it, and this as often as they go. We set too much by our women and children to have them served in this way any longer.

It also spoils our fishing, for white people think they have as good a right to our plantations and fishing privileges as ourselves, and of course throng us, and injure us all more or less.

This law also declares our whole plantation to be a public highway, and the inhabitants to be thieves and robbers, according to the plea made by Mr. Warren, the District Attorney, appointed by the Governor and Council; and this too, for merely inquiring into our rights, and shuts us up in prison. This law discourages our people, so that many of them have left their homes, and say they will not live under such oppressive laws, (the Overseers never encouraging industry,) and we believe it is the design of the Overseers so to oppress us as to drive all our people from the plantation. So that this law only adds disgrace to disgrace, and grinds us to the dust. The Overseers have also incurred many needless expenses by hiring other houses to have our meetings in, when we had them of our own, and appointed several men to do our business, and paid them out of our funds, when we might have done it ourselves; such as mending roads, carting wood, it being far from market, and by the time the poor got it there who had no team of their own, they had but little indeed left for themselves.

There are several tons of our most excellent ship timber that is cut and carried off yearly, and other valuable timber that we do not want cut; for we do not know but we shall want to build a ship ourselves, if we get able; and if not, we want the profit of it, for we have never learnt that any account has been rendered for any of it, to any one. Our cedar swamps share the same fate. Many of our most enlightened and virtuous men have been and cut and corded wood for themselves, and the Overseers have taken it from us, and sold it to whom they pleased; and even torn our fencing stuff from our fences, and carried it off, and sold it, and all the satisfaction we could get was, hold your peace, or you shall have nothing. This law admits just as much wood as the Overseers are a mind to cut and sell, and we believe it will average yearly, not less than twelve hundred cords per year of cord wood, besides other wood that is sold for fires around about us; and if we want any, we have to pay one dollar per cord for pine wood, and one dollar fifty cents for oak, out of our commons, and then sell it to just such men as the Overseers say, and to no others; and we think that such a tax is enormous, to pay for our own wood.

It also admits the white people to take away from our meadows all the hay, if they choose, leaving only enough for one cow, if any of us happen to have one; and if we have any more stock, we have to go ten or twelve miles to cut hay upon shares, or buy it. This we are compelled to do, or our cattle must suffer and die; and from these men we have no encouragement to raise stock, or be enterprising in any way whatever. It also admits the white people to greater privileges in possessing our pastures, than ourselves; for our wood, and hay, and pastures, are all set up at auction, and the white people have the means to out-bid us, and take every thing from us; and the Overseers will not give us any change, for our lives, in these things. As to the poor, we are all poor together; for we, in general, take care of ourselves in farming, hunting, fishing, and some in going to sea. We have some poor that are not able to maintain themselves. The Overseers assist a little in helping us to take care of them, but if we do not help them, they must suffer; and in the manner things are conducted, it makes it hard for all. If things were conducted differently, it would make it easy for all; but we cannot have it otherwise under present law and task-masters, although we believe there has been enough to maintain our poor, and if we had what has been squandered, as we believe from circumstantial evidence, we all should be in a better condition than we are now.

How much the proceeds of our plantation would amount to, yearly, we are not able to give an account, but from circumstances that we have had before us, we think we can come somewhere near it. We will say twelve hundred cords of wood, at nine shillings per cord, amount to eighteen hundred dollars; two hundred tons of hay, at four dollars per ton, amount to eight hundred dollars; there are twelve farms, at fourteen dollars per farm, amount to one hundred and sixty eight dollars; we have much pasture, we will say one hundred dollars for that, although we think we are within bounds; ship timber, we will put one hundred more; the whole amounting to twenty nine hundred and sixty eight dollars. We think the property ought to fetch that, certainly.

How much our expenses would be, when all told, we are not able to account accurately, but we believe we can come very near it. Our schools are kept in the following manner: in the winter we have two, the teachers receiving pay from twelve to fourteen dollars for three months each; in the summer we have two female teachers, they receiving one dollar per week for about sixteen weeks, making one hundred and ten dollars. There are seven poor, we believe, assisted by the Overseers; three are supported principally from the fund; for them is paid one dollar per week out of the funds, the others receive from two shillings to fifty cents, making about two hundred and fifty six dollars for their table expenses. As to clothing, they get but a little; they get a suit of course factory cloth, amounts to four or five dollars per suit, we will say thirty dollars; the Overseers let us have a few boards and shingles, to stop a few holes in our old houses, we would say it would be one hundred and fifty per year. We have a doctor that comes amongst us; we should presume he received about seventy five per year. The Overseers pay out of our funds about twenty five dollars per year, for mending our roads; the whole of the expenses amounting to six hundred and forty six dollars per year.

We think there is a great contrast between our expenses and the income of our plantation. But how much the Overseers charge for their services we know not, (we presume they take care of themselves) but they take the remainder—the funds are generally all away.

And now, Honored Gentlemen, we think we have been in slavery long enough. As to the Overseers, we have no confidence in them whatever—we do not believe they have dealt honestly by us, and we believe if they have a mind to swindle, none has a better chance than themselves, for they keep debt and credit, and how easy it is for them to conspire together to do us wrong, if they choose! At any rate, after suffering so much, we are jealous of them, and do assure your Honors we want them no longer. The Overseers say there is a general satisfaction amongst us, and that the excitement is of recent date. But we say, for more than five years there has been a very great dissatisfaction amongst us, and if we should add five more to it, it would be nothing out of the way: and it appears from the movements of the Overseers, that their influence in past times respecting our petitions, has been against us—that we have been represented as being a set of indolent, drunken Indians; but we say it is not the case—for many, very many of our people, are temperate, and sober, and industrious, and are willing to do, if they (the Overseers) would not prevent us. And now, if we wish to take care of ourselves, we cannot see why we may not have that privilege.

We presume the above charges and complaints are sufficient to warrant us a redress, and the abrogation of an unconstitutional law. If not, we have no doubt but the Overseers would strip us of all our living in five years more; and we have no doubt but it was the intention of the Overseers to strip us from our all; and we most solemnly believe we have been wronged out of thousands and tens of thousands of dollars in the course of this Overseership—every man seeking his own wealth instead of another man's.

Honor to whom honor is due, custom to whom custom, fear to whom fear; and we would render therefore unto Caesar the things that belong to Caesar, and unto God the things that are God's.

Therefore we can say there is one item in the law that is good—that is this: that no one should be permitted to sell his land without mutual consent, and we wish that item still to be retained for a few years, till our people become more enlightened, for many of them are ignorant in making trades, although we are happy to state to this Honorable Body, that we have many who are capable of doing business any where, and any kind of common and merchantable or seafaring business—to navigate a ship to any part of the globe.

And now we want a chance to instruct those who are ignorant, before that item is removed, for there are many that would not hesitate to strip us, who are ignorant, of our last morsel—and we shall consider it a favor indeed to have that item remain, and give us a chance for our lives in acting for ourselves.

And we do not want Overseers—as for them, we want them discharged, and never want their names mentioned amongst us again. And we would say of the preacher, Mr. Fish, we think no more of him than we do of the Overseers, believing they are all linked together; and we want him discharged, for we want our house to meet in ourselves.

Yours Most Obediently,
THE MARSHPEE INDIANS.

We, the Marshpee Tribe,
Also pray for a grant of the liberties of the Constitution, to form a Municipal Code of Laws amongst ourselves, that we may have a government that will be useful to us as a people; for we are sure we have never had any since our original Sachem fathers fell asleep.

Also, we desire that this Honorable Body would grant us the privilege of choosing an Attorney, to advise with us in our municipal regulations, and to instruct us still further in the laws; and this gentleman to be chosen yearly, or as long as we may deem it proper for the safety of the Town, and to be supported out of our funds (his expenses).

We wish that some provision could be made for the appointment of one or two Magistrates amongst us.

We also pray, that our Town may be incorporated and called Marshpee.

We have made these requests, believing the white men are knowing to our oppression in the general; and that if such laws are still enforced upon us, it is still murdering us by inches. And we do not know why the people of this Commonwealth want to cruelize us any longer, for we are sure that our fathers *fought, bled, and died for the liberties* of their now weeping and suffering children, the same as did your fathers for their children, whom ye are, who are now sitting to make laws to suit your own convenience, and secure your liberties. *Oh, White man! white man!* the blood of our fathers, spilt in the Revolutionary War, cries from the ground of our native soil, to break the chains of oppression, and let our children go *free.*

Yours we are, most respectfully,
THE MARSHPEE INDIANS

Notes

Introduction. Negative Work

Unless otherwise indicated, William Apess quotations are taken from *A Son of the Forest* (*SOF*), *The Increase of the Kingdom of Christ: A Sermon and The Indians: The Ten Lost Tribes* (*IKC*), *The Experiences of Five Christian Indians of the Pequot Tribe* (*FCI*), *Indian Nullification of the Unconstitutional Laws of Massachusetts Relative to the Marshpee Tribe; or, The Pretended Riot Explained* (*IN*), and *Eulogy on King Philip, as Pronounced at the Odeon, in Federal Street, Boston* (*EKP*), as they appear in *On Our Own Ground: The Complete Writings of William Apess, a Pequot*, ed. Barry O'Connell (Amherst: University of Massachusetts Press, 1992).

1. Walt Whitman, "Walt Whitman to Ralph Waldo Emerson," *Walt Whitman: The Complete Poems* (New York: Penguin Books, 2004), 767–68.
2. Whitman, "Osceola," in *Walt Whitman*, 561.
3. Alexis de Tocqueville, *Democracy in America*, vol. 1 (New York: Vintage Books, 1945), 26.
4. For a discussion on the choice of either civilization or extinction for nineteenth-century Natives, see Lucy Maddox, *Removals: Nineteenth-Century American Literature and the Politics of Indian Affairs* (New York: Oxford University Press, 1991), 3–49.
5. Barry O'Connell, ed., introduction to *On Our Own Ground: The Complete Writings of William Apess, a Pequot* (Amherst: University of Massachusetts Press, 1992), xli.
6. An 1880 catalogue of books on the American Indian declares of Apess that he "was a humbug" whose claims to "Pequod" ancestry were typical of the fallacy of Indian "tradition." Samuel Gardiner Drake, the mid-nineteenth-century "Indian historian," helped to propagate this perception by challenging Apess's reliance on Native "tradition," something Drake regarded as a leaky vessel of historical knowledge. Many twentieth-century critics tackling Apess's literary contribution continued to regard his work as problematically subjugated and incapable of authentically rendering Pequot experience. David Brumble saw Native authors writing in the Christian tradition in the wake of colonialism as being separated from the more pristine state of their ancestors' "preliterate" traditions. Cheryl Walker argues that Apess received his notions of tradition secondhand through textual productions rather than experiential contact—a view that this book complicates. Arnold Krupat acknowledges Apess's cosmopolitanism but suggests that the Native "lost his voice" when he lost the land. Walker and Krupat both offer generative readings of Apess's work but also isolate him from Native tradition, as though that tradition itself were something locked in the past or subtracted, in some poststructuralist arithmetic, from the equation of print discourse. While there are good reasons to problematize notions of "authenticity," this line of criticism seems to divorce contemporary Natives from claims to identity on interpretive grounds not equally applied to writers of the dominant culture. A

later wave of Native scholars, including Barry O'Connell, who was in many ways ahead of his time when he published his introduction to Apess's works, realized the generative possibilities of locating Apess "on his own ground," exposed to the tradition of his people as it manifested itself at that time. Cheryl Walker, *Indian Nation: Native American Literature and Nineteenth-Century Nationalisms* (Durham, NC: Duke University Press, 1997), 44. H. David Brumble III, *American Indian Autobiography* (Berkley: University of California Press, 1998), 63. Arnold Krupat, *The Voice in the Margin: Native American Literature and the Canon* (Irvine: University of California Press, 1989), 147. O'Connell, introduction to *On Our Own Ground*.

7. "Survivance" is a term brought into the service of Native studies by the Anishinaabe scholar, poet, and critic Gerald Vizenor, who describes it as "more than survival, more than endurance or mere response; the stories of survivance are an active presence." Gerald Vizenor, *Fugitive Poses: Native American Indian Scenes of Absence and Presence* (Lincoln: University of Nebraska Press, 1998), 15.

8. Robert Warrior, *Tribal Secrets: Recovering American Indian Intellectual Traditions* (Minneapolis: University of Minnesota Press, 1995), xxiii.

9. Robert Warrior, *The People and the Word: Reading Native Nonfiction* (Minneapolis: University of Minnesota Press, 2005), 27.

10. Ibid., 8.

11. Ibid., 3.

12. Lisa Brooks, *The Common Pot: The Recovery of Native Space in the Northeast* (Minneapolis: University of Minnesota Press, 2008), 163.

13. See Maureen Konkle, *Writing Indian Nations: Native Intellectuals and the Politics of Historiography, 1827–1863* (Chapel Hill: University of North Carolina Press, 2004); Phillip H. Round, *Removable Type: Histories of the Book in Indian Country, 1663–1880* (Chapel Hill: University of North Carolina Press, 2010); Jean M. O'Brien, *Firsting and Lasting: Writing Indians out of Existence in New England* (Minneapolis: University of Minnesota Press, 2010); Anne Marie Dannenberg, "'Where, then, shall we place the hero of the wilderness?': William Apess's *Eulogy on King Philip* and Doctrines of Racial Destiny?," *Early Native American Writing, New Critical Essays*, ed. Helen Jaskoski (Cambridge: Cambridge University Press, 1996); Karim M. Tiro, *The People of the Standing Stone: The Oneida Nation from the Revolution through the Era of Removal* (Amherst: University of Massachusetts Press, 2011); Mark J. Miller, "'Mouth for God': Temperate Labor, Race, and Methodist Reform in William Apess's *A Son of the Forest*," *Journal of the Early Republic*, 30, no. 2 (Summer 2010): 225–51.

14. Michel Foucault, *The Archeology of Knowledge and the Discourse on Language,* trans. A. M. Sheridan Smith (New York: Pantheon Books, 1972), 21 (emphasis added).

15. Jean M. O'Brien, *Dispossession by Degrees: Indian Land and Identity in Natick, Massachusetts, 1650–1790* (Lincoln: University of Nebraska Press, 1997).

16. *SOF,* 44.

17. Ibid., 11.

18. Ibid., 44.

19. John Augustus Stone, *Metamora: The Last of the Wampanoag* (New York: Feedback Theaterbooks & Prospero Press, 1996), 39.

20. *EKP,* 280.

21. Apess's "rebirth" in Ontario is asserted by Lisa Brooks in *The Common Pot,* 173.

22. *FCI,* 157.

23. Ibid., 160.

24. Scott Richard Lyons, *X-Marks: Native Signatures of Assent* (Minneapolis: University of Minnesota Press, 2010), 1.

25. Ibid., 24–25, 3.

26. John Mason, "A Breif History of the Pequot Warr," in *History of the Pequot War,* ed. Charles Orr (Cleveland, OH: Helman-Taylor, 1980), 35.

27. *EKP,* 278.

28. Warrior, *People and the Word,* 11, 44.

1. The Baskets Copy Our Stories

1. This passage is taken from *SOF,* 6, except for the last line, "my poor little body was mangled and my little arm broken into three pieces," which is taken from a retelling of this event that appears in *FCI,* 121.

2. *SOF,* 7.

3. John Mason, "A Brief History of the Pequot War: Especially of the memorable Taking of their Fort at Mistick in Connecticut in 1637," in *The History of the Pequot War,* ed. Charles Orr (Cleveland: Helman-Taylor, 1897), 35. See also Laura M. Stevens, *The Poor Indians: British Missionaries, Native Americans, and Colonial Sensibility* (Philadelphia: University of Pennsylvania Press, 2004).

4. *SOF,* 5.

5. Ibid., 7.

6. Ibid.

7. Ibid., 6–7 (emphasis added).

8. Edward Winslow, *Good News from New England: A Scholarly Edition,* ed. Kelly Wisecup (Amherst: University of Massachusetts Press, 2014), 57.

9. Ibid., 55.

10. See Charles W. Mills, *The Racial Contract* (Ithaca, NY: Cornell University Press, 1997). Roy Harvey Pearce's *Savagism and Civilization* stands at the forefront of a long-running scholarly discourse concerning the construction of "savagery" as a powerful historical and literary trope that comes to define Native identity in the mainstream American consciousness. Pearce recognized "savagism" as a kind of discourse in constant operation in America's textual productions, but did little to address the destructive agency of this discourse for Native peoples. Richard Slotkin's *Regeneration through Violence* moved the conversation forward by recognizing the central place the trope of "savagism" held in America's self-mythologizing structure. Other works, such as Francis Jennings's *The Conquest of America,* James Axtell's *The Invasion Within,* and William Cronon's *Changes in the Land,* among others, have worked to bring into relief the highly subjective cognitive frameworks by which colonialism justified acts of violence and appropriation against Native peoples. It was largely thanks to the contributions of a number of Native scholars, however, such as Gerald Vizenor, Linda Tuhiwai Smith, Craig Womack, Robert Warrior, Jace Weaver, and Lisa Brooks, that Native traditions and epistemologies have come to be privileged and placed at the center of the discourse, rupturing the persistent construct that equates Native culture with savagery.

11. Mills, *The Racial Contract,* 70–71.

12. Quoted in Thomas Jefferson, *The Selected Writings of Thomas Jefferson,* ed. Wayne Franklin (New York: W. W. Norton, 2010), 63.

13. William Stanhope Smith, *An Essay on the Causes of Variety of Complexion and Figure in the Human Species* (New Brunswick, NJ: J. Simpson, 1810), 357.

14. Ibid., 397.

15. George Bancroft, *History of the United States from the Discovery of the Continent* (New York: D. Appleton, 1888), 3.

16. Ibid., 5.

17. James Fenimore Cooper, *The Last of the Mohicans* (New York: Bantam Books, 1989), 25.

18. Edward Winslow, *Mourt's Relation: A Relation or Journall of the Beginning and Proceeding of the English Plantation Setled at Plimoth* (London: John Bellamie, 1622), 21.

19. Winslow, *Good News,* 102.

20. Bancroft, *History of the United States,* 434.

21. Ibid., 198.

22. Hector St. John de Crèvecoeur, "Letters from an American Farmer," in *Letters from an American Farmer and Other Essays*, ed. Dennis D. Moore (Cambridge, MA: Belknap Press of Harvard University Press, 2013), 80.

23. Quoted in "The Declaration of Independence," in Franklin, *Selected Writings of Thomas Jefferson*, 21 (emphasis added).

24. Mills, *Racial Contract*, 66–67.

25. *FCI*, 120.

26. *SOF* (1829), 10.

27. See Gladys Tantaquidgeon and Jayne G. Fawcett, "Symbolic Motifs on Painted Baskets of the Mohegan-Pequot," in *A Key into the Language of Woodsplint Baskets*, ed. Ann McMullen and Russell G. Handsmen (Washington, CT: American Indian Archaeological Institute, 1987), 99.

28. Roger Williams, *A Key into the Language of America* (Bedford, MA: Applewood Books, 1936), 135.

29. Stephanie Fitzgerald, "The Cultural Work of a Mohegan Painted Basket," in *Early Native Literacies in New England: A Documentary and Critical Anthology*, ed. Kristina Bross and Hillary E. Wyss (Amherst: University of Massachusetts Press, 2008), 53.

30. Winslow, *Mourt's Relation*, 22.

31. Ibid., 29.

32. See Dena F. Dincauze, "A Capsule Prehistory of Southern New England," in *The Pequots in Southern New England: The Fall and Rise of an American Indian Nation*, ed. Laurence M. Hauptman and James D. Wherry (Norman: University of Oklahoma Press, 1990), 19–32. Also see Kathleen J. Bragdon, *Native People of Southern New England, 1500–1650* (Norman: University of Oklahoma Press, 1996).

33. Alfred Cave refers to linguistic research, suggesting that the Pequot were not related to western tribes such as the Mahicans or the Delaware but rather had a long duration in southern Connecticut. See Alfred A. Cave, *The Pequot War* (Amherst: University of Massachusetts Press, 1996), 42.

34. William Simmons, "The Mystic Voice: Pequot Folklore from the Seventeenth Century to the Present," in Hauptman and Wherry, *Pequots in Southern New England*, 143.

35. The English merchant Thomas Morton somewhat ironically likened these practices to those of English nobility who would remove to their summer estates when the season dictated. Thomas Morton, *New English Canaan by Thomas Morton of "Merrymount": Texts, Notes, Biography, and Criticism*, ed. Jack Dempsey (Stoneham, MA: Jack Dempsey, 1999), 22.

36. Nicholaes van Wassenaer, "Historisch Verhael," in *Narratives of New Netherland, 1609–1664*, ed. J. Franklin Jameson (New York: Barnes & Noble, 1909), 69, 72.

37. Emphasis added.

38. The Haudenosaunee folklorist, historian, and ethnographer Arthur Parker, in his study on the Iroquois uses of maize, notes that "the Iroquois generally planted their squashes in the same hills with corn and some kinds of beans. Beside the land and labor saved by this custom there was a belief that these three vegetables were guarded by three inseparable spirit sisters and that the plants would not thrive apart in consequence." Arthur C. Parker, "The Iroquois Uses of Maize and Other Food Plants," in *Parker on the Iroquois*, ed. William N. Fenton (Syracuse, NY: Syracuse University Press, 1968), 91–92. Early settler accounts speak of land management practices of the Natives, from clearing land through controlled burns (Winslow, *Mourt's Relation*, 46) to using fish to fortify the soil with nutrients (ibid., 82).

39. Trudi Lamb Richmond and Amy E. Den Ouden maintain that power in northeastern Native communities was achieved through perceived wisdom and admirable character traits rather than simply inherited through bloodline. Therefore, women were often as eligible for the position of sachem as men. But corn surpluses were also a source of influence, and "Native women's daily labor embodied their true power: power over reproduction

of community life as well as the subsistence economy." Trudi Lamb Richmond and Amy E. Den Ouden, "Recovering Gendered Political Histories: Local Struggles and Native Women's Resistance in Colonial Southern New England," in *Reinterpreting New England Indians and the Colonial Experience,* ed. Colin G. Calloway and Neal Salisbury (Boston: Colonial Society of America, 2003), 180–81.

40. Roger Williams may have hit upon the most helpful characterization of this dynamic when he observed, "The Sachims, although they have an absolute Monarchie over the people; yet they will not conclude of ought that concerns all, either Lawes, or Subsidies, or warres, unto which the people are averse, and gentle perswasion cannot be brought." To what extent "absolute Monarchie" and "gentle perswasion" agree I am at pains to suggest. Roger Williams, *Key,* 142.

41. Cave, *Pequot War,* 82.

42. Johannes de Laet, "New World," in *Narratives of New Netherland, 1609–1664,* ed. J. Franklin Jameson (New York: Barnes & Noble, 1909), 43.

43. Ibid., 44.

44. Neal Salisbury, *Manitou and Providence: Indians, Europeans, and the Making of New England, 1500–1643* (New York: Oxford University Press, 1982), 10.

45. Paul Le Jeune, *Jesuit Relations and Allied Documents: Travels and Explorations of the Jesuit Missionaries in New France, 1610–1791,* vol. 6, ed. Reuben Gold Thwaites, trans. Finlow Alexander, Percy Favor Bicknell, William Frederic Giese, Crawford Lindsay, and William Price (New York: Pageant, 1959), 5.

46. Lisa Brooks, *The Common Pot: The Recovery of Native Space in the Northeast* (Minneapolis: University of Minnesota Press, 2008), 4.

47. Williams, *Key,* 159–63.

48. For more on wampum and its production, Margaret Bruchac's blog "On the Wampum Trail: Restorative Research in Northeastern Museums" provides the best contemporary account of an ongoing account of our growing understanding of wampum and its uses in precolonial and colonial America: https://wampumtrail.wordpress.com/.

49. Arthur Parker, "The Constitution of the Five Nations," in Fenton, *Parker on the Iroquois,* 20.

50. William A. Starna makes the distinction between "tribute" and "reciprocity" in "The Pequots in the Early Seventeenth Century," in Hauptman and Wherry, *Pequots in Southern New England,* 42.

51. de Laet, "New World," in Jameson, *Narratives of New Netherland,* 47.

52. See Lynn Ceci, "Native Wampum as a Peripheral Resource in the Seventeenth-Century World System," in Hauptman and Wherry, *Pequots in Southern New England,* 48–50; Bragdon, *Native People of Southern New England,* 97–99; Salisbury, *Manitou and Providence.*

53. William Bradford, *Of Plymouth Plantation,* ed. Caleb Johnson (Xlibris, 2006), 329–30.

54. See John Winthrop, *Winthrop's Journal: History of New England, 1630–1649,* vol. 1, ed. James K. Hosmer (New York: Elibron Classics, 2005), 118, 138–39. John Underhill, *Newes From America* (New York: De Capo Press, 1971). Increase Mather, *A Relation of the Troubles which have hapned in New-England By reason of the Indians there* (New York: Arno Press, 1972); Drew Lopenzina, *Red Ink: Native Americans Picking up the Pen in the Colonial Period* (Albany: SUNY Press, 2012), 75–85.

55. Underhill, *Newes,* 84. Increase Mather reports that "some 40 Narragansett were wounded or killed in the fight, while, strange to relate, only twenty-four Englishmen were wounded and two or three killed." Mather, *Relation,* 47.

56. Bradford, *Plymouth Plantation,* 355.

57. The newly formed Connecticut General Court at Hartford determined in 1637 that the Pequot were responsible for thirty English deaths. Many of these were clearly not direct or even indirect acts that could be attributed to the Pequot. See Benjamin Trumbull, *A Complete History of Connecticut Civil and Ecclesiastical from the Emigration of Its First Planters*

from England in the Year 1630 to the Year 1764 and to the Close of Indian Wars (New Haven, CT: Maltby, Goldsmith and Co. and Samuel Wadsworth, 1818), 79.

58. Mason, "Brief History," 35.

59. Ibid.

60. Ibid., 44.

61. Roger Williams, *The Complete Writings of Roger Williams: The Letters of Roger Williams,* vol. 6 (Eugene, OR: Wipf and Stock, 1963), 92.

62. Mason, "Brief History," 38.

63. Mather, *Relation,* 53.

64. "The Massachusetts Body of Liberties" (1641), Hanover Historical Texts Projects, http://history.hanover.edu/texts/masslib.html.

65. Winthrop, *Journal,* 227.

66. "New England's First Fruits," in *The Eliot Tracts: With Letters from John Eliot to Thomas Thorowgood and Richard Baxter,* ed. Michael P. Clark (Westport, CT: Praeger, 2003), 59.

67. Cockenoe was a captive of the Pequot War who, as a servant to Richard Calicot of Dorchester, acquired the skill of English literacy and helped John Eliot translate some of the Christian Bible into the Algonquian language before moving on to negotiate a number of land deals for the Montauk on Long Island. See William Wallace Tooker, *Cockenoe de Long Island: John Eliot's First Indian Teacher and the Story of His Career from the Early Records* (New York: Francis Harper, 1896); and Lopenzina, *Red Ink,* 72.

68. For more on this, see Lopenzina, *Red Ink,* 69–73.

69. Winthrop, *Journal,* 225–26.

70. Williams, *Complete Writings,* 79–80.

71. *SOF,* 5.

72. Ibid., 7.

73. *Eliot Tracts,* 97–98, 116.

74. Ibid., 117.

75. Ibid., 151.

76. One such case involved a Native servant in Boston identified only as "Maria" who went on trial for infanticide in 1711 but was ultimately exonerated when her master vehemently defended her. As Sharon M. Harris observes, in the case of Native servants, it was often deemed more important that a master "retained his property, which was of greater concern than the death of a Native American child." Another case involved Patience Boston, a Wampanoag accused of killing two of her children but condemned and executed only when she poisoned a white child in 1732. Sarah Pharoah was a Narragansett women of Rhode Island Colony brought to court for allegedly murdering her infant child in 1743. Forced to conceal her pregnancy (and, afterward, the dead issue of her womb), her secret was nonetheless discovered by a group of children who found the dead baby in an "Indian barn," or storage pit. Pharoah maintained her innocence and ultimately was allowed to go free, but her case speaks to the kind of scrutiny that servant women were under. See Sharon M. Harris, *Executing Race: Early American Women's Narratives of Race, Society, and the Law* (Columbus: Ohio State University Press, 2005), 25–68. Ann Marie Plane, *Colonial Intimacies: Indian Marriage in Early New England* (Ithaca, NY: Cornell University Press, 2000), 123–27.

77. Jack Campisi, *Pequots,* 118. The Connecticut General Court officially granted this land to the Eastern Pequot in 1659. See J. Hammond Trumbull, ed., *The Public Records of the Colony of Connecticut, prior to the Union with New Haven Colony* (Hartford, CT: Brown & Parsons, 1850), 335–36.

78. The quoted materials concerning Katherine Garret's testimony and all other related items, except where otherwise indicated, are taken from *Early Native Literacies in New England: A Documentary and Critical Anthology,* ed. Kristina Bross and Hillary E. Wyss (Amherst: University of Massachusetts Press, 2008), 142–48.

79. Plane, *Colonial Intimacies,* 126–26, 117.

80. Scott Richard Lyons, *XMarks: Native Signatures of Assent* (Minneapolis: University of Minnesota Press, 2010).
81. *FCI,* 155.
82. Ibid., 151.
83. Quoted ibid., 153.

2. Birthright, Bondage, and Beyond

1. See Lisa Brooks, *The Common Pot: The Recovery of Native Space in the Northeast* (Minneapolis: University of Minnesota Press, 2008), 14–24.
2. Ibid., 35.
3. Certain Colrain tracts were apparently purchased in the wake of the Deerfield Conference and conveyed to the colony of Massachusetts by two "Scautecook" women, Mauhammetpeet and Mequnnisqua, in August of 1735. Such transfers of land, however they were understood by the Native agents involved, are never referenced in the Colrain histories, providing yet another form of "lasting." See Harry Andrew Wright, ed., *Indian Deeds of Hampden County* (Springfield, MA: Wright, 1905),120–24.
4. Charles H. McClellan, *Early Settlers of Colrain, Massachusetts* (Greenfield, MA: W. S. Carson, 1885), 11.
5. Jean M. O'Brien, *Firsting and Lasting: Writing Indians out of Existence in New England* (Minneapolis: University of Minnesota Press, 2010), 6.
6. Fanny B. Shippee, "Rhythmical Reminiscences of Catamount Hill," in *A Sketch of the Origin and Growth of the Catamount Hill Association of Colrain, Massachusetts, Compiled by Dr. A. F. Davenport and Miss Charlotte Augusta Dunton of North Adams, Massachusetts* (North Adams: Walden & Crawley Printers, 1901), 36.
7. Lois McClellan Patrie and Ursula Russell, *A History of Colrain, Massachusetts, with Genealogies of Early Families* (Salem, MA: Higgenson Book, 1974), 21.
8. *SOF,* 4.
9. See Liza Ketchum, *Where the Great Hawk Flies* (New York: Scholastic, 2005).
10. A published version of the Griswold tale is told by Sarah H. Rowell, "The Griswold Family," in *The Vermont Historical Gazeteer: A Magazine Embracing a History of Each Town, Civil, Ecclesiastical, Biographical, and Military*, vol. 2, ed. Abby Maria Hemenway (Burlington, VT: Miss A. M. Hemenway, 1871), 1009. An oral account of the story was told to me by John Moody in spring 2014.
11. *The Griswold Family: England-America,* compiled by Glenn E. Griswold, the Griswold Family Association (privately published, held at Griswold Memorial Library, Colrain, MA), 149. See also Mrs. Charles Delmar Townsend, *The Griswold Family, England-America* (Burlington, VT: Griswold Family Association of America, 1962), and Ruth Lee Griswold, *A Narrative of the Griswold Family* (Rutland, VT: Tuttle, 1931).
12. R. L. Griswold, *Narrative,* 157.
13. Jean M. O'Brien, *Dispossession by Degrees: Indian Land and Identity in Natick, Massachusetts, 1650–1790* (New York: Cambridge University Press, 1997), 127.
14. Connecticut State Library (CSL), Connecticut Vital Records (CVR), Stonington Probate District Packets 1766–1875, reel 1383.
15. Yale Indian Papers Project (hereafter cited as YIPP), "Apess, Samuel,–1773," http://yipp. yale.edu/bio/bibliography/apes-samuel-1773.
16. CSL, CVR, Stonington Probate District Packets 1766–1875, reel 1383.
17. *SOF,* 4. Philip Gura, in his short biography of Apess, suggests that this was Apess's grandfather, but Gura seems not to have noticed the tribal designation of "Pequot" on the military roles. For this to have been his grandfather, Apess would have had to have been mistaken about his grandfather being "white," which seems doubtful. Philip F. Gura, *The Life of William Apess, Pequot* (Chapel Hill: University of North Carolina Press, 2015), 4–5.
18. Information concerning the military service of the Apes family is taken from *Rolls of*

Connecticut Men in the French and Indian War, 1755–1762, vol. 2, ed. Albert C. Bates, (Hartford, CT: 1903, 1905). The exception is Peter Apes, who is found in *Forgotten Patriots: African American and American Indian Patriots in the Revolutionary War* (National Society Daughters of the American Revolution, 2008), 270, available at http://www.dar.org/sites/default/files/media/library/DARpublications/Forgotten_Patriots_ISBN-978-1-892237-10-1.pdf. See also Barbara W. Brown and James M. Rose, *Black Roots in Southeastern Connecticut, 1650–1900* (Detroit: Gale Research, 1980), 11. Samson Occom, Joseph Johnson, and Samuel Ashpo were all influential Christian Mohegan leaders of the generation before Apess. Occom and Johnson were involved in the exodus to the Brothertown settlement, and Occom, an ordained Presbyterian minister, was often thought of as the most famous Indian of his day. Their families remained influential in the communities in which they served for generations to come.

19. YIPP, "Joseph Fish's Tenth Eastern Pequot Journal," http://yipp.yale.edu/bio/bibliography/apes-samuel-1773. See also CSL, CVR for Preston, microfilm reel 3839, sec. 4, slide 3.

20. This is taken from Occom's journal, dated July 17, 1785. See Samson Occom, *The Collected Writings of Samson Occom, Mohegan,* ed. Joanna Brooks (New York: Oxford University Press, 2006), 296. For Sally George's indenture (entered as "Sarah George") with the Park family, see Brown and Rose, *Black Roots,* 161.

21. Brown and Rose, *Black Roots,* 265.

22. CSL, CVR for Preston, microfilm reel 3839, 4:3.

23. See Brown and Rose, *Black Roots,* 11. Connecticut Historical Society (CHS), Colchester, CT. Selectmen. Health Certificate, February 18, 1805, DS, 1 page (Ms 79497). According to Eva Butler, who, with the noted anthropologist Frank Speck, co-authored a book on Eastern Algonquian basket decorations in 1947, Apess's mother was a sister to Sally George. This reference may have blurred the line, however, between "sister" and "sister in law." Frank Speck and Eva Baker, *Eastern Algonquian Block-Stamp Decoration: A New World Original or an Acculturated Art* (Trenton: Archeological Society of New Jersey, 1947), 40.

24. *SOF,* 4.

25. For instance, a 1985 edition of *A Eulogy on King Philip* claims in the introduction that Apess's mother was "a pure blooded Pequot." Carl Benn has recently called into question the idea that Candace could be Apess's mother because, as he notes, Apess "affirmed his mother was of pure native ancestry." Nancy Shoemaker has also forwarded the claim that Candace "was probably not" Apess's mother on the basis of her status as a black slave. Barry O'Connell, in a footnote to his edited edition of *A Son of the Forest and other Writings,* notes that "according to her son she was . . . a full-blooded Pequot woman." One can see how critics are misled into assuming this, but read correctly, Apess never actually makes this assertion. He simply claims that his mother was not white. See Lincoln A. Dexter, *A Eulogy on King Philip* (Brookfield, MA: Lincoln A. Dexter, 1985), ix; Carl Benn, ed., *Native Memoirs from the War of 1812: Black Hawk and William Apess* (Baltimore, MD: John Hopkins University Press, 2014), 83. Nancy Shoemaker, "Race and Indigeneity in the Life of Elisha Apes," *Ethnohistory* 60, no. 1 (Winter 2013): 28–50. Barry O'Connell, ed., *A Son of the Forest and Other Writings by William Apess, a Pequot* (Amherst: University of Massachusetts Press, 1992), xi.

26. Brown and Rose, *Black Roots,* xv.

27. *SOF,* 4.

28. CSL, "May 10, 1804 Letter from Samuel Mott to Judge William Hillhouse," Connecticut Archives, Historical Reference F91 C-56 Indians 1666–1820, series 2, vol. 2, microfilm reel 32. See also See Brad D. E. Jarvis, *The Brothertown Nation of Indians: Land Ownership and Nationalism in Early America, 1740–1840* (Lincoln: University of Nebraska Press, 2010), 21–27.

29. Charles R. Stark, *Groton Connecticut, 1705–1905* (Stonington, CT: Palmer Press, 1922), 55.

30. See Karim M. Tiro, *The People of the Standing Stone: The Oneida Nation from the Revolution*

through the Era of Removal (Amherst: University of Massachusetts Press, 2011). Tiro writes that shortly after the 1768 Treaty of Fort Stanwix, which drew the "Line of Property" dividing Haudenosuanee and colonial possessions, the Oneidas moved to "buttress the Line of Property by placing more Natives on it" or, in other words, by inviting the Brothertown Natives to move in (34–35).

31. Occom, *Collected Writings*, 308–9.
32. See Drew Lopenzina, " 'The Whole Wilderness Shall Blossom as the Rose': Samson Occom, Joseph Johnson, and the Question of Native Settlement on Cooper's Frontier," *American Quarterly* 58, no. 4 (December 2006): 1119–45.
33. *FCI*, 120.
34. See William DeLoss Love, *Samson Occom and the Christian Indians of New England* (Syracuse, NY: Syracuse University Press, 2000), 364–66. Stark too notes that in 1786 "a large number of Pequots, with a few Mohegans . . . removed to Oneida County, NY . . . forming the nucleus of what has since been known as the Brothertown tribe." Stark, *Groton*, 59.
35. Jarvis, *Brothertown*, 140.
36. Ibid., 141–42.
37. CSL, "May 1811 Letter from Samuel Mott to Conecticut General Assembly," Connecticut Archives, Historical Reference F91 C-56 Indians 1666–1820, series 2, vol. 2, microfilm reel 36.
38. It is worth noting that, in Virginia, the Pamunkey tribe's effort to gain federal recognition was held up for many years by concerns about past clauses to exclude intermarriage with blacks. While members of the Congressional Black Caucus labeled this clause "disturbing," the Pamunkeys countered that the clause dated back to efforts in the first half of the twentieth century to label as "colored" any Pamunkey with black ancestry, thereby erasing any legal presence as Pamunkey. Attempts to disenfranchise Native communities in this manner have been going on since at least the late eighteenth century. Frederic J. Frommer, "Black Lawmakers Rebuke Virginia Tribe," *Virginian-Pilot* (Norfolk), November 11, 2014.
39. *A Sketch of the Origin and Growth of the Catamount Hill Association of Colrain, MA,* ed. Dr. A. F. Davenport and Charlotte Augusta Dunton (North Adams, MA: Walden & Crawley Printers, 1903), 53.
40. Ritchie Garrison observes that the population of Franklin County jumped 325 percent between the years 1765 and 1790, most of this due to young men leaving their family farms, where there was no opportunity for them to advance, and moving to hilltop settlements. See Ritchie J. Garrison, *Landscape and Material Life in Franklin County, Massachusetts, 1770–1860* (Knoxville: University of Tennessee Press, 1991), 96–98. See also Elmer F. Davenport, *The Puzzle of Catamount Hill: Being a Report of Pioneer Life in Franklin County, Massachusetts, during the Century after the War of Independence, 1780–1880* (self-published, 1969).
41. E. Davenport, *Puzzle of Catamount Hill,* 12–25. MA State Tax Valuations of 1811, Samuel Brown's lot, Misc. Documents, Griswold Memorial Library, Colrain, MA. Eliel B. Smith, "A Brief Historical Sketch," in "Colrain Historical Sketches" (assembled for the Griswold Memorial Library, Colrain, MA), 96.
42. *SOF* (1829), 9.
43. Ibid., 8.
44. *SOF,* 3–4.
45. *SOF* (1829), 8
46. Carl G. Smith, "From Homesteads to Cellar Holes on Catamount Hill, Colrain, Massachusetts," *New England Historical and Genealogical Register,* vol. 96 (1942), 69.
47. E. Davenport, *Puzzle of Catamount Hill,* 9.
48. William Tyler Arms, *History of Leyden, Massachusetts, 1676–1959* (Orange, MA: Enterprise and Journal, 1959), 172.
49. *FCI,* 99.
50. *SOF,* 4.

51. Stark, *Groton*, 52.
52. Margaret Bruchac, "Hilltown Touchstone: Reconsidering William Apess's Relations to Colrain," manuscript, used by permission of the author.
53. The place of birth of Apess's children can be found in Town of Leyden Births—Deaths, 1777–1848, Town Clerk's Office Book no. 3, 98.
54. Arms, *History of Leyden*, 172.
55. *SOF*, 5.
56. Ibid.
57. Brown and Rose, *Black Roots*, 11.
58. *FCI*, 120.
59. Town Clerk of Salem, CT, Land Records, vol. 4, 758.
60. Brown and Rose, *Black Roots*, 11.
61. *SOF* (1829), 10.
62. *SOF*, 5; *FCI*, 120.
63. Town of Colrain Clerk's Office, bound record book labeled Buckland, Colrain, Montague Vital Records, 193.
64. "Death Notice," *Greenfield (MA) Gazette*, September 12, 1803.
65. *SOF*, 5.
66. *SOF* (1829), 14; *SOF*, 5
67. *SOF*, 5.
68. See Colchester Town Records, 1797–1805, for the year 1802, entries 10, 18, and 32. I have cross-referenced the name Lemuel Ashbo with Mohegan tribal historians, but they have no record of him, and he appears to have slipped out of view of the archive after boarding Apess for a short period, a fate not unusual for Natives at this time.
69. Interestingly, William Apes also owned land in this area that he would later sell to Daniel Taylor (brother of Candace's owner, Joseph Taylor) for two hundred dollars. Town of Colchester Clerk's Office, sale dated October 27, 1811, Town of Colchester Land Records, vol. 17, p. 293. There exists a convergence of names on land records that, I suspect, tells a deeper story of inheritance, disenfranchisement, and displacement, although I have not been able to crack the code as of yet. Names such as Gillet, Freeman, Chamberlain, and Taylor all show up on land transactions involving the Apess family, as well as in Apess's autobiography.
70. *SOF*, 6.
71. Ibid., 7.
72. Ibid., 6
73. Ibid., and *FCI*, 61 (emphasis added).
74. *SOF*, 13.
75. Ibid., 9.
76. Ibid., 10.
77. Ibid., 12–13.
78. Ibid., 10.
79. *SOF* (1829), 25.
80. *SOF*, 10–11.
81. Ibid., 13. *SOF* (1829), 28.
82. Judith Herman, M.D., *Trauma and Recovery: The Aftermath of Violence—From Domestic Abuse to Political Terror* (New York: Basic Books, 1992), 1.
83. Ibid., 96 (emphasis added).
84. *SOF*, 14.
85. Ibid., 13.
86. *FCI*, 129.
87. *SOF*, 19–20.
88. Herman, *Trauma and Recovery*, 35.
89. *SOF*, 20.

90. To get a sense of what a more conventional conversion experience, within the framework of Methodism, looked like at the time, we might visit Sarah Knight's 1829 memoir. Knight was born the same year as Apess, in 1798; lived in the town of Colchester, Connecticut, where Apess spent much of his youth,; and her memoir was published by her husband a year after her death in 1829, the same year that Apess first published *A Son of the Forest*. Knight's conversion and subsequent carriage upon her deathbed were regarded as exemplary and prompted her husband to publish a small account of her life, including passages from her journal and from letters that she wrote to a few devout friends. Sarah Knight, *Memoir of Sarah Knight, Wife of Thomas Knight of Colchester Who Died in the 28th of the Fifth Month, 1828* (Philadelphia: Thomas Kite, 1829).

91. *SOF,* 14.

92. James Abraham Hillhouse, *Sachem's Wood: A Short Poem with Notes* (New Haven, CT: B & W Noyes, 1838), 16, 28.

93. It has commonly been reported that Occom's sermon went through seventeen editions, but Mike Kelly, curator of the rare book collection at Amherst College, has recently recorded a number of heretofore unknown editions, bringing the current total up to twenty-two.

94. CSL, "May 17, 1796 Letter from William Hillhouse to the Honorable Governor and Council of his Majesty's Colony of Connecticut," Connecticut Archives, Historical Reference F91 C-56 Indians 1666–1820, series 1, vol. 2, microfilm reel 286.

95. Samson Occom, "Autobiographical Narrative, Second Draft (September 17, 1768)," in *The Collected Writings of Samson Occom, Mohegan: Leadership and Literature in Eighteenth-Century Native America* (Oxford: Oxford University Press, 2006), 58.

96. Margaret Ellen Newell, "The Changing Nature of Slavery in New England, 1670–1720," in *Reinterpreting New England Indians and the Colonial Experience,* ed. Colin G. Calloway and Neal Salisbury (Boston: Colonial Society of Massachusetts, 2003), 108, 124. See also David J. Silverman, "The Impact of Indentured Servitude on the Society and Culture of Southern New England Indians, 1680–1810," *New England Quarterly* 74, no. 4 (December 2001): 622–66; O'Brien, *Dispossession by Degrees*; Amy E. Den Ouden, *Beyond Conquest: Native Peoples and the Struggle for History in New England* (Lincoln: University of Nebraska Press, 2005); Anne Marie Plane, *Colonial Intimacies: Indian Marriage in Early New England* (Ithaca, NY: Cornell University Press, 2000).

97. *SOF,* 10.

98. Ruth Wallis Herndon and Ella Wilcox Sekatau, "Colonizing the Children: Indian Youngsters in Servitude in Colonial Rhode Island," in Calloway and Salisbury, *Reinterpreting New England Indians,* 143.

99. Ibid., 149.

100. David Menschel, "Abolition without Deliverance: The Law of Connecticut Slavery 1784–1848," *Yale Law Journal* 1, no. 183 (September 2001): 188.

101. Ibid., 191.

102. According to the 1774 census, of the three thousand residents in Colchester, two hundred and one were slaves. Colchester Town Library, Special Collections, "Historical and Architectural Survey" (manuscript), 28.

103. *SOF,* 15.

104. Ibid., 16.

105. *FCI,* 64.

106. *SOF,* 16.

107. Ibid., 17.

108. Ibid., 22.

109. Ibid., 18

110. Ibid., 17

111. Ibid., 19.

112. Ibid.

113. Ibid., 18.
114. Joseph Snelling, *Life of Reverend Joseph Snelling: Being a Sketch of His Christian Experience and Labors in the Ministry* (Boston: John M. Leish, 1847), 109.
115. *SOF,* 21.
116. Ibid., 20.
117. Ibid., 22.

3. The Broad Theater of the World

1. "Advertisement," *Connecticut Gazette* (New London), April 21, 1813.
2. *SOF,* 23.
3. Samson Occom, "Indians Must Have Teachers of Their Own Coular or Nation," in *The Collected Writings of Samson Occom, Mohegan: Leadership and Literature in Eighteenth-Century Native America* (New York: Oxford University Press, 2006), 133.
4. "Speech of the President of the United States to Both Houses of Congress," *Albany (NY) Gazette,* November 3, 1791.
5. Ibid.
6. Arthur C. Parker, *The History of the Seneca Indians* (Port Washington, NY: Ira J. Friedman, 1926), 132.
7. Chief Irving Powless Jr., "Treaty Making," in *Treaty of Canandaigua 1794: 200 Years of Treaty Relations between the Iroquois Confederacy and the United States,* ed. G. Peter Jemison and Anna M. Schein (Santa Fe: Clear Light Publishing, 2000), 28.
8. Henry Wiencek, *An Imperfect God: George Washington, His Slaves, and the Creation of America* (New York: Farrar, Straus and Giroux, 2003), 19.
9. George Washington, *The Journal of Major George Washington* (London: T. Jeffreys, 1754), 9.
10. Powless Jr., "Treaty Making," 28.
11. Karim M. Tiro, *The People of the Standing Stone: The Oneida Nation from the Revolution through the Era of Removal* (Amherst: University of Massachusetts Press, 2011), 55.
12. Arthur Parker, "Iroquois Uses of Maize," in *Parker on the Iroquois,* ed. William F. Fenton (Syracuse: Syracuse University Press, 1968), 20.
13. Barbara Alice Mann, *George Washington's War on Native America* (Lincoln: University of Nebraska Press, 2005), 74.
14. Parker, *History of the Seneca Indians,* 126; Tiro, *Standing Stone,* 55; John Mohawk, "The Canandaigua Treaty in Historical Perspective," in Jemison and Schein, *Treaty of Canandaigua,* 46–47; Carl Benn, *The Iroquois in the War of 1812* (Toronto: University of Toronto Press, 1998), 17–18.
15. Mohawk, "Canandaigua Treaty," 48–49. See also Benn, *Iroquois,* 10–28.
16. Alan Taylor, *The Civil War of 1812: American Citizens, British Subjects, Irish Rebels, and Indian Allies* (New York: Alfred A. Knopf, 2010), 10.
17. Quoted in Taylor, *Civil War,* 140.
18. Sandy Antal, *A Wampum Denied: Proctor's War of 1812* (Montreal: McGill-Queens University Press, 1998), 14.
19. *SOF,* 23
20. Ibid.
21. Ibid., 24.
22. Johan de Laet, "From the 'New World' by Johan de Laet, 1625, 1630, 1633, 1640," in *Narratives of New Netherland, 1609–1664,* ed. J. Franklin Jameson (New York: Barnes & Noble, 1909), 44.
23. Daniel Denton, *A Brief Description of New-York: Formerly Called New-Netherlands* (London: First Shop on Popes-Head Alley, 1670), 7.
24. Washington Irving, "Knickerbocker's History of New York," in *The Complete Works of Washington Irving, in One Volume* (Paris: Baudry's European Library, 1834), 577.

25. Paul A. W. Wallace, *White Roots of Peace: The Iroquois Book of Life* (Santa Fe: Clear Light, 1994), 34.

26. Charles G. Leland, *Algonquian Legends of New England: Myth and Folk Lore of the Micmac, Passamaquoddy, and Penobscot Tribes* (Boston: Houghton, Mifflin, 1884), 128.

27. I have found only one reference to this story, published in the *New York Advocate* and picked up by a handful of other newspapers at the time as a miscellany feature. "Crossing the Line," *Bangor (ME) Weekly Register*, May 26, 1825.

28. *SOF*, 22.

29. Ibid., 24.

30. Melissa Jayne Fawcett, *Medicine Trail: The Life and Lessons of Gladys Tantaquidgeon* (Tucson: University of Arizona Press, 2000), 35.

31. See William L. Stone, *History of New York City from the Discovery to the Present Day* (New York: Virtue & Yortson, 1872), 335–70.

32. *SOF*, 25.

33. Ibid.

34. Ibid.

35. *SOF* (1829), 56.

36. *SOF*, 25.

37. Ibid., 26. Apess's description of the execution perfectly matches a description of formal proceedings for military execution given in Anastasio Carlos Mariano Azoy, *Three Centuries under the Flag: The Story of Governors Island* (Governors Island, NY: Headquarters First Army, 1951), 46–47. It also closely follows the proceedings witnessed by Jarvis Hanks, a young boy of thirteen who was enlisted, as was Apess, as a drummer boy but later made to serve in the ranks. Jarvis Hanks, "A Tale of Five Deserters: Niagra's Frontier, June 1814," in *The War of 1812: Writings from America's Second War of Independence*, ed. Donald R. Hickey (New York: Library of America, 2013), 442–43.

38. *SOF*, 26.

39. Ibid., 27.

40. Talyor, *Civil War*, 203.

41. Carl Benn, "Missed Opportunities and the Problem of the Mohawk Chief John Norton's Cherokee Ancestry," *Ethnohistory* 59, no. 2 (Spring 2012): 260–91.

42. Ibid., 273. John Norton, *Journal of Major John Norton,* ed. Carl F. Klink and James J. Talman (Toronto: Champlain Society, 2011), 289.

43. Norton, *Journal,* 174–75 (emphasis added).

44. Ibid., 289–90.

45. For more on Gnaddenhutten, see Mann, *George Washington's War,* 147–80.

46. Norton, *Journal,* 289–90.

47. James Madison, "James Madison: War Message to Congress, June 1812," in Hickey, *War of 1812,* 7.

48. Taylor, *Civil War,* 210.

49. William Henry Harrison, "Governor Harrison to the Secretary of War, 29 August 1812," in *The First American Frontier: Documents Relating to the Invasion of Canada and the Surrender of Detroit, 1812,* ed. Ernest A. Cruikshank (Ottawa: Government Printing Bureau, 1912), 204.

50. Antal, *Wampum Denied,* 131.

51. Benson J. Lossing, *Lossing's Pictorial Field Book of the War of 1812,* vol. 2 (Gretna, LA: Pelican Publishing , 2001), 546n2. Malden was the name the Americans gave to the fort at Amherstburg where scalp bounties were issued.

52. Black Hawk, *The Life of Black Hawk or Ma-ka-tai-me-she-kia-kiak,* ed. J. Gerald Kennedy (New York: Penguin, 2008), 28.

53. Charles Askin, "Extract from an Original Journal of Charles Askin, in the Canadian Archive," in Cruikshank, *First American Frontier,* 241.

54. Ibid., 240.

55. Norton, *Journal,* 314–15.

56. Ibid., 315.

57. Ibid., 312.

58. Ibid., 343.

59. Isaac Brock, "Major-General Brock to the Earl of Liverpool, August 29, 1812," in Cruikshank, *First American Frontier,* 192.

60. Quoted in Antal, *Wampum Denied,* 73–74.

61. "Speech of Indians on the Wabash in Reply to Message of Colonel M. Elliott, S.I.A.," in Cruikshank, *First American Frontier,* 35–36.

62. Antal, *Wampum Denied,* 115.

63. *SOF,* 58.

64. *EKP,* 278.

65. *SOF,* 27.

66. Lossing, *Field Book,* 642. *SOF,* 27.

67. *SOF,* 16, 27.

68. Robert Purdy, "Letter from Robert Purdy to James Wilkinson, Oct. 26, 1813," in Hickey, *War of 1812,* 339–34. Lossing, *Field Book,* 658.

69. *SOF,* 28.

70. Paul Fussell, *The Great War and Modern Memory* (New York: Oxford University Press, 1975), 3–35.

71. *SOF,* 28.

72. Ibid., 27.

73. Keith A. Herkalo, *The Battles at Plattsburgh, September 11, 1814* (Charleston, SC: History Press, 2012), 37.

74. *SOF,* 28.

75. Ibid., 28–29. George McFeely, "George McFeely's Diary," in Hickey, *War of 1812,* 415.

76. Quoted in John Halloway Hanson, *The Lost Prince: Fact Tending to Prove the Identity of Louis the Seventeenth, of France, and the Rev. Eleazar Williams, Missionary among the Indians of North America* (New York: G. P. Putnam, 1854), 222.

77. Ibid., 225–28.

78. Ibid., 240–41.

79. Ibid., 242–51.

80. Ibid., 260.

81. *SOF,* 29.

82. Hanson, *Lost Prince,* 258–61.

83. Jack Bilow, *Whispers in the Dark: A War of 1812 Death Register* (Plattsburgh, NY: Jack Bilow, 2011), 54. Hanson, *Lost Prince,* 262–63.

84. Apess's name can be seen in the "Payroll of a Corps of Artillery Commanded by Capt. Alexander S. Brooks, June 30, 1814" where he is listed as a private. *A List of Pensioners of the War of 1812,* ed. Byron N. Clark (Burlington, VT: Research Publishing, 1904). Brooks's Corps of Artillery was assigned to Fort Brown during the Battle of Plattsburgh. John C. Fredriksen, *The United States Army in the War of 1812: Concise Biographies of Commanders and Operational Histories of Regiments, with Bibliographies of Published Primary Sources* (Jefferson, NC: McFarland, 2009).

85. *SOF,* 29. Bilow, *Whispers,* 54–55.

86. Hanson, *Lost Prince,* 264–66.

87. Ibid., 266.

88. *SOF,* 30.

89. Hanson, *Lost Prince,* 267.

90. Ibid.

4. "And They Held All Things in Common"

1. Keith A. Herkalo, *The Battles at Plattsburgh, September 11, 1814* (Charleston, SC: History Press, 2012), 13.
2. *SOF,* 30 (emphasis added).
3. Ibid. (emphasis added).
4. Gloria Anzaldúa, *Borderlands/La Frontera: The New Mestiza* (San Francisco: Aunt Lute Books, 1987), 25.
5. See Kevin Bruyneel, *Third Space of Sovereignty: The Postcolonial Politics of US-Indigenous Relations* (Minneapolis: University of Minnesota Press, 2007).
6. Anzaldúa, *Borderlands,* 24.
7. Rachel St. John, *Line in the Sand: A History of the U.S.-Mexico Border* (Princeton, NJ: Princeton University Press, 2011), 5.
8. See Alan Taylor, *The Civil War of 1812: American Citizens, British Subjects, Irish Rebels, and Indian Allies* (New York: Alfred A. Knopf, 2010), 6–12.
9. Laurence M. Hauptman, *Seven Generations of Iroquois Leadership: The Six Nations since 1800* (Syracuse, NY: Syracuse University Press, 2008), 1.
10. Arthur Parker writes, "There had been no actual break until the War of 1812, but when arraigned against one another and fighting on opposite sides, then bitterness was gall indeed." Arthur Parker, "The Seneca in the War of 1812," in *Proceedings of the New York State Historical Association,* vol. 15 (Albany: New York Historical Association, 1916), 88.
11. Six Nations reservation land also exists today in Wisconsin and Oklahoma.
12. See Karim M. Tiro, *The People of the Standing Stone: The Oneida Nation from the Revolution through the Era of Removal* (Amherst: University of Massachusetts Press, 2011), 129–30. Carl Benn, *The Iroquois in the War of 1812* (Toronto: University of Toronto Press, 1998), 174–75.
13. Hauptman, *Seven Generations,* 122.
14. Eileen M. Luna-Firebaugh, "The Border Crossed Us: Border Crossing Issues of the Indigenous Peoples of the Americas," *Wicazo Sa Review* 17, no. 1 (Spring 2002): 162.
15. Ibid., 165.
16. *SOF,* 30.
17. *U.S. Army Register of Enlistment Records, 1798–1914,* for William Apess, National Archives Microfilm Publication M233 (ancestry.com)
18. See *SOF,* 30. Taylor, *Civil War of 1812,* 325.
19. *SOF,* 31.
20. Ibid. (emphasis added).
21. Red Jacket, "Message to Erastus Granger, October 1813," in *The War of 1812: Writings from America's Second War of Independence* (New York: Library of America, 2013), 333–34.
22. Hauptman, *Seven Generations,* 53–58.
23. *SOF,* 31.
24. Herkalo, *Battles at Plattsburgh,* 67.
25. *SOF,* 32.
26. Ibid.
27. *SOF,* 32.
28. *FCI,* 131.
29. Out of respect for the wishes of the Mohawk Nation, rather than provide the given name of the culture hero of this narrative, I refer to him here and elsewhere by his title of "Peacemaker."
30. Arthur Parker, "The Constitution of the Five Nations," in *Parker on the Iroquois,* ed. William F. Fenton (Syracuse: Syracuse University Press, 1968), 14.
31. Ibid., 8.
32. According to Mohawk tradition, there is a spot in Lake Ontario at the Bay of Quinte that never freezes over in the winter as a result of the fact that it was here the grandmother tried to drown the Peacemaker.

33. Parker, "Constitution," 14–15.
34. Ibid., 67–68.
35. Ibid., 23.
36. Ibid., 20.
37. Ibid., 7.
38. Lisa Brooks, *The Common Pot: The Recovery of Native Space in the Northeast* (Minneapolis: University of Minnesota Press, 2008), 10.
39. Parker "Constitution," 61–63.
40. Ibid., 13.
41. Thomas King, *The Truth about Stories: A Native Narrative* (Minneapolis: University of Minnesota Press, 2003), 2.
42. Jonathan Shay, *Achilles in Vietnam: Combat Trauma and the Undoing of Character* (New York: Scribner, 1994), 5, 16.
43. Ibid., 190.
44. Maria Yellow Horse Brave Heart and Lymera DeBruyn, "The American Indian Holocaust: Healing Unresolved Grief," *American Indian and Alaskan Native Mental Health Research* 8, no. 2 (1998): 60–82.
45. Shay, *Achilles,* 4.
46. Parker, "Constitution," 20.
47. Ibid., 112.
48. This and following quotations from the meeting are taken from "A Meeting of the Following Indian Nations from the Grand River at Niagara on the 31 August and 1 Sept. 1815," National Archives of Canada, C series, vol. 258, 204–8.
49. *SOF,* 32.
50. Parker, "War of 1812," 88.
51. *SOF,* 32–33.
52. Brooks, *Common Pot,* 173.
53. *SOF,* 33.
54. Brooks, *Common Pot,* 174.
55. Barry O'Connell suggests that this community would have been either the Mohawk community on the northeast side of the bay or a band of Mississaugas on the southwest shore. But given some of the cultural landmarks Apess describes, I conclude it was the Tyendinaga Mohawk reservation. *SOF,* 33n26.
56. *SOF,* 35.
57. Melissa Jayne Fawcett, *Medicine Trail: The Life and Lessons of Gladys Tantaquidgeon* (Tucson: University of Arizona Press, 2000), 24.
58. Brooks, *Common Pot,* 175.
59. *SOF* (1829), 70.
60. Shay, *Achilles,* 193.
61. Judith Herman, *Trauma and Recovery: The Aftermath of Violence—from Domestic Abuse to Political Terror* (New York: Basic Books, 1992), 2.
62. See Benn, *Iroquois,* 19. See also the official website of the Tyendinaga Nation, http://www.mbq-tmt.org/community/history-of-tyendinaga.
63. Brooks, *Common Pot,* 184.
64. *SOF,* 33.
65. Ibid.

5. Becoming a Son of the Forest

1. *FCI,* 131; *SOF* (1829), 74.
2. *FCI,* 131.
3. *SOF,* 35–36.

4. Ibid., 36.

5. Ibid.

6. Joseph Johnson, *To Do Good to My Indian Brethren: The Writings of Joseph Johnson, 1751–1776*, ed. Laura J. Murray (Amherst: University of Massachusetts Press, 1998), 126.

7. *SOF*, 37.

8. Barbara W. Brown and James M. Rose, *Black Roots in Southeastern Connecticut, 1650–1900* (Detroit: Gale Research, 1980), 10.

9. *IN*, 187.

10. See Connecticut State Library, "Connecticut Archives: Index No. 24 Indians 1666–1820," ser. 2, vol. 1, Historical Reference F91 C-56 v. 1 reel 70, ser. 2, slides 32, 36.

11. Chief Irving Powless Jr., "Treaty Making," in *Treaty of Canandaigua 1794: Two Hundred Years of Treaty Relations between the Iroquois Confederacy and the United States,* ed. G. Peter Jemison and Anna M. Schein (Santa Fe, NM: Clear Light, 2000), 21.

12. Ibid., 23. *Teiohâte* in Mohawk means "two paths" or "two roads"; *Kaswenta* means "wampum belt." See also Rick Hill, "Talking Points on History and Meaning of the Two Row Wampum Belt" (Ohsweken, ON: Indigenous Knowledge Center, 2013).

13. See Drew Lopenzina, *Red Ink: Native Americans Picking Up the Pen in the Colonial Period* (Albany, NY: SUNY Press, 2012), 200–207.

14. The earliest recorded instance of the phrase of which I am aware occurs in an address by then President James Madison to a delegation of Creek and Cherokee in 1817 in which he lays out the proposed space for new homelands for both of these nations in Arkansas and claims, "You are now in a country where you can be happy; no white man will ever disturb you . . . as long as water flows, or grass grows upon the earth." Quoted in Stan Hoig, *Beyond the Frontier* (Norman: University of Oklahoma Press, 1998), 11.

15. Samson Occom, *The Collected Writings of Samson Occom, Mohegan: Leadership and Literature in Eighteenth-Century America,* ed. Joanna Brooks (Oxford: Oxford University Press, 2006), 55.

16. *FCI*, 155.

17. Ibid., 156.

18. Brown and Rose, *Black Roots,* 161. *SOF*, 40.

19. *FCI*, 150.

20. *SOF*, 38.

21. *FCI*, 131.

22. Karim M. Tiro, "Denominated 'SAVAGE': Methodism, Writing, and Identity in the Works of William Apess, a Pequot," *American Quarterly* 48, no. 4 (December 1996): 656.

23. *SOF*, 39.

24. Ibid.

25. Frederick A. Norwood, *The Story of American Methodism: A History of the United Methodists and Their Relations* (New York: Abingdon Press, 1974), 163.

26. "Camp Meetings," *Christian Advocate* (New York), October 7, 1826.

27. *SOF*, 39.

28. Samuel Gardiner Ayres, *Methodist Heroes of Other Days* (New York: Methodist Book Concern, 1916), 9.

29. George Claude Baker Jr., *Early Methodism in New England* (Durham, NC: Duke University Press, 1941), 32.

30. Ibid., 23.

31. W. McDonald, *History of Methodism in Providence, Rhode Island from Its Introduction in 1787 to 1867* (Boston: Phipps & Pride, 1868), 7–13.

32. Edward Sharman, *The Christian World Unmasked, or an Enquiry into the Foundation of Methodist Camp Meetings With a Plan for Their Correction and Improvement as Recommended by Mr. John Wesley; and a Looking Glass for Talkative Professors of Religion* (Watertown, NY: printed by the author, 1819), 7, 13.

33. Norwood, *American Methodism,* 15–16.

34. Ibid., 40.

35. *SOF,* 40.

36. According to Baker, women could enter into prayer meetings and exhortations within the Methodist organization, which other denominations of the time considered quite inappropriate. Baker, *Early Methodism,* 21.

37. *SOF,* 40.

38. *FCI,* 150.

39. Ibid., 132; *SOF,* 40.

40. Barry O'Connell, ed., *On Our Own Ground: The Complete Writings of William Apess, a Pequot* (Amherst: University of Massachusetts Press, 1992), lxi.

41. *SOF,* 42.

42. *FCI,* 132

43. Ibid.

44. *SOF,* 42.

45. *A Sketch of the Origin and Growth of the Catamount Hill Association of Colrain, MA,* ed. Dr. A. F. Davenport and Charlotte Augusta Dunton (North Adams, MA: Walden & Crowley Printers, 1901), 28.

46. *SOF,* 42.

47. Apess writes in the passage that to turn around at this point, if possible, were as "dangerous as to go over," echoing a line from Shakespeare wherein Macbeth realizes himself so mired in his murderous plot that to turn back would be as dangerous as to proceed. "I am in blood / Stepp'd in so far, that, should I wade no more, / Returning were as tedious as go o'er" (*Macbeth,* 3.4).

48. O'Connell, *On Our Own Ground,* lii.

49. Ron Welburn, *Roanoke and Wampum: Topics in Native American Heritage and Literatures* (New York: Peter Lang, 2001), 98.

50. Ibid., 88.

51. *SOF,* 43.

52. Dr. A. F. Davenport, "Reminiscence of a Barefoot Boy," in Davenport and Dunton, *Sketch,* 87–90.

53. *SOF,* 43. Lois McClellan Patrie, *A History of Colrain Massachusetts with Genealogies of Local Families* (Salem, MA: Higgenson Book Co., 1974), 104. Elmer F. Davenport, *The Puzzle of Catamount Hill: Being a Report of Pioneer Life in Franklin County, Massachusetts during the Century after the War of Independence, 1780–1880* (self-published, 1969), 35.

54. Ibid., 43.

55. Ibid., 44.

56. *FCI,* 132.

57. *SOF,* 44.

58. Emma Manning, "The Autobiography of the Old School House," in Davenport and Dunton, *Sketch,* 31.

59. *SOF,* 44.

60. Ibid., 45.

61. Ibid., 46.

62. Ibid. See also Connecticut State Library, Connecticut Vital Records, Salem, CSL reel 4828, Waterford, Salem 2.9.

63. *FCI,* 133.

64. Ibid., 134.

65. Ibid., 135.

66. *SOF,* 47.

67. Ibid.

68. Leyden Town Clerk's Office, Town of Leyden Births Deaths, 1777–1848, book 3, 98.

69. *FCI,* 148.

70. Ibid.

71. Samson Occom, "Autobiographical Narrative, First Draft (November 28, 1765)," in *Collected Writings of Samson Occom*, 51–52.

72. *FCI*, 149. The rhetorical convention Aunt Sally George uses is echoed in some measure by Jarena Lee, another self-taught women preacher of the Black Methodist community in Pennsylvania, who offers a similar account of wanting to end her life by drowning prior to her salvation. In Lee's case, however, no transcendent value adheres to the space of her conversion, and the stream itself has no particular spiritual significance. See Jarena Lee, "The Life and Religious Experience of Jarena Lee, a Coloured Lady," in *Sisters of the Spirit: Three Black Women's Autobiographies of the Nineteenth Century*, ed. William L. Andrews (Bloomington: Indiana University Press, 1986), 28–30.

73. *FCI*, 150 (emphasis added).

74. *SOF*, 41.

75. John Wood Sweet, *Bodies Politic: Negotiating Race in the American North, 1730–1830* (Philadelphia: University of Pennsylvania Press, 2003), 354–55.

76. Ibid., 377.

77. Quoted ibid., 374.

78. Norwood, *American Methodism*, 129–30.

79. Ibid., 131.

80. McDonald, *Methodism in Providence*, 63.

81. *Minutes of the Annual Conferences of the Methodist Episcopal Church for the Years 1773–1828*, vol. 1 (New York: T. Mason and G. Lane, 1840), 317.

82. *SOF*, 48.

83. Ibid. (emphasis added).

84. Ibid.

85. Quoted in Mason L. Weems, introduction to *The Life of Washington*, ed. Marcus Cunliffe (Cambridge, MA: Belknap Press of Harvard University Press, 1962), xii–xiv.

86. Tiro, "Denominated 'SAVAGE,'" 665.

87. *SOF*, 48.

88. Ibid., 48–50.

89. *SOF* (1829), 104, 102.

90. *SOF*, 50–51.

91. Ibid., 17.

92. O'Connell, *On Our Own Ground*, 99.

93. *IKC*, "Ten Lost Tribes," 113.

94. Ibid., 102.

95. Ibid., 104.

96. *Constitution and Discipline of the Protestant Methodist Church Baltimore* (John J. Harrod, 1830), 21, 29.

97. *SOF* (1829), 112.

98. Ibid.

99. Apess writes that he left the Methodist Episcopal Church on April 11, 1829, but the Troy conference was actually held in May. *SOF*, 51.

100. Ibid., 52.

6. Indian Preacher

1. *SOF*, 54.

2. Cooper in fact characterizes captivity by Indians as a "fate worse than a thousand deaths" for the heroines of his novel *The Last of the Mohicans*. Although such thoughts are too delicate to be explicitly stated, the implication is always that the intermixing of white women and red men would violate everything held as sacred to a civilized people and degrade the women in question beyond the hope of redemption. "Name not that horrid alternative again" we are warned in Cooper's novel. This attitude remains consistently in place throughout most of the literature of the period and can still be seen operating in current

conflicts. In regard to Jessica Lynch, supposedly held captive by the Iraqis in 2003, her biographer Rick Bragg sardonically notes that "everyone knew what Sadaam's soldiers did to woman captives." The specter of men of color sexually violating white women seems to stand in contrast to an unspoken assumption that "civilized" white soldiers are somehow incapable of such moral aberration. James Fenimore Cooper, *The Last of the Mohicans* (Oxford: Oxford University Press, 1983), 125. Rick Bragg, *I Am a Soldier, Too: The Jessica Lynch Story* (New York: Vintage Books, 2003), 10.

3. Maureen Konkle, *Writing Indian Nations: Native intellectuals and the Politics of Historiography, 1827–1863* (Chapel Hill: University of North Carolina Press, 2004), 99.

4. *SOF*, 7.

5. John J. Kucich, "Sons of the Forest: Environment and Transculturation in Jonathan Edwards, Samson Occom and William Apess," in *Assimilation and Subversion in Earlier American Literature,* ed. Robin DeRose (Newcastle, UK: Cambridge Scholars Publishing, 2008), 15.

6. Advertisement, *American Traveller* (Boston), June 8, 1832.

7. Phillip H. Round, *Removable Type: Histories of the Book in Indian Country, 1633–1880* (Chapel Hill: University of North Carolina Press, 2010), 158. I say "almost" unprecedented, because, as Round observes, David Cusick had copyrighted his *Historical Sketches* the previous year.

8. "A Son of the Forest," *Salem (MA) Gazette,* October 11, 1831.

9. "Apes, The Indian," *Boston Recorder,* January 23, 1833.

10. *SOF*, 3.

11. "Article X—*A Son of the Forest: The Experience of William Apes, a Native of the Forest,*" *American Monthly Review,* August 1832.

12. William Joseph Snelling, "Article IV—*Life of Black Hawk: The Life of Mal-ka-tai-me-she-kia-kiuk or Black Hawk, Dictated by Himself,*" *North American Review,* January 1835.

13. William O'Bryan, *A Narrative of Travels in the United States of America with Some Account of American Manners and Polity and Advice to Immigrants and Travellers Going to That Interesting Country* (London: S. Thorne, Shebbear, Hatherleigh, Devon, Gilbert, and Co., 1836), 322.

14. U.S. Federal Census 1830, Ward 8, New York, ser. M19, roll 97, p.152, Family History Library Film 0017157, Ancestry.com.

15. Patrick Rael, "The Long Death of Slavery," in *Slavery in New York,* ed. Ira Berlin (New York: New Press, 2005), 144.

16. Ibid., 128.

17. Ibid.

18. *FCI,* 133.

19. Ibid., 160.

20. See advertisement, *Evening Post* (New York City), July 3, 1830, and *New York Evangelist,* June 26, 1830.

21. Douglass was in New York City in 1838 at the same time as Apess, and attended Methodist lectures. It is interesting to think that not only might he have heard Apess speak, but that he might have borrowed in some ways from Apess's style of address. See Frederick Douglass, "My Slave Experience in Maryland: Speech before the American Anti-Slavery Society, May 6, 1845," in *Frederick Douglass: Selected Speeches and Writings,* ed. Philip S. Foner (Chicago: Lawrence Hill Books, 1999), 11.

22. "Henry Hallet School Dist. Comm. for 5th District," Ledyard Board of Education Records for August 14, 1830, Special Collections, Bill Library Historical Room, Ledyard, CT.

23. Advertisement, *Christian Secretary,* September 25, 1830, ,; news/opinion, *Salem Gazette* (originally *Hartford [CT] Mirror*), October 1, 1830.

24. See Roger Williams, "To the Reader," in *A Key into the Language of America* (Bedford, MA: Applewood Books, 1936).

25. Rochelle Raineri Zuck, "William Apess, the 'Lost Tribes,' and Indigenous Survivance," *Studies in American Indian Literature* 25, no. 1 (Spring 2013): 4.

26. William Apess, "The Indians—The Ten Lost Tribes," *Monthly Repository, and Library of Entertaining Knowledge* 1, no. 3 (August 1830): 63–65.

27. "Rabbi Noah at a Discount," *Herald* (New York City), March 8, 1837.

28. Interestingly, on the back page of Apess's *Increase of the Kingdom of Christ* is an advertisement for the *Monthly Repository, and Library of Entertaining Knowledge*, suggesting the elaborate networks by which Apess was engaging with the literary world of his time.

29. William Case, "Methodist Indian Missions," *Christian Advocate*, April 21, 1827.

30. See "News," *New York Morning Herald*, September 10, 1830.

31. Mark J. Miller, "'Mouth for God': Temperate Labor, Race, and Methodist Reform in William Apess's *A Son of the Forest*," *Journal of the Early Republic* 30, no. 2 (Summer 2010): 225–51.

32. Nathan Bangs, *Christian Advocate and Journal*, December 27, 1833.

33. *The Seventeenth Annual Report of the Mercantile Library Association, Clinton Hall, New York* (New York: James Van Norden, 1838), 11–14; *New York as It Is in 1835* (New York: J. Dusternell, 1835), 155.

34. American Antiquarian Society, *United States Telegraph*, March 28, 1831.

35. *Somerset County Historical Quarterly*, vol. 7, ed. A. Van Doren Honeyman (Plainfield, NJ: Somerset County Historical Society, 1918), 60.

36. *IN*, 248.

37. *FCI*, 151 (see also Barry O'Connell's footnote on that page).

38. Lisa Brooks, "At the Gathering Place," in Jace Weaver, Craig S. Womack, and Robert Warrior, *American Indian Literary Nationalism* (Albuquerque: University of New Mexico Press, 2006), 232.

39. *FCI*, 139.

40. Ibid., 146–47.

41. *SOF*, 40.

42. *FCI*, 152.

43. Ibid.

44. Joseph Snelling, *Life of Reverend Joseph Snelling: Being a Sketch of His Christian Experience and Labors in the Ministry* (Boston: John McLeish, 1847), 109.

45. Ibid.

46. Ibid., 110.

47. Ibid., 111–12.

48. Connecticut State Library, Connecticut Archives, RG003 New London County Court Files, box 3, folder 18.

49. Jason Richard Mancini, *Beyond Reservation: Indian Survivance in Southern New England and Eastern Long Island, 1713–1861* (PhD diss., University of Connecticut, 2009), 158.

50. Connecticut State Library, Connecticut Archives, RG003 New London County Court Files, box 3, folder 19.

51. Lyon Gardener, "Gardener's Narrative," in *The History of the Pequot War*, ed. Charles Orr (Cleveland, OH: Helman Taylor, 1897), 118–19.

52. *FCI*, 132.

53. *SOF* (1829), 114.

54. John Reynolds, "Communication," *Christian Watchman* (Boston), August 19, 1831. See also American Antiquarian Society, Ira Moore Barton Papers, box 1, folder 1, Committee on Affairs of Marshpee Indians.

55. US Congress, "Indian Removal Act: May 28, 1830," in *The Cherokee Removal: A Brief History with Documents*, ed. Theda Perdue (Boston: Bedford / St. Martins, 1995), 116.

56. Andrew Jackson, "State of the Union Address, December 6, 1830," in Perdue, *Cherokee Removal*, 119–20.

57. Lewis Cass, "'Removal of the Indians,' January 1830," in Perdue, *Cherokee Removal*, 109, 107.

58. See Anthony F. C. Wallace, *The Long Bitter Trail: Andrew Jackson and the Indians* (New York: Hill and Wang, 1993), 4–6. Theda Perdue and Michael Green, *The Cherokee Nation*

and the Trail of Tears (New York: Penguin, 2007), 49–50. Henry L. Watson, *Liberty and Power: The Politics of Jacksonian America* (New York: Hill and Wang, 1990), 106–7.

59. Cass, "Removal of the Indians," 110.

60. Ralph Waldo Emerson, "To Charles Chauncy Emerson, Boston January 19, 1832," in *The Letters of Ralph Waldo Emerson,* ed. Ralph L. Rusk (New York: Columbia University Press, 1939), 346.

61. Konkle, *Writing Indian Nations,* 100; *Christian Register,* May 5, 1832.

62. American Antiquarian Society, "Louisa Park, Park Family Papers 1800–1890," folder 1, letter dated April 29, 1832.

63. Ibid. See also Theresa Strouth Gaul, "Editing as Indian Performance: Elias Boudinot, Poetry, and the *Cherokee Phoenix,*" in *Native Acts: Indian Performance, 1603–1832,* ed. Joshua David Bellin and Laura L. Mielke (Lincoln: University of Nebraska Press, 2011), 281–307.

64. William Lloyd Garrison, *Liberator,* issue 20 (May 19, 1832), 79.

65. "A Solemn Appeal," *Liberator,* issue 23 (June 9, 1832).

66. Andy Doolen, *Fugitive Empire: Locating Early American Imperialism* (Minneapolis: University of Minnesota Press, 2005), 156.

67. Extracted from Hyde's journal for July 10, 1832 (emphasis added). See Christopher, "'A Son of the Forest' and 'An Intelligent Son of Abraham': Orson Hyde and Samuel Smith Meet William Apess, 1832," *Juvenile Instructor: Organ for Young Latter-Day Scholars,* November 21, 2013, http://juvenileinstructor.org/a-son-of-the-forest-and-an-intelligent-son-of-abraham-william-hyde-and-samuel-smith-meet-william-apess-1832/.

68. *Liberator,* issue 27 (July 7, 1832), 107; *Liberator,* issue 28 (July 14, 1832), 111; *Christian Watchman* (Boston), August 17, 1832; *American Traveller,* September 7, 1832.

69. The pooling of money to buy lottery tickets may have been a common fundraising tactic in African American church organizations in the 1830s. William J. Brown, recalling his youth in Providence, remarked that "the colored people [himself included], under the leadership of Minor Hall, a Methodist man, formed a society, each member paying into the treasury 25 cents a month. This money was given to a committee of three to buy lottery tickets." This would have occurred remarkably close to the time when Apess filled the role of "Teacher" at the Methodist church in Providence. William J. Brown, *The Life of William J. Brown of Providence: With Personal Recollections of Incidents in Rhode Island* (Durham, NC: University of New Hampshire Press, 2006), 30.

70. "Charge of Libel," *Newburyport (MA) Herald,* October, 9, 1832.

71. *Norwich (CN) Courier,* January 1, 1833.

72. "Apes, the Indian," *Boston Recorder,* January 23, 1833.

73. "Letter from Benjamin Franklin to Jane Franklin Meacom, Nov. 1, 1773," quoted in Jill Lepore, *Book of Ages: The Life and Opinions of Jane Franklin* (New York: Knopf, 2014), 163.

74. *FCI,* 157.

75. Ibid.

76. Ibid., 158–59

77. Ibid., 160.

78. Ibid., 160–61.

79. *IN,* 169.

80. According to Kerri Helme, a great-great-great-granddaughter of Oakley, the Mashpee had recruited Apess to come to their community and assist in ousting their overseers. Oakley was connected to Apess's ministry in Connecticut and may have alerted Amos and the Attaquins of Apess's skill as a preacher and agitator for Indian rights.

81. *IN,* 169.

82. Such language was often employed by the first New England settlers in their desultory efforts to convert the local Natives. This particular quote comes from a tract known as "First Fruits." "New England's First Fruits," in *The Eliot Tracts,* ed. Michael P. Clark (Westport, CN: Praeger, 2003), 58.

83. *IN*, 170–71.
84. Ibid., 171
85. Ibid., 172.
86. *Barnstable (MA) Patriot*, June 26, 1833, available in Sturgis Library's *Barnstable Patriot* Digital Newspaper Archive.
87. *IN*, 168.
88. Ibid., 177.
89. Ibid., 173.
90. Ibid., 174–75.
91. Ibid., 176–77.
92. "Marshpee Indians," *Liberator*, issue 25 (June 22, 1833), 99.
93. *Barnstable Patriot*, June 26, 1833.
94. See *IN*, 178–80. See also Earl Mills Sr. and Alicja Mann, *Son of Mashpee: Reflections of Chief Flying Eagle, a Wampanoag* (North Falmouth, MA: Word Studio, 1996), 10.
95. "Trouble in the Wigwam," *Columbian Centinel* (Boston), July 7, 1833. According to the *Barnstable Patriot*, the "Nullifying Ordinance" read as follows: "Having been heretofore degraded and despised, and a much abused people, we have determined to make our own laws and govern ourselves. For this purpose we have seen the Governor, who has no objection to our governing our own affairs. This is to give notice we have resolved if any person is seen on our plantation after the first of July, carting or cutting wood, without our leave, or in any way trespassing upon our lands, they shall be bound hand and foot and thrown off. Signed Daniel Amos, President, Moses Amos, Secretary."
96. *IN*, 181.
97. Theresa Strouth Gaul, "Dialogue and Public Discourse in William Apess's Indian Nullification," *American Transcendental Quarterly* 15, no. 4 (December 2001): 281.
98. *IN*, 182.
99. Ibid., 180–81.
100. Ibid., 183.
101. Ibid., 184.
102. Ibid., 195.
103. Ibid., 187.
104. Ibid., 189.
105. Ibid., 187.
106. "Massachusetts's Indians," *Globe* (Washington, DC), issue 30 (July 18, 1833).
107. "Hostilities Commenced in Marshpee," *Baltimore Gazette and Daily Advertiser*, July 10, 1833; "Indian War in Massachusetts!," *Hampshire Gazette* (Northhampton, MA), July 10, 1833; "Trouble in the Wigwam."
108. "Indians in Massachusetts," *Jerseyman* (Morristown, NJ), July 24, 1833.
109. "Marshpee," *Philadelphia Inquirer*, July 11, 1833.
110. "The Poor Indians," *Hampden Whig* (Springfield, MA), July 24, 1833 (emphasis added).
111. "Marshpee Indians; Hon. J. J. Fiske; Council," *Newburyport (MA) Herald*, July 15, 1833; "The Marshpee Indians," *Hampshire Gazette*, July 17, 1833; *IN*, 207; *Portsmouth Journal of Literature and Politics*, July 13, 1833; *IN*, 227.
112. *IN*, 169.
113. Strouth Gaul, for one, whose work on *Indian Nullification* has influenced my own sense of the text in generative ways, nevertheless maintains that Apess's dream is one of "American Indian participation in American public and political life." Strouth Gaul, "Dialogue and Public Discourse," 291. Also see Jean M. O'Brien, *Firsting and Lasting: Writing Indians Out of Existence in New England* (Minneapolis: University of Minnesota Press, 2010).
114. *IN*, 205.
115. Strouth Gaul, "Dialogue and Public Discourse," 275.
116. *IN*, 228.
117. Ibid., 212.
118. "Marshpee Indians," *Liberator*, issue 25 (June 22, 1833), 9.

7. The Bizarre Theater of Empire

1. Arthur C. Parker, "The Constitution of the Five Nations," in *Parker on the Iroquois,* ed. William N. Fenton (Syracuse, NY: Syracuse University Press, 1968), 16.

2. "Marshpee Indians," *National Aegis and Massachusetts Yeoman* (Worcester, MA), December 11, 1833.

3. Barnstable Court House Document, Case 633, "Commonwealth vrs. William Apess," see index "Defendants A–K 1827–1886."

4. The fact that the petition was written by Apess while in prison is asserted by Phineas Fish in his own memorial to the Boston legislature. While an undisputed critic of Apess, Fish, too, was close to the events as they unfolded and had little to gain by inventing this particular detail (the fact that the memorial was written by Apess is asserted by the editor of the *Liberator* as well). Fish wrote, "Apes, while in prison, is said to have drawn a lengthy petition to the Legislature." See "Memorial: To the Honorable the Senate and House of Representatives, in General Court Assembled" *Liberator,* issue 5 (February 1, 1834).

5. "Committee on Affairs of Mashpee Indians, Feb. 5, 1834," Ira Moore Barton Papers, box 1, folder 1, American Antiquarian Society, Worcester, MA.

6. *IN,* 206; "The Marshpee Indians," *Liberator,* issue 4 (January 25, 1834), 15.

7. *IN,* 208.

8. See Appendix 1 and "Memorial of the Mashpee Indians," *Liberator,* issue 5 (February 1, 1834), 20.

9. *IN,* 202, 227–29. Benjamin Hallett also notes that "every person on the jury, who said he thought the Indians ought to have their liberty, was set aside." *IN,* 167.

10. "The Marshpee Indians," *Trumpet and Universalist Magazine* (Boston), August 17, 1833, 31.

11. *IN,* 203.

12. Ibid., 227–28.

13. "Monday; Indian; Preacher; Baptist; Gospel," *Rhode Island Republican* (Newport), October 30, 1833. See also "Marshpee Indians," *National Aegis and Massachusetts Yeoman* (Worcester, MA), December 11, 1833. "Marshpee Indians," *Salem (MA) Gazette*, December 17, 1833.

14. "Marshpee Indians," *New Hampshire Observer* (Concord), January 10, 1834.

15. *IN,* 226.

16. "The Marshpee Indians," *Liberator,* issue 4 (January 25, 1834), 15.

17. Benjamin F. Hallett, *Rights of the Marshpee Indians* (Boston: J. Howe Printer, 1834), 6.

18. Ibid., 13.

19. Ibid., 15.

20. Ibid., 17.

21. Ibid., 32.

22. Earl Mills Sr. and Alicja Mann, *Son of Mashpee: Reflections of Chief Flying Eagle, a Wampanoag* (North Falmouth, MA: Word Studio, 1996), 10.

23. "Marshipee Indians," *Hampden Whig* (Springfield, MA), November 26, 1834.

24. *EKP,* 282.

25. "Marshipee Indians," *Hampden Whig,* November 26, 1834; *IN,* 240.

26. The authorship of *Indian Nullification* has been disputed, and the Library of Congress catalog record still offers the caveat that the book is "sometimes attributed to William Joseph Snelling." Snelling was the author of the 1830 *Tales of the Northwest; or Sketches of Indian Life and Character.* The book traffics in standard negative stereotypes of Lakota life based on experience the author gained as a trader out of Fort Snelling (commanded by his father, Col. Josiah Snelling). Snelling later became an abolitionist and newspaper editor in New England. The attribution of authorship to *Indian Nullification* can be traced back to Samuel Gardiner Drake, the "Indian Historian" and antiquarian who, in his copy of the book, left a note indicating that Snelling was the "real" author. There is nothing in the text of *Indian Nullification* to suggest Snelling could have written any part of it.

27. "Marshpee," *Boston Recorder,* May 29, 1835.

28. *IN,* 166–67.

29. Ibid., 242.

30. Ibid., 247.

31. Ibid., 245.

32. Ibid., 274.

33. "Mr. William Apes," *Boston Recorder,* June 5, 1835.

34. "The Marshpee Indians," *Portsmouth (NH) Journal,* July 18, 1835.

35. "Indian Nullification," *New-Hampshire Gazette* (Portsmouth), July 21, 1835.

36. "Indian Nullification," *New England Magazine* 9 (July 1835): 79.

37. "Notices of Publications: *Indian Nullification,*" *New England Galaxy and United States Literary Advertiser,* June 11, 1835.

38. "Rev. William Apes; Gov. Lincoln; Violent," *Massachusetts Spy* (Worcester), June 17, 1835.

39. A newspaper advertisement reads, "The author of the work called 'Indian Nullification'; will pronounce an Eulogy upon King Philip, tomorrow evening at 8 o'clock, in the Universalist Meeting House." "Indian Nullification; Eulogy; King Philip; Universalist Meeting," *New Hampshire Gazette* (Portsmouth), July 21, 1835.

40. *EKP,* 277.

41. Lepore notes how Forrest absorbed a great deal of literature about King Philip's War, took to speaking in what he considered to be an Indian accent, and called his real-life mistress by the name of Philip's wife in the play, Nahmeokee. Apparently he also lived for a time with a Choctaw man, of whom he made an intimate study. See Jill Lepore, *The Name of War: King Philip's War and the Origins of American Identity* (New York: Vintage Books, 1998), 200–202.

42. Ibid., 210.

43. Douglas Edward Leach, *Flintlock and Tomahawk: New England in King Philip's War* (Hyannis, MA: Parnassus Imprints, 1958), 88.

44. Edward Everett, *An Address Delivered at Bloody Brook in South Deerfield, Sept. 30, 1835, in Commemoration of the Fall of the "Flower of Essex" at That Spot in King Philip's War, Sept. 18 (O.S.), 1675* (Boston: Russell, Shattuck and Williams, 1835), 39.

45. "South Deerfield Celebration," *Commercial Advertiser* (New York), October 7, 1835.

46. All parts of Everett's speech can be found in Everett, *Address,* 1–38.

47. Andrew Jackson, "State of the Union Address, Dec. 6, 1830," in *The Cherokee Removal: A Brief History with Documents,* ed. Theda Perdue and Michael D. Green (Boston: Bedford / St. Martins, 1995), 119–20.

48. For a genealogy of Philip's development as a figure in colonial times, see Drew Lopenzina, *Red Ink: Native Americans Picking Up the Pen in the Colonial Period* (Albany: SUNY Press, 2012), 137–93.

49. *Liberator,* issue 42 (October 17, 1835), 168.

50. Lisa Brooks, *The Common Pot: The Recovery of Native Space in the Northeast* (Minneapolis: University of Minnesota Press, 2008), 199.

51. On January 1, 1836, the *Christian Watchman* announced, "A Eulogy will be pronounced upon King Philip, by an Indian preacher, at the Odeon this evening at 7:00." See "The Indian King Philip," *Christian Watchman.* A "specimen" of Philip's language was promised—in fact, a recital of the Lord's Prayer taken from Samuel Drake's *Book of the Indians,* who in turn received the translation into the Algonquian language from the 1663 Eliot Bible.

52. "Eulogy on King Philip," *Standard* (Boston), January 6, 1836. The article alludes to the fact that following King Philip's War, Philip's head was impaled on a stake outside the gates of Plymouth Colony and remained there for twenty years. (Thanks to Daniel Radus for first alerting me to this news story.)

53. "The Indian King Philip," *Columbian Sentinel* (Boston), January 23, 1836.

54. "The Indian King Philip," *Salem (MA) Gazette,* January 26, 1836 (emphasis added).

55. *Massachusetts Spy,* February 22 , 1836.
56. "The Indian King Philip," *Hartford (CT) Times,* March 5, 1836.
57. *SOF,* 60.
58. *EKP,* 279.
59. Reynolds, speaking of New York theater in the 1830s and 1840s, notes that the "roughs of the gallery went to theater as much to engage in deviltry as to see plays. They expressed their praise and displeasure with the greatest possible noise. It was not unusual for the din of clapping, yelling, cheering, or hissing to drown out the actors. At the slightest provocation, unruly elements in the audience would throw things onto the stage." David S. Reynolds, *Walt Whitman's America: A Cultural Biography* (New York: Vintage Books, 1995), 157.
60. *EKP,* 277.
61. Ibid., 283.
62. Ibid., 304.
63. Ibid., 286.
64. Ibid.
65. Ibid., 300.
66. Ibid., 294.
67. See Benjamin Church, "Entertaining Passages Relating to Philip's War," in *So Dreadfull a Judgment: Puritan Responses to King Philip's War, 1676–1677,* ed. Richard Slotkin and James K. Folsom (Hanover, NH: Wesleyan University Press, 1978), 451.
68. *EKP,* 304.
69. Ibid., 301.
70. Ibid., 283
71. Ibid., 280.
72. Ibid., 306.
73. Parker, "Constitution," 49.
74. *EKP,* 306.
75. Ibid., 310.
76. "Mohegan Petition," March 28, 1836, in *The New England Indian Papers Series,* ed. Paul Grant-Costa and Tobias Glaza,Yale University Library Digital Collections, http://findit. library.yale.edu/yipp.
77. "Marshpee Indians," *Hampden Whig* (Springfield, MA), November 26, 1834.
78. "Marshpee Indians," *Liberator,* issue 27 (July 2, 1836), 107.
79. Ibid.
80. Barnstable County Registry of Deeds, book 18, 126. See also Mashpee Town Clerk's Office, Record of Mortgages 1834–1862, 4.
81. Mashpee Town Clerk's Office, "Mortgage Deed of William Apess to Richard Johnson," Record of Mortgages, 1834–1862, September 1836, p. 4.
82. *Barnstable Patriot,* November 23, 1836, available in Sturgis Library's *Barnstable Patriot* Digital Newspaper Archive.
83. "Indian Lectures," *Evening Star* (New York, NY), February 21, 1837.
84. *New Orleans Times Picayune,* March 24, 1837.
85. *New York Colored American,* April 22, 1837.
86. Timothy Alden, "Mission to the Senecas," in *The Christian Herald,* ed. John E. Caldwell, vol. 2 (New York: J. Seymore, 1816), 282.
87. "A Rabbi in the Rostrum," *New York Herald,* February 14, 1837.
88. "Rabbi Noah at Discount—Indian Lecture at Clinton Hall," *New York Herald,* March 18, 1837.
89. "Indian Lecture," *New York Herald,* March 1, 1837.
90. "Great Public Meeting—Twenty Thousand Assembled—The Revolution Begun," *New York Herald,* February 14, 1837.
91. Parker, "Constitution," 23.

92. Judith Herman, M.D., *Trauma and Recovery: The Aftermath of Violence—From Domestic Abuse to Political Terror* (New York: Basic Books, 1992), 42.

93. Parker, "Constitution," 20.

94. *FCI*, 100.

Conclusion. "He Possessed the Real Traits of the Indian Character"

1. "An Inquisition on the View of the Body of Wm Apes, May 10, 1839," New York Deaths and Burials, 1795–1952, New-York-EASy, Indexing Project Number B73407-7, microfilm 13184360. Barry O'Connell, in a 1997 essay, gives credit to Reginald H. Pitts for discovering the coroner's inquest for Apess's death in the Municipal Archives of the City of New York. See Barry O'Connell, "'Once More Let Us Consider': William Apess in the Writing of New England Native American History," in *After King Philip's War: Presence and Persistence in Indian New England*, ed. Colin G. Calloway (Hanover, NH: University Press of New England, 1997), 162–77.

2. "Death of a Pequot Indian," *Albany (NY) Evening Journal*, April 14, 1839.

3. "An Inquistion."

4. Ibid.

5. "Death of a Pequot Indian," *Albany (NY) Evening Journal*, April, 13, 1839.

6. "Lobelia Again," *North American* (Philadelphia), April 12, 1839.

7. "Death of Apes," *Christian Watchman* (Boston), April 19, 1839.

8. "The Late Reverend William Apes," *Olive Branch*, May 18, 1839.

9. article title? *Boston Recorder*, June 6, 1844.

10. Robert Warrior, *The People and the Word: Reading Native Nonfiction* (Minneapolis: University of Minnesota Press, 2005), 4, 44.

11. "Washington D.C.," *Sun* (Baltimore), December 5, 1837. See also "Scene with the Indians," *Newark (NJ) Daily Advertiser*, December 14, 1837. .

12. "The Late Reverend William Apes," *Olive Branch*, May 18, 1839.

13. Ibid.

14. Connecticut State Library, Connecticut Archives, RG003 New London County, County Court Files, Native Americans, box 4, folder 24.

15. Nancy Shoemaker, "Race and Indigeneity in the Life of Elisha Apes," *Ethnohistory* 60, no. 1 (Winter 2013): 28–50. See also "Research Travels: New Zealand," blog, posted June 28, 2013, *The Indian Mariner's Project*, http://indianmarinersproject.com. Shoemaker asserts that William Elisha was Apess's brother rather than his son. I do not think this was the case, but the archival evidence is unclear. It seems that there were two William Elishas, one Apess's younger brother, and the other his son. A William Elisha is listed as a seaman set to ship out on the *Ann Maria* destined for New Zealand with a projected departure date of May 27, 1839. The William Elisha aboard this ship was involved in a mutiny and ended up making a new life for himself in New Zealand. Barry O'Connell suggests that family tradition understood this William Elisha to be Apess's son. Another Elisha Apes is listed as living in New London, Connecticut, in the 1840 census. This I believe to be the brother to William Apess who married Julia Worthington in 1837 and, although also a whaler, continued out his days in the United States. There is not a lot to go on here, but I am further persuaded by the fact that the William Elisha who ultimately married in New Zealand named his firstborn Mary, which would seem to be after his mother, Mary Wood. Shoemaker makes what I believe to be a mistake when she interprets a document from the Massachusetts Vital Records in Leveret (this record is incorrectly marked, as I have located the original at the Town Clerk's Office in Leyden, MA) to mean that William Apes Sr. had a second marriage after Candace to a woman named Mary and went on to have six children. Evidence suggests these are, in fact, the children born to William Apess and Mary Wood. But even here we run into difficulty, as the first child listed in this record is an Elisha who was born in May 7, 1815, roughly two years before Apess even met Mary

Wood. This may suggest that Elisha was a child of another father, or the date may simply be wrong. But the children on this record do not align with the children known to be born to William Apes Sr. and listed in Brown and Rose's *Black Roots*. Other questions arise. The mariner who traveled to New Zealand in 1839 is listed as being twenty-four years of age. This conforms with the 1815 birthdate earlier mentioned, but Apes might also have lied about his age (as his father did when entering the army).

16. See Shoemaker, "Race and Indigeneity," 28–50; also "New London Crew Lists Index: 1803–1878," http://library.mysticseaport.org.

Index